London in Cinema

London in Cinema

The Cinematic City Since 1945

Charlotte Brunsdon

First published in 2007 by the
BRITISH FILM INSTITUTE
21 Stephen Street, London W1T 1LN

The British Film Institute's purpose is to champion moving image culture in all its richness and diversity across the UK, for the benefit of as wide an audience as possible, and to create and encourage debate.

Cover design: Eureka!
Cover image: *Wonderland* (Michael Winterbottom, 1999, © PolyGram Films [UK] Limited)

Set by Fakenham Photosetting, Fakenham, Norfolk
Printed in the UK by The Cromwell Press, Trowbridge, Wiltshire

British Library Cataloguing-in-Publication Data
A catalogue record for this book is available from the British Library

ISBN 978–1–84457–183–3 (pbk)
ISBN 978–1–84457–182–6 (hbk)

Contents

Acknowledgments

The final stages of the writing of this book were supported by the Arts and Humanities Research Council under the Research Leave Scheme, which provided a matching term to study leave granted by the University of Warwick. I would also like to acknowledge Henry Bacon, Anna McCarthy, Nina Wakeford, Chantal Cornut-Gentille, Felix Driver, Lynn Spigel, Monica Seidl and Roman Horak, Peter Hutchings, Asu Aksoy and Kevin Robins for inviting me to present this research at, respectively, the Universities of Helsinki, New York, Surrey (Incite), Burgos (IBACS), London (Institute of Historical Research), Vienna; Northwestern University, Tate Britain, Berlin (The British Council), and to the commentary and questions of participants at these events. Aspects of the work presented here have previously been published, and I thank Steve Chibnall and Robert Murphy, John Hill, Ysanne Holt and Jackie Stacey for commissioning and/or editing these articles:

> 'Space and place in the British crime film' in Steve Chibnall and Robert Murphy, *British Crime Cinema* (London: Routledge, 1999).
> 'London films: from private gardens to utopian moments', Supplement on British Cinema edited by John Hill, *Cinéaste* vol. XXVI no. 4, Autumn 2001, pp. 43–46.
> 'The poignancy of place: London in the cinema', *Visual Culture in Britain* vol. 5 no. 2, 2004: pp. 59–73.
> '"A fine and private place": the cinematic spaces of the London Underground' *Screen* vol. 47 no. 1, (2006), pp. 1–17.

I am also indebted to the many Warwick students who have responded to my urban enthusiasms with grace and insight, and to those who have checked various elements of the book: Sarah Thomas, Eimear Ballard and Tom Hughes. The book has been in production while the future of British Film Institute Publishing has been in doubt. I must thank Andrew Lockett for the original commission, Sarah Watt for her work on the book, but most particularly Rebecca Barden and Sophia Contento, who worked on the book while their own jobs were in jeopardy. If this book is published under the BFI imprint, it is thanks to them.

Also at the BFI, at a time when the interdependence of its internationally recognised collections (film, television, paper and stills) and the expertise of its staff seems under threat, I must thank, in particular, Kathleen Dixon and Steve Tollervey (Research Viewings) and Janet Moat (Special Collections).

A very long London list could be made from the names of the many people who have mentioned relevant films, television and other material to me: thanks to all who did this. In a more limited list, I am indebted to the following who have helped in many different ways: Karen Alexander, José Arroyo, Anne Birchall, Lucy Bland, Jon Burrows, Pam Cook, John Corner, Richard Dyer, Christine Geraghty, Sue Harper, Andrew Higson, Peter Hutchings, Bob Lumley, Angela McRobbie, Frank Mort, Robert Murphy, Geoffrey Nowell-Smith, Richard Perkins, V.F. Perkins, Helen Scalway, Amy Sargeant, Lynn Spigel, Carolyn Steedman, Ginette Vincendeau, Nick Wadham-Smith and Jerry White. I am very grateful to those who supported my attempts to get funding to undertake the research and to those who read parts – and the whole – of the manuscript. John Caughie was both kind and unflinching in his identification of foggy patches. I have not always followed suggestions made, and of course, the errors are all mine.

For company and encouragement over many post codes, thanks, as ever, to D.M.

And finally, I salute David, Jane, Paul, Simon and Deke, in memory of days when London and the cinema were ours.

Introduction: Impossible Geographies

The LadyKillers (1955), the last of the Ealing comedies, is set in the area of London around King's Cross and St Pancras stations and has a noticeably impossible geography. Mrs Wilberforce (Katie Johnson), the absent-minded, elderly heroine, lives in a subsiding Victorian house near the railway stations. This house is the film's main setting and it is here that Mrs Wilberforce's lodger, Professor Marcus (Alec Guinness), and his mixed gang of collaborators plan a daring hold-up of a security van. 'Mrs Lop-sided', as she is called by the conspirators, inadvertently foils their plans, mainly through her continuous hospitality, and it is in the house, and in the garden and wasteland behind the house, overlooking the railway lines, that each of the gang members in turn meets their death. The narrative of the film makes use of the proximity of the railway lines at the back of the house to create Mrs Wilberforce's own farcical killing field in which the precipitous drop down to tracks, the steam from the engines and even the signals contribute to murder. The house is positioned at the head of a cul-de-sac, with the train lines behind it, and compared to the grim, tall terraced houses on either side of the cul-de-sac, Mrs Wilberforce's house seems, on first appearances, rather sweet and idiosyncratic.

From the front of the house – not immediately revealed – the spectacular pinky-red Victorian Gothic of St Pancras Station is directly opposite. The impossibility of the film's geography lies in the fact that the house both backs onto the railway lines, which head away from the station, and lies opposite the front of the station. So, in a referential geography, the house is simultaneously both north and south of St Pancras and King's Cross stations, with railway lines behind and in front of it. As a cinematic geography, though, this double aspect of Mrs Wilberforce's house is both economical and effective. Viewed from the street, the small house at the end of the cul-de-sac, with its slightly tilting angles, is like a gingerbread house in a forest of tenements. It is an old house, a unique house, a house which is different to the others in the street. And so it proves when entered, as the Victorian décor, the antimacassars, the net curtains, the paintings, the birdcages and the bulky mahogany furniture crowd the *mise en scène*. This Victorian interior is matched and echoed by the view from the house, of St Pancras Station and the former Midland Grand Hotel, an outstanding example of

Victorian Gothic, built in 1868–72 to a design by Sir George Gilbert Scott. The large red-brick structure, with a clock tower, another tower, and pinnacles, gables and turrets, offers an external equivalent to the Victorian interior of the house. While monumental, it is also architecturally rather busy, just as the tiny Mrs Wilberforce is constantly, hospitably fussy.

Critical analysis of *The Ladykillers* has emphasised the significance of the Victorian within the film. Charles Barr's reading of the film sees the gang as the post-war Labour government, with its cross-class mix, while the Victorian Mrs Wilberforce – who ends up with the money – represents the 'the startling, paralysing charisma of "natural" governing class'.[1] He notes the careful construction of Mrs Wilberforce's milieu, 'It's an entrancing portrait of a Victorian civilisation lingering on, tottering into the post-war world',[2] while also noting the suffocating resistance to change of this world. Barr calls his state-of-the-nation reading 'admittedly fanciful', but more than fifty years after the film was made, his reading is still attractive. Christine Geraghty's more recent comments on the film echo Barr, while embedding the film more tightly into a general tendency within 1950s British cinema to resist modernity.[3] She is less concerned with a reading in relation to the post-war Labour government, than with the more widespread phenomenon of an embrace of the old, as is Richards with his notion of 'cul-de-sac' England.[4] The filmic construction of Mrs Wilberforce's Victorian environment: the little old house, the interior décor, the view of St Pancras and the performances of Katie Johnson (and Edie Martin, and the other old ladies), is the cinematic presentation of this theme of the persistence of the old. The doubled location of the house, repeatedly Victorian, but also disposing of post-war modernity – the gang – through that symbol of Victorian modernity, the railways, embodies the victory of Mrs Wilberforce over the newer class

The Ladykillers: Mrs Wilberforce's house with the railway lines behind

The arrival of Mr Harvey (Herbert Lom) with his violin case, and St Pancras in the background

alliances in mid-twentieth-century Britain. The referential geographical impossibility of the film is a dramatic strength. And most viewers, anyway, won't notice, or won't know about the house on both sides of a station.

There is more that can be said about where *The Ladykillers* is set, though. Barr concludes his book on Ealing Studios with the film, observing that it provides an appropriate farewell 'both sardonic and affectionate' for its director, Alexander Mackendrick, who left for the USA and *The Sweet Smell of Success* (1957). He leaves behind 'the little England' of Ealing Studios and Mrs Wilberforce's King's Cross. There are some photographic records of the shoot reproduced in Sorensen's *London in Film*. Mrs Wilberforce's house was built as a set at the end of Frederica Street, slightly north-east of King's Cross and St Pancras stations in Barnsbury – and near the railway lines – and there is a rather charming photograph of staff and crew apparently catering for a street party for the residents after the shoot was finished.[5] We also know that the hold-up itself was partly location shot behind the stations in Goods Way and Cheney Road, cobble stoned streets that have been used repeatedly in British cinema until they were blocked off and partly destroyed early in the twenty-first century in the building of the Eurostar terminal.[6]

The film was released in 1955, shortly after the Conservative government's relaxation of building controls in 1954, leading to the first post-war London property boom, which lasted until 1964.[7] This led to a transformation of the material fabric of the city, driven by office building. Euston Station, the oldest London terminus, just along the road from St Pancras, was demolished in 1963. The fate of St Pancras itself was uncertain for many years, particularly in the 1960s and 1970s when the Victorian was very unfashionable. When Mrs Wilberforce leaves her house to go to the nearby police station where she is so gently tolerated, she walks

The Ladykillers: the hold-up, filmed in Cheney Road, behind King's Cross with the gasholders visible

down a curved little street, which Barr describes as having an 'idealised "village" quality',[8] and it was a clip of this pedestrian journey that the sculptor Richard Wentworth used on a looped tape in his 2002 King's Cross installation, *An Area of Outstanding Unnatural Beauty*.[9] This exhibition, by an artist who had worked in King's Cross for many years, was a response to the redevelopment of the area to accommodate the new international terminal for the Channel Tunnel. He transformed the General Plumbing Supplies Building in York Way into an exploration of the many spaces, and modes of spatiality, of King's Cross. So alongside Mrs Wilberforce, perpetually going down to the police station, there were ping-pong tables, maps for aircraft routes over London and a periscope, which looked over the roofs. In the context of the grey warehouse-like brick building, the colour of the film stock (on video) was very striking. King's Cross in 1955 seemed a brighter, richer and more resonant place. The landmark pink gothic of St Pancras may have survived the twentieth century, but some of the little streets and communities behind and around it have not, and Wentworth's exhibition staged an impassioned documentation and mapping of the area's inner-city ecology.

So, in combination with the film's impossible and expressive geography and its mixture of location and studio shooting, the images in *The Ladykillers* of vanished locations are some of the few remaining traces of the old King's Cross area. It is somewhere between these different ways of seeing the London of *The Ladykillers* that this book is positioned. It is a book about London in post-war British feature films. 'Mostly post-war', 'mainly British', 'mainly feature films, and only some of them' would be the accurate qualifications. I look at some of the many different Londons found in the cinema in the second half of the twentieth century, and explore, often in considerable textual detail, the way in which London is invoked by a film, and the ways in which it works in the narrative.

Andrew Higson has reminded us that, in the cinema, narrative always 'takes place'.[10] How might that work when the analytic concern is with both the imagined world of the film and also with referential aspects of that 'taking place'? My interest is in films in which that 'place' is London. So across a series of detailed analyses of individual films, I trace something of the cinematic geography of post-war London, to investigate how the spaces that are, in the cinema, created through *mise en scène*, cinematography and editing, invoke and stage this city. But in offering this outline of some of the ways that cinematic London might be approached, I have also wanted to recognise that cinematic Londons are only one contribution to the myriad histories and textualities of the city. Mrs Wilberforce's house, with its impossible geography and its disappeared streets, points to one of the key difficulties of this book: the way in which attention, when considering London in film, can – must – slip between the diegetic location of the fiction and the real (extra-diegetic) location that it invokes, to which it refers and from which it is sometimes, in some parts, made. While location shooting was used in *The Ladykillers*, so were the full resources of a film studio, including a set for what is called the 'shopping centre' in the script (the little street down which Mrs Wilberforce walks), and 'process shots' for some of the exteriors, as well as a careful mixture of exterior location shots and work with a studio parapet for the final death scenes.[11] Mrs Wilberforce's London is an imagined London, which draws on, and contributes to, our ideas of what London is and was like. Does the disappearance of parts of the material city in which *The Ladykillers* is set make its Ealing vision of a local community seem truer? Does the colour of the film stock, 'the rich dark reds and browns', tell us 'that the London of terraced streets is no longer a real location for events carrying connotations of actuality', as John Ellis suggests?[12] Does the very absence of *The Ladykillers'* London make it seem as if it did once exist, with its kindly police-man and its little old ladies? How might the relationship between the cinematic city and the material city be most productively understood?

This book approaches these questions through the detailed textual analysis of selected London-set films in which attention is paid to the rendering of space and place in the imagination of cinematic London. I argue that cinematic London has a discernible shape, and it is this that the book explores. Some readers may wish to skip the rest of the introduction, moving to the chapter outline at its end, rather than read the intervening account of some of the other scholarship with which it is in conversation.

What the Book Doesn't Do

I have subtitled the book *The Cinematic City Since 1945* to ward off the disappointment of those who might expect a book called *London in Cinema* to be a survey of all the different films in which London appears. I survey neither films in which London appears, nor London build-ings, districts and sights as they appear in films. What I have written is based on the systematic viewing of London-set films, and so general observations I make should have some grounding, but I didn't want to write a 'list-book' – of which more below. Nor is this a sourcebook about where particular films were shot, although I have researched this where possible, and have also drawn on published location research from a range of sources.[13] This is a book about where films are set, rather than where they are shot. And, finally, in the list of what the book is not, this is not a book in which film is used primarily as an illustration of London's social or architectural history. I didn't start the book thinking 'What's been happening to London since the Second World War?' and then go and look at lots of movies. I started the book, while teaching British cinema, as a result of trying to see whether it was possible to give a coherent account of the 'Londons' found in post-war British cinema. So the films came first, and there is sometimes only rather fleeting reference to significant aspects of London's cultural history and geography. Movies and cities have different kinds of temporalities, and are constituted, through quite different imperatives, of different kinds of spaces and events. If it is possible for the London historian Jerry White to observe, in a discussion of immigration and London's changing ethnic composition after 1940, 'Of all the changes to London and Londoners in the twentieth century, this was the greatest',[14] there is no simple or singular cinematic response to this fact. Indeed, British cinema itself is partly made by immigrants: it is itself a product of these movements of people.[15] While the changing population of London, a city with a significant early migrant myth in the arrival of Dick Whittington from 'the country', continues to be both a theme and context for London-set films, it can be apprehended in diverse ways. For instance, the topos of the airport, and the changing significance and meaning of London airports in cinematic geographies, from the elite venue of *Spring in Park Lane* (1948) through to the more middle-class Heathrow of *Out of the Clouds* (1955) to the crowded non-places of *Dirty Pretty Things* (2002), would repay further study.[16] So would the careers, for example, of Joseph Losey, Stephen Frears, Gurinder Chadha, Pawel Pawlikowski or the members of the 1980s Black Audio Film Collective. The retrospective nostalgia of 1980s heritage cinema, with the reiterated whiteness of the Englishness invoked, might be argued to be one of the most significant responses to this changing Britain. One way it is approached in this book is through analysis of the discernably ethnicised movement of different characters through different spaces. The point is that film-making has its own economic and creative dynamics, and although British cinema has established documentary and social-realist traditions, the generic engagement with 'the real' through these traditions is only a minor part of cinema, even though the medium itself constantly promises that what one sees is real. I didn't set out to track historical changes through their representation in cinema, but instead to investigate the kinds of London that are found in cinema and, using critical categories such as genre, explore significant patterning in these cinematic Londons over the sixty years of the study.

The historical geographer Miles Ogborn, in an afterword to a collection of essays on 'the spatial imaginary', has reflected on the relationships 'between Geography and Literary Studies, or to be more inclusive of the broad interdisciplinary field which is involved, of the relationships between words and spaces'.[17] Ogborn argues that current research has transcended earlier paradigms of 'representation' (images of the city) and 'metaphor' (the city as text, 'mapping fiction'), arguing instead that 'neither spaces nor texts can be the *a priori* basis for the other. Instead, texts are part of the cultural production of spaces and spaces are part of the cultural production of texts.'[18] In this argument, both spaces and texts are cultural productions, and should be treated in parallel. While the contribution of cultural and historical geography to our understanding of the 'production' of space has been significant to my project, the specificity of the cinema complicates this argument when it is not 'words and spaces' but 'images and spaces' that are the analytic concern. For cinema seems so readily to render up the real and is, in one sense, constituted through the production of spaces. And these cinematic spaces are produced through the manipulation of other spaces and processes: editing, camera movement, sets, models, back-projection, paintings, refilming, computer-generated imagery and, occasionally, locations. What I try to do in this book is pay attention to the specificity of cinema, but also to think about its Londons in relation to other Londons, some of them cinematic, some of longer duration – and some, bricks and mortar, tunnels and rivers and streets.

My starting point is with films seen primarily as aesthetic objects, and so my question is always about how London, as space and place, is both constituted in any particular film and how it works within the fiction. Mrs Wilberforce's London is shown to be a local neighbourhood in which she can walk from her house to the local police station, although the film commences with a very high establishing shot of her house with the railway lines behind it. The only clues that this is London come from the accents of the characters, the style of the buildings and the scale of the railway lines. None of these do more than suggest geographical location (England, a city, the South-east, probably London), although dramatic location is finely realised through the variety of the characters she meets and greets in the street, with the tone of the film indicated by the way in which the baby she greets responds by

The Ladykillers: Mrs Wilberforce (Katie Johnson) walking to the police station through the 'shopping centre' set

bawling. The drama of the location of her house has attention drawn to it in the opening high-angle shot, but this accented significance is at this stage empty of narrative potential. How could this story of a sweet little old lady turn the location of her house into a technology of death? It is only with the appearance of Professor Marcus that St Pancras is seen to loom opposite the house, identifying the location as King's Cross. All that the plot requires is 'a major railway station' (which is what the script specifies), so that it is plausible both that bullion would be there to be stolen, and that the elaborate detail of Professor Marcus's plan can be realised in the crowded bustle. The choice to use the façade of St Pancras enhances the Victorian aspects of the setting in the manner I have already discussed. My interest in what follows, then, is in both how attention to the construction of place-that-is-London in a film can inflect our understanding of how the film works, as well as how the film's London contributes to broader patterns of cinematic Londons.

London and Los Angeles

This starting point, an interest in the simultaneous fictiveness and referentiality of cinema, is different to that of the London writer Iain Sinclair, who has written about several of the films discussed in this book. In an influential body of work, which has tested the distinctions between poetry, literary fiction, criticism and reportage since the 1970s, Sinclair has engaged with, and produced, images of a fin-de-siècle London centred on the City and further east, downriver.[19] For Sinclair, London comes first. The cinema is mainly interesting to the extent to which it can reveal or express the essence of the city. This means that he has a preference for location shooting and, because of his view of the city, for the dark genres. In a review of *Dirty Pretty Things*, he observes, '[U]sing the city as a set diminishes it.'[20] This is basically a repudiation of cinema as a fictional medium: no *My Fair Lady* (1964) here, then. In this context, it is not surprising that Sinclair judges Patrick Keiller's 1994 *London* (in which there are no identified characters shown on screen) '*the* film of its period – essay, document, critique, poem'.[21] While I agree that *London* is a wonderful film, my interest is in a broader range of cinematic Londons, and in this book I explore some of them, interested, precisely, in London as a set, and its relationship to other imagined and lived Londons.

Thom Andersen's 2003 film *Los Angeles Plays Itself* scrutinises feature films for their representation of Los Angeles. Nearly three hours long, it is composed of clips from movies ranging from Maya Deren's *Meshes of the Afternoon* (1943) to 1970s pornography, from Mack Sennett to Charles Burnett's *Killer of Sheep* (1977), overlaid with a commentary about the different ways in which Los Angeles has appeared in the movies. Andersen is well aware of the perversity of his project, observing in the opening that he knows that 'movies aren't about places, they're about stories', and that there is something wrong with the film if you are thinking about where it is shot. However, he perseveres in his endeavour to 'watch with our voluntary attention' directed to place and to 'apprecia[te] fiction films for their documentary revelations'. Andersen's title condenses both his project and one of his key hypotheses, that Los Angeles, although home of the movies, appears as itself quite rarely: 'We might wonder if the movies have ever really depicted Los Angeles.' It is his own oblique gaze, reading against the narrative subordination of setting to story, that reveals the Los Angeles of the movies, which he organises through three main categories: the city as background; the city as character; and the city as subject. While Andersen's gaze is instructive, and recalls something of the hesitation that I described in looking at the setting of Mrs Wilberforce's house in *The Ladykillers*, there are also significant differences, which are mainly to do with the cities of Los Angeles and London, their very different histories and their different relations to the movie industry.

Although London has had a film industry from the earliest days of the medium and there is a north-western arc of studios and former studios, in most cases about an hour's journey from the smoke and pollution of the city, London has never been a player in the movie business to match Los Angeles. Los Angeles – Hollywood – is the movies, and thus Andersen's project is an attempt to find the material city within the celluloid stories. By contrast, London is an old imperial city, capital of a country dominant in pre-cinematic days, already imagined and given many shapes in poems, paintings, novels, memoirs, diaries, prints, plays, statues, histories and plans before the movies were invented. Patrick Wright has written eloquently of the role of tradition and history in Englishness in *On Living in an Old Country*, and London is predominantly 'an old city'.[22] While Los Angeles, within international cinematic geography, may represent the future – even if it is now the old future of the twentieth century – London represents the past, a time before cinema, or in its scratchy, black-and-white beginnings. So while in some ways I am trying to do what Andersen does, to trace some of the patterns of filmic representation of a particular city in fiction film and to attend to the inadvertent documentary role of feature films, the material encountered is quite different, and I am more interested than Andersen in individual films as wholes. If in some sense the movies made Los Angeles, movies made of London encounter a city already thick with stories and images. The foggy streets of old London town are never far from the screen when London is depicted in the cinema, as Colin McArthur has suggested.[23] In this sense, Katherine Shonfield is right to choose Mary Poppins's descent through the fog to epitomise Hollywood's London,[24] and one of the more significant choices I have made in this book, as its exponential growth threatened to take over the whole South-east, is to eliminate chapters on heritage and Victorian Londons. I made this choice mainly because one of the more generative areas of British cinema scholarship has been work on the films variously identified as 'historical', 'costume' and 'heritage' cinema.[25] However, Victorian London lingers on in the book from the discussion of fog in the first chapter to Jack the Ripper films towards the end. Mrs Wilberforce's elimination of the opposition in *The Ladykillers* can be helpful here too. For her victory over the mixed gang of criminals who plan their robbery in her Victorian house can be read as indicative of generic patterning within cinematic London. Within a cinematically self-conscious film, of the gang members, Louis (Herbert Lom) can be seen to represent a certain foreign nastiness of film noir, the Major (Cecil Parker), indigenous, middle class and polite, has seen better days, while 'One-round' (Danny Green) is a dim London heavy in the gangster tradition. The Professor, the most important member of the gang, who looms up at Mrs Wilberforce's front door with the lighting and camera angles of horror film, introduces another, significant, generic inheritance. In distinction to the film noir continental or American city, cinematic London is more shaped by the gothic imagination, and is both more Victorian and more shaped by the horror genre. Nice Mrs Wilberforce – and gothic horror – have been more significant for London in the cinema than film noir.[26]

Los Angeles Plays Itself is made by a lover of the city who has both lived and researched its history. Andersen's commentary, at points, recognises wryly that not everyone will share his enthusiasms: 'Images of thing that aren't there any more mean a lot to those of us who live in Los Angeles and almost nothing to everyone else.' He points to a difficulty in studying a particular city and the cinema, rather than '*the* city and the cinema'. For particularity and detail can, as he suggests, 'mean a lot' to people who recognise what is being discussed, and 'almost nothing to everyone else'. For many non-British readers, London is probably just a mixture of some of the landmarks discussed in Chapter 1. However, in the case of London, there is a further complication because of London's role in relation to the rest of Britain. Detailed location discussion can work to confirm the widely recognised London bias of British culture. Because it is the capital, and because of the dominance of the South-east region more generally, more assumptions are made about the recognisability of London than other British cities and, within British culture, those who can't make these recognitions, or understand the discriminations in a distinction between, say, 'Greenwich' and 'Deptford', are rendered 'provincial'. Londoners, in contrast, gain a spurious authority through the ability to say 'well that's really in Hammersmith' in a way which often closes down the more interesting critical question of how the location is being used in the film. In this context, while I make no apology for writing a book about London, there is a delicacy in the way in which the detail of location is cited that I wish to explore a little here. Most film setting is unspecific. Scenes are set in 'a terraced street', 'a market', 'a pub', 'an attic' or 'an office'. This setting is commonly given a geographical location either through an establishing shot, which includes a recognisable landmark, the use of a title, 'London, 1888', or perhaps through use of dialogue. A film usually only requires its viewers to recognise, for example, that characters are crossing the River Thames, rather than which bridge they use. This doesn't mean that the choice of bridge isn't significant. Westminster Bridge provides excellent views of the Houses of Parliament; Waterloo Bridge, which is relatively unornamented, a good aspect of St Paul's. Many London bridges, and their views, are recognisable to audiences who would not be able to name them. And this can be tricky in the writing, as the referential naming of locations can suggest that the point of the writing is to identify the bridge, when the symbolic and expressive aspects of 'crossing the water' are usually more significant. For example, the park that is the site of the investigation in *Blow-Up* (1966) is not identified diegetically. Within the world of the film, the point about this park is that it is not one of the recognisable London parks. It is one of those little, anonymous, local-authority-maintained parks, which used to figure quite significantly in local London life. Location sleuthing has identified the park as Maryon Park in Woolwich, and now writing about the film frequently mentions this in a way which distorts the role of the park within the film. It was its unfamiliarity that was significant. Of course, there would always have been viewers who could identify Maryon Park, and perhaps for them *Blow-Up* was overshadowed by this recognition. Charles Tashiro, writing about production design, comments:

> At best, a pre-existing street expresses a script imperfectly. The street will be read as itself before it reads as a particular street in a particular story; that is the purpose of using a location, to

achieve lived, social recognizability. However, if recognized, the location brings the narrative to a halt, as the space as physical fact triumphs over narrative service.[27]

Thus, while some locations must be recognised to serve their part in a narrative fiction – say Tower Bridge (even if it is mis-recognised as 'London Bridge', which is how it generally functions in movies) – others must not be, and their recognition disrupts the imagined world of the film.

The best example of this unbalancing, a swerve into the literal, that I have come across in the research for this book was a comment by John Trevelyan (Secretary to the British Board of Film Censors) in relation to the film *Alfie*, and concerns not parks but a station. There were many issues for the censors in this 1966 film, most significantly its treatment of an abortion when these were illegal. However, in the midst of the detailed commentary on the script submitted for the film version of *Alfie* comes: 'Although this is not a censorship point, I am doubtful whether you can get a train from Waterloo Station to Forest Hill Station. I would have thought that Victoria was more likely.'[28] It is not that these details are without importance: it is partly through these details that the cinematic real is produced, and sometimes what Thom Andersen calls 'silly geography' reveals considerable contempt for a local audience. However, it is not the purpose of this book to invoke a fantasy cinema of geographical veracity, and then to track down deviations. The point of cinematic geography is that it is made up.

London in the Cinema

If 'London in the cinema' is a smaller category than 'London and the cinema', excluding, for example, the history of London film studios and some of the interesting work being done on practices of film exhibition, as well as the often rather melancholy documenting of past picture palaces undertaken by cinema historians like Allen Eyles, it is still a huge and amorphous area of study.[29] The London historian Colin Sorensen, who for many years ran film screenings of 'London on Film' at the Museum of London, had a very catholic approach, but in his book *London on Film*, which is subtitled '100 Years of Film-making in London', chose to concentrate on films from the first half of the twentieth century, stating that 'it has been frankly impossible to resist the temptation to explore the vanished London that can be revisited when looking at these earlier films'.[30] His interest was primarily with the cinema as document in which can be traced both vanished London and film-making in London, and I address some of these concerns in Chaper 6, on the river, and the Afterword. I have chosen to start this study with films made after the Second World War – with bombsites rather than the Blitz. The London Blitz is the source of images of London, and particularly London as a capital city, which continue to dominate representations of the city for many decades to come – and arguably still do.[31] While I do discuss some of this imagery, particularly in Chapter 4, on the London Underground, and also refer to some earlier films, this book starts in the period of austerity of the 1945–51 Labour government, part of a decade often seen as a 'golden age' of British cinema.[32]

Methodologically, the difficulty of thinking about London in the cinema seems to generate lists. There are London studios such as Ealing and Gainsborough, each of which have recognisable cinematic Londons, and then, in a wider arc to the west and north-west, Bray, Denham, Pinewood, Shepperton, Teddington and Twickenham. There are production companies and groupings with recognisable London signatures: London Films, Working Title, Palace Pictures, the London Film-makers Co-op and Black Audio Film Collective. There are film-makers (directors, producers, writers) with significant London oeuvres, including: Alfred Hitchcock, Mike Leigh, Hanif Kureishi, Robert Hamer, Michael Balcon, Jill Craigie, Richard Curtis, Sally Potter, Joseph Losey, Gurinder Chadha, Stephen Frears, Isaac Julien, Richard Lester, Powell and Pressburger, Penelope Mortimer, Herbert Wilcox/Anna Neagle, Derek Jarman, Humphrey Jennings, Julien Temple, Neil Jordan, Steve Wooley, Nik Powell. There are visiting film-makers who have made notable Londons, such as Michelangelo Antonioni, Jerzy Skolimowski and Roman Polanski. There are many other professionals involved in film production who have made distinctive contributions to London in the cinema, including production designers such as Hugo Luczyc-Wyhowski, costume designers such as Sandy Powell and cameramen such as Douglas Slocombe. There are the writers of books and stories, which gain screen life either through repeated adaptation or one significant work: pre-eminently, Charles Dickens, but also including Sir Arthur Conan Doyle, Joseph Conrad, Len Deighton, Patrick Hamilton, Henry James, Gerard Kersch, Arthur La Bern, Pamela Travers, Virginia Woolf. There are performers associated with the city, some also associated with earlier popular forms like music hall or later, with television: Betty Balfour, Norman Beaton, Michael Caine, Stanley Holloway, Bob Hoskins, Marianne Jean-Baptiste, Tommy Trinder, Barbara Windsor and Ray Winstone. And there are locations, some of which, as Thom Andersen puts it, usually play themselves: Tower Bridge, St Pancras, Piccadilly Circus; and some of which appear in many roles, such as Senate House, Carlton House Terrace, Newman Passage, the Reform Club and Thamesmead. These can in turn generate their own lists of their many appearances.

I could go on – and readers will have many additions. The point is that these lists are endless, and none of them are adequate. It would even be possible to make a list of quotations about the vastness and the illimitable-ness of London, the way in which it always exceeds attempts to exert 'some kind of epistemological authority' over it, to render it knowable.[33] London lists, compendia and encyclopaedias are a characteristic of the field of London studies as a whole, just as the study of films generates its own endless lists.[34] As the previous paragraph demonstrates, lists do not make scholarly writing either more interesting or more attractive, and, within what follows, I have chosen to limit the sometimes overwhelming troops of examples and counter-examples that I have found storming nearly every point. Instead, I have tried to give a shape to how one might think about London in the cinema.

This I have done partly by thinking about place in the cinema as relational. It is a truism of film studies that off-screen space is significant in the construction of meaning. In classical cinema, the gaze out of frame constructs the place of the view, what is seen, which is usually the next shot. When considering place in the cinema at what might be called the next level, each particular location in a film is made meaningful in relation to the film's other locations (home/not home: Kansas/Oz). These locations in turn have referential aspects, which can be general (other homes, streets, imaginary kingdoms) or particular (Buckingham Palace). For London, historically, the key relations of place are between the

West and East Ends, north and south of the river, and the West End, the City and the suburbs. These internal relations of place are partly shaped both by London in Britain, and by London and Empire. But cinema cannot be approached as if it should map these relations of place; the question must be, what are the meaningful relations of place within London-set cinema? And how should those that are specific to London be understood? It is in response to these questions that I arrived at the structure for the book as a whole.

To contribute to this shape, I use, at points, the idea of London as a 'biographical city'. The biographical city is proposed as a city understood from the point of view of a life lived in it. The Queen's London is different to Patrick Keiller's London, and each of these is different to the London of Stephen Frears. In relation to the cinema, it permits an understanding of the imagined London of a film as a city in which individual characters understand their lives partly topographically, through journeys that they make, or can't make, or aspire to make. The biographical city has destinations of habit, impossible destinations and destinations of desire and memory.[35] As a way of thinking about the city, the notion of the 'biographical city' can be contrasted with the city of the flâneur, the leisured urban stroller, who could be seen as the hero of much scholarship on the city.[36] The biographical city is more banal, and includes journeys of necessity and labour. It encompasses the flâneur's city: the flâneur's city is just one of the many biographical cities, and one which is distinguished by, in some cases, its disavowal of its particularity and privilege.[37] I explore the biographical city particularly in relation to the notion of 'going up west' in Chapter 3, where I explore the way in which the fantasy of this journey can be as powerful as any journey made.

As London is a capital city, it has a strong metaphoric and metonymic presence in the cinema, standing variously for England, Britain, the British Empire, the government, and it is the signifying of this London that is the main topic of my first chapter on 'Landmark London'. Much work on British cinema includes discussion of the cinematic representation of London, although this is usually dispersed and frequently articulated through a problematic of 'national cinema' or, more recently, 'national identity' as in the work of Andrew Higson, John Hill, Claire Monk, Robert Murphy and Sarah Street.[38] Amy Sargeant's recent *British Cinema* is unusual in that it consciously comments on cinematic London and Robert Murphy's work, partly because he has a continuing interest in crime genres, is also notably sensitive to London locations.[39] However, there is also an intermittent periodisation of significant cinematic Londons possible, although not with the clarity James Saunders achieves for New York,[40] so there is also interesting discussion of particular temporal Londons, such as the increased use of location shooting in the 1960s, or the 1990s romantic-comedy London.[41] Similarly, without wanting to lapse once more into lists, there are studies of individual film-makers and studios, which offer analysis of the treatment of London. The cinematic London of a particular imaginary, be it an individual, studio, genre, cycle or period, can be, and has been, the subject of analysis. The difficulty, though, is in moving beyond this to sketch broader contours.

This becomes clear in any review of attempts to think 'London in the cinema' in more detail. Pierre Sorlin's discussion avoids some of these problems because he places London in the context of a more general exploration of post-1939 European cinema.[42] One of his conclusions is that by the time of *Blow-Up* 'a concerted, systematic representation of an urbanized space seemed so hazardous that few cinematographers attempted it'.[43] The 'cinema and the city' literature, with its favoured protagonist of the flâneur, and its canon that runs from 'city symphonies' through post-war cinematic modernism to *Blade Runner* (1982) and *Wings of Desire* (1987), usually, for London, only includes Humphrey Jennings and 1940s planning films,[44] although latterly, in what John Orr has called 'the revival of the cinematic city', Patrick Keiller's *London*, Mike Leigh's *Naked* (1993) and Gary Oldman's *Nil By Mouth* (1997) have attracted commentary.[45] Colin McArthur points to the complex, pre-cinematic origins of what he refers to as 'London discourse' in the cinema in his 'Chinese Boxes and Russian Dolls', while also showing the importance of Hollywood in reproducing it.[46] Ewa Mazierska and Laura Rascaroli give a brief survey of cinematic Londons before concentrating on what they propose as two groups of millennial films, 'posh London' (*Sliding Doors*, 1997, and *Notting Hill*, 1999) and 'chaotic London' (*Beautiful People*, 1999, and *Wonderland*, 1999).[47] Pamela Church Gibson offers a not dissimilar distinction between 'de-romanticized' and 'heritage' London.[48] Ian Christie ranges over the whole twentieth century in his discussion of London for the Cahiers du cinéma encyclopaedia on *La Ville au cinéma*, using different categories to organise his survey in ways that partly recall Sorensen. He points to the historical interplay of place and cinema, suggesting that 'locating cineastes' favourite areas across the years permits one to bring out a cultural geography of London, with particular stories tied to areas which in their turn become emblematic of these stories'.[49] Christie's article, with its pragmatic shifts between different ways of approaching its topic, has similarities with the organisation of the Cahiers du cinéma volume as a whole, where the list-like characteristics of attention to cities in the cinema – this is, after all, an encyclopaedia – is countered by the different types of categories that are employed, ranging from individual cities, cineastes, places and people to framing, archives, film noir, prostitutes, parking and serial killers. The point, though, is that no one system of classification or approach is adequate. London in the cinema is interesting in different ways in different films at different historical moments. It can't be unified.

Structuring the Cinematic City

I'm interested in the meanings of London, what the city signifies, the stories that recur as 'London' stories and their relation to that much broader, international corpus of 'city stories' (such as the arrival in the city, or the stranger in the crowd), as well as to ways of thinking about cities more generally. My questions include, 'How does this film show that it is set in London, and how is this setting used?' and 'How does this presentation of London relate to others?' However, as one of my main purposes is film analysis, I'm also interested in what a perspective 'from London' does to a reading of a film. How does the direct invocation of the spatial inflect the emphases of an analysis? What aspects of this film are specific to its London setting? These questions act as a filter for the selection of films for detailed analysis: I have chosen films which I think are 'about' London in some way, and which I think would reward further analysis. This 'about' is realised in different ways, and my selection has been made with attention to different types of range (for example, genre and period) and existing and forthcoming scholarship. I've refrained from reiterating discussion of some very obvious 'London films' (with some regret) and hope that my analysis will persuade readers that other films are more 'about' London than they might first appear.

One of the most enjoyable aspects of researching this book – not quite as good as walking round London, but excellent to think about on routes that had more roaring dual carriageway than anticipated – was the question of how to organise the material. I have found that although I started out with what could be called a primarily cinematic organisation, with chapters on, for example, London noir, naturalist London, 'olde London Towne', 1960s London films, 'the streets of London', as I have been working on it, a rather more spatial organisation has asserted itself. The book contains more discussion of identifiable areas of London than I originally anticipated and its shape, somewhat to my surprise, owes as much to the city as to the cinema, although, within the chapters, the analysis is of the London of individual films. My original intention was to give substantial attention to wholly studio-set Londons such as that of *My Fair Lady*, believing, with Pierre Sorlin, that 'a setting is not more "true" because it exists in actuality',[50] and also wanting to avoid the geographical literalism that potentially haunts the project. While many of the films discussed do use the studio, I have been drawn increasingly to films that, through location shooting, yield up what Geoffrey Nowell-Smith has called 'a sense of place', issues that I discuss in more detail in Chapter 6.[51] In saying this, I am not claiming that London, perhaps as characterised by Peter Ackroyd ('infinite' and 'illimitable'),[52] has somehow taken charge of the book's structure. However, I am saying something about the resistance of the real, about the recalcitrance of the city to being textualised. The big theoretical issue for scholarship on the cinema and the city is the relationship between the two terms. This is not, in my view, something that can be satisfactorily addressed solely at a theoretical level, which becomes particularly evident when the focus shifts from 'the city' to 'a particular city, London'. Just as there are many cinematic Londons, so there are many different relationships between London and the cinema, and between the writer, the city and the cinema. My starting point in what follows is that these relationships can most usefully be approached historically and textually.

The result is a book with a rather hybrid organisation, and this hybridity enacts many qualities of both the topic and the different ways in which I have tried to approach it. There is a centre/periphery distinction discernible in the relationship between the first three chapters, on 'Landmark London', 'Local London' and 'Going Up West'. However, these chapters are also concerned with different kinds of cinematic space and time. Within and across these chapters, there is attention to different genres (including science fiction, romantic comedy and film noir) and different film-makers. Chapters 4 and 6 are organised to examine the spaces and times of the city through the two symbolic structuring spatial networks and thoroughfares of the city, the London Underground and the River Thames. The labyrinthine Underground, which is also a significant landmark in its diagrammatic manifestation, is explored for its generic, spatial and narrative propensities, some of which it shares with metro systems the world over, some of which are London-specific. The river, a richly generative site in London's cultural history, is seen as the privileged locus for stories of industrial and imperial decline. It is in the context of the river that I discuss the docks and docklands, although a different organisation would recognise the docks as a constitutive element of the East End. The East End, Landmark London's mythical dark other, now a landmark itself, is approached in Chapter 5 through three different narrative figures, the gangster, the ripper and, less well documented but still discernible behind the flayed whore, the woman in a pinny.

London tends not to fare well in discussions of the cinematic city: Paris, Berlin and Los Angeles are more readily proposed in a range of contexts. However, running through this book is another view of cinematic London, which would provide a different outline of its structure. Through a reading of selected films which emphasise different aspects of this cinematic city, I explore the way in which cinematic London can contribute to our understanding of some of the relationships between the cinema and the city more generally. Through the shape, conventions and histories of cinematic London, we can explore different modalities of this relationship. Cinema is a time-based art form with its origins in the Victorian period. Victorian London lingers on throughout the twentieth century, and perhaps these origins of cinema are most apparent in relation to this city, resistant as it has proved to many modes of planned modernity, and resurgent as extreme contrasts of wealth and poverty are at the turn of the century. The first two chapters consider the different ways in which what could be seen as the raw materials of cinema, space, time and image are articulated to give different senses of place, and to signify different kinds of London. The first chapter emphasises the construction of identifiable place through the editing of recognisable landmark icons; the second, the use of repetition to create a sense of locality. A different relation between cinema and city, one close to metaphor, is proposed in the next two chapters. Chapter 3 explores the interplay between the bright lights of the West End and cinema itself. At its simplest, this is offered as the metaphorical relationship between 'going to the cinema' and 'going up west'. But there is also the homology of the relationship between the darkness of cinema and travel through underground space explored in Chapter 4. The role of genre in the construction of cinematic space and narrative pleasures is discussed in Chapter 5, on the East End, while the final chapter considers the cinematic image as document in relation to the changing city and riverscape. In the Afterword, some of these topics are revisited in a reflection on studying an old – and changing – city in what is now an old – and changing – medium. In this way of thinking about the book, I am proposing that these London-set films, themselves, when considered together, offer ways of understanding possible relationships between the cinema and the city.

Throughout the work on the book, the changing fabric of the city has drawn attention to itself: the viewer who scrutinises the cinematic image for its revelation of place cannot but notice changing places. This has both melancholy and exciting aspects, which is what I explore in the Afterword, returning to King's Cross with which this Introduction started. The shape that I have given to my discussion of London in the cinema is not proposed as the only shape that would be possible, and I will resist the temptation to indulge in another list of the omitted. However, it will, I hope, provoke a reconsideration of London as a cinematic city; one that, in its formation as Victorian darkness as much as the bright lights of modernity, witnesses both the history of cinema and the end of Britain's imperial power, and which now, at the end of a celluloid century, imagines neo-liberal London through an almost Dickensian syntax. In the project, I have been influenced by Franco Moretti's suggestive book, *Atlas of the European Novel 1800–1900*, in which he explores geographies of literature through attention to both 'space in literature' and 'literature in space'.[53] Moretti, in his introduction, recognises that in his project 'method is all',[54] proceeding to insist that the success or otherwise of his method will be judged by the reader, not by his own 'theoretical promises'.

His account of his method emphasises this point: 'Placing a literary phenomenon in its specific space – mapping it – is not the conclusion of geographical work; it's the *beginning*. After which begins in fact the most challenging part of the whole enterprise: one looks at the map, *and thinks*.'[55] The shape that cinematic London is given in the structure of this book is both my method and my conclusion.

Notes

1. Charles Barr, *Ealing Studios* (Newton Abbot: Cameron and Tayleur in association with David and Charles, 1977), p. 171.
2. Ibid.
3. Christine Geraghty, *British Cinema in the Fifties* (London: Routledge, 2000), pp. 69–70. See also Philip Kemp, *Lethal Innocence* (London: Methuen, 1991), pp. 120–3.
4. Jeffrey Richards, 'Cul-de-sac England: *The Ladykillers*', in A. Aldgate and J. Richards, *The Best of British* (London: I. B. Tauris, 2002), pp. 148–65.
5. Colin Sorensen, *London on Film* (London: Museum of London, 1996), pp. 124, 126, 127 (the party).
6. Mark Adams, *Location London* (London: New Holland, 2003), pp. 58–62, and Sorensen, *London on Film*.
7. Oliver Marriott, *The Property Boom* (London: Hamish Hamilton, 1967).
8. Barr, *Ealing Studios*, p. 170.
9. Richard Wentworth, *An Area of Outstanding Unnatural Beauty* (Artangel), General Plumbing Supplies Building, York Way, 4 September–17 November 2002. Wentworth discusses the role of this locality in his work with Joe Kerr in '"The accident of where I live" – journeys on the caledonian Road', in Iain Borden, Joe Kerr, Jane Rendell with Alice Pivaro (eds), *Unknown City* (Cambridge, MA: MIT Press, 2001), pp. 386–404.
10. Andrew Higson, 'Place, space and spectacle: landscape and townscape in the "kitchen sink" film', in Andrew Higson (ed.), *Dissolving Views* (London: Cassell, 1996), p. 138.
11. *The Ladykillers* shooting script, 5 April 1955, annotated by A. Mackendrick, BFI Library, S16643.
12. John Ellis, 'Made in Ealing', *Screen* vol. 16 no. 1, Spring 1975, p. 89.
13. Studies of individual films, studios and directors often include production information and are referenced where relevant throughout the book. See also, Brian Pendreigh, *On Location: The Film Fan's Guide to Britain and Ireland* (Edinburgh: Mainstream Publishing, 1995), Adams, *Location London* and Tony Reeves *The Worldwide Guide to Movie Locations Presents London* (London: Titan, 2003). Film London provides extensive location information for films produced with its support: <www.filmlondon.org.uk>.
14. Jerry White, *London in the Twentieth Century* (London: Penguin, 2002), p. 13.
15. See, for example, Jill Balcon's speculation on the significance to her father, Michael Balcon, of his own experience of migration in contributing to the image of England fostered in the Ealing films. *Omnibus: Made in Ealing*, BBC, 2 May 1986.
16. On airports as spaces see David Pascoe, *Airspaces* (London: Reaktion, 2001).
17. Miles Ogborn, 'Mapping Words', *New Formations* no. 57, Winter 2005–6, p. 145.
18. Ibid., p. 146.
19. Sinclair's most sustained discussion of cinema appears in 'Cinema Purgatorio', in *Lights Out for the Territory* (London: Granta, 1997), pp. 279–329. He is also the maker, with Chris Petit, of the film *London Orbital* (2002).
20. Iain Sinclair, 'Heartsnatch Hotel', *Sight & Sound* vol. 12 no. 12 (NS), December 2002, p. 34.

21. Sinclair, *Lights Out for the Territory*, p. 306.

22. Patrick Wright, *On Living in an Old Country* (London: Verso, 1985) and *A Journey through the Ruins* (London: Radius, 1991). See also the persistence of the old in *Peter Ackroyd's London* (BBC, 7 May 2004, 14 May 2004, 21 May 2004).

23. Colin McArthur, 'Chinese boxes and Russian dolls', in D. Clarke (ed.), *The Cinematic City* (London: Routledge, 1997), p. 34–5.

24. Katherine Shonfield, *Walls Have Feelings* (London: Routledge, 2000), p. 135.

25. See Sue Harper, *Picturing the Past* (London: BFI, 1994); Pam Cook, *Fashioning the Nation* (London: BFI, 1996); John Hill, *British Cinema in the 1980s* (Oxford: Clarendon Press, 1999); Guy Barefoot, *Gaslight Melodrama* (London and New York: Continuum, 2001); Claire Monk and Amy Sargeant (eds), *British Historical Cinema* (London: Routledge, 2002); Andrew Higson, *English Heritage, English Cinema* (Oxford: Oxford University Press, 2003).

26. See Raymond Durgnat on the vigour of British horror in *A Mirror For England* (London: Faber and Faber, 1970) and 'Paint it Black: the family tree of film noir', in Alain Silver and James Ursini (eds), *Film Noir Reader* (New York: Limelight, 1996); David Pirie, *A Heritage of Horror* (London: Gordon Fraser, 1973); Peter Hutchings, *Hammer and Beyond* (Manchester: Manchester University Press, 1993); and Steve Chibnall and Julian Petley, *British Horror Cinema* (London: Routledge, 2002).

27. Charles Tashiro, *Pretty Pictures* (Austin: University of Texas Press, 1998), p. 33.

28. BBFC file on *Alfie* quoted by Anthony Aldgate, *Censorship and the Permissive Society* (Oxford: Clarendon Press, 1995), p. 113.

29. On London exhibition, see Jon Burrows, 'Penny pleasures: film exhibition in London during the nickelodeon era, 1906–1914', *Film History* vol. 16 no. 1, 2004, pp. 60–91, and 'Penny Pleasures II', *Film History* vol. 16 no. 2, 2004, pp. 172–97. Allen Eyles has documented London cinemas in his books on the cinema chains of Britain, including *Odeon Cinemas 1* (London: Cinema Theatre Association, 2002) and *Gaumont British Cinemas* (London: Cinema Theatre Association, 1996).

30. Sorensen, *London on Film*, p. 10.

31. The most difficult aspect of this decision was the exclusion of Humphrey Jennings, whose films have been enormously influential in the imaging of London at war, and whose footage is frequently re-edited into other films and television without acknowledgment. There is a substantial literature, see for example, Brian Winston, *"Fires Were Started–"* (London: BFI, 1999), and John Corner's analysis of Michael Grigsby's references to Jennings in *The Art of Record* (Manchester: Manchester University Press, 1996), pp. 108–24.

32. Charles Drazin, *The Finest Years* (London: André Deutsch, 1998).

33. The phrase is Simon Grimble's, 'Somewhere to stand: descriptive writing and cultural criticism in Iain Sinclair's *Lights Out for the Territory*', in Mark Dorrian and Gillian Rose (eds), *Landscapes and Politics* (London: Black Dog, 2003), p. 175.

34. Raymond Durgnat includes, as one of the appendices of *A Mirror for England*, a section entitled 'Lists', pp. 263–7.

35. See the idea of a 'geographical life' explored by Stephen Daniels and Catherine Nash, 'Lifepaths: geography and biography', *Journal of Historical Geography* vol. 30 no. 3, 2004, pp. 449–58.

36. There is an extensive literature here, but the core originary texts are: Charles Baudelaire, 'The painter of modern life', trans. and ed. Jonathan Mayne, in *The Painter of Modern Life and Other Essays* (London: Phaidon, 1964 [1863]), pp. 1–41; Walter Benjamin, *Charles Baudelaire* (London: New Left

Books, 1973); Walter Benjamin, *The Arcades Project*, trans. Howard Eiland and Kevin McLaughlin (Cambridge, MA: Harvard University Press, 1999).

37. See Frank Mort and Miles Ogborn for a discussion that positions the flâneur in the context of some other urban actors, 'Transforming metropolitan London 1750–1960', *Journal of British Studies* vol. 43 no. 1, 2005, pp. 1–14, and James Donald on this figure in city/cinema scholarship, 'Talking the talk, walking the walk', *Screen* vol. 40 no. 3, 1999, pp. 295–303. The extensive feminist interrogation of this figure includes: Janet Wolff, 'The invisible flâneuse: women and the literature of modernity', *Theory, Culture and Society* vol. 2 no. 3, 1985, pp. 37–46; Griselda Pollock, 'Modernity and the spaces of femininity', in her *Vision and Difference* (London: Routledge, 1988), pp. 50–90; Elizabeth Wilson, 'The invisible flâneur', *New Left Review* no. 191, 1992, pp. 90–110; Jenny Ryan, 'Women, modernity and the city', *Theory, Culture and Society* vol. 11 no. 4, 1994, pp. 35–63; and Anke Gleber, *The Art of Taking a Walk: Flânerie, Literature and Film in Weimar Germany* (Princeton, NJ: Princeton University Press, 1999). See also John Sutherland's acerbic analysis of Mrs Dalloway's journey, 'Clarissa's invisible taxi', *Can Jane Eyre Be Happy?* (Oxford: Oxford University Press, 1997).

38. Andrew Higson, *Waving the Flag* (Oxford: Clarendon Press, 1995); Hill, *British Cinema in the 1980s*; Robert Murphy, *Realism and Tinsel* (London: Routledge, 1989) and *Sixties British Cinema* (London: BFI, 1992); Sarah Street, *British National Cinema* (London: Routledge, 1997); Claire Monk, 'From underworld to underclass', in S. Chibnall and R. Murphy (eds), *British Crime Cinema* (London: Routledge, 1999), pp. 172–88.

39. Amy Sargeant, *British Cinema* (London: BFI, 2005); Robert Murphy, 'Riff-raff', in Charles Barr (ed.), *All Our Yesterdays* (London: BFI, 1986), pp. 286–305, and (not on film) *Smash and Grab* (London: Faber and Faber, 1993).

40. James Saunders, *Celluloid Skyline* (New York: Knopf, 2001).

41. Murphy, *Sixties British Cinema*; Moya Luckett, 'Travel and Mobility: Femininity and National Identity in Swinging London Films', in Justine Ashby and Andrew Higson (eds), *British Cinema: Past and Present* (London: Routledge, 2000); Shonfield, *Walls Have Feelings*; Robert Murphy, 'City life: urban fairytales in late 90s British cinema', in his *British Cinema Book*, 2nd edn (London: BFI, 2001), pp. 292–300.

42. Pierre Sorlin, *European Cinemas, European Societies 1939–90* (London: Routledge, 1991). See also Anthony Sutcliffe, 'The metropolis in the cinema', in A. Sutcliffe (ed.), *Metropolis: 1890–1940* (London: Mansell, 1984), pp. 147–71, where he suggests that his relative neglect of British cinema is because 'British film-making was not very accomplished before 1940', p. 164.

43. Sorlin, *European Cinemas*, p. 132.

44. In Edward Timms (ed.), *Unreal City* (Manchester: Manchester University Press, 1984), the chapter on film is Michael Minden, 'The city in early cinema: *Metropolis, Berlin* and *October*', pp. 193–213. In David Clarke (ed.), *The Cinematic City* (London: Routledge, 1997), the only dedicated chapter on London is John R. Gold and Stephen V. Ward, 'Of plans and planners: documentary film and the challenge of the urban future 1935–52'. Nicholas Bullock, 'Imagining the post-war world: architecture, reconstruction and the British documentary movement', pp. 52–61, is the only essay on London in François Penz and Maureen Thomas (eds), *Cinema and Architecture* (London: BFI, 1997); Dietrich Neumann (ed.), *Film Architecture: Set Designs from Metropolis to Blade Runner* (Munich: Prestel Verlag, 1999), deals, as its title suggests with the Weimar/USA axis. In Myrto Konstantarakos (ed.), *Spaces in European Cinema* (Exeter: Intellect, 2000), the only essay on British films is Elizabeth Lebas, 'The clinic, the street and the garden: municipal film-making in Britain between the wars'.

Mark Shiel and Tony Fitzmaurice (eds), *Screening the City* (London: Verso, 2003), has no chapters on London, while the companion volume, *Cinema and the City* (Oxford: Blackwell, 2001), includes Leo Enticknap, 'Postwar urban redevelopment, the British Film Institute and *The Way We Live*', and Mike Mason, '*Naked*: social realism and the urban wasteland'.

45. John Orr, 'The revival of the cinematic city', in his *The Art and Politics of Film* (Edinburgh: Edinburgh University Press, 2000), pp. 136–54. Stephen Barber's *Projected Cities* (London: Reaktion, 2002) discusses *London* and John Maybury's *Remembrance of Things Fast*, pp. 96–101; Luana Babini, 'The urban soul of British cinema in the 1990s: London as cinematic city in Mike Leigh's *Naked* and Gary Oldman's *Nil By Mouth*', is the only essay on London in Wendy Everett and Axel Goodbody (eds), *Revisiting Space* (Bern: Peter Lang, 2005).

46. McArthur, 'Chinese boxes and Russian dolls'

47. Ewa Mazierska and Laura Rascaroli, *From Moscow to Madrid* (London: I. B. Tauris, 2003).

48. Pamela Church Gibson, 'Imaginary landscapes, jumbled topographies: cinematic London', in Joe Kerr and Andrew Gibson (eds), *London from Punk to Blair* (London: Reaktion, 2003), pp. 363–9.

49. Ian Christie, 'Londres', in Thierry Jousse and Thierry Paquot (eds), *La Ville au cinéma* (Paris: Cahiers du cinéma, 2005), p. 438 (my translation).

50. Sorlin, *European Cinemas*, p. 112.

51. Geoffrey Nowell-Smith, 'Cities real and imagined', in Shiel and Fitzmaurice, *Cinema and the City*, p. 103.

52. Peter Ackroyd, *London: The Biography* (London: Chatto and Windus, 2000), p. 779.

53. Franco Moretti, *Atlas of the European Novel 1800–1900* (London: Verso, 1998), p. 3.

54. Ibid., p. 5.

55. Ibid., p. 7. What the author of earlier books such as *Signs Taken For Wonders* (London: Verso, 1983) and *The Way of the World* (London: Verso, 1987) thinks *with* is another matter.

1

Landmark London

When a film shows Big Ben and the Houses of Parliament, Tower Bridge, Trafalgar Square, St Paul's Cathedral, Piccadilly Circus, red buses and black taxis, you know you are in London. This is the shorthand iconography of location, 'landmark London', which allows film-makers to indicate that their stories, or particular parts of their story, are set in London. Films that are entirely studio-shot may insert a little stock footage, location shooting or model work to reference this landmark iconography, to place their stories in London. Location-shot films may go to great pains to offer fresh views of familiar landmarks, or attempt to eschew them altogether in favour of accent and character as ways of establishing setting. For the paradox of landmark imagery is that it must be already familiar in order to elicit recognition, and 'already familiar' is often, already, overfamiliar. Thus, in Seth Holt's 1958 film, *Nowhere to Go*, the location of a solicitor's office in the City of London is shown through the reflected image of St Paul's in the brass door plate, employing a landmark image but doing so in a way that demands a fresh attention, as well as indicating a certain self-consciousness about the device.

In using these recognisable images, a film both refers to the urban imaginary of a specific city and also stages it, contributing to the many images, characters and tales that constitute that urban imaginary. This is nicely recognised in the opening of Alfred Hitchcock's *Stage Fright* (1950). The film opens in a theatre with a frontal shot of the proscenium arch. The title credits are played over the safety curtain of the theatre stage. As the credits roll, the curtain rises in front of the unmoving camera. The spectacle revealed behind the curtain is not a stage dressed for a performance, but location footage of St Paul's Cathedral rising above surrounding bombsites and traffic. The London setting of the film is revealed in a gesture that, five years after the end of the Second World War, uses formal invention to draw attention to the survival of the cathedral among the ruins. While this shot is the first of three, which move in to a two-shot of the occupants of a sports car, the narrative significance of the speeding car is overwhelmed by the dramatic, self-conscious staging of St Paul's in post-war London. The joke of the theatrical curtain rising on cinematic reality, rather than theatrical artifice, can only confirm the accomplishment of the cinematic artifice employed.

Stage Fright: the curtain (just visible at the top of the image) rises on St Paul's

This landmark iconography, like that of all capital cities, is an historically formed, multi-media iconography which is always about location but never just about location. While all cities have their landmarks, those of capital cities also carry complex and sometimes contested national and international meanings. Britain's imperial past and London's global significance in the Victorian period is strongly represented in London landmark imagery, with the Palace of Westminster, Tower Bridge and Trafalgar Square and Nelson's Column dating from the nineteenth century,[1] but there is also an earlier historical repertoire (the Tower of London, St Paul's) that confirms London's status as an 'old city'; and there is an emerging one of millennial modernity, which includes Richard Rogers' 1986 Lloyd's Building, the Millennium Wheel, Tate Modern and 30 St Mary Axe (the Gherkin).

Landmark iconography is not specific to cinema, although there are specifically cinematic ways of deploying it, as I will explore. Principal of these is a 'landmark montage', which functions as an establishing shot sequence at the beginning of a film, or to mark a move in location. Single shots of key landmarks, such as the Palace of Westminster, or St Paul's, can also be inserted into the space and time of film narratives, while other films integrate landmark imagery within narrative space and time. Landmark iconography is produced historically in a range of ways across many sites and practices, including postcards, engravings, guided tours, museums and souvenir shops. The historical marketing of London analysed in the study of London guidebooks by scholars such as David Gilbert, Fiona Henderson and John

Eade[2] provides one set of sources for tracing the transformations to landmark London, just as the agency Film London, established to facilitate filming in London, provides another. 'Grands projets' architecture (such as Millennium wheels), T-shirts with tube maps, miniature red telephone kiosks key rings and the televising of Parliament all contribute to the production and circulation of the landmark images of London. The artist Banksy, spraying 'This is not a photo-opportunity' on a lamp-post opposite Parliament, draws attention to the role of everyday photography in reproducing London as a city of tourist views.[3] The representative status of particular landmarks has its own history and their iconographic presence can wax and wane at particular times, as Stephen Daniels has shown with the extra-cinematic history of St Paul's Cathedral.[4] For the cinema, the cathedral, which was London's tallest building until 1958, has a silhouette which can be easily referenced and recreated in the studio. Following its iconic significance in the photography and cinema of the Second World War and the immediate post-war period, it has recently gained a new view with the redevelopment of the South Bank, the building of the Millennium footbridge and 30 St Mary Axe. In this view, St Paul's (old) is recruited to a funkier, modern London represented by the steel lines of the bridge or the dark glass curves of 30 St Mary Axe. Modern, professional Londoners, such as the characters in *Closer* (2004), can be filmed with the cathedral as a fashionably accented backdrop, and it is this mixture of ancient and modern, with a little bit of shopping thrown in, which is characteristic of twenty-first-century landmark London montages.

One of my arguments in this book is that all films that claim London as their setting must engage with this hegemonic discourse of location – with that river, that clock, that bridge, those buses and those taxis – but that there are various ways of going about it. The exclusion of what Katherine Shonfield has called 'the tourist hardware'[5] is often more significant in a London-set film than is its inclusion, and there are very different tonalities with

Closer: a twenty-first-century landmark London view

which iconographic elements can be used in narratives, as will be discussed below. Just which image or sound, in which combination, in which period, means 'this is London', is one of the ways in which the historical and documentary aspect of fiction film can be traced through its dramatic *mise en scène*.

This chapter has three parts. I start by examining some 'this is London' sequences from a range of films. The very ubiquity of some of these images in the cinema could lead to some rather dull lists, so instead I have chosen to look in detail at particular sequences in a few films with the aim of highlighting the contrasting ways in which different films use the same imagery. I then proceed to discuss three London 'landmarks' that are less monumental than Tower Bridge and Big Ben: the red London bus, the pub and the fog. While the red double-decker bus is always cited as a cliché of London-ness, I will argue that its appearance in the cinema is often managed with considerable subtlety. The complex spatiality of public houses, where status and belonging can be negotiated with a glance, provides a rich setting for a medium in which space is constructed through the interplay of looks and gazes, and demands discussion in a book on London in the cinema, even though pubs are by no means specific to London-set films. A brief consideration of foggy days in London films shows the way in which landmark London imagery signifies time as well as place. For if there is a predominance of Victorian landmarks in the cinematic signifying of London, there is also a substantial tradition of the cinematic presentation of London as a Victorian city, within which fog is a key motif. This London requires only a gas street lamp, a cobbled street, a horse-drawn carriage and a wisp of mist to be identified, and begins to demonstrate the way in which landmarks signify genre as well as time and place.

In later chapters, I will discuss the way in which the eschewing of landmark London can be as significant as its imaging, particularly in films that make the realist claim to show an authentic London and, thus, want to avoid familiar images such as Tower Bridge and Piccadilly Circus. But here I want to concentrate on the familiar and often clichéd images that signify 'This is London' and the chapter closes with a discussion of the role of landmark imagery in the staging of an uncanny London in two films made fifty years apart, *Seven Days to Noon* (1950) and *Twenty-Eight Days Later …* (2002).

'This is London'

Night and the City (1950) was the first of blacklisted director Jules Dassin's European films and was made, with some location shooting, at Shepperton by Twentieth Century-Fox. It is interesting here for its complex presentation of a doubled London. London landmarks are shown as the superficial attractions – the surface – of a much grubbier underworld, while generically it is both American film noir and, through the use of location and character actors, British realist. This doubling is introduced at the beginning of the film through the relationship between landmark London images and a voice-over narration. The film's title sequence gives cast and crew credits over a brief, dark montage of night-time London views, including the Embankment, Tower Bridge and Piccadilly Circus, returning, for the final shot of the sequence, to the Palace of Westminster from the Albert Embankment. The up-tempo orchestrated musical accompaniment to the title sequence hints at (rather non-British) excitement to come, but also introduces a more plangent violin theme, which suggests that the outcomes of the film may not be entirely happy. London is established as the location for the film through this dark, five-shot montage, but the narration, which begins after the title sequence over a lighter image of Westminster, disregards the 'London' that has been carefully established, beginning instead with the more general noir proposition: 'Night and the city. The night is tonight, tomorrow night or any night.'

This narration, over images that foreground the River Thames in its misty beauty, promises the generalised urban anomie of film noir. Only after the dominance of 'night and the city' in general has been established does the narrator specify, over a cut to Piccadilly Circus, with Eros centred, and a double-decker bus moving from right to left to obscure it, that 'The city is London'. There are two kinds of 'establishing' going on here – one of place, the other of genre. While the images are recognisable landmark London images: the place of government, the River Thames and the slightly more risqué centre of the West End, the voice-over promises something less straightforward. The darkness of the images – this is clearly London at night – offers generic clues as to the type of narrative that will be set here, but it is the narration that both fixes, and disavows, the location. This is London – but it is London within a repertoire that includes New York and Los Angeles, rather than Cardiff and Edinburgh. A cut to a figure running across monumental steps and then a silhouetted St Paul's confirms the 'noirish' promise of the voice-over narration and the existential randomness of the temporal setting, 'any night'. We understand that while this time, tonight, it is London – and a London

Night and the City: 'the night is tonight, tomorrow night or any night'

rendered with some precision, as I discuss in Chapter 3 – the story we are being told is a perennial city tale, a story of 'the city' in general.

This view of Westminster from across the water is used in innumerable films, sometimes with just a shot, unrelated to other aspects of the *mise en scène*, to signify arrival or location in London. There is a sudden shot of Westminster in the 1946 Ealing film, *The Captive Heart*, which is set mainly in a German prisoner-of-war camp, where a captured Czech officer, Captain Hasek (Michael Redgrave), corresponds to his supposed wife Celia Mitchell (Rachel Kempson) in an English village (to escape death he has masqueraded as her dead husband). The film is notable for the evocation of English village life with which Captain Hasek falls in love, cricket on the village green, the changing seasons, gardening; as he does with the woman who describes it to him. This rural imaginary of England is the counterpart to landmark London, and within the narrativised spaces of the film is set against the prison camp. However, suddenly, about forty minutes in, there is a single shot of the Palace of Westminster and Big Ben from Westminster Bridge in the twilight. The following brief scene, which is necessary to establish that Hasek is a bona fide anti-Nazi, is set in Army headquarters, by implication, in Whitehall, and then the film returns to the prison-camp location. This is a simple use of landmark iconography in which a widely recognised view of the British Parliament is used to signify location economically and without contradiction. The signifier of place is the place of government, and the story does at this point require senior Army personnel – people who are in command. The gloomy twilight of the image befits the wartime story of stoicism and deprivation, while also referring to that long history of foggy, twilit Londons.

Sally Potter's witty short dance film, *The London Story* (1986), also uses shots of Westminster to signify the place of government, opening with canted shots of the clock tower. A tale of espionage, dramatising Britain's position between Europe and the USA in a drama of stolen documents, secret assignations and subsequent changes to government policy, the film is cut to a soundtrack of Prokofiev's ballet music, *Romeo and Juliet*. Before the spying starts, this Soviet soundtrack is used as counterpoint to three shots of the River Thames, two with Westminster in the background. Misty twilit and night views, the composition of the image accentuated by the strings of light-bulbs on the Embankment reflected in the water, these landmark views of the 'British government' are both familiar and, in their sequence, and the length of the shots, offered for fresh contemplation. The three shots form a beautiful pause in which other images of the same view can be recalled, and the viewer can meditate on the qualities of the image and their immanent narrative role.

Pierre Sorlin has suggested that the same image within landmark iconography can either block or incite the viewer's engagement:

> [I]mages can also conceal the world, since permanent recourse to the same words and pictures, a repetition of the same clichés, prevents us from seeing. The same Tower can be an incitement (we know where we are, now let us explore the visual presentation of the town) or a block (we are in London and that is enough).[6]

London Story: the landmark river

The logo for London Films

gle shot of Westminster in *The Captive Heart* would be an example of blocking in this
ve are in London and that is enough. The function of the shot could have been
covered with a title 'Army High Command, London, 1943'. The point is 'change of location:
forward with the story'. An even more abbreviated example of blocking would be the use of
an image of Big Ben as the logo for Alexander Korda's company, London Films. Here, the
image, the chimes and the gothic-inflected script of 'A London Film' at the beginning of a
film served as a branding that is only residually concerned with place. Potter's Westminster,
in contrast, encourages reflection on the imbrication of aesthetic history, monumental stone,
government, nationality and the loyalty of citizens.

Incitement, Sorlin suggests, is more interesting in that we know where we are, and can
now explore the visual presentation of the city. In the example of Potter's film, this 'incitement' is possible because the experimental form of the film produces an interpretative space
that is more open than many popular narrative films. The opening of Patrick Keiller's film
London (1994) is an example of the invocation of landmark imagery with a voice-over that
incites an unfamiliar engagement with the image. Filmed in 1992, when the Conservative
government unexpectedly won an election for another five years in power and the IRA
bombed the financial district, the City, *London* documents the city journeys of the narrator
(Paul Scofield) and his friend, the flâneur, Robinson, repeatedly finding traces of the modernist imagination in locations ranging from Atlantic Avenue in Brixton to the shopping malls
of Brent Cross. The film is composed of a series of unmoving tripod-mounted shots of different scales and duration, which are presented as a London image track to a narration of three
expeditions taken by Robinson and the narrator, neither of whom is ever seen. Patrick Keiller
trained as an architect and his films and his writing on film shows a consistent concern with
relationships between architectural space and film space.[7] *London*, evidently somewhat to its
maker's surprise, has become a canonical film for those interested in London, within the
'city/cinema' canon and a series of related fields.[8] This is partly because it incites so much
reflection on the presentation of the city through the rather deadpan poise with which it
locates its fictional, journal-like narration in a setting, London, which it does not use as a set.

It opens with a shot of Tower Bridge and the River Thames looking east as a cruise liner
moves through the Pool of London. Tower Bridge has become, if possible, an even more
favoured London landmark image towards the end of the twentieth century, perhaps increasingly attractive as it offers Victorian Gothic (like the Houses of Parliament), but is not associated with government. Its position easily marks entry to the city, and its presentation here
serves to locate the film and to declare, in combination with the film's title, that this film will
be about London, not merely set there. But how it will be about London is immediately
thrown into question by the tone of the narration.

The first image is a symmetrically framed view of Tower Bridge with its roadway down, closed
to ships, with faint noises of river and road traffic. This is a postcard view of London, and the plain
white title on black background which follows confirms this location. But then the narration
starts, and the first words, in the rich, mellifluous received pronunciation of Paul Scofield, propose not a tourist's arrival at the threshold of a great city, but something rather darker: 'It was a
journey to the end of the world.' At the very point of recognition of Tower Bridge as a great ship
comes into anchor, there is an echo of the journey in Joseph Conrad's *Heart of Darkness* which

opens on the 'lower reaches of the Thames'. Marlowe begins his story, 'And this also has been one of the dark places of the earth.'[9] These beginnings share the device of rendering the heart of empire foreign. The opening shot is returned to, the slow approach of a cruise liner with its pilot vessels continuing, and the narrator begins his story, starting with the friendship that will provide a point of engagement for the viewer, and setting up the enigma of Robinson's investigations.

> It is seven years since I saw Robinson on the day I left England … now he has written that he urgently wishes to see me, that he is on the verge of a breakthrough in his investigations, and that I should come as soon as possible, before it is too late.

The image is held for a few seconds after this section of narration finishes – still a postcard, still Tower Bridge, but now an image that has become enigmatic to the viewer and that incites curiosity. A new title, '11 January 1992', follows and the very low tones of the cello in a Beethoven string quartet are heard. In the next image, the bridge is raised and the cruise ship is coming through when the narrator moves into a third modality and declares, 'Dirty old Blighty – under-educated, economically backward – bizarre,' as the third title appears, 'The great malady – horror of home'. This indictment continues over the third view of the ship, now through the closing bridge,

> a catalogue of modern miseries, with its fake traditions, its Irish war, its militarism and secrecy, its silly old judges, its hatred of intellectuals, its ill health and bad food, its sexual repression, its hypocrisy and racism and its indolence. It's so exotic, so home-made.

The intimacy of this condemnation of Blighty, the use of classic critiques of the English (bad food, bad teeth, bad sex) with the colloquialism of 'silly old judges' and Scofield's patrician tones unsettles the meaning of the image, even as the liner seems to glide serenely up-river. Tower Bridge is shorn of its landmark grandeur and becomes a 'fake tradition' – possibly even a silly old bridge, with its stone-clad Gothic towers concealing the sophisticated Victorian engineering of its steel frame. After a flash of black leader, which concludes the indictment, the final image of the sequence, a wider shot from further away, is of the cruise ship at anchor, with Tower Bridge still dominating the composition, the whole in a warmer, less misty light, while the narrator identifies himself as a ship's photographer working on a cruise liner 'in which the berths cost £4,000 a week'. The exquisite timing of this opening, in which the 'unblocking' of the image of Tower Bridge is achieved through a narration which reveals something of the backstory, the project and the politics of the film, is demonstrated through the 'pause' of the final image of the sequence which inaugurates the next sequence introducing Robinson in more detail.

This opening informs the viewer of the way in which images and soundtrack will work in the film, with the dense, ironic, literary narration counterpointing the tableaux images from the unmoving documentary camera. It also gives an indication of the way in which landmark imagery is handled by the film. Moving beyond the first moment of recognition of the image, the narration incites a re-recognition of images such as Tower Bridge or Whitehall, placing them back into the rich material history of London as a literary and imperial city, a city in which something as banal as the fencing round some council blocks turns out to be stretcher frames from the Second World War. The film traces forgotten rivers and local parks, seeks out the former residences of writers and poets, but also visits tourist spots like Leicester Square and places of indigenous pilgrimage like the shopping mall of Brent Cross, tracing that other pre-Victorian London when British culture might have developed differently. Its choice of images refuses to conform to any accepted combination of significant London images. The film combines a Francophile lament for a romantic and symbolist London that hardly existed with an angry, melancholic and loving documenting of the rubbish-strewn, bomb-damaged city of the postscript to the Thatcher years. As many commentators have noted, the unmoving camera produces the visual track of the film as a series of postcards. These are of differing scales and types, each meticulously planned and composed, their editing together refusing any single system, although there is a discernible interest in presenting, in a single image, the extraordinary juxtapositions that reveal themselves in a city. For example, in a two-shot sequence near the end of the film, a 1930s semi-detached house is shown, tightly framed, with a (palm-like) yucca tree in its front garden. The house has been customised by its owners, the tiling on the bay painted in gloss paint, the brickwork covered in crazy-paved stone cladding. The tight framing accentuates the detail of the vernacular embellishment. In the following shot, taken further back to show the house as one

London: Myrtle Avenue, Hatton

of a terrace, a huge aeroplane dominates the sky about the house, taking off from Heathrow. The laconic edit, collating the two images, the personalised ordinary house and then the astonishing shot of the row of houses dominated by the plane, condenses the film's proposition: this is London.

In a different strategy, which is used at the opening of the film in a manner that instructs the viewer of both the intellectual formation of the film and its visual modes, city signage is regarded within its visual environment rather than proposed for directional reading. In the three-shot 'Montaigne' sequence, the camera set-up is repeated for the first and third shots. In this shot, the camera faces a corner wall, one side of which is covered with old posters and notices. The part of the wall facing the camera is adorned with notices about learning English, '*Aprenda Ingl*', and part of a sign reading 'The Mont School of English' and complemented by a little model of figure in black scholar's robes similarly encouraging the learning of English; the narration mentions that Robinson is reading Montaigne, citing with approval 'that it is good to be born in depraved times' before there is a cut to the seedy doorway with its plastic sign for 'The Montaigne School of English'. What Stephen Daniels has called the 'Paris-envy' of the film is made explicit by the narrator in the recital of the connections of Verlaine, Mallarmé, Rimbaud and Baudelaire with London over this shot.[10] When the camera set-up of the first shot is repeated, the truncated word on the sign 'Mont' has now been confirmed as the first part of Montaigne, and the viewer is given cause, and pause, to reflect on the aspiration to learn English as taught by, or in the former house of, or in some other mysterious relation to Montaigne in seedy central London. The ridiculous bathos of the seediness of the signage and the institution, in combination with the fact that such attention has been paid to it, and a literary history extrapolated from it, gives something of the tone of the film's vision. Another thread of the film is comprised of close-ups of city nature, sometimes miniatures – a snowdrop – sometimes with a framing that permits an oscillation in the image between a represented sight, say horse-chestnut flowers, and an abstractly patterned visual field. This series of seasonal flowers – the film follows the chronological structure of the year – is matched by another, of the Thames framed tightly in a similar way. So the Thames appears in the film, not just as a series of views, but as a series of water shots: rippling, with raindrops, swirling, with flotsam and jetsam.[11] In each shot, the water fills the

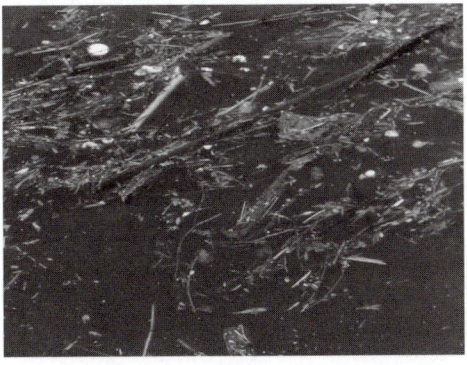 

London: flotsam and jetsam (left) and the view of the Thames at Richmond (right)

frame: there is no horizon, no bank, just the variety of the textured surface of the 'strong brown God'. These series offer interludes for the viewer in which the everyday beauty of the city is noticed and made available for contemplation, while also, continuously, drawing attention to the dimensions and boundaries of the cinematic image and the flatness of the screen.

And so as a whole the film continues to make new our images of the city as its opening promised. Both at the level of its form, and what it chooses to show of the city, the film offers an interrogation of what we might understand as London, and the type of postcards that might be sent of its landmarks. The narrator informs us that Robinson is indeed preparing 'his own series of postcards of contemporary London'. In some ways an encyclopaedia for the eye, with a narration often counterpointing the image, waylaid by a chance encounter, or caught in another footnote of London literary history, the film solves its 'problem of London' through a rigorous but opaque structuring of the apparently random.

London is a perverse city symphony film. Through the exercise of tight aesthetic control, it documents the epiphenomena of everyday life in the city, while assessing the future in relation to a past that partly didn't happen and a present regarded pessimistically. If Vertov's 'kino-eye' in *Man with a Movie Camera* (1929) could, through mechanical vision, render the modern city in a manner that augments human vision, emphasising the speed and beauty of the machine, Keiller's steady camera and melancholy, slightly grumpy travellers reinstall the human eye to a vision of the city that attempts not to encompass the whole, but instead to accumulate and record material which cannot be classified under any one system. Within these structured refusals, though, the film includes a good deal of 'landmark' material such as Trafalgar Square, the Trooping of the Colour, Monet's view of the Thames and Routemaster buses. But these postcard images are never left alone. Either they are contextualised into dissident histories (England as the place of the failed bourgeois revolution, the shame of the bombing of civilian populations of Germany, the inconvenience of the amount of space the royal family occupy); or they are shown from an unfamiliar angle – the Trooping of the Colour showing bearskinned soldiers, shuffling to align themselves like a minimalist dance; or their un-postcard-like reality is evoked: the smell of urine and cigarettes in the 'neo-Georgian phone boxes'. And these landmark images are countered, and contextualised, by the surreal beauty of the banal juxtapositions of city life. The accomplishment of the film lies in the way in which its formal strategies, the combination of unmoving camera and long take, both convince the viewer of the reality of what is shown – they really are Trooping the Colour, on a parade ground framed by rustling Virginia creeper on buildings – and, at the same time, constantly remind the viewer of the framing of the image. This is an encounter between modernism, documentary and the nation which, despite the tonal differences partly attributable to being made at the beginning and the end of the dream of the Welfare State, has most in common with the British film-maker cited within the film, Humphrey Jennings.

Bruzzi points to the perversity of a journey film with an unmoving camera; Paul Dave, who discusses the film alongside Keiller's later films, *Robinson in Space* (1997) and *The Dilapidated Dwelling* (2002), argues that the film is characterised by a defeated 'aestheticisation of the social'.[12] In relation to cinematic Londons, one of the film's distinctions lies in a fastidious aesthetic relativism, rendering up for contemplation both flotsam in muddy water and the pastoral view of the River Thames at Richmond. In a film that could be seen as a meditation on a postcard, London's landmarks are rendered almost arbitrary, the traces and residues of a history which could have been otherwise, and are augmented, in a record of journeys that could have gone elsewhere, by more idiosyncratic signs of place such as sacred bus-routes and whispering gate-posts.

Katherine Shonfield addresses landmark imagery in a different way in *Walls Have Feelings: Architecture, Film and the City.* She is concerned throughout the book to investigate the way in which borders are articulated and maintained – in building construction, in films and in architecture, and she discusses the use of centre/periphery models in the envisioning of London from the 1943 LCC County of London Plan to the building of the Millennium Dome and the conversion of Bankside Power Station into Tate Modern. Shonfield suggests that the singling out of particular areas for special planning treatment, together with adoption of conservation areas, 'have effectively objectified museum London to be cherished and encouraged, from rubbish London – the other side of the planners' borders'.[13] Shonfield goes on to argue that the opposition between 'museum London' and 'rubbish London' is also produced by the way in which Hollywood views London, illustrating her argument with a discussion of the opening of *Mary Poppins* (1964):

> every part of London that is not deemed a recognisable object is swathed in useful fog.
>
> Through the mist emerges Hollywood's judgement on what are London's big four: the Houses of Parliament, St Paul's, the Tower of London and Tower Bridge. Mary Poppins's London uncannily re-emerged as a prevailing image on the cover of the 1996 *Strategic Guidance.* In both, London is done away with in favour of the same familiar lumps of tourist hardware.[14]

Thirty years after *Mary Poppins, Trainspotting* (1995) chose Big Ben, Boadicea, Tower Bridge and Nelson's Column as the relevant 'lumps of tourist hardware' – but also Carnaby Street, motorbike couriers, a steel-drum player, the Lloyd's Building and a pearly king and queen. *Trainspotting* is set mainly in Leith, the port of Edinburgh, and is partly distinctive in its refusal to traffic in the ravishing beauty of parts of the Edinburgh city centre and the surrounding countryside, offering instead the grim squalor of the heroin and alcohol cultures of the estates. The film is staged against the Bonnie Scotland of shortbread biscuit tins in both its setting and narrative; its Edinburgh is dirty flats, filthy pubs, drug hallucinations and overdoses. London, in contrast, is first shown through a very fast landmark montage cut to an Ice MC soundtrack. The first shot of the sequence is Big Ben, but a hint of the approach is given by the angle of the shot of Queen Boadicea and her chariot rearing up across the screen. The film makes it clear that this is a knowing recycling of the landmark imagery that signifies London location. Punctuated with shots of an open double-decker bus with 'Official London Sightseeing Bus' inscribed across its side, the sequence offers a fantasy tour bus with the boring bits left out. The narrative demanded that Renton's arrival in London be briefly conveyed, and this the film does with an upbeat montage of hackneyed and more modern images showing that the conventions of arrival in London were being used, but that everyone concerned was cool enough to know that these were the conventions used to convey location change.[15] Sometimes the signalling of location is so perfunctory that no more than street signs are shown – 'Piccadilly Circus', 'Regent Street' – the street sign more important than the place, which might itself be unrecognisable.[16] Sometimes camera movement or angle is used to freshen an image: Eros starts upside down, as do his surrounding tourists, but this device too is cynical, attempting not to incite our interest, but just to jazz things up a little. London iconography is here a third order system of signification, in which the familiar postcard images are used, but in a way which recognises their commodification, and indeed inscribes a knowingness about this commodification in the image in a way that parallels an earlier sequence set in the Scottish countryside ('It's shite being Scottish'). This knowingness can be seen in the use of two landmark London characters, the British bobby and the cockney. There are two policemen in the sequence, one mounted on horseback and the other giving directions in a crowd. The direction-giving policeman is performing a useful civic task. The potentially more menacing mounted policeman, shot from below on his chestnut horse, allays anxiety by giving a cheerful wave – in happy London tourist town, the policemen are friends. The friendly wave at the viewer is more developed in the case of the cheery cockneys, a pearly king and queen, dressed in traditional manner, with mother-of-pearl buttons sewn all over their clothes. First seen outside St Paul's Cathedral, bowing and ingratiatingly welcoming spectators, they appear later in the sequence waving from the platform of a double-decker red bus. Their welcoming wave is later echoed by both a busload of tourists and the thumbs-up given by a doorman of the Lloyd's Building – the film is both signifying London in the traditional way, and winking at its audience.

The soundtrack, though, and images such as the leather-dressed motorbike couriers and the steel-drum player, juxtapose traditional heritage London with post-1960s London. The music breaks just before kicking in on a Carnaby Street sign, while the steel-drum player invokes the inheritance of the West Indies and carnival in what might be called a figure of 'integrated Empire'. So *Trainspotting*, made in the moment just before 'Cool Britannia', also invokes Swinging London and a more hybrid Britishness than is usually signified by Nelson's Column, just as the use of Richard Rogers's Lloyd's Building acknowledges the City in its post-Big Bang manifestation.[17] Renton has moved to Mrs Thatcher's London, and in the comparison the film offers between stealing, drug-dealing and estate agency, a boom profession of the Thatcher years, estate agency does not emerge as the more honourable profession.

Murray Smith uses an opposition very similar to Shonfield's distinction between 'objectified museum London' and 'rubbish London' when he points out that after Renton's arrival most of the London action takes place in his cramped flat, and that '[o]nce Begbie and Sick Boy arrive, this space comes to resemble more and more the decrepit hovels they inhabited in Edinburgh. Heritage is once again overwhelmed and undercut by its doppelganger, garbage.'[18] This violent opposition, between what Shonfield, writing in 2000, calls 'museum/ rubbish', and Smith (2002) 'heritage/garbage', is an historically and nationally specific form of the traditional city image of the juxtaposition of rich and poor (the rich man and the beggar; the palace and the hovel). In cinematic London it can be seen to govern genre as well as locality, in, for example, the contrast between romantic comedy London (*Notting Hill*, 1999) and naturalist London (*Nil By Mouth*, 1997). In the next two chapters, I will explore this opposition further through the more general, historical contrast between 'Landmark London' and local and everyday Londons.

Trainspotting's landmark sequence self-consciously references memories of 1960s 'Swinging London' films. This is a disparate group of films, with a wide range of tone, usually seen to include *The Knack* (1965), *Georgy Girl* (1966), *Darling* (1966), *Alfie* (1966), *Blow-Up* (1967), *I'll Never Forget What's 'is name* (1967) and *Smashing Time* (1967)[19]. *Blow-Up*, with the accentuated green of its empty park, and its photograhers, models and pop-groups, renders a London both uncanny and swinging.[20] The most interesting accounts of the British films, like Dick Lester's five-part television series, *Hollywood U.K.* (1993), contextualises them within a much broader view of British film and television in the period, while also attending to the way in which the films present London[21]. This scholarship connects the construction of London as a city of youth culture and consumption with the cinematic construction of the North as the site of authenticity. There is debate about how these connections should be understood, and to what extent there is a cinematic Swinging London, as opposed to a fantasised memory of one[22]. For my purposes in this chapter, which I am not suggesting is necessarily a central concern of the films themselves, they are interesting for the tone of their engagement with landmark London. They do it – when they do it – zanily. The protagonists encounter key elements of 1960s landmark London – parking meters, telephone kiosks, the Royal Albert Hall – and fool around in some way – such as driving too fast round Trafalgar Square in an MG in *Georgy Girl*. This produces landmark images which can function within the cultural memory of the1960s

Flirting in front of a London landmark: Alfie (Michael Caine) and Ruby (Shelley Winters) in *Alfie*

quite separately from the narratives in which they are embedded. The icons of traditional landmark London are invoked, but the gaze directed at them is different. In a period when the expectation that the cinema audience would stand still and silent at the end of the evening during the national anthem was being challenged, the gaze at icons of Britishness was also less deferential. In *Alfie*, one of the hero's careers is as a street photographer, stalking the Embankment to inveigle passers-by into having their photographs taken. Landmark London, in the form of Tower Bridge, provides a background for Alfie's risqué flirtation with one of his customers. The spectacle of heritage, in a move that contributes to the continuing popularity of images of 1960s Britain, was both rendered old fashioned and spectacularised by a pop sensibility, epitomised by the junk shop in *Blow-Up*, while the newer icons of the 1960s, women in mini-skirts, pop groups, Carnaby Street and parking meters, were recruited to the identity of the city[23]. In *Darling* Diana Scott's (Julie Christie) adultery is signified with a close-up on a parking meter as the indicator switches mechanically first to 'excess charge' and then to 'penalty'. The film also shows the pleasures of consumption in a more affluent Britain, with a scene set in Fortnum and Mason where the privilege and stuffiness of the British upper classes are mocked as the heroine and her gay friend (Murray Melvin) get the giggles as they shoplift luxury food. Their behaviour here disrupts the recognised cultural cachet of Fortnum and Mason, used, for example, in *The Reluctant Debutante*, Vincente Minnelli's 1958 film, in which Sandra Dee is introduced to the London Season. Dee is taken by another young woman to have tea in Fortnum and Mason after they have inspected the Household Cavalry: the shop is signified through a single lattice partition in its trademark aqua colour scheme.[24] Like the scene set in a supermarket in *The Ipcress File* (1967), where Harry Palmer (Michael Caine) picks up his tin of button mushrooms, or the lure of Carnaby Street in *Smashing Time*, this scene in *Darling* marks the beginning of the social extension of the 'shopping for pleasure' trope in the identity of landmark London. Shopping in London is coming to mean more than just the upper classes in Harrods and Fortnum and Mason.

The final example of landmark London I will discuss comes from the very successful 2001 Bollywood film made for a Hindi-speaking audience, *Kabhi Khushi Kabhie Gham* (directed by Karan Johar). The shopping trope is here transformed from the 'fun' social extensiveness of the 1960s films to dominate the presentation of the city. Here, the hero's arrival in London is marked by a classic landmark sequence (aerial shots of Tower Bridge, the river, the Palace of Westminster, the Millennium Wheel, Big Ben), which is presented as a musical number, 'Vande Mataram', which includes a chorus of young Asian women singing on the Embankment, and other tropes of the genre. Landmark London segues into London as a world city, a welcoming city for wealthy tourists, as the London icons such as buses and phone boxes are intercut with the attractions of branded consumption in the West End: shows (*Cats*, *Les Miserables*, *Chicago*), coffee bars (Coffee Republic, Starbucks) and shops – Dolce and Gabbana, Armani, MaxMara. The hero joins in a series of dance and song routines with different groups of women, including one in Trafalgar Square and one on the banks of the Thames, and is shown to be at home and welcomed in London. This use of landmark London as a set for song and dance numbers is characteristic of millennial Bollywood London-set films, and can also be found in films such as *Ramji London Waley* (directed by Sanjay Dayma, 2004), where the 'London' number is staged across a number of locations, including Piccadilly

The number 'Deewana Hai Dekho' set in the Great Court of the British Museum in *Kabhi Khushi Kabhie Gham*

Circus and Tower Bridge, and also uses a trailer and a boat to render the musical number mobile across the city. In *Kabhi Khushi Kabhie Gham*, though, tourist hardware is less important in London's attractions than the promise of branded international consumption, an emphasis confirmed through the location of the final climactic meetings in the Bluewater Shopping Complex. London here has been extended to mean the shopping boxes on the M25, but this film's postmodern geography is most perfectly expressed in the song 'Deewana Hai Dekho', which includes a routine set in the Great Court of the British Museum, where Norman Foster's roof encloses much older Portland stone buildings modelled on classical architecture.

These Bollywood landmark London montages, in which London is one of many generic settings for musical numbers, could be seen as extreme examples of Sorlin's notion of 'blocking', in which the image of the city does not encourage reflection on the city.[25] They also, like the opening of *Night and the City*, establish both location and genre. However, they can also be read historically to exhibit London not so much as a location, but as a site of consumption, in which what were formerly signifiers of location (red phone boxes, Tower Bridge, Trafalgar Square) are rearticulated into a string of sights, of attractions, and take their place alongside shows and multinational shops and international franchises. This begins to raise the question, to which I will return in Chapter 3, not of London's distinctiveness, but, at the end of the twentieth century, its sameness. David Martin-Jones, in a discussion of preferred modes of national identity in *Sliding Doors* (1997), argues that 'the film does not aim to sell what is specifically different about London – its culturally specific tourist attractions, its history or its heritage – rather, it focuses on those aspects that establish London as comparable with other global cities.'[26] Looked at in this way, the increasing inclusion of brand names and advertising in landmark montages rebalances the sequences, so that the signifiers of location become merely the quaint context for global consumption.

Landmark London montages thus raise issues about the historical city as well as more general questions about cinematic space, location and time. The modulation, from film to film and from period to period, of what is chosen to mean 'this is London' and the tone in which images are handled can offer more and less sensitive indices of change and attitude. 'This is London' always tells the viewer something of the type of London that is being imagined, even as it seems to offer only a referential image. Edward Dimendberg uses the notion of 'synoptic' city views in his discussion of the US film noir city, suggesting

> [t]hat so many films noir begin with elevated, aerial, or skyline views suggests that an essential feature of the film cycle entails the movement from a clearly delimited synoptic overview of the metropolis towards dark street corners, alleyways, and other relatively inaccessible interior spaces.[27]

While this is a productive contrast for his argument about the spaces of film noir, and there clearly are some possible analogies for London, in general, the signifying of London through landmark images is more variable and necessarily more eclectic than this. I have already referred to Shonfield's discussion of the opening of *Mary Poppins*, where all but the selected landmarks are shrouded in mist. A twenty-first-century version of this de facto montage is given at the beginning of the Olsen twins' vehicle, *Winning London* (2001), where photographic images of Big Ben, the Tower, a Routemaster bus and Tower Bridge appear on a black screen as computer icons which can be clicked. Instead of mist, cyberspace articulates 'the bits between' the landmarks. The tourist hardware has remained constant: only its medium of delivery has changed.

These abstractions of landmark London do, however, show something of how location is being used in these sequences. For although a quick succession of shots of Tower Bridge, Piccadilly Circus and the Millennium Wheel may signify a location for a narrative, this meaning paradoxically signifies the city abstractly: 'this is London', rather than in terms of the spaces in which the narrative will take place. There are, of course, exceptions to this. For example, the 1954 film *Hidden Cargo* has a dramatic final car chase in which an alcoholic drug smuggler tries to 'jump the gap' as Tower Bridge is raised; *An American Werewolf in London* (1979) does involve panic in Piccadilly Circus, and Big Ben has featured in more than one narrative climax.[28] But landmark images, although they are images of place, mobilised to inform viewers where a film is set, are in general, not a part of the narrative spaces of the film.[29] The images used in landmark London sequences may, ultimately, say more about genre, orientation and period than about place.

The Bus, the Pub and the Fog

The London bus, the London pub and the London fog are also landmark images of London, if of a slightly different order. The red double-decker London bus is widely recognised as a signifier of London, and is often referenced when people wish to speak scathingly of clichéd London imagery in the cinema. The pub is perhaps more properly regarded as a British landmark, but there are some notable uses of London pubs in the cinema, which I want just to touch on because the pub is such a significant 'low-life' landmark in British cinema and films set in Britain. London fog, as many have recognised, has a rich pre-cinematic history, and James Donald commences his book on *Imagining the Modern City* with an analysis of Charles Dickens's evocation of the London fog in *Bleak House*.[30] Each merits much more space than I can give it here, but the point of the grouping of the bus, the pub and the fog is that these are different types of entities that can all mean 'London'. Their appearance in a film works to identify the setting, but each also, in different ways, can function as both metaphor and metonym for the city.

The Bus

> The moment you saw a red London bus go through the shot – the moment you saw that [points to image of 73 Routemaster bus] – you knew you were in for a rotten time.[31]

The film director Alan Parker delivers this condemnation of 'red bus films' in his 1986 television polemic about British film culture, *A Turnip Head's Guide to British Cinema*. While he is correct to point to the ubiquity of the red double-decker bus to show a cinema audience that a film is set in London, his contemptuous comment underrates the flexibility of the London bus as a signifier of place, as well as dismissing the chic colour co-ordination of mid-twentieth-century London, with the colour of the buses picked up in street furniture such as pillar-boxes and phone boxes and contrasted with the black of taxis.

A bus does not have to be a central plot element, as it is in *Summer Holiday* (1962), when Cliff Richard and the Shadows take a bus to Europe, to be significant within a film. The slightest flash of the corner of a red double-decker bus shows that the setting is London. The colour and the mobility of the vehicle permit a very quick reference to landmark London that doesn't disturb a more naturalist or realist project. *Intimacy* (2000), the Patrice Chéreau film based on Hanif Kureishi stories, with its lengthy interior sex scenes, is firmly within a grubby realist stylistic repertoire, but uses a red bus in the first moment of its first exterior shot to confirm the location already alluded to by the initial soundtrack of the Clash's 'London Calling'.[32] The punchline, if it can be called that, of Steve McQueen's super-8 film/ video *Exodus* (1992–7) is when the two men the camera has been following through Brick Lane suddenly discard the palms they are carrying, get on a bus and wave from the top deck. But buses, like Underground trains, as will be discussed in Chapter 4, are also full of narrative possibilities, particularly those of the coincidence and the chase. In *Dance Hall* (1950), it is on the top of a bus that the factory girls run into their former workmate Eve, who has given up work and dancing now she has got married (see Chapter 3). In *Pool of London* (1950), the flirtatious ways of the Leslie Phillips character are revealed early in the film on a trolley-bus, when he changes his destination after learning where his pretty neighbour is bound (see Chapter 6). In *23 Paces to Baker Street* (1956), a suspect is tailed across London to Barkers in High Street Kensington on the 73 bus.[33] This narrative potential is shared by public transport systems the world over, but each manifestation in each particular city can also work to give the particular setting local authenticity. René Clément uses a bus in *Knave of Hearts* (1954) to show how at home his French hero (Gerard Philippe) is in his adopted city. M. Ripois (Philippe) hails his liberation from the office by nipping into a telephone kiosk, declaring, 'Leaving the office for me was like waking from a nightmare, and to celebrate my release, I was going to change.' With a clean collar and tie, he wanders through the city near Charing Cross, 'like a lord, invited out to dine by another lord, but I was invited by a whole city, London'. The high point of his exuberant flânerie is when he swings himself onto the platform of a bus, and resumes his city observations from his new position – relaxed, at home and enjoying one of the pleasures of a native Londoner as the bus rolls on and he gazes at the city crowds.

M. Ripois, a good-looking charmer, lives off women, and the film (which is being narrated by Philippe in a final seduction) traces his pursuits and fortunes in London as he moves from one woman to another. *Knave of Hearts* has several notable location sequences filmed in the streets of the West End with concealed cameras, of which this is the first. A jazz soundtrack adds to the presentation of London as an attractive and seductive city here, and it is this city which M. Ripois combs for women who will support him. The film caused a stir on release, much of it outrage at the mistreatment of English women by a French cad, some bridling at a London in which prostitutes openly walked the streets of the West End.[34] As M. Ripois observes, 'There was one kind of woman who didn't interest me, the kind who was after money, because I was too.' Nevertheless, when other options have been exhausted, and he has spent a night on the streets, he takes refuge with a French prostitute, Marcelle, who is kind to a fellow-countryman, and feeds him food he can tolerate. Marcelle takes him to a pub in Charlotte Street, shot with chiaroscuro lighting, to give a rather Parisian shadowy tableau of the prostitutes with their pimps, sitting round a table waiting to start work. M. Ripois's London mobilises landmark imagery, but in a way which, in Sorlin's terms, incites interest, particularly in the first half of the film, when it shows the delight of the central character at the possibilities it offers. He is not, like so many characters in London-set films, constrained by the city, but free to follow his whim: to leap on and off the platform of a bus as it pleases him.

Joseph Losey's 1959 *Blind Date* opens with a similar 'foreigner on a London bus' trope, but also shows how the mobility of the bus can be used in confident location shooting. The first shot starts on the branches of a plane tree against the sky, panning down to show the tree's dappled bark also dappled with sunlight, until it shows a bus travelling towards it, with a young man, Hardy Kruger, visible on the bus platform. The jazz soundtrack gives this already recognisable London a light modernity and, still in the same shot, the young man leaps off the bus, cheerful in the sun, and takes a few steps forward to the camera into close-up before turning round to retrace his footsteps, hopping. Through a slight reframing, he is revealed as returning to retrieve his shoe which he has lost in the enthusiasm of his dismounting. The camera then pans right back horizontally, following him, and as he leaves the shot, the pan continues, specifying its position on the Victoria Embankment as the shot finishes on the river and the South Bank. This long opening shot hints at character and establishes location, as well as intimating the narrative to come. Although the rest of the young man's journey, which takes him past a London landmark series (a flower lady, the Palace of Westminster, bowler-hatted gentlemen and a zebra crossing) to where he is meeting his lover, is conducted with the same light-hearted gait, it is this initial stumble that is prophetic. In this opening shot, with its fluid vertical and horizontal pans, we have been shown that he feels sufficiently at home to leap from bus platforms, but there turns out to be more than his shoe at stake; his carefree jump from the bus proves overconfident of his place in London.

The liminal quality of the bus platform is used in a different way in Neil Jordan's *Breakfast on Pluto* (2006), where there is a repeated shot of the central protagonist's mother, in a checked coat, standing on the platform of a crowded bus.[35] The film is about the search of Kitten (Cillian Murphy) for his mother, who abandoned him at birth. Once again, this is an extremely economical image, condensing both the London location of his mother, and the impossibility of a reconciliation as she is both there, on the bus, so near, and gone, swept away in the movement of the vehicle. This recounted image – a glimpse described to Kitten – signifies the impossibility of Kitten's desire for this woman, and is later matched by a glimpse of a woman who could be his mother on an Underground train, showing the way in which the most mundane modes of transport can be used to render the inaccessibility of desire.

Jasmin Dizdar's *Beautiful People* (1999) introduces a slightly different way of using a London bus, in which the bus functions more as a metaphor for the city. It also demonstrates the way in which the character role of the bus conductor can do its own work in the construction of a London setting.[36] 'Hold on tight', 'Any more fares' or 'Room for one more inside' are twentieth-century street cries of characters who may also comment on action and character. *Beautiful People* places the London bus in a broader political arena, starting with the depiction of a normal, slightly stressful bus journey, everyone involved in their own worlds: a young man eating a hamburger while on the phone, older men reading newspapers, a child noisily annoying a woman who is trying to work, the bus driver listening to the radio. This is a classic use of a London bus to indicate location. The set-up is presented as casual, almost incidental, so that location is established apparently without attention to it, cued by the red of the bus and the English voice on the radio, which the bus driver has hanging in his cab. Into this banal setting erupts the war in Bosnia, as two passengers recognise each other as former village neighbours from the former Yugoslavia. Through the windows of the bus central London has been visible, but this had no immediate significance, but now landmark London becomes a curiously displaced background to the physical fight between the two refugees. While the bus driver asserts, 'This is London transport, we don't behave like this here,' the identities reawakened in the meeting on the bus defy this injunction.

In the opening of *Beautiful People*, there is a sense in which the bus is London, a trope that is further developed in *Wonderland* (1999). This film, which is also discussed in the concluding chapter, attempts an integrated London, in which landmark iconography is never isolated from its context. So although the dome of St Paul's is shown, it is shot from a character's south London flat, just as Trafalgar Square and the National Gallery are almost unrecognisable in the rain. This approach attempts to ground landmark London in a lived, material, everyday city so that there is an inhabited London between the landmarks. The film, which is set over one November weekend, follows the everyday lives of one south London family and its neighbours. Mainly naturalist in style, the film also includes, at fairly regular intervals,[37] sequences in which time-lapse and slow-motion photographic effects are used in combination with a prominent Michael Nyman score replacing naturalistic sound. In these moments, the film moves from the stories of particular characters to a more general concern with the representation of the city. I want to look in detail at this movement in a sequence that starts in a central London flat and finishes on the upper deck of a London bus.

Nadia (Gina McKee), the character in the film whose life is followed in most detail, has spent an evening with a new man. She has previously met Tim (Stuart Townsend) for a drink at lunchtime, and unlike her first date in the film, clearly considers him to have some potential. The next time we see them together in his central London flat, he has cooked them both a meal and they have then had sex. The scene, as is characteristic of the film, is shot in edgy close-ups and medium shots, with characters rarely centred in the image, which gives a slightly nervous, unpredictable impression. Tim, fully clothed, walks over to the kitchen area, leaving Nadia half undressed and a little dishevelled sitting on the bed. Standing in the kitchen, he loads himself a plate of left-over food from a saucepan, and then gets himself a beer from the fridge, turning up the living room light as he comes back. Nadia, who has been offered neither food nor drink, says that she had better go and starts struggling, as Tim watches, snacking, to pull up her knickers and tights. As she leans forward to do this, he tidies a cushion behind her. He offers to call her a cab, but she says she'll take the bus. When she has gone, he turns the lighting back down. The detail of this scene – the food shovelled out of the saucepan, the unoffered drink, the adjusted cushion and Tim's manipulation of the lighting – gives precision to Nadia's humiliation, as does her struggle to put her tights back on. This is clearly Nadia's story. However, the next sequence does something rather different. Central London is identified as a bus stop just off Trafalgar Square, with both the dome of the National Gallery and the bus itself working as iconographic London images, but Nadia's lonely journey home through the rain on the last bus begins to generalise her predicament. What starts as a sequence that reaffirms the public geographical location of the personal drama moves into a more perennial 'city' sequence, which invokes one of the great city themes of loneliness in a crowd. Hunched in her seat, Nadia is filmed surrounded, accosted and ignored by other travellers, who are filmed with time lapse, lack of continuity and the Nyman score. On the one hand, it has been clearly established that this is Saturday-night London nightlife; on the other, the disassociation of the *mise en scène* and particularly the use of non-diegetic music encourages a reading at a more general level. Although the events of Nadia's evening have been shown in considerable detail so that it is easy to understand why she is tearful, at the same time, there is a distancing invoked through which Nadia becomes just one person in a huge city. The soundtrack is crucial in changing the type of time and space of the film from a very particular set of events in one character's life to a more general, abstract meditation on city life. The sequence pulls together a topical story – Nadia's particular Saturday evening in London – with a perennial city theme, the loneliness and anomie of the city.[38] In this movement, the bus is both particular and metaphorical, London and the city. The qualities of the music, its soaring and swooping orchestral score, played over the rainy dark London streets and the chaotic Saturday night bus, both generalises and transcends Nadia's story.

So far from being solely the indicator of a 'rotten film', the London bus exists variously within cinematic space, both showing where a film is set, but also, in many different ways, showing something of how the city is inhabited. The colour and mobility of the bus are its greatest assets as a London landmark, meaning that so very little can be used to indicate location if the film-makers don't want to stray into 'Tower Bridge' territory, just a flash of red or the height of the shadow: just there for a moment, saying 'this is London', here, and then gone.

The Pub

> Ever been in a pub before? Here it is – the heart of Merry Old England. Complete with dirty glasses, watery beer, draughts under the door and a twenty-three-inch television.[39]

Persisting across all periods of cinematic London is the pub or tavern. When Phil Redmond first set up the Liverpool-set Channel 4 soap opera *Brookside* (1982–2003), his controversial innovation to British soap-land was the decision not to include a pub as one of the permanent sets, unlike the Rover's Return in the Granada soap *Coronation Street* (1960–). However, this decision proved to have difficult consequences dramatically, which, for a period, were resolved through the addition of a pillar-box to enable people to meet each other as they posted letters. Pubs, as well as being a recognised part of most British neighbourhoods, are dramatically extremely convenient. Free to enter, they usually have more than one door, and offer a combination of the constant (the bar, the bar staff) and the variable (the customers). Characters can pop into pubs to look for people or spend the whole evening in there observing comings and goings. Historically often many-chambered, with saloon and public bars, snugs, smoking rooms, off-sales doors, many pubs are also very striking visually, be it with the etched glass, mirrors, brasswork and marble of Victorian public houses, or the smaller darker labyrinths of coaching inns and taverns. Pubs are social spaces which permit chance interactions and can easily be produced in the studio.[40] They are often used as a type of 'low-life' landmark in films that eschew all other London landmarks, except maybe elements of London transport. There are many films which have important pub locations or scenes, and some, such as *Saloon Bar* (1940) and *Last Orders* (2001), are principally set in pubs. The sing-song in the pub is trope of community across a wide range of films. I will discuss, in some detail, another use of the pub in just one film, *Victim* (1961), as it provides an example of the way in which the use of particular locations can speak to sectional audiences, as well as demonstrating the choral functions often associated with pubs in films. My argument is that there are many aspects of the use of the pub in this film which are characteristic of the filmic use of London pubs generally. However, because the film was made as a purposeful intervention into the debates about the status of homosexuality, in which the distinction between 'private' and 'public' spaces was key, the spatiality of the film is particularly significant. The Checkers is a 'doubled' landmark in this film. It is a London landmark, a beautiful Victorian pub, but it is also a subcultural 'queer' landmark, for The Checkers is filmed in a well-known homosexual pub, the Salisbury.[41]

Victim, which was made after the publication of the Wolfenden Report on Homosexual Offences and Prostitution in 1957, but before the limited decriminalisation of homosexuality in 1967, centres on the decision of a successful, married lawyer, Melville Farr (Dirk Bogarde), to pursue some blackmailers, following the suicide of a young man, Jack 'Boy' Barrett (Peter McEnery), that he had been seeing and who died in an attempt to protect Farr. The film explicitly addresses the current state of the law and is one of a series of 'social problem' films made by the team of Basil Dearden and Michael Relph.[42] The film is set in London, although the hapless Barrett does try to escape, and it uses a wide range of locations. Trafalgar Square, St Paul's and St Martin-in-the-Fields are 'mentioned' visually, as is the gay pub The Marquis of Granby, but always, as befits a film with a realist project, in narratively integrated shots, rather than landmark montage; and the film is more concerned with the contrasting social geography of the well-connected Farr, who lives in Chiswick Mall and works in the Inns of Court, and the building labourer Barrett, who lives in rented accommodation and works on the site of one of the new office blocks transforming the city. *Victim* has attracted considerable critical commentary in relation to its representation of homosexuality, and it is pioneering in its location shooting of known gay venues such as the pubs.[43]

There are three scenes set in The Checkers, all in the first hour of the film. The first introduces the pub through Boy Barrett's use of its telephone. Boy then enters the saloon bar to sit with his friend Eddie, and is observed by two other groupings. One, PH and Mickey, are a couple ostensibly bound by the blind PH's dependence on the younger Mickey. PH's blindness motivates his role as a chorus as he comments to Mickey on what he can hear and deduce from those around him.[44] The other grouping is based at the bar, and includes the barman and two regulars, a car salesman and Madge, a blonde model who buys more than her fair share of drinks. The pub is Victorian, with etched glass and mirroring, and feature lighting provided by very recognisable gilded nymph statuettes, which are repeatedly framed in shot with each group of customers. In this scene, although some of the key players are present, their connections are invisible, and the topic of homosexuality has not been broached.

In the second Checkers scene, the blackmail plot has now been developed, Barrett is dead and a red herring in relation to Mickey and PH has been set up. This second scene, though, introduces two new elements alongside the choral function of both Mickey and PH's conversation and that at the bar between the barman, Madge and others. The barman, when left alone temporarily with Madge, reveals that he 'can't stand "them"', while Eddie exchanges glances with a bowler-hatted, pin-striped suit, who, at the end of the film, is revealed to be an undercover policeman. The space of The Checkers is revealed as criss-crossed with glances and their auditory equivalent, the homosexual men engaged constantly in a monitoring of the space and discriminating between gay patrons and the 'noise' of straight patrons who block views and voices. This aspect of the space is reinforced in the third pub scene, when PH comments to Mickey that 'there's a real charnel house atmosphere in this place today', and Eddie realises that another regular is also a victim of the blackmailers. These scenes explore the way in which the standard social division in pubs, exploited in many a movie, between regulars and temporary visitors, is, in The Checkers, mapped over a secret queer culture.

The pub provides a place for a chorus: a chorus both inside and outside queer London. Melville Farr is never associated with the pub, and it is made clear that he did not meet Boy Barrett there. The Checkers is a place that permits a promiscuous public cross-class mixing, and in this, it is contrasted with the private homosexuality of the upper- and upper-middle-class men with whom Farr mixes. When Farr, who is investigating the blackmailers' web, is summoned by a senior colleague, he discovers that men with whom he has worked for many years also have secrets. These men meet in public as the ruling class in exclusive Mayfair gentlemen's clubs – it is only in the privacy of a fashionable mews flat that their sexuality is revealed. This distinction, which was to be enshrined in law in the recognition of the legitimacy of homosexual acts 'between consenting adults in private', is precisely made in the film. Although we see Barrett's bed-sit, we never see him at home, and his desperate flight at the beginning of the film, linking together his disparate acquaintances, stages homosexuality for someone of his class as involving a series of public spaces. It is through the pub that people become caught in the blackmail, as one of the 'bar group' is, in desperation, feeding names to the blackmailers. And so the film both displays a homosexual world and, through its topography, advocates privacy. It is lack of discretion, being publicly identifiable as homosexual, that fuels disgust and even blackmail.

The pub in this film works in another way as well. While much location shooting has to position itself between the authenticity given by the location and a necessary opacity about precise geographies, there will always be some part of an audience that recognises a location. As Richard Dyer suggested in 1972 in his pioneering article on the film, the ability to identify The Checkers in this film as The Salisbury in St Martin's Lane, 'one of London's old theatrical gay bars',[45] might be an attribute of 'gay men on the gay scene'.[46] This naming of the 'real' pub is a moment of subcultural belonging in Dyer's own article, a moment when another geography of London is invoked, its landmarks not Tower Bridge and Big Ben, but the pubs, clubs and lavatories of 'the gay scene', or what Matt Houlbrook has recently historicised as 'Queer London' and which Frank Mort describes being mapped in the proceedings of the Wolfenden Committee.[47] The 'real' pub in this film, The Salisbury, is present in the same shots as the fictional pub, The Checkers, to those with subcultural knowledge, just as subcultural gay London has its own topography across 'landmark London'.

The Fog

It is not just buildings, vehicles and bodies that comprise London landmarks. Cinematic London also has identifying weather: rain and fog. Fog is both a temporal and a generic signifier.[48] Fog usually indicates a setting in the past, and often that murder will be done; the Shepperton-shot *Footsteps in the Fog* (1955), despite its title, has only one fog sequence, but within this sequence a murder is accomplished. The Sherlock Holmes/Jack the Ripper film *A Study in Terror* (1965) was released in the USA with the title *Fog*. It is foggy in Victorian London, in the East End (see Chapter 5) and down by the river (see Chapter 6). But it can rain everywhere in London at any time, and often does. In *It Always Rains on Sunday* (1947) it rains on most characters for most of the day, as its title suggests. But, as many have noticed, it also rains at the end of *Passport to Pimlico* (1949), when the glorious fantasy of outdoor dining to celebrate returning to Britain is rained off. Fifty years later, it rains when Hugh Grant and Andie McDowell finally get together at the end of *Four Weddings and a Funeral* (1994), as if to demonstrate to the American Carrie (McDowell) what she is taking on if she marries an Englishman. But it rains at the beginning of romances too, as it does in *My Fair Lady* (1964), when rich and poor are thrown together by the rain in Covent Garden. In *Mary Poppins* it rains when the characters must return from their fantasy of 'Jolly Holiday' to everyday London, and the rain washes off Dick van Dyke's pavement drawing, which inaugurated the fantasy. Rain can be used expressionistically, as well as to indicate location; it rains in this way in both *Nil By Mouth* and *Naked*. Generally, though, when it rains, characters in British movies make the best of it: rain provides an opportunity to be British about the weather. Fog is a different matter. Fog, rather than revealing character, characterises the experience of the city.

Figures can loom up and disappear; landmarks and familiar surroundings are obscured – the viewer can be lost in the image. In *The Tiger in the Smoke* (1956), almost the whole film is set in a London fog so thick that characters can be misrecognised and can disappear from view. While the main protagonists in this film are contemporary, in the fog there also travel a troupe of almost Victorian street beggars and musicians, pointing to the way in which Victorian London haunts later Londons, with the fog providing what could be seen as a liminal temporality. In *The Libertine* (2005), the arrival of the central characters in (Restoration) London is marked by a quick establishing shot sequence of fog, mud and a tavern. In *Hangover Square* (1945) fog in the turn-of-the-century streets shrouds murder and amnesia. In the cinema, fog tells us that it is London, and fog shows us that London is an old city. It is foggy in 'Olde London Towne'. Guy Barefoot has discussed the *mise en scène* of Victorian London in his *Gaslight Melodrama*, showing how different versions of the Victorian city can reveal conflicting and contradictory attitudes to the past.[49] My point is simply that fog can be used with more or less subtlety in a significant strand of cinematic Londons, and that as an aspect of *mise en scène* it both prepares the audience for the type of narrative events that will follow and can function metaphorically to give a sense of the city. However, fog is also an aspect of cinematic *mise en scène* that manifests pre-cinematic London (Victorian London) in a form that draws attention to the cinema itself as a mode of representation, and to its painterly heritage. *Murder By Decree* (1978), in which Sherlock Holmes investigates the Whitechapel Murders, makes the expected use of foggy East End streets. But there is an establishing shot of London, when Holmes and Watson are returning from a visit to an asylum, that shows a view of London in which the image is almost obscured. Here, fog is an aspect of landmark London, along with the silhouettes of Big Ben and the Palace of Westminster. This image is economical in its obscurity: London *is* Big Ben, the river and the fog, framed by the 'victorian'

Murder By Decree: the foggy city skyline

lamp-posts of the Embankment. So little can be seen that the limits of the frame draw attention to the composition of the image and the screen as surface, rather than window. This is at once both a Victorian and a minimalist London. Fog is the medium that both evokes a pre-cinematic London, and draws attention to the medium in which this urban imaginary is evoked.

Within the paradigms of national cinema studies, particularly in the context of discussion of Britain's wartime cinema, there has been some discussion of metaphors of the nation. While many wartime films propose the motivated camaraderie of fighting and working units such as aircraft crew, firemen or conscripted factory workers as the model for the nation, there are also films such as *This Happy Breed* (1944) in which an identification is proposed between family, house and nation.[50] Films such as *The Happy Family* (1952), in which the Lord family resist the demolition of their house to make way for the Festival of Britain, or *Forever and a Day* (1943), the portmanteau film set in a single London house made to support the British war effort, also carry this set of identifications.[51] The house, the family, the nation: this string of meaning has considerable resonance. For the city, the house will not do as metaphor, unless it is a boarding house, like that in *London Belongs to Me* (1948). Instead, the bus, with its random and temporary association of strangers, has much richer metaphorical potential and is much more city-like. Similarly, the city pub, always somebody's 'local', with its elaborate patterning of belongings and exclusions, regulars and visitors, can represent the city, just as the fog not only signifies 'olde London Towne', but also permits the appearance and disappearance of strangers, just like a city crowd.

Uncanny London: Undoing the City

Landmark London can also be staged in negativity as an uncanny London. There are a small number of films celebrated for their glimpses of a deserted and empty city, including *Seven Days to Noon* and, half a century on, *Twenty-Eight Days Later ...*, which both make careful and self-conscious use of landmark London imagery to evoke an unpeopled city. Peter Hutchings has written interestingly about what he calls the 'uncanny landscape' in British cinema, which he describes as 'a landscape suffused with a sense of profound and sometimes apocalyptic anxiety; it is also a landscape of a comprehensive dispossession and vacancy'. Discussing both urban and rural settings, he explores this landscape in relation to national identity, suggesting, 'This is not a landscape where we find ourselves as modern national subjects.'[52] My interest, while it overlaps with Hutchings' concerns, is with the way in which these films use landmark imagery in their staging of London, and what the trope of the abandoned capital contributes to our understanding of the city more generally. Hutchings comments,

> While scenes involving dehumanized crowds fit quite easily into some of the more broadly negative ways of representing the city and the modernity it represents, scenes of urban abandonment are perhaps more unusual and striking, if only because they are unexpected.[53]

In the context of a discussion of landmark London, it is the necessary inclusion of landmark images in the creation of this uncanny on which I will concentrate.

Seven Days to Noon is a film that has been seen as most interesting for its shots of deserted London and, contextually, as an early 'nuclear threat' film.[54] It addresses these anxieties through the story of a senior government scientist who attempts to blackmail the British government into unilateral nuclear disarmament by threatening to explode a nuclear bomb in London. The title refers to the week that the government has to meet this demand before the bomb is exploded in the heart of government, Westminster, on a Sunday at 12.00. The government response to the threat is to search 'the haystack' that is London for Willingdon (Barry Jones), the scientist, and then to evacuate London, as they anticipate that the city would be wiped out, 'from Rotherhithe to Notting Hill Gate'.[55] The London of *Seven Days to Noon* is a post-war London with bombsites still visible, a blitzed 'St Stephens' Westminster, an important plot setting and synecdochical use of a silhouette of St Paul's as London. This is most evident in the latter part of film in which Willingdon is hiding in an attic room (studio shot) with a view of St Paul's from its window. It is at this window that Professor Willingdon spends much of his time, looking at the London that is symbolised by this dome; 'London, she either makes you or she breaks you, that's what they all say,' comments Goldie, whose room it is. So although the film makes extensive use of location shooting, it is the image of the dome of the cathedral in studio-shot scenes that is used to symbolise the city for a man struggling with his conscience.

The film is post-war in another sense though, in that its plot, and particularly the evacuation of the population of London, provides an opportunity to rerun aspects of the war with the benefit of hindsight (and the convenient absence of enemy action). Planning, order and organisation are the characteristics of the response to the danger. London itself, in a film made only six years after the publication of the LCC County of London Plan,[56] is shown divided up into concentric circles on a map in military HQ. The Army will move rationally and progressively through the city from the outside inwards.[57] The messy, recalcitrant population is evacuated, forced to leave their pets and sports equipment behind. The evacuation, which consciously references Dunkirk more than once, also offers an intensified vision of urban life with queues, crowds and packed, busy public transport accentuating the crowded turmoil of city experience. In contrast, the empty city, while a matter of regret – shown through cameos of separated children, abandoned pets and a man giving a final water to his window-box – is also a blank canvas, which can be dealt with rationally, at least at the planning stage, although the execution of the plan is shown to be only human.[58] The deserted city is imaged through landmark London: on the Sunday morning, the three shots are Piccadilly Circus, the Admiralty Arch onto the Mall and Horse Guards Parade. Britain as a monarchy is figured here, while later images, such as Trafalgar Square and Westminster Bridge, give a broader sense of 'the seat of government'. Guy, who heralds the film as 'a rich film for London-spotters', later observes that 'an astonishing number of tourist spots flit across the screen, all devoid of their usual humanity, hustle and bustle'.[59] In fact, the film presents an empty London rather systematically. The previous day, desertion had been evoked through shots of empty attractions such as London Zoo and Wembley Stadium, as well as iconographic work-places such as Covent Garden, the Docks, the sewers and more ordinary images such as a street of terraced houses and a deserted Underground station. This spread of imagery is quite ambitious, combining as it does landmark and ordinary London, because for the image of deserted London to be significant, the viewer must have another memory, of this image 'peopled'. It is partly to establish this that the film commences with familiar 'working day in the city' images, of a commuter train coming into a mainline terminus, of the commuters rushing from the station and then of a crowded bridge over the Thames. Similarly, busy city streets and a tube station, as well as landmark locations such as Westminster Bridge, Trafalgar Square and Downing Street, are all shown early in the film, setting up the later contrast. The uncanny city can only be imaged through the memory of that other city, 'all that mighty heart'.

Twenty-Eight Days Later ... is set in a present-day England devastated by a 'rage' virus after some chimpanzees that have been deliberately infected are freed by Animal Rights activists. The prelude to the film shows the raid on the Cambridge animal laboratory and the extreme and horrible speed with which the virus works. The next scene, '28 days later', shows Jim (Cillian Murphy), a bicycle courier, waking up in what turns out to be a deserted hospital. Jim finds himself some hospital scrubs to wear, fills a white plastic carrier bag with discarded cans of cola, and sets out from the hospital to find out what has happened, shouting 'hello' as he wanders through the city. Jim's London wanderings, a four-minute montage sequence, include a series of landmark images. Indeed, the sequence is in many ways a classic landmark sequence indicating arrival in London, except that he meets no one else, and the only human noise is his own repeated shout of 'hello'.

The sequence is structured through a loose alternation of landmark views and shots of Jim walking with his carrier bag, his green, flapping hospital outfit indicating either that he shouldn't be on the streets, or that something more profound is wrong. The opening shots are river shots: a cityscape shot from Waterloo Bridge with golden light illuminating the centrally positioned dome of St Paul's; a shot of the Millennium Wheel by the river in the same golden light; the statue of a lion; and then, in one of the 'Jim walking' shots, the camera focused on the ground as he walks through metallic-sounding debris. This shot wittily anticipates what follows, which is the shot used for publicity purposes of Jim's head framed with Big Ben immediately behind it. For the debris that Jim walks through is shown to be, through the inclusion of a couple of Union Jack flags, the discarded stock of a souvenir seller, and he is treading on, and kicking out of his way, lots of miniature Big Bens, little models of national identity, just like the Eiffel Towers in Ealing's *The Lavender Hill Mob* (1951). This shot shows the same self-consciousness about the use of landmark imagery as the sequence from the same film-makers' landmark sequence in *Trainspotting*. The little Big Bens, tinnily noisy on the pavement, tell the viewer that the film-makers know that their evocation of post-disaster London is dependent on a series of familiar images. And on they come: a red bus on its side in Whitehall, the Cenotaph, the Mall, St Paul's, the Bank of England, Centrepoint. The huge smiling faces of a Benetton hoarding gaze unseeingly across the empty city as Jim walks on, his bag now stuffed with £20 notes that he has found. The sequence finishes in Piccadilly Circus after Jim reads the headline on an old newspaper: 'Evacuation'. The Circus too is deserted, but the hoarding round the statue of Eros flutters with pieces of papers and photographs, which have been stuck on, little notes and pleas and messages for and about lost loved ones. The music, which has been single string for much of the sequence, comes to a climax, and Jim begins to grasp that he might be in London, but not as he has known it.

Mark Kermode, in his favourable review of the film, discusses the use of digital video for shooting and pays particular attention to the empty streets:

the early scenes in particular, in which a wasteland-like London is laid out before us much as T. S. Eliot's proverbial 'patient etherised upon a table', are striking not only for their practical accomplishment (is it a digital effect, or are those streets *really* empty?) but also for their haunt-ingly poetic resonance. Rarely has the West End, cleansed of human traffic, seemed so terrifyingly tranquil.[60]

Kermode's question here, 'is it a digital effect, or are those streets *really* empty?' points to the uncanny fascination of the empty streets, which he here translates into a question of pro-duction through which his fascination still shines. The uncanniness of the deserted city street has been discussed in relation to the work of photographers such as Bill Brandt, Eugene Atget and Brassai, but that street is usually a night-time street. The generic imagi-nary of *Twenty-Eight Days Later . . .* produces a deserted, technicolour, daytime London. Here, in the context of cinematic landmark London, the sequential repetition of empty tourist vistas raises the question of the relationship between people and buildings in our understanding of what cities are. The well-documented evils of the city, the anonymity, the lonely crowd, the alienation, are evoked both in their absence and their virulent, monstrous return, 'the infected', the post-human mob, which gathers to hunt any survivors.

These two films use similar filmic strategies to render the city uncanny: the montage sequence of London landmarks in empty streets. This often requires longer and wider shots than those typically used for landmark images, as there must be a foreground to be empty. The uncanny city, in these two films, is a daytime city from which people have been evacu-ated. Without people, without crowds, without the anonymity of the press of people, the city is revealed as recognisable, but eerie: a city which is only buildings. These images of the empty city are uncanny because they reveal the ways in which the city is and isn't made of buildings. As in the classic definitions of the uncanny, the city is strangely familiar.[61] How-ever, this analysis has also shown that while the uncanny city here imaged raises questions for our apprehension of the city in general, it can also be seen that many of the elements of 'uncanniness' are historically specific. *Seven Days to Noon* offers a post-war uncanny, in which the government is strong, decisive and cabinet-based, the Army efficient but also world-weary, and, in the ranks, willing to skive; and the memory of evacuation and deprivation is strong.[62] The city, however, is knowable and mappable. It can be divided up and it can be searched in a planned, rational fashion. This is both a fantasy of the past and the future. *Twenty-Eight Days Later . . .* , in contrast, has no faith in governments, and no faith in plan-ning. The litter that gusts round the empty streets indicates a different sense of public space. The working class is banished to tower-blocks, food is sugary, fizzy or irradiated and con-sumption, in several different ways, provides landmarks that rival the architectural. This later film is both more confident in its deployment of landmark imagery, and more self-con-scious about it. Landmark London has in some senses become rubbish London, and the film intimates strongly that this transition pre-dates the evacuation. *Seven Days to Noon* makes a much more substantially inclusive effort to represent local as well as landmark London.

Goldie (Olive Sloan) at the end of *Seven Days to Noon*

It is also much more about London, which can be seen in the role of Big Ben in the last few minutes as the noon of the title approaches, when there is cross-cutting between the clock and the bomb. For *Twenty-Eight Days Later . . .* , the abandoned city registers panic not planning, its deserted beauty a register of a failed civilisation. The film's generic drive lies in the zombie/uninfected confrontations, which take place all over the country: in that sense landmark London is used to signify the former seat of government, the capital of a country in which government has been abandoned. So the uncanny city has historically specific forms. The landmarks left desolate by the flight of the population, are, in each film, articulated slightly differently, revealing different understandings of the capital city and its past and future. However, the very feel of the city without people shows that a city is more than its buildings, and London is shown to be more than its landmarks.

Reviewing Woody Allen's 2005 London excursion, *Match Point*, Philip French complains of its use of the 'new clichés' of 'the London Eye, the London Gherkin and Tate Modern'.[63] The new clichés of twenty-first-century landmark London, like the old clichés such as the red Routemaster bus, do not derive their iconic status solely from their deployment in the cinema. 'Iconicity' is made and remade across many sites, from postage stamps to pilgrimages. To be instantly recognisable in the cinema as a signifier of place – to justify its inclusion in the syntagm 'this is London' – an image must, to most audiences, already mean 'this is London'. This, in turn, means that these images, in the very moment that they elicit recognition, also confirm their status as clichés. French notes that the new clichés are deployed alongside older landmarks such as 'a Thames-side flat overlooking the Houses of Parliament and a Guards band in bearskins and scarlet tunics'. New landmarks can be located by their juxtaposition with more familiar ones. So here, an old view, the Houses of Parliament, is given a new angle from a 'post-Docks' residential property, while the bearskins and scarlet tunics give a traditional, imperial texture and colour to all that glass and steel of new landmarks. Landmark London, in its necessary overfamiliarity, is and isn't the essence of cinematic London. While characters in many movies may look at the dome of St Paul's, and film-makers may insert shots of it in many more, in movie London, not much actually happens there. St Paul's may mean 'London', and 'England', and 'Britain' in different ways, to different characters and audiences at different times in different genres, but it is relatively rare for it to be used as a location within the imagined world of a film.

Landmark London presents itself, and is presented, as being about place. The exploration of this signifying of place in this chapter reveals that this cinematic place is always, also, historical. This is, of course, partly what is complained of in the notion of the *same old* clichés. But it is precisely the waning and the persistence of certain images that reveals something of the historicity of the idea of 'London', just as it is the choice of how to combine the signifiers of London that tells an audience something of how the film situates itself in the city.

Notes

1. The Palace of Westminster (in its present form) was completed 1847–60; Tower Bridge opened in 1894; and Trafalgar Square and Nelson's Column were constructed between 1839 and 1845. Throughout this book I will use the convention of referring to the clock tower of the Palace of Westminster as 'Big Ben'.

2. David Gilbert and Fiona Henderson, 'London and the tourist imagination', in Pamela K. Gilbert (ed.), *Imagined Londons* (Albany: State University of New York Press, 2002), pp. 121–36, and John Eade, *Placing London* (Oxford and New York: Berghahn Books, 2000).

3. Banksy, *Wall and Piece* (London: Century, 2005), p. 101; see also John Urry, *The Tourist Gaze* (London: Sage, 1990), and Kevin Lynch, *The Image of the City* (Cambridge, MA: MIT Press, 1960).

4. Stephen Daniels traces the changing historical significance of St Paul's in his *Fields of Vision* (Cambridge: Polity Press, 1993), 'The Prince of Wales and the shadow of St Paul's', pp. 11–42. See also Annette Kuhn, 'A phantasmagoria of memory', in her *Family Secrets* (London: Verso, 1995), pp. 104–21; John Taylor, 'History under fire', *A Dream of England* (Manchester: Manchester University Press, 1994), pp. 182–211; and David Matless, 'Landscapes of war', *Landscape and Englishness* (London: Reaktion, 1998), pp. 173–200.

5. Katherine Shonfield, *Walls Have Feelings* (London: Routledge, 2000), p. 135.

6. Sorlin is discussing the Swinging London setting of the 1965 Richard Lester film, *The Knack and How to Get It*. Pierre Sorlin, *European Cinemas, European Societies 1939–90* (London: Routledge, 1991), p. 12.

7. Patrick Keiller, 'Photogenie', *Cambridge Architecture Journal* vol. 8, 1996/7, pp. 43–6, and 'London in the early 1990s', in Joe Kerr and Andrew Gibson (eds), *London from Punk to Blair* (London: Reaktion, 2003), pp. 353–61; see also interviews by Colin Sorensen, *London on Film* (London: Museum of London, 1996), pp. 160–1; Claire Barwell, *Pix* no. 2, 1997, pp. 160–5; and David Martin-Jones, *Journal of Popular British Cinema* no. 5, 2002, pp. 123–32.

8. 'It was made for export really. I didn't make it for a local audience, and I was touched that so many people came to see it here. I couldn't believe it.' Interview with Sorensen, *London on Film*, p. 161. See, on the film, Iain Sinclair, 'Necropolis of fretful ghosts', *Sight and Sound* vol. 4 no. 6, June 1994, pp. 12–15; Stephen Daniels, 'Paris envy: Patrick Keiller's *London*', *History Workshop Journal* no. 40, 1995, pp. 220–2; Stella Bruzzi, *New Documentary* (London: Routledge, 2000), pp. 115–23; Paul Dave, 'Representations of capitalism, history and nation in the work of Patrick Keiller', in Justine Ashby and Andrew Higson (eds), *British Cinema: Past and Present* (London: Routledge, 2000), pp. 339–51; Steve Pile, '"The problem of London", or, how to explore the moods of the city', in N. Leach (ed.), *The Hieroglyphics of Space* (London: Routledge, 2002), pp. 139–57; Peter Brooker, *Modernity and Metropolis* (Basingstoke: Palgrave, 2002), pp. 105–9; Julian Wolfreys, *Writing London volume 2* (Basingstoke: Palgrave, 2004), pp. 227–32; and Paul Dave, *Visions of England* (Oxford: Berg, 2006).

9. Joseph Conrad, *Heart of Darkness* (London: Penguin, 1983 [1902]), p. 29.

10. Daniels, 'Paris envy'.

11. Of course, because of the framing of the shots, there is no way of identifying the water as Thames water rather than the water of, say, the River Brent (also visited).

12. Dave, *Visions of England*, p. 136.

13. Shonfield, *Walls Have Feelings*, p. 133.

14. Ibid., p. 135.

15. John Hill points out that 'the script refers to this interlude as a "contemporary retake of all those 'Swinging London' montages". John Hodge, *Trainspotting and Shallow Grave* (London: Faber and Faber, 1996), p.76, quoted by Hill in 'British cinema as national cinema: production, audience and representation', in Robert Murphy (ed.), *The British Cinema Book* (London: BFI, 2001 [1997]), p. 254.

16. Hodge cites 'street names made famous by Monopoly', *Trainspotting and Shallow Grave*, p. 76.

17. On 'cool Britannia' in the cinema, see Moya Luckett, 'Image and nation in 90s British cinema', in Robert Murphy (ed.), *British Cinema of the 90s* (London: BFI, 2000),

18. Murray Smith, *Trainspotting* (London: BFI, 2002), p. 26.

19. These well-known features are shadowed by more obscure films such as *Primitive London* (1965), *The Sorcerers* (1967) and Peter Whitehead's *Tonite Let's All Make Love in London* (1968).

20. There is a substantial literature on *Blow-Up*. See, for example, Seymour Chatman, *Antonioni or, The Surface of the World* (Berkeley: University of California Press, 1985), pp. 138–58, but also Peter Lev, '*Blow-Up*, Swinging London, and the film generation', *Literature/Film Quarterly* vol. 17 no. 2 (1989), pp. 134–7; Peter Theobald, 'Antonioni in London' (photographs), *Sight and Sound* vol. 35 no. 3, 1966, pp. 28–9.

21. Dick Lester, *Hollywood UK* (BBC, 1993); Robert Murphy, *Sixties British Cinema* (London: BFI, 1992), pp. 139–60; Amy Sargeant, *British Cinema* (London: BFI, 2005), pp. 233–64; Christine Geraghty, 'Women and sixties British cinema: the development of the *Darling* girl' in Robert Murphy (ed.), *The British Cinema Book* (London: BFI, 1997). See also Alexander Walker, *Hollywood UK* (London: Harrap, 1986 [1974]); Jeffrey Richards, *Film and British National Identity* (Manchester: MUP, 1997), ch. 6; Bruce Carson, 'Comedy, sexuality and "Swinging London" films', *Journal of Popular British Cinema* no. 1, 1998, pp. 48–62; Pamela Church Gibson, 'New stars, new fashions and the female audience' in Christopher Brewer and David Gilbert (eds), *Fashion's World Cities* (Oxford: Berg, 2006), pp. 89–106.

22. Moya Luckett argues that 'Swinging London' films feature mobile female characters who travel to the city in search of glamour and modernity, and contrasts these new young women with the fixed

traditional working-class masculinities of the New Wave films, while Pamela Church Gibson argues that there are much greater continuities between the New Wave films and the London cycle. See Luckett, 'Travel and mobility: femininity and national identity in Swinging London films' in Ashby and Higson (eds), *British Cinema: Past and Present*, pp. 233–45, and Church Gibson, 'From up north to up west? London on screen 1965–1967', *The London Journal* vol. 31 no. 1, 2006, pp. 85–108

23. This memory of the 1960s is produced in films like *Scandal* (1989), based on the 1963 Profumo affair, which uses a London montage cut to Lennon/McCartney's 'Listen, do you want to know a secret?' when the scandal breaks. Daytime shots of Westminster, Trafalgar Square and Piccadilly Circus, and, then, at the end of the sequence, Piccadilly by night, provide. through the juxtaposition of the song, newspaper headlines and the locations, the connection between government and the sins of Piccadilly. The tune of the song, the repetition of the red of the buses, the speed of the cutting and fading make the sequence upbeat and jaunty: a landmark London sequence which casts the Profumo affair as the moment of transition into 'Swinging London'. But the story of the connection between Westminster and Piccadilly, and its discovery, of which this is the climax of the film, is a story of hypocrisy and exploitation.

24. On *The Reluctant Debutante*, see Christine Geraghty, 'Paris, Hollywood and Kay Kendall' in Rachel Moseley (ed.), *Fashioning Film Stars* (London: BFI, 2005), pp. 121–32.

25. Sorlin, *European Cinemas*, p. 91.

26. David Martin-Jones, *Deleuze, Cinema and National Identity* (Edinburgh: Edinburgh University Press, 2006), p. 95.

27. Edward Dimendberg, *Film Noir and the Spaces of Modernity* (Cambridge, MA: Harvard University Press, 2004), p. 69.

28. Ian Conrich has discussed (the slightly different narrative modality of) the destruction of landmarks in 'Trashing London: the British colossal creature film and fantasies of mass destruction', in I. Q. Hunter (ed.), *British Science Fiction Cinema* (London: Routledge, 1999), pp. 88–98.

29. Mark Glancy, discussing British actors such as Nigel Bruce and Dame May Whitty in Hollywood, observes, 'It would be difficult to find a single "British" film of the 1930s and 1940s that did not have the names of at least two or three of these character actors towards the lower end of the credits. They were as essential to conveying the British setting as the opening, establishing shots of Big Ben and Tower Bridge.' *When Hollywood Loved Britain* (Manchester: Manchester University Press, 1999), p. 166. Some of my later discussion of Bob Hoskins picks up this 'actor as landmark' point, which is here neglected.

30. James Donald, *Imagining the Modern City* (London: Athlone Press, 1999), pp. 1–4.

31. Alan Parker, A *Turnip Head's Guide to British Cinema*, 12 March 1986.

32. See Richard Falcon, 'Last Tango in Lewisham', *Sight and Sound* vol. 11 no. 7 (NS), July 2000, pp. 20–4.

33. Routemaster enthusiasts will note that a film that has a notorious 'American' cinematic geography, with a Portman Square flat overlooking the Thames, has an accurate 73 bus route.

34. Robert Muller summarises some reviews, 'L'Amour in London', *Picture Post*, 19 June 1954, pp. 21–2. His article is headed, '*The Knave of Hearts* is a Frenchman's view of love in London. It is also the first British X film to be booked by one of the big cinema circuits. The critics thought you would be shocked by it' (p. 21).

35. A dramatic possibility lost for ever with the final phasing out of the Routemaster bus in December 2005, with considerable public lamentation. See for example, *Evening Standard*, 'Farewell', 7 December

2005, p. 1, and BBC 4's 'Bus Night', 9 December 2005. Travis Elborough points out that many examples given of Routemasters in films are 'the wrong bus', *The Bus We Loved* (London: Granta, 2005), pp. 95–7.

36. Elborough (Ibid.) points out that while Alfie works as a chauffeur, Gilda settles down with a 'safe' bus conductor in *Alfie*. He argues that in the 1960s, 'buses were for losers and tourists', p. 123.

37. After the first fifty-five minutes, these sequences are regularly placed about every seven to eight minutes. There are four in the earlier part of the film. This book's cover image is taken from one.

38. Mette Hjort discusses topical and perennial themes in her discussion of the extent to which contemporary Danish films are 'about' Danishness. M. Hjort, 'Themes of nation', in M. Hjort and S. Mackenzie (eds), *Cinema and Nation* (London: Routledge, 2000).

39. Superintendant Newhouse (Laurence Olivier) to the disturbed young American Ann Lake (Carol Lynley), who has just arrived in London, in *Bunny Lake is Missing* (Otto Preminger, 1965, script John and Penelope Mortimer). The pub is a Victorian gin palace with etched glass and tiling; on television is 'Swinging London', in the form of the cult music programme, *Ready, Steady, Go!*.

40. Dick Hobbs provides a detailed analysis of the complexity of a London pub as a social space in *Doing the Business* (Oxford: Oxford University Press, 1992 [1988]), ch. 7.

41. For a discussion of the use of the term 'queer London', see Matt Houlbrook, *Queer London* (London and Chicago: Chicago University Press, 2005), pp. 1–13.

42. John Hill, *Sex, Class and Realism* (London: BFI, 1986), pp. 90–4; Murphy, *Sixties British Cinema*, pp. 40–2; Raymond Durgnat, 'Two "social problem" films: *Sapphire* and *Victim*', in Alan Burton, Tim O'Sullivan and Paul Wells (eds), *Liberal Directions* (Trowbridge: Flicks Books, 1997), pp. 59–88.

43. Richard Dyer, *The Matter of Images* (London: Routledge, 1993), pp. 93–110; Andy Medhurst, '*Victim*: text as context', *Screen* vol. 25 nos. 4–5, July–October 1984, pp. 22–35; Stephen Bourne, *Brief Encounters* (London: Cassell, 1996), pp. 155–62 and Appendices; James C. Robertson, *The Hidden Cinema* (London: Routledge, 1989), pp. 119–26; Robin Griffiths (ed.), *British Queer Cinema* (London: Routledge, 2006).

44. The figure of the blind man in the pub recurs and augments the choral role of pubs (see *Saloon Bar* and *23 Paces to Baker Street*) and should perhaps be considered in relation to Lynda Nead's discussion of the blind man in the Victorian city in *Victorian Babylon* (New Haven and London: Yale University Press, 2000), pp. 59–62.

45. Tony Reeves, *Worldwide Guide to Movie Locations Presents London* (London: Titan, 2003), p. 12.

46. Richard Dyer, *The Matter of Images*, p. 107.

47. Houlbrook, *Queer London*; Frank Mort, 'Mapping sexual London: the Wolfenden Committee on Homosexual Offences and Prostitution, 1954–57', *New Formations* no. 37, Spring 1999, pp. 92–113.

48. Anthony Sutcliffe observes, '[*The Lodger*] helped confirm London as the breeding ground for maniacs of Jack-the-Ripper lineage, and as the home of atmospheric, and also money-saving fogs. These features were exploited by subsequent directors to an extent which it would be tedious even to begin to investigate, but the upshot was that cinematic London appeared even gloomier than the reality.' 'The metropolis in the cinema', in A. Sutcliffe (ed.), *Metropolis: 1890–1940* (London: Mansell, 1984), p. 164.

49. Guy Barefoot, *Gaslight Melodrama* (London and New York: Continuum, 2001).

50. See Andrew Higson, *Waving the Flag* (Oxford: Clarendon Press, 1995), ch. 5.

51. On *Forever and a Day*, see Glancy, *When Hollywood Loved Britain*, pp. 170–80.

52. Peter Hutchings, 'Uncanny landscapes in British film and television', *Visual Culture in Britain* vol. 5. no. 2, 2004, p. 29.

53. Ibid., p. 34.

54. Stephen Guy points out that the film was both a critical and a popular success on release in
    '"Someone presses a button and it's goodbye Sally": *Seven Days to Noon* and the threat of the atomic
    bomb', in Alan Burton, Tim O'Sullivan and Paul Wells (eds), *The Family Way: The Boulting Brothers and
    British Film Culture* (Trowbridge: Flicks Books, 2000), pp. 143–54.

55. Guy argues that the government's refusal to negotiate is politically significant and that Willingdon
    has a classic Campaign for Nuclear Disarmament (CND) profile (Ibid.).

56. The 1945 documentary *The Proud City* presents the principles behind the 1943 County of London
    Plan. See Shonfield, *Walls Have Feelings*, pp. 130–3; Frank Mort, 'Fantasies of metropolitan life:
    planning London in the 1940s', *Journal of British Studies* 43, January 2004, pp. 120–51; Matless,
    Landscape and Englishness.

57. When the groups of soldiers start joining up in Westminster it is like a premonition of Francis Alys'
    piece *Guards*, which can also be seen as a meditation on landmark London. Francis Alys, *Seven Walks*
    London, 2004–5 Portman Square, London (Artangel).

58. There are a series of jokes as the soldiers prove to be both idle and tempted by goods they discover.
    Raymond Durgnat is interesting on the Boultings' attitudes to 'mediocre decency', *A Mirror for
    England* (London: Faber and Faber, 1970), pp. 234–7. See also Matless, 'Is planning English?',
    Landscape and Englishness, pp. 195–8.

59. Guy, '"Someone presses a button"', p. 149.

60. Mark Kermode, *Sight & Sound* vol. 12 no. 12 (NS), 2002, p. 60. The DVD audio commentary by Danny
    Boyle and Alex Garland gives some details on the early morning shooting of these scenes.

61. There has been considerable discussion of the uncanny in relation to the space, architecture and
    the urban. See, for example, Anthony Vidler, *The Architectural Uncanny* (Cambridge, MA: MIT Press,
    1992); Donald, *Imagining the Modern City*, and the London-based 'Strangely Familiar' project with
    publications including: Iain Borden, Joe Kerr, Alicia Pivaro and Jane Rendell, *Strangely Familiar*
    (London: Routledge, 1996) and *The Unknown City* (Cambridge, MA: MIT Press, 2001). In relation to
    London, Roger Luckhurst provides an interesting commentary in 'Occult London', in Kerr and
    Gibson, pp. 335–40.

62. See Conrich, 'Trashing London', for an argument that late 1950s monster movies also replay the
    Blitz, p. 97.

63. Philip French, 'New balls, Woody', *The Observer* Review, 8 January 2006, p. 17.

2

Local London

In contrast to landmark London, there is another, less spectacular cinematic London, a local London. This is the setting for small narratives and everyday life, a London of terraced houses, blocks of flats, high streets, corner shops, pubs, bus stops, launderettes, cafés and recreation grounds. Generically, local London is a realist London, although this realist impulse is realised in different ways in different periods and by different film-makers. The realism of local London is partly its point, its defining feature – this is London as it is lived. The who and how of this living, as well as contemporary cinematic conventions, determine what is seen as realistic in each particular version of local London. An enquiry into these different 'true stories' will be one of the concerns of this chapter.

Local London is partly defined in the negative: it is not landmark London. Instead of the exceptional, local London offers the ordinary and the quotidian, the unspectacular. The time of local London is a time of repetition: of going to work, or to sign on, of shopping, of hanging about, of meal times and washing-up, of games of darts and snooker, of television, of visiting relatives and the pub. 'Local London' is dominated by a narrative time, which is like Mikhail Bakhtin's description of the time of the provincial town in the writings of Flaubert: 'Such towns are the locus for cyclical everyday time. Here there are no events, only "doings" that constantly repeat themselves.'[1] He continues, 'It is a viscous and sticky time that drags itself slowly through space.'[2] This 'viscous and sticky time' is most apparent in the south London films I discuss in the last part of the chapter, but throughout I shall be exploring the way in which, in the cinema, a sense of local space can be produced through temporal and spatial repetition.

The authenticity of 'local London' is often guaranteed by its eschewal of landmark iconography. No Westminster or Tower Bridges here, although buses, as I discussed in the last chapter, do feature, and the absence of landmark London is often marked in some way. Thus *Bend It Like Beckham* (2002), which is set firmly in Hounslow, includes one brief, transgressive trip to the West End to buy football boots, and is throughout haunted by Heathrow Airport, where Jess's father works. The huge planes are juxtaposed with local life throughout the film, testifying to arrivals and anticipating the departures on which the film ends. Similarly, *Good-*

bye Charlie Bright (2001), which is set in south-east London, includes a Docklands Light Railway panorama of the Dome in a trip out to Essex. Characters do leave local London to go 'up West' (as discussed in the next chapter), for days out, or sometimes by just imagining themselves elsewhere. These excursions and fantasies, though, often work to confirm the inescapability of local origins and to show that everyday local life is 'real life'. The localness of local London is thus partly constituted through the apprehension of an elsewhere, but the films on which I will concentrate remain within the local.

Local London is also, often, a temporally limited part of a film's narrative time. Local London, or perhaps more properly here, 'ordinary London', is where narratives start – or where they started, as we learn in flashbacks – and quite often where they finish. *Shaun of the Dead* (2004), a twenty-first-century zombie film, must establish its absolutely undistinctive local, suburban London with its familiar topography of local shops and a pub before this can be transformed by the appearance of the zombies. Here, the recognisable rendition of a local London is a prerequisite for its generic transformation. In other instances, such as *Love Actually* (2003), local London is an origin that an individual character transcends, as in the case of the Prime Minister's secretary, Natalie (Martine McCutcheon), who describes herself as coming from 'Wandsworth – the dodgy end', and the test of the Prime Minister's love for her is his journey across the river to the streets of uniform terraced houses. His romantic quest demands leaving the landmark London of Downing Street and travelling, across the illuminated Albert Bridge, to local London, the place of origins and ordinariness. As this is a Richard Curtis film, even local London is illuminated and magical and there is also a nostalgic quality to the rendering of the street, partly achieved through the special behaviour associated with Christmas. Generally, though, local London is a duller and less special place, a place of all the other days that are not Christmas.

If local London is produced in the cinema partly through contrasts with landmark London and the West End, it is also made through the ordinariness of its inhabitants. Local London in the cinema is where ordinary people live: working-class and lower-middle-class people in undistinguished homes: terraced streets, flats and estates. Its point, as setting, is that it is nowhere special and, often, nowhere specified. 'The city' of much scholarship on 'the cinema and the city' is conceived of in terms of mobility, modernity, crowds, streets, anonymity and strangers. It is characterised rather glamorously, as I discuss in more detail in the following chapter, as the 'city of attractions'. The personae of this city include flâneurs (and, contestedly, flâneuses), men about town, rogues, shoppers, prostitutes and gangsters. In this chapter, I look at that other, less glamorous city, the local London of homes, jobs, routines and families, which is also, unsurprisingly, where female characters are found in greater numbers – and stay alive throughout the film. This London, in its preoccupations with homes and families, is also where feature films incidentally document changes in residential housing stock. This is particularly noticeable in the 1960s rehousing of working-class Londoners from Victorian terraces and tenements into tower-blocks and estates. Sometimes, these upheavals are referred to directly by characters or plots. Charlie (James Booth), returning home to the East End in *Sparrows Can't Sing* (1963), asks, amazed, 'Where's all the houses? This used to be my street.'[3] Or, as Dave (Tony Selby) puts it, in the 1965 version of *Up the Junction*, when he takes a girl to the semi-derelict house where he grew up, 'They've moved us out to crummy Roehampton.'[4] However, it is not changes in housing stock that are my primary interest here, but rather the cinema of banal everyday life in post-war, post-imperial London.

Local London is often produced as a setting to be taken for granted. Because its essence lies in its ordinariness, it is often seen as not noticeable. In this chapter, I want to pay attention to the changing contours of this ordinariness – to notice it. For, arguably, what is most ordinary at any particular moment is also what is most historical, and it is here, in the rendition of everyday life, that the 'cultural production of spaces' that is London in the cinema is achieved. The films discussed in this chapter range from the 1950 Ealing film *Dance Hall* to Mike Leigh's 2002 *All or Nothing*. I want to explore the idea of a cinematic 'local London' in three groups of films: the output of the best-known London film studio, Ealing Studios; the feature films of the Trinidadian-born director Horace Ové, *Pressure* (1974) and *Playing Away* (1986); and films set in a particular part of London, south London, at the turn of the twentieth century.

In grouping together such a diverse group of films as representing 'local London', I am not suggesting that local London is one place. However, I will be exploring the extent to which the local – different locals – are produced in the cinema in similar ways or using similar strategies. These films are unified by being set in a London that is primarily conceived and imagined on a local scale – an estate, a block of flats, a neighbourhood, a cul-de-sac, a high street – rather than as a tourist destination and the capital of a nation state. Residential settings are significant in the cinematic construction of the local, as are the rhythms of everyday life. This local London, though, is frequently offered metonymically as more than local, giving an account of something in the state of the nation, and something, it is often implied, more authentically rendered for its grounding in the local. Local London is constituted differently in each group of films I discuss, and these various locals are formed in a complex interplay of factors which range from the availability of lighter, portable 16mm cameras to historical transformations in the role of the British high street. The local, too, has many modalities, and can be reassuring or constricting, familiar or claustrophobic – and sometimes all of these things at once.

A Little London: Ealing Studios

Passport to Pimlico (1949) opens with a characteristic Ealing joke about Britishness. After a dedicatory shot of a wreath 'In memory of ' ration books, Latin American music provides a soundtrack to a shot of a nearly cloudless sky. A suited man walks into shot, wiping the sweat from the back of his neck, and then pulls down a venetian blind, moving to peer through it. From his point of view, we see below him a parasol shading a man. A cut catches the gesture of a banana skin (a post-war delicacy) thrown to an uninterested dog and then there is the cut to the final, bravura shot of the sequence, which opens on a sunbathing woman lying on a lilo with a palm-like shadow. Moving down her body, the camera then cranes down a faded stripey awning to reveal the shutters of a shop being opened. A sign reading 'Frying Today' becomes visible as the music stops, and the voice of a BBC announcer tells us that we have been listening to 'Les Norman and his Bethnal Green Bambinos'. These four shots promise an exotic, noirish narrative: the evident heat; the blinds on the window;

the passive woman and the watching man; the hint of a palm tree; and the music. But 'Frying Today', in combination with the BBC voice, brings us back to post-war Britain with a bump, promising the British delicacy of fish and chips and allowing us to understand that it's not just fish that are frying, but Londoners too, as the crane turns into a pan across a London street, coming to a stop outside a general ironmongers to the chimes of Big Ben.

This opening condenses the narrative of the film into a few shots. It shows us an everyday London transformed into an exotic elsewhere, and, at a different level, intimates how setting might determine story. We think we are in a different place to where we really are, and in that moment, we expect a different kind of story. *Passport to Pimlico*'s well-known narrative of the discovery by the inhabitants of Miramont Place, Pimlico, that they are in fact Burgundians when an unexploded bomb reveals ancient treasure and documents, has been extensively discussed, usually in relation to British national identity, attitudes to the Second World War and as a typical Ealing comedy.[5] Charles Barr offers an elegant analysis of the film's presentation of Ealing's post-war 'daydream of a benevolent community', showing how Ealing Studios, Miramont Place and England are intimately related. The film is so explicitly about how to be British in a post-war context that its contribution as a London film is sometimes overlooked. Barr, however, does point out the two key aspects of the presentation of London, in addition to the overarching theme of community. First, like its predecessor, *Hue and Cry* (1947), the film 'brings alive a London community centred on a bombsite.'[6] In this, the film uses a key iconographic element in the post-Second World War representation of London, the bombsite.[7] And, second, its vision of a London community is 'a village within a village: the tiny community of Miramont Place, where all the people know each other and trade with each other.'[8] Ealing's London, as the BBC announcer in the opening of the film reminds us, is deeply parochial: Les Norman's Bambinos are from Bethnal Green in the East End. When Pimlico is under siege, other parts of London send food and goods. These are collected and stored with labels indicating where in London they have come from, characterising the image of each district in few objects: Finchley, stuffy and respectable, donates a standard lamp and a grandfather clock; Ealing's gift are mainly chintzy curtains; while poor old Lambeth contributes only second-hand boots and shoes.

Ealing's 'daydream of a benevolent community' is founded, in this film, on a sense of the local: local people, local amenities – or lack of them – and local knowledge. Ealing's Pimlico is bereft of what are often seen as the key characteristics of the city: anonymity, the crowd, loneliness. These are present in the film, particularly in the mob attracted by the promise of ration-free trading, Whitehall and the West End cinema where the evacuated children watch a newsreel, but these are what the little community of Pimlico/Burgundy must unite to fight against. Pimlico London, as Barr observes, is a village London, and in this is opposed to 'city London'. Ealing's London is distinguished by its scale and its knowability, and is often, as here, a little London. I want to explore Ealing's 'little London' in two 1950 films, *Dance Hall* (Charles Crichton) and *The Blue Lamp* (Basil Dearden).

Dance Hall, set in West London round the 'Chiswick Palais', tells the story of four young women who enjoy going out to dance. Their lives are closely intertwined and at the start of the film, Eve (Natasha Parry), Mary (Jane Hylton), Carole (Diana Dors) and Georgie (Petula Clark) work together in a factory and live in the same flats. Unusually for Ealing, the film focuses on the four women, and in this recalls home front films such as *Millions Like Us* (1943) and *The Gentle Sex* (1943), in which each character represents a different type of femininity.[9] Here, Eve must choose between her love of dancing – in which she is partnered by Alec (Bonar Colleano) – and her rather dull, clumsy aircraft engineer boyfriend Phil (Donald Houston), who wants to take her to Biggin Hill every weekend to watch planes. The childlike Georgie must decide whether to wear the frumpy dress her hard-up, decent parents have bought her for the dance competition, or to betray them by accepting the loan of a much more glamorous frock from the Palais manager. Carole is looking for a man who can match her flamboyant, American-identified style, while Mary longs for romance and is in love with Phil. Pat Kirkham's illuminating discussion of the film shows how costume is used to reveal the different desires and destinies of the female characters within a context transitional between post-war austerity and the intimations of 1950s affluence.[10]

The film was shot mainly at Ealing Studios, with some limited location work, using the original Ealing Studios (the Will Barker studios at Ealing Green) for night sequences. Hammersmith Palais is explicitly acknowledged in the credits, although the press book is at pains to point out that 'the hall in the film is in no way meant to be a replica of that famous dance haunt.'[11] I want to explore how what Barr describes as 'a decent film in a familiar Ealing format' constructs its sense of place. Ealing films are often marked not just by the much-discussed projection of Britishness, but also by a strong sense of London, which is particularly manifest in a delight about its parochial rivalries and the loving juxtaposition of the native with the foreign. In *Dance Hall* it is the heats for Greater London Amateur Ballroom Dancing Competition that provide a key narrative structure and, in the Final, the passionate advocacy of outer London boroughs ('Come on Cricklewood', 'Come on Wimbledon') is a mild joke, which matches the district labels attached to the piles of donated goods in *Passport to Pimlico*. The native/foreign juxtaposition, often accomplished through verbal play, embodied in film titles such as *The Lavender Hill Mob* (1951) or the band name, 'Les Norman and his Bethnal Green Bambinos', is found in *Dance Hall* in the exhibition dancers, Juan and Chiquita. As they prepare to slip through the curtain into the spotlight, glamorously dressed in evening clothes, Juan asks Chiquita, in a local London accent, 'Are you ready, Ducks?' The humour here, the puncturing of more exotic expectations of their appearance and billing, is also found, in a reverse move, in *Dance Hall*'s narrative detail, that it is a case of kippers from Aberdeen that excites suspicions of adultery.

The opening of the film establishes the core topography within the first few minutes. The young women's lives are mapped within the triangle of work, home and dancing. The opening titles run over shots of the *palais de danse* out of hours: chairs piled up on tables for sweeping, the only rhythmic movement that of the women cleaners as they vacuum and mop the deserted floors. The vast space is empty, its curvaceous *moderne* balconies and columned recesses being prepared and waiting, like us, for the narrative that will take place there. The soundtrack of musicians tuning up drifts into 'I'm Only Dreaming', the film's theme, and then cuts abruptly to the noise of machinery as the titles finish and the second location is revealed through a close-up on the big oily machine Georgie is operating. A slow track down the workshop reveals each protagonist in turn, Georgie, Carole, Mary and Eve, singing while they perform heavy, dirty work and clocking off with alacrity as the hooter goes. The third element in the core topography of the film is then produced with a quick series of three scenes in three different homes. Carole talks to her sister about the attractions of the new saxophonist, while she sits at her dressing table making up; Georgie dances round her parents explaining her hopes for the dance competition, telling them that Eve also has a chance if only she can find the right partner; Eve too is trying to get ready in a bedroom crowded with two of her sisters, and trips over her brother lying on the floor as she rushes past her harassed mother to join the others. In each of the scenes, railings and other windows are discernible through the window, and these views are brought together in the final shot of the sequence, an external view of the tenement buildings where all the girls live. Mary is waiting in the courtyard as the others rush along the railinged walkways and down the stairs.

This triangular topography structures the spaces of the film, with the homes crowded, work noisy and most time spent in the dance hall itself. As the press book notes,

> A *palais de danse* caters for many types. Primarily it is a place of relaxation for youngsters who seek healthy diversion in an atmosphere of gaiety and bright music, a haven in which many can forget the more humdrum surroundings of their home and work.[12]

Eve's crowded bedroom in *Dance Hall*, with the railing of the walkways visible outside

Judicious location shooting and set-dressing secures these generic 'humdrum' spaces of work, home and play as set in London. On a Sunday morning early in the film, Phil, who often works away, gets a lift back to London and is dropped by the river. The churches are ringing out and a band of cyclists sweep past him. This sequence associates Phil with the bright morning, the outdoors and healthy exercise, while the bombed-out wasteland juxtaposed with a church against the river confirms that this is post-war London. Much later in the film, Eve shops in a high street, intending to go to MacFisheries to buy the supper. Here, a helmeted policeman directs traffic, which includes a Routemaster bus. Although the spatial relationships between work, home and the dance hall are not given detail, the girls can walk to the Palais and take a bus to work. These locations are lit realistically: bright and even at home, harshly at work and more dramatically for exhibition dances at the Palais. This is Ealing's local London: friendly, neighbourly, modest. As Georgie's parents say to each other, 'We shouldn't expect too much.' In contrast to this, the film offers a different kind of space, a different kind of London, which is associated with Alec Vinas and his seduction of Eve.

On his first entrance, it is established that Alec Vinas is a ladies' man.[13] As he stands surveying the dance floor from the stairs, he rests his elbow on the baluster in a way that knocks the head of a woman standing below him. She turns, recognising him, and greets him by name, 'Hello, Alec'. Hardly interrupting his scanning of the dancers, he replies absently, 'Hello, Jean', and gazes on into the distance. But it is when we first see Alec giving Eve a lift home in his open-top sports car that his danger is made explicit. The scene immediately follows Phil's announcement of his distrust of Alec – a comment made in the bright open air. The next shot is dark – Eve and Alec in the car, unfamiliar streets around them. As they turn into the mews to Alec's garage and flat, Eve asks, 'Where's this?' as indeed she might, for the *mise en scène* is quite different to the film so far, offering a glimpse of a noir London backstreet in which she is invited upstairs to listen to a record. An invitation, which, this time, she declines.

The dance hall, even though it hosts a particularly riotous New Year's Eve party at the climax of the film, is the safe bright place for pleasure.[14] But its pleasures of music, movement and bodily proximity – which seduce even the cleaners – have a more dangerous potential beyond its bright lights, and it is this danger that Alec represents. Eve's dilemma, her choice between bright Phil and dark Alec, is presented through the casting, costume and performance of Donald Houston and Bonar Colleano, but also through lighting and spatially. Alec not only dances better than Phil, he literally takes her to places she would not otherwise go. Her assent to the seduction is signified by her choosing to leave the Palais with him. With great economy, the scene is shot in front of an upstairs window in the Palais with Alec and Eve standing in front of a window through which a dark London skyline is visible. Alec gestures to the outside, and Eve, turning to look out, makes an almost imperceptible movement to convey assent. Christine Geraghty has analysed Natasha Parry's performance in this scene in the context of her convincing argument about the emotional power of an extremely restrained acting style in post-war Ealing films. She observes,

> Eve's decision to 'go with' Alec occurs in a wordless scene and is registered through Parry's blank face and averted gaze; a movement in the throat and a parting of the lips indicates desire, until finally she turns her head towards him to indicate acceptance.[15]

This skilled performance is conducted in relation to an elsewhere to the dance hall, the dark skyline at which both actors gaze, and it is the promise of this dark city, in combination with their skill, which gives this scene its eroticism. Consent given, Eve and Alec leave the frame and the camera moves through the window into the night.

Eve is the only female character who finds herself outside in the dark space of the city in this film. After Alec introduces her to the night, she finds herself there alone twice in the film. In the first instance, she rows with Phil at the Palais when he (wrongly) suspects infidelity, and she runs out into a dark, rain-glistening side alley. Her flight takes her from the alley outside the dance hall exit onto the high street and eventually back to her parents' flat. This is a journey from the safe, local public space of the dance hall to, fleetingly, the city streets, more dangerous and more anonymous. Locality is reasserted though, with the appearance of the tenement buildings shown at the beginning of the film. The consequence of Eve's earlier, dangerous fascination with Alec is shown spatially: when she leaves the dance hall, she is potentially lost to local London, alone on the streets of the city. This spatialisation of Eve's sexual experience is repeated at the climax of the film in a sequence when she is subjected to an almost comic humiliation at the New Year's Eve dance. In this scene, which immediately precedes her final reconciliation with Phil, she is shut out of the Palais on the roof, and is shown shouting, getting drenched in heavy rain and putting her foot through a discarded box, in her attempt to regain entry.[16]

The invitation to enter the dark city in *Dance Hall* (Bonar Colleano [Alec] and Natasha Parry [Eve])

So, in *Dance Hall*, the sense of Ealing's safe little London is created partly through the suggestion that just outside it – visible through the dance-hall window, through an exit door, sometimes occupying the same streets – is another London, a dark city of sex and solitude. Eve, the film's central figure, moves in and out of the dark city. The grim conclusion of her story, though, is the similarity between Eve's life with Phil and that of her mother, even to the extent of a matching shot of Eve almost tied to an ironing board, with the electric flex hanging down from the light socket. The dark, tempting city may be what Eve must resist, but life with Phil is dark in its own way and it is difficult not to sympathise with her as she gazes longingly at the bright lights of the Palais.

The Blue Lamp is on a larger scale than *Dance Hall*. It is more explicitly a state-of-the-nation narrative, offering both an anatomy of what was just being named as juvenile delinquency and its spectacular containment by a united society in the dramatic finale in the White City Stadium. Like *Dance Hall* it is also a west London film, with repeated reference to the environs of Paddington Green police station – the Edgware Road, the Harrow Road, Ladbroke Grove – and considerable location shooting for the chase scenes and along the Grand Union Canal. It even has a little west London joke at the end during the final chase, when a close-up of a police map shows that the fugitives are fleeing straight towards Wormwood Scrubs, the main prison in west London. Like *Dance Hall*, *The Blue Lamp* is concerned with the destiny of young people in post-war Britain. There is also an echo of the good/bad masculinity of Alec and Phil in *Dance Hall* with the dark, delinquent Tom Riley (Dirk Bogarde) contrasted to the fair, decent young police recruit Andy Mitchell (Jimmy Hanley). But *Dance Hall* was centred on the dreams and dilemmas of young women and thus took place mainly inside: its heroines gazed in mirrors and fantasised about winning dance competitions and getting married. No respectable young woman could have dreams that could be realised on the streets of London, and the dance hall itself provided a protected indoor public space. Eve's fall, temptation and punishment, as we have seen, takes place outside this protected space and puts her literally in the streets. The young woman in *The Blue Lamp*, Diana Lewis (Peggy Evans), has run away from home at the start of the film and is first seen loitering in the street. Diana, who 'doesn't want to be helped', is already living outside the respectable domestic; in this film it is only the police who have decent home lives.

The Blue Lamp is dedicated to the Metropolitan Police, made with their co-operation, and addresses the problem of the new, asocial criminality of young people brought up during the war years.[17] The film offers a detailed account of metropolitan policing, showing the division of labour between uniformed beat officers and the CID, the role of the local police station of Paddington Green within the community and of New Scotland Yard in London. Steve Chibnall argues that police involvement in the film was such that it represented a strategic intervention by the Metropolitan Police Commissioner and 'is more an animated recruitment poster than an analysis of youthful crime'.[18] Police officers are shown undertaking a wide variety of tasks ranging from ordinary beat work and traffic duty to liaising with the underworld and dramatic car chases. There is also considerable attention paid to the technologies of policing, with film of telephone switchboards, emergency services, car radio announcements, police telephones and forensic examinations, some of it location shot. *The Blue Lamp*'s retrospective fame produced by the long-running BBC television serial *Dixon of Dock Green* as

the film that first introduced and then killed off Jack Warner as George Dixon, has sometimes obscured its considerable success on first release.[19] Within the terms of my argument,
the film is most interesting in the way in which the rhythms and practices of a local London,
most strongly associated within the film with George Dixon himself, are asserted against the
deracinated, Americanised urban violence represented by the three young villains.

The film's local London, and Dixon's role within it, is mobilised within a general argument proposed by a narrator at the beginning of the film, over an image of the Old Bailey,
when a judge is quoted on the importance of the 'regular uniformed policeman on the beat'
in protecting citizens against the 'crime wave'. Thus the whole local narrative of the film is
an example given to prove a general case about the need for more police and the importance
of the local bobby. This structure is embodied in the opening of the film, which offers in
quick succession the blue lamp of a police station and a police car leaving; a location-shot
fatal car chase; a 'crime-wave' montage of newspaper headlines and the image of the Old
Bailey, which leads to the transition into the local story of George Dixon. In contrast to this
crime-wave introduction, which promises the viewer car chases and gunfire, Dixon is introduced with precise geographical specificity.[20] The film has a clear narrative and topograph-
ical heart in Paddington Green police station. It is about Paddington Green's 'manor': the
police, the citizens, who show up drunk, lost, driving badly and losing their dogs, and the
criminals, both established and new. George Dixon is first shown in a way that places him in
relation to local landmarks: the children's hospital and the Green itself, giving directions to
Paddington Station over the iron bridge. Dixon is a model local copper, so embedded in the
area that he knows the names of most of those he meets and understands their tricks and
evasions. The narrative of the film is partly the story of an apprenticeship, in which young
PC Mitchell must learn this local belonging from Dixon. As many have commented, Mitchell's
apprenticeship can be deemed complete by the end of the film, when he is approached for
directions to Paddington Station and gives them in an exact repetition of George Dixon's
words at the beginning.[21] So place, and its repetitions, here signify a way of policing. Like the
London of *Passport*, Paddington Green is a little London, where children get jam buns at the
police station and old ladies are excused their overdue dog licences. The village quality is
enhanced by, for example, having a police horse being groomed in the background throughout a scene of a CID breakthrough, and the particular quality of the night patrol, which I will
discuss in more detail below. But, as with *Passport*, there is another London, London the city,
here signified by the bright lights and jazzy soundtrack of the West End. Riley and Spud are
shown briefly in Piccadilly Circus, when they are hawking their plans for a robbery around,
and the shadowy pool hall where they try to make a deal can be identified as Soho because
of the diversity of its patrons.[22] It is in the West End that we first see Diana Lewis walking
aimlessly along the pavement, and all three young people then meet in a shiny Americanised Milk Bar Café.

Several writers have commented on the contrast between the Dixon and the Tom Riley
(Dirk Bogarde) elements of the film.[23] It is a contrast between two Londons, the village and the
city, shown clearly in an early night-time sequence. The policemen are on night-duty,
and are shown serially having different night-time encounters. Taffy, the Welsh policeman,
comes across a young couple kissing in a shop doorway and dispatches them home with torch-

light. Dixon, patrolling residential streets, passes road-works and chooses to tip-toe past in order not to rouse the snoozing night-watchman. Andy Mitchell disturbs yowling cats. Mitchell and Dixon meet in the stuccoed streets of Maida Vale and Dixon reveals that he passes the time making up little ditties. These interactions all take place in detailed night environments, where it is possible to see shop window displays, sleeping night-watchmen, canal boats, star constellations and front gardens. In contrast, in the middle of this sequence, Tom Riley waits for his friend to pick him up in a stolen car, and the space is empty and anonymous: a city street, made meaningful through long shadows and a slight mist. The very emptiness of the shot and its lack of detail point to a shift from the detailed realism of the policemen's night to the generically immanent world of the villain: a crime is about to be committed.

The celebrated finale of the film, shot on location in the White City Stadium, has been eloquently anatomised by Charles Barr who comments:

> It makes an extraordinary climax, and extraordinary vision. Police, stadium authorities, the 'underworld', the anonymous crowd, all unite to bring to justice a criminal who has transgressed the *code* referred to in the early commentary and expressed in action throughout the film.[24]

The scale of the mobilisation against Riley is what is so impressive. As Barr observes, 'The stadium is the place Riley has reached: he thinks he can lose himself within this anonymous crowd, within a recognised sub-criminal milieu … The police now have to find this one man in a crowd of many thousands.' He continues:

> At the stadium, Mike [Randall], the film's senior underworld man, is presiding over a network of operations. His wariness with the police is transformed when he hears who it is they are seeking; he immediately puts his network into service to track Riley down. A montage of eager signals shows the bookies and their tic-tac men passing the word round the stadium. Riley is spotted, the message comes back, Mike tells the police, and they close in.[25]

This sequence is fulfilling not just because, narratively, the villain is caught, but because it brings together the village and the city, and reveals that the city still abides by village rules. Riley seeks refuge in the crowd of the city, but it turns out to be not anomic, but purposeful.[26] This is the 'daydream' of *The Blue Lamp* – that the city is not a city, but a village. Although early in the film, while being questioned by the police, the senior underworld figure (Randall) had dismissed the perpetrators of a robbery with violence (committed by Riley and Spud) as 'local lads', this conclusion suggests the opposite. Riley may be young and unprofessional, which is Randall's implication, but this finale unites all sections of the local community, police, punters and criminals, to expel Riley from the local.

Horace Ové's London: *Pressure*

> I didn't make the film sitting in my room: I went out with Samuel Selvon and researched it. I was aware of the political situation, I know what's going down. So when it was made, and people started saying, 'That's not true,' I knew that either they didn't know what they were talking about,

or they didn't want to admit to things. *Pressure* has had a lot of pressure. It's a touchy film, about something that's happening here.

Horace Ové, 1978[27]

Horace Ové's 1975 film *Pressure* also creates a local London.[28] This too is a west London and the street names of *The Blue Lamp* recur – Ladbroke Grove, Harrow Road – in a film that also features young people and the police. *Pressure's* local London, though, is confining rather than comfortable. After the Second World War, North Kensington, which includes Notting Dale, Ladbroke Grove and Notting Hill, had become one of the primary areas for Caribbean settlement in London.[29] The historical poverty, particularly in the north of an area long associated with immigration, has moved ethnicities: from being a poor Irish area it becomes – in part – a poor black area. Basil Dearden's 1959 film about racial prejudice, *Sapphire*, locates the overcrowded lodgings of West Indian immigrants in Notting Hill; it is in a multi-occupied North Kensington terraced house that a Jamaican labourer discovers the bodies of Reginald Christie's victims, and the film-makers of *10, Rillington Place* (1970) specify that some filming was done in Rillington Place;[30] much of *Performance* (1970), seen by some as one of the outstanding London films, is mainly set in a Notting Hill house where the shifting population is the core of the narrative;[31] *Jemima and Johnny* (1964), a short film by the actor Lionel Ngakane, which contrasts the innocent friendship of a little black boy and white girl with the prejudices of their parents, was set there. *Pressure* is thus part of an identifiable thread of post-war British and Caribbean artwork – including the work of Colin MacInnes, Sam Selvon and Charlie Phillips – which explores Notting Hill as a particular London site for the negotiation of a post-imperial British culture, a tradition continued in later works such as Menelik Shabazz's 1981 *Burning an Illusion*, Isaac Julien's *Territories* (1984), Julien Temple's version of *Absolute Beginners* (1986), the film based on the Profumo affair, *Scandal* (1988), and Hanif Kureishi's directorial debut, *London Kills Me* (1991). The 1958 Notting Hill 'race riots', All Saints Road as a 'front line' and the Notting Hill Carnival hover behind, and sometimes structure, these artworks, just as the M40 motorway careers through the cityscape.

North Kensington was transformed by the enlargement of the A40 westward exit from London and the building of the Marylebone flyover and the Westway in the late 1960s. Paddington Green all but disappeared, reduced to a little slip of land overshadowed by the flyover and the rebuilt police station, a secure tower-block used for detaining terrorist suspects. The Edgware Road is cut in two by this inner London section of the Westway. Further west, the motorway bifurcates Dixon's old manor, cutting off the northern stretches of Ladbroke Grove and Portobello Road from the historically more affluent higher, southern, Notting Hill, and blocking the sky with stark concrete archways. The wastelands under the Westway, particularly round Portobello Road market, feature in a range of films filmed in Notting Hill, including *Sammy and Rosie Get Laid* (1987), *London Kills Me* and here in *Pressure*.[32] Erno Goldfinger's celebrated and reviled Trellick Tower, with its distinctive two-part silhouette, has towered over the Golborne Road since its completion in 1972; its own transition, from hated council flats to refurbished luxury apartments, a metonym for the gentrification of the area that meets its apogee in *Notting Hill* (Roger Michell, 1999).

Pressure, made with the support of the British Film Institute, is marked as the first British-made feature film by a black director.[33] It was scripted by Horace Ové, who had made the short films *Baldwin's Nigger* (1969) and *Reggae* (1970), and the writer Samuel Selvon, famous for his 1956 book about the experience of West Indian immigrants in London, *The Lonely Londoners*. The film is realist in style, except for a dream sequence, and set in Ladbroke Grove before it became 'Notting Hill'. It focuses on Tony (Herbert Norville), a sixteen-year-old British-born black youth who is unable to find work after leaving school, despite being top of his class and passing all his O-level exams. Brought up by law-abiding, Christian Trinidadian immigrant parents, Tony is torn between his desires to please them and get a respectable job, and accepting the explanations of his failure to do this given by his brother Colin (Oscar James), who is involved with the local Black Power movement; or falling into a life of petty thieving along with other unemployed local black youth that he knows. In some ways, the film offers a classical narrative of 'coming to consciousness', although the tiny picket of drenched campaigners outside the Old Bailey in the pouring rain at the end of the film, seeking justice for Colin among others, offers a very downbeat view of what that consciousness can achieve. Critical response to the film, while recognising its landmark status, has concentrated on the extent to which its stylistic realism confines it to retelling familiar stories. Thus Jim Pines observed, 'It is a classic "race relations" drama which draws on a number of familiar themes – e.g. the "immigrant problem" motif and the problem of assimilation – and reworks them into the film's documentary-like fictional narrative', but proceeded to suggest that the film had a 'timely message' in its black perspective.[34] Kobena Mercer suggests that the film cannot find 'a successful means of escaping from the master codes that circumscribe it'.[35] Certainly, as Mercer points out, the dream sequence, in which Tony enters a mansion set in a formal garden, and frenziedly stabs at what turns out to be a pig's carcass (in a bed), is problematic and does perhaps indicate 'a certain powerlessness on the part of the film itself'. Thirty years on, though, the film's realist codes, articulated through its low-budget aesthetics, offer an interesting account of a particular 1970s' local London as a contested space. In addition to its explicit agenda about the widespread and institutional racism of 1970s Britain, the film offers a clear spatialisation of the position of black youth, and it is on this use of space that my analysis will concentrate.

Pressure is an angry film, which, while it has some obvious villains, has no simple solutions. Its angry localness is the sometimes forgotten historical backstory to the apparently unproblematic inclusion of steel drums in *Trainspotting*'s 1995 montage of 'Landmark London'. *Pressure*, like Menelik Shabazz's *Burning an Illusion*, also filmed in Notting Hill, and the Brixton-set *Babylon* (Franco Rosso, 1980), is testament to the struggles that precede the marketing of London, at the end of the twentieth century, as a city with an achieved multiculturalism.[36] The films speak from a post-imperial moment in which there is, or has been, an imagination of settlement, of accommodation, of coexistence, even if obstructed at every turn. In these 1970s/early 1980s post-colonial London films, however angry they are, there is a narrative of entitlement. Identities exist quite variously, but one of the key and repeated narrative motivations of characters is the claim for recognition, a recognition, often as British, sometimes as a passport holder, sometimes as 'born here', but, whichever, as equal and as a citizen, someone who is entitled to have a voice and to be heard. In this, these films mark an historical moment in the negotiation of post-imperial Britishness which involves some quite different vectors than those in the emerging US black cinema with which they are sometimes compared. While there is, frequently, within the British films, an invocation of the African diaspora, it is mediated through concerns with the claiming of an entitlement to British identities. It is within this context that *Pressure's* attention to the local is so significant. It is this history that was vanished in the internationally successful romantic comedy set in the same area, *Notting Hill*.

At the beginning of the film, through the use of close-ups on frying egg and bacon, *Pressure* signals that food will be used to signify identity and identifications. In the opening set-up, a clear contrast is established between Colin, the Trinidadian-born elder brother, and British-born Tony. Colin takes an avocado from their father's West Indian food shop, and teases Tony as he eats the bacon and eggs their mother has cooked. By the end of the film, Tony is taking West Indian Pepper Sauce with his food, although he is still arguing against racial absolutism. This explicit symbolising of Tony's conflict is matched by a more implicit spatialising of his restricted choices and destiny. Tony's quest, in the film, can be seen as an attempt to gain a legitimate access to inside spaces, now that he is growing up, has left school and must contribute to, rather than be sheltered by, his parents in their home. The logic of a racialising culture is shown to be a repeated return of a young black man to the streets. These streets can be occupied in different ways: Tony's anomie as he wanders alone after another humiliating job interview; Colin and Sister Louise's political activism selling papers on a market stall; the hanging about and petty pilfering and criminality of other black youth; or the final, dismal, rained-on political protest. As Lola Young has pointed out, *Pressure* figures black experience as black male experience, offering little sympathy to Tony's mother and characterising Sister Louise as an (American) seductress, but it offers a vivid account of the streets of London as the only space for young black men.[37] As we saw with Diana Lewis in *The Blue Lamp*, wandering the streets of London is rarely a good activity in the cinema. The poignancy of *Pressure* is that Tony wishes to do something else – to come inside.

Tony first leaves his parents' home to go to a job interview, but is shown to have difficulty even being admitted to the office building. After the interview, we see him wandering, aimlessly, round crowded shopping streets.[38] There is a little mood sequence as Tony walks disconsolately down the street, excluded from the consumption he sees around him. In the latter part of the sequence the soundtrack, with the lyrics of 'Pressure' written by Ové, is explicitly carrying Tony's experience of rejection and remaking it as one of the sounds of black London. And it is, of course, this music that has proved more mobile than youths in Tony's situation. Meeting former school friends at the community centre, Tony is invited to go to a disco at the Bird's Nest, but is unable to accept until they – all white, and already in work – offer to pay for him. This outing, which requires catching a bus, is the only time, apart from the job interview, that Tony leaves the local area. After the Bird's Nest, he walks home Sheila, the (white) girl whom he fancied at school and with whom he was dancing. Unlike the boys, Sheila is upwardly mobile and has managed to move out of the area, expressing her achievement as relief, 'I hated it in Ladbroke Grove – it was crummy'. Her invitation to coffee is blocked by her landlady who is explicitly hostile to Tony, but will not name her prejudice. This landlady is a mixture of two types in British cinema, the bossy landlady who'll have no hanky-panky in her house – for example, Ted's landlady in *It Always Rains on Sunday* (1947) – and the 'negrophobic' white woman that Lola Young has shown is often, along with working-class youths, identified as the source of racism in British films.[39] Her hysterical response to Tony puts him out on the streets again, and so Tony has been kept out of work, of leisure and romance. These exclusions lead him to consort with the youths who support themselves through more and less organised pilfering – and who turn out to live, not at home, but in a derelict house on the Harrow Road.[40] Their refuge has a roof, but is hardly inside. Towards the climax of the film, the Community Centre, which is the one inside space Tony has access to apart from his home, is invaded by the police after a political meeting and Tony's home is aggressively searched by the police, who leave it wrecked after destroying many of his parents' precious possessions. The police – rude, violent and hostile – have penetrated each refuge. By the end of the film, there are no inside spaces left for Tony except for an activist's flat, where protest placards are made and the politics of ethnicity debated.

Tony's London, as indicated by a brief flashback, experienced during his schooldays as an integrated local London where he moved between home, school and leisure, has become a confining set of streets that he cannot escape, and in which he cannot feel safe. However, within this local London, constructed so differently to the same streets patrolled by Dixon's paternalistic gaze, there is at least a debate about exclusion and entitlement. The film's investment in the question of identity, of how to be black in Britain, is developed partly through Atlantic affiliations: the West Indies or black America. Tony's drama is a drama of

Tony (Herbert Norville) on the streets in *Pressure*

identity and identification. It is about a stake in Britain, and how to achieve it. It is about being recognised as an equal citizen. This marks the film's discursive repertoire as quite distinct from what I am calling the 'global London' films, discussed in the next chapter, where asylum seekers and illegal immigrants are characterised as, above all, seeking to avoid recognition. *Pressure* is about establishing that difference is institutionalised: it makes an argument that there is systematic discrimination against young black people at every level of the education system, which is then followed by discrimination in the job market. However, this argument has as its basis an expectation of equality and inclusion, and Tony, like other characters in this first wave of black British feature films, is granted subjectivity, aspiration and the ability to reflect on his own identity and heritage. While the film does have moments of didacticism, one of its achievements is the rendering of Tony's situation aesthetically through its deployment of the space of local London.

Playing Away, Ové's second feature, is, as its title suggests, set mainly away from home. It too, though, is concerned with the local, and the way in which a sense of the local is constructed through the interplay of what is taken for granted, what is *heimlich*, and what is elsewhere. Again, Ové works with an established writer with his own record in relation to these themes, this time the novelist Caryl Phillips.[41] Made ten years after *Pressure*, with funding from Channel 4, in the paradoxical flourishing of oppositional arts that marked the second half of the Thatcher government, *Playing Away* is a less overtly angry film. However, it too is concerned to reveal the complex imbrication of global and local, this time through the metaphor of a game of cricket, the English game which the British Empire exported, only to discover that colonial history is no guarantee of subsequent sporting victory. The film follows the fortunes of a cricket team from Brixton, south London, when they travel to Sneddington, a village in Suffolk, for an away match. Caryl Phillips describes his final aesthetic choice as 'Which one of the teams would play away? It was easy. The team that had been playing away the longest'.[42] The local here is constructed, ambitiously, in two modes, which are juxtaposed in the opening sequence as the film cuts between the two 'locals' of the teams who will meet in a cricket match on the Sunday. A traditional village England with half-timbered houses, a single pub and a vicar is contrasted with the urban milieu of the Brixton Conquistadors, who meet to plan their trip in a local pub, some still wearing London Transport work uniform.

The Brixton team are billeted on their opposite numbers in Sneddington, and, on the evening before the game, have a range of experiences of English rural life – some extremely unpleasant, frightening and humiliating. Although the Brixton sequence of the film is short and confined to the beginning, the film is relevant here because of its explicit contrast of the urban and rural villages, and the routines, characters and locales that constitute the local in each. For Sneddington, the 'non-local' is London and the Africa that was once part of the British Empire. These are exquisitely combined in the villagers' sense that it would be appropriate to play cricket against a Brixton team as a contribution to Africa Famine Week. For the Conquistadors, the utter foreignness of the English countryside is juxtaposed with the troubled longing of the older immigrants for the West Indies, and the difficulty of reversing decisions first made forty years earlier. The younger Brixtonians have no such worries, and suffer only the same rural boredom as afflicts the young people of Sneddington.

Playing Away takes Brixton, as a centre of London West Indian and British black culture, for granted. Its use of the locations of the pub, where the team meet to plan the trip, and the blues party where some members continue the evening, permits the development of individual character story lines, and some broader themes such as the tension between older and younger members of the team and the marginal place of women. Key Brixton landmarks, such as the railway bridge and the edge of the market, form part of a local topography of streets, pubs, flats and the Recreation Centre, which are mobilised within the film as setting for a story that will take place mainly elsewhere. The structure of the film, with the picturesque English village, in the main, fairly inhospitable to the visitors, makes this taken-for-granted Brixton doubly homely by the end of the film. It is a relief to return, to see the railway bridge again, the rain, the traffic, the urban congestion, which somehow has more room than the countryside. *Playing Away*'s Brixton is significant in its achieved localness. In this, it contrasts with other cinematic presentations of the area as either a site of exotic difference, or a site of turmoil and danger, particularly for black characters. In *The Long Good Friday* (1979), which is discussed in detail in Chapter 6, Harold Shand (Bob Hoskins), a gangster based in east London, goes to Brixton to interrogate Erroll the Ponce (Paul Barber). One of the few locations in the film with trees, Brixton, in comparison with east London, is sunny and shabby with music blaring in the streets. 'This used to be a nice street,' says Harold, before proceeding to order the razor whipping of the naked Erroll, the scene directly reminiscent of the imagery of slavery.[43] In Patrick Keiller's *London* (1994), Brixton is hailed as delightful for its 'modernity', and the narrator celebrates both the arcades of Brixton market, which remind him of the Parisian arcades so suggestive to Walter Benjamin, and the international modernity of street names such as Electric Avenue. In Franco Rosso's *Babylon* the streets of Brixton offer reverse flânerie for the central character, Blue (Brinsley Forde), as his meandering journey home, peering into shop windows as he wanders back after a night out, is transformed into a nightmare chase through the streets and back-alleys in which his pursuers turn out to be the police. In some ways, the glimpsed Brixton of *Playing Away* is closest to that of the 1977 Brixton of *Black Joy* (directed by Anthony Simmons based on a play by Jamal Ali), which has a classic 'country dweller comes to the city' narrative, told as the tale of new and established West Indian immigration to Brixton.[44] In both *Black Joy* and *Playing Away*, Brixton is where ordinary people live their often rather messed-up lives, a place that has become local to those who arrived as immigrants, and a locality in which the memory of Empire lives on in more than the street names such as Atlantic Road and Coldharbour Lane.

South London: A Changing Grammar of the Local

> [T]he sinister, noisy, hopeless and rowdy night of South London.
>
> Joseph Conrad, *The Secret Agent* (1907), p. 117

In the final part of this chapter on local London, I turn to two films made at the turn of the twenty-first century, which take south London (but not Brixton) as their setting: Gary Oldman's explicitly autobiographical 1997 *Nil By Mouth* and Mike Leigh's 2002 *All or Nothing*, both of which are about white working-class families living on south London estates.[45] These are both rather grim films, and will thus inflect my discussion of south London rather differently than if I had chosen *Waterloo Road* (1945), with its anticipation of a better post-war world, or one of the versions of *Up the Junction* (1965 and 1967), or *South West 9* (2001), which Paul Dave celebrates for its narrative use of symbolic Brixton locations.[46]

Before looking in detail at these films though, I want to note briefly what, following Rob Shields, we might call the 'place-image' of south London, and its cinematic role as a location for the ordinary.[47] A useful starting point here is a film from more than fifty years before, *This Happy Breed* (1944), made just as the Second World War was ending, which proposes that its story of one south London family should be taken as representative of the nation as a whole.[48] The opening aerial shot over London, looking south-west from the north-east, showing the cranes of the docks, the winding river and the fumes of the factories and power stations is placed in 1918 by Laurence Olivier's voice-over: 'After four long years, the men are coming home. Thousands of houses are becoming homes again ...'. Strong, bass choral singing of the returning soldiers rises over the image, as, with a series of cuts, this panoramic view of London becomes more and more localised, moving from the city, south of the river to a district and then to a street. The grey uniformity of the terraced houses is countered by the flourishing varied green of the back gardens, and it is from the back garden that the camera swoops down and enters a house through the bathroom window. The camera greets the Gibbons family, whose story the film will follow from 1918 to 1939, from the inside, as Mr Gibbons, just demobbed, opens the door of number 17, Sycamore Grove, where the ghostly shapes of previous tenants' furniture are still visible on the walls. Sycamore Grove is in Clapham, south London, and this brief opening sequence condenses many of the key features of cinematic south London. It is dull, uniform and massed with few distinguishing features or landmarks.[49] Indeed, much of the drama in *This Happy Breed* comes from the determination of one of the Gibbonses' daughters, Queenie, to escape from her origins: not to be ordinary.

In *Sapphire*, the Dearden/Relph 'social problem' film about 'race' and 'passing', the central white family live in south London, in a street not unlike Sycamore Grove. This film, which has been discussed mainly in terms of its explicit engagement with issues of race and racism, uses a murder mystery to discover the identity and killer of a young woman found dead on Hampstead Heath.[50] Through the use of costume, such as the incongruous red petticoat worn by the victim underneath her 'good plain things', it transpires that she – Sapphire – although 'passing' for white, had black parents. The police task thus becomes not just a murder inquiry, but an investigation into Sapphire's life and the attitudes of those who knew her; most notably the ordinary south London family of her fiancé, David Harris (Paul Massie). Sapphire's London has an ethnicised topography. Dead – and white – on Hampstead Heath, it turns out that she was also white with David's Royal College of Music friends in the West End and the coffee bars of Soho, but black at the London University International Club, and known to be passing at Tulips, the underground black club where she loved to dance. David's family live in a south London terraced house, which, the investigation reveals, Sapphire was not welcome to visit after her ethnicity is 'revealed'. This house is very pale inside, lit and dressed so that its dominant tone is a light blue. The murderer turns out to be David's sister, but his father too, so ambitious for his boy, is also implicated. The sister, Millie (Yvonne

Mitchell) works in a dairy, again, all pale and white. For this family, south London is where ordinary white families live – from which people like Sapphire must be removed. The project of the film is to reveal, and show as mistaken, the colour prejudice found within ordinary British people, both police and public, and show its consequences. Several writers have commented that in doing this, the film is dependent on the very oppositions it is trying to undo, as its message that difference doesn't matter is undone by its constant investigation and detection.[51] While all critics comment on the role of Sapphire's red petticoat in revealing her ethnicity, the film also mobilises a topography of ethnicity that is indicative of major transformations in the understanding of what is ordinary and local in London. Bill Schwarz in a discussion conducted across several different articles of what he calls in one the 're-racialization of England', suggests that in the 1950s,

> the populist re-imagining of what it was to be *white* owed much to the unconscious presence of a received colonial syntax. The frontier ceased to be the stuff of fiction and came to be relocated at the end of the street, palpable and present. Through a complex process of symbolic displacement, the neighbourhood became imagined as a colonial frontier.[52]

It is this topography, enacted through the *mise en scène* of colour in this film, which is contested in some of the Brixton films noted in the last section, and which could be seen as one of the recurrent geographies of local London. The most influential film in this context is *My Beautiful Laundrette* (1985), directed by Stephen Frears from a script by Hanif Kureishi.

My Beautiful Laundrette, with its narrative of the transformation that Omar (Gordon Warnecke) and Johnny (Daniel Day-Lewis) effect on a scuzzy launderette in a run-down south London high street, in the context of Thatcherite Asian enterprise and fascist sympathies among white youth, is perhaps *the* London film of the 1980s. It is also, as many scholars have noted, significant for many other reasons: it was Working Title's first feature film; it was made for television on 16mm, but won theatrical release; it has a gay love story in which nobody dies; it is one of a group of 'anti-Thatcher' London films from the mid-1980s. John Hill discusses the film in relation to ideas of the 'interstitial space' of cities, the places 'in-between', and contemporary theorisations of black and Asian British identities, and Christine Geraghty has analysed the film's *mise en scène* and construction of space at far more length than is available to me here.[53] I want to comment on the film in relation to ideas of local London, for *Laundrette* both contributes to this cinematic London, and transcends it – and indeed takes the possibility of this transcendence as its topic. While this transcendence has an obvious symbol in the launderette itself, which is the film's most fully 'local' setting, with its repeated cast of characters, having the same conversations, it is also achieved through a range of stylistic choices, such as the clear references to Hollywood cinema and the expressionist use of colour.

My Beautiful Laundrette is rigorous in its avoidance of iconic London views, drawing attention to this strategy with one high shot, twenty-five minutes in, which gives a view of south London looking north to the neglected landmark of Battersea Power Station, with its unmistakable four chimneys. However, the London of *My Beautiful Laundrette* is, from the beginning, much more substantially constructed across an axis of the local and 'elsewhere' than some

of the other 'local Londons' I discuss. The pre-title sequence is an eviction, requiring characters to move from a squatted 'home' to where? Simply somewhere else. The next location,
home for Omar and 'Papa' (Roshan Seth) is a flat with its balcony up against the railway
lines. But against the literal elsewhere promised by the train tracks, there is, in this flat, and
in all the other domestic locations of the film, the elsewhere of Pakistan. For nearly all the
Asian characters that Omar and Johnny deal with, England, 'this damn country', is a pragmatic alternative to the remembered home of Pakistan. It is the unemployed white youth
who are trapped in the local, forever caught either in the street of the launderette, which as
Geraghty points out, is like a main street in a Western, or under the railway viaduct, where
strongly contrasting sodium lighting dramatises their threat expressionistically.

There has been a tendency to read *My Beautiful Laundrette* as social realist cinema, which
both Hill and Geraghty contest, despite its textual properties and clear indications from
those involved in its making,[54] which may be partly attributable to the social extensiveness
of its range of Asian characters. What seems more interesting is the possibility that aesthetically the film effects the same transformation of social realist cinematic south London as
Omar and Johnny perform on the launderette. This is a transformation of the everyday into
the exceptional and the local into the utopian, when the banality of washing dirty clothes is
also the opportunity for a waltz. Hill's arguments about the way in which the film is distinguished by a formal hybridity, and Geraghty's stress on the significance of 'transformation'
at every level of the film's history and textuality, can be reread as a 'mixing up' of what cinematic south London looks like. This is also a moment in which 'the local' is seen as constricting – but also enabling – in relation to the allure of the promiscuous mixing of
metropolitan identities.

So, in an accelerated history of cinematic south London in three films, I am suggesting
that one of the key post-war south London stories is that of ordinariness, and who gets to be
ordinary – who lives in south London. This, necessarily, involves a variety of negotiations,
across a range of texts, about the heritage of empire. I am not suggesting that these concerns
are confined to, or specific to, south London films. However, I am proposing that south
London in the cinema is primarily working-class London, and the naturalist and realist
visual tropes of British working-class life, elaborated in discussion of the Northern working
class from *Coronation Street* to *Saturday Night and Sunday Morning* (1961) to *East Is East* (1999),
here find their southern embodiment.[55] This is in contrast, generically, to the narratives of
the (historically working-class) East End of London, as I discuss further in Chapter 5, dominated as they are by 'the poor', Jack the Ripper, 'Limehouse nights' and criminality. So my
argument is, in Shields' terms, partly an argument about the different 'place-images' of parts
of London, but it is understood through the notion of cinematic genre. I am not suggesting
that life is more ordinary in south London than the East End, but that in the cinematic topography of London, south London tends to be produced through that matrix of stylistic practices associated with realism, naturalism and documentary in British cinema and television,
and, as a cinematic topos, lacks the strongly marked generic codes associated with the East
End.[56] That is partly why *Laundrette* is such an interesting south London film, as it does and
doesn't partake of these traditions. The films on which the rest of the chapter concentrates
are, in different ways, significant contributions to the realist and naturalist traditions in

British film and television, but they also partake of Bakhtin's 'viscous and sticky time that drags itself slowly through space'.[57]

Gary Oldman has described his 1997 film *Nil By Mouth* as his 'blues', immediately invoking the local: 'what was outside my window'.[58] As the film also concludes with a dedication to his father, and is known to have used as a location one of his father's regular pubs, the local here is intimately connected with the personal and autobiographical. But if we follow Doreen Massey's arguments from her influential article about Kilburn High Road, the local here is also profoundly shaped by global processes.[59] This is post-industrial south London, from which skilled and unskilled working-class jobs outside the service industry have mainly long gone. Just as the terraced houses have now disappeared so too now have the jobs, and with them the traditional recreations and public spaces. What could be called the grammar of the local, in which place and time are imbricated together through the rhythms of work, rest and play, exists only in a residual form and only for some characters, as we shall explore.

The film follows, episodically, an extended family centring on Raymond (Ray Winstone), his pregnant wife Valerie (Kathy Burke) and her heroin-addict brother Billy (Charlie Creed-Miles). The only person in legal paid employment is Janet (Laila Morse), Val and Billy's mother, and she is under constant pressure to use her wages to support Billy's habit. Most of the film is set in interiors filmed on the now demolished Bonamy Estate. Val, who loses her baby as a result of a jealous beating from Raymond, is filmed almost exclusively inside. The production designer Hugo Luczyc-Wyhowski has discussed the methods of achieving the very dark, close-up, mainly location-shot look of the film, revealing that two rules were 'no trees' and to stop filming if it was sunny.[60] This south London is a place where it is often difficult to tell whether it is night or day and where public space is mainly desolate graffitied corridors, bits of wasteland and phone boxes on busy roads. This is a local London from which no escape seems imaginable.

Masculine culture in this film is soaked in alcohol. There is no social space in which people are not drinking, and some spaces designed for other purposes, such as a launderette, have been recruited for drinking and waiting for the delivery of drugs. This drink-sodden culture is introduced as tightly framed and local. The opening, through which the credits are interspersed, shows Raymond buying a round at a social club. In extreme close-up, Ray is filmed going through the list of drinks, sweat visible on his face as he asks 'Ain't you got no ice?' The camera does not move from his face as he accumulates his round, and the tightness of the framing anticipates the spatial constraints of the film. John Orr has analysed the use of close-up in this film, suggesting, of this social club sequence: 'obscenely, it brings them close enough for us to touch, taste and smell. With the same discomfort which they, unacknowledged, experience their tight surroundings, we, explicitly, are forced to experience them.'[61] The women do drink, but on a different scale to the men, and not with the same constancy and ubiquity. Thus the women are shown drinking in a pub and the social club, but at home they drink tea: there is a sense of appropriate behaviours for particular places.

The social club is part of the residual local topography of film, offering, along with the pub where Valerie plays snooker with her family on one occasion (and is then brutally beaten) and the dystopian launderette on the Old Kent Road, an escape from the domestic. Glen Creeber has discussed the gendering of space in this film, suggesting that there is transformation of the masculine dominance of the first half of the film to a more female-centred space in the second part.[62] He argues that this is shown partly through the telling of anecdotes. When the film opens, the men tell the stories; as it closes, it is the women. While Creeber is right that the final, domestic scene of the film, when the women prepare to visit Billy in prison, is dominated by the women's stories of Billy's prison predicaments, I want to look at some of the other spaces of the film. The unseen prison visit on which the film finishes could be seen as a counterpart to the men's earlier trip to Soho, which is discussed in the next chapter. This tawdry night-time sortie takes the men out of the grim naturalism of Deptford into a cinematically familiar, neon, night-life – but their behaviour remains the same – they carry on drinking, recounting tall tales and taking drugs. We do not see the women leave local space, and their motivation, as with all their actions, is family maintenance. It is the men who can leave the local for pleasure, but it is also the men, Raymond, Mark (Jamie Foreman) and Billy, whose lives are presented as desperately lacking the boundaries that permit the making of homes and the maintenance of families. Raymond is shown to be unable to distinguish between friendliness, affection and lust and, in a fit of alcoholic fury, wrecks the flat in which he lives with Val and their daughter. Billy, the most mobile character in the film, can never rest from the constant labour of the quest for the next fix. It is through Billy that much of the external spatiality of the film is explored as he pounds down corridors and up escalators, begs from passengers in tube trains and beds down in the basement entrails of the estate: a dimly lit, anomic world in which he has no home of his own and cannot even always sleep inside. Billy is restlessly mobile throughout the film, but the city through which he moves is not the flâneur's city, but instead a grim, dark, empty, disorienting place in which he can find no rest.

In some ways, Billy's situation is not unlike Tony's in *Pressure*. Both are young men on the streets. But in *Pressure* there is a strong sense of the social and the local. In *Nil By Mouth* shared public space is degraded and empty: in fact not shared at all. An early revelation of the debasing of the social is set in the nearly deserted asphalted playground of the estate. Billy has been thrown out of his sister's after a fight with Raymond, and wanders, junk-less and penniless and with a scabby, bloody nose, into the playground where a lone father is watching his child play. Billy bums a cigarette, brief civilities are exchanged, and then Billy asks for money, saying that he only lives in the flats. The man says nothing, merely summoning the child off the apparatus and then leading him away. The child is shot looking backwards at Billy, the expression on his little pinched white face quite unreadable. This is an interaction in which Billy is shown to be incapable of observing the mores and boundaries of neighbourliness. He just can't stop himself pressing an ordinary civil interaction, in which a neighbour has given him a cigarette, to breaking point, by asking for money. The silent child, his own leisure abruptly terminated, is present as both victim and witness of this betrayal of local, social space as a neighbourly place. In contrast to Billy's hyper-mobility and Raymond's abuse of his own home and neighbours, the women are shown in homes which they make and remake as places of refuge. The co-ordinates of what I am calling 'local London', dailiness, repetition, regularity, are almost erased, and the local retreats to become co-terminous with the domestic. The film portrays an exterior world, outside people's flats and the occasional pub, which has been abandoned by the practices of 'place-making', the banal, everyday encounters which render an area local, rather than anomic. Eric Clapton's bluesy soundtrack for the film, much of it extra-diegetic, accentuates this abandonment of the social, producing a distancing from some of the narrative events, like Billy's endless searches for money, in which musical repetition is used to suggest the quality of time in these lives.

The south London estates of Britain's 'banlieues' are also the setting for Mike Leigh's *All or Nothing*. Nearly all of Mike Leigh's film work is set in London, but he is thought of as an actors' film-maker, rather than a London film-maker. Discussion of Leigh's work is dominated by his working method and the collaborative character preparation he undertakes with actors, many of whom, such as Lesley Manville, Phil Daniels, Ruth Sheen and Timothy Spall, work with him repeatedly. Setting, in Leigh's films, often seems primarily important as a meticulously realised, naturalist environment for character. Spatially, his films sometimes seem like an assembly of domestic environments, for it is within these separate spaces that the family interactions, which are his main concern, are enacted. Place in this work is almost always local, although often slightly abstractly so: a suburban house, a flat in a converted Victorian terrace, an inner-city terraced house. These are, to an extent, homes presented as typical, and their class provenance is more significant than their geographical location.[63] The other principal critical discussion about Leigh concerns his attitude to his mainly working-class characters. John Caughie writes of *Life is Sweet* (1990), 'the revelation that people without taste are not necessarily people without feeling seems patronising and predictable',[64] while Michael Collins, in his angry book about attitudes to the white working class, observes, 'He has barely made one film that that didn't include a dysfunctional family that had run to fat and moved to Essex.'[65] An early film, *High Hopes* (1988), is discussed in the final chapter, but here I will look at *All or Nothing*, a 2002 film set in south London, which, while it retains this primary interest in homes as settings for character, constructs its local London in relation to a broader view of the city and treats its characters with some tenderness.

All or Nothing opens with a long static shot of a corridor with a clean shiny linoleum floor. At the far end of the corridor there is wider space in which a fat girl is cleaning. An elderly woman in a dressing gown comes into this space, and the girl offers to help her. There is a cut to Timothy Spall driving a cab, shot from the windscreen so we see his face and his passengers, who in this first sequence include some arguing Arabs and a very angry white man. The third location introduced is a supermarket, where Lesley Manville and Ruth Sheen are working the checkouts. Like *Dance Hall*, this film opens with a grammar of the local, the workplaces and homes of the main protagonists. However, here, there is not the shared public space of the dance hall, but instead the parched yellowing grass and graffitied walls of the estate where the three main families live. The opening shot, in which Rachel (Alison Garland) is constrained by the strong verticals of the corridor walls, confined by the frame within a frame, but within that, willing, helpful and pleasant, both introduces us to Rachel, and shows something of the limited expectations of the characters. This intimation of restricted vision is repeated in the supermarket sequence when the two friends leave work together by the side exit. Maureen (Ruth Sheen), played as cheery optimist throughout, observes 'Ain't it nice' as they step outside, but the camera remains fixed on the women, the nondescript exit into the car park, the blank brick façade. It might be nice – but we don't see it; there is no glimpse of the sky or any growing thing. The repeated withholding of wide shots, shots in which the sky is visible and shots that contextualise characters in their surroundings makes the world of *All or Nothing* restricted in its localness. The local, for most of the characters most of the time, is all there is. Safeway, where Penny and Maureen work, is such an obvious landmark within this world that it is given no geographical qualifier when she needs a cab to the hospital in a hurry ('Can anyone go Safeway?'); Jason, the aggressive boyfriend of Maureen's daughter Donna, complains that he's had to 'drive all the way round here, nearly two miles'. The only character not bound by the local is Phil (Timothy Spall) the cab-driver, who on the day on which his overweight son Rory has a heart attack – the main narrative event of the film – has a fare to the West End. Phil's cab has already been used as a type of city interlude up to this point in the film, so there is at first no hint that this journey will be any different. The cab is, throughout the film, a city interlude in the sense that a series of different passengers – the strangers of the city streets – take up positions in the back seat and Phil, often wordlessly, drives them to their destinations. As his wife observes at the end of the film, he has 'all sorts' in the cab. The repeated fixed camera position from the windscreen gives an image like the driver's rear-view mirror, although we also see Phil's face as he monitors his fares. The strength of the passengers' different moods, the contrasting lives and types, and Phil's relative impotence, gives a sense of the city, with its characteristics of anonymity and alienation, passing through the cab.[66] Phil is philosophical. 'I'm free,' he radios to base after he tells a fare-dodger to 'hop it'.

All or Nothing is centred on the lives of the Barrett family (Phil, Penny, Rachel and Rory) and their neighbours on an estate in south-east London. The action takes place over a few summer days in which life continues as normal except that Rory has a heart attack in the estate's open grassland and Donna reveals that she is pregnant. Rory's heart attack mobilises the Barretts' neighbours to help them, involving each of the two other principal families. The scrubby, bald grass onto which flats look down suddenly becomes something more like shared public space as Maureen, Carol and Samantha ring for the emergency services, try to comfort Rory and contact his parents. Phil has, however, left the local – switching it off – after a fare up to the West End with a French woman. Their conversation is a mixture of the intimate and the banal. She is initially sceptical that he knows the way to the West End, and he reveals that he had once walked the Blackwall Tunnel through which they are driving: 'Walked through it from south to north. My face turned completely black. My mate's face was already black.' The contrast with the tunnel means that the arrival north of the river is marked by space and light, and central London is marked by the light-dappled leaves of plane trees: it is another type of place than the London where Phil lives. We see that Cécile's personal questions – and her own revelations – lead Phil to reflect on his life, and after he drops her he turns his phone and radio off and heads out to the coast. Phil's journeys provide a spatial frame for the local that he has left behind, a frame which is lighter, brighter and with more sky. His journey is intercut with Rory's drama, and a contrast is maintained between the hospital interior and the wide sky and shingle beach where Phil stares out to sea and meditates. His privilege of mobility gives a spatial form to his reflection.

Phil's journey and Rory's heart attack provide a turning point for the film and afterwards, very painfully, particularly for Penny and Phil, the family begins to come together in a way that is more attentive to each other, and with more self-respect for themselves. Rory, who is

Rachel (Alison Garland) with the Dome in the background (*All or Nothing*)

very overweight, reveals that he has eaten a meal comprising fish and broccoli. Phil is shown clean-shaven and with his hair newly washed. If this is an ending, filmed in interior space, with an element of redemption for the family, the future is not clear. Nor is there any indication of any improvement in their environment. In this, the film finds a perfect local landmark in the Millennium Dome, the then-empty architectural extravaganza built on reclaimed dockland on the south-east peninsula, which is shown three times without comment.

Other Local Londons

There are many more local Londons in the cinema than those discussed here. To mention only relatively recent work, films like Hettie MacDonald and Jonathan Harvey's *Beautiful Thing* (1995), Julian Henriques' *Babymother* (1998), Jamie Thraves' *The Low-Down* (2000) and Saul Gibbs' *Bullet Boy* (2004) all offer different versions of different local Londons.[67] The conventions of cinematic Southall – the crowded bazaar of the High Street, alternated with well-ordered semi-detached houses in some local proximity – began to emerge in the 1990s in films such as *Wild West* (written by Harwaint Bains, directed by David Attwood, 1992) and the internationally successful *Bend it Like Beckham* (directed by Chadha), as well as being hailed as a site of long-sought community for Robinson and the narrator in *London*. In *London*, it is Diwali that transforms Southall into the city of attractions, but in *Bend it Like Beckham*, a wedding in the central Sikh family is used as a visual and musical focus for west London British Asian identity – in juxtaposition with football and cricket on a 'village green'.

Local London is a topic on which it is particularly difficult to omit television, but on which this distinction must be enforced not just because the televisual rendition of the local is so very rich, but because it has medium-specific qualities. While the Battersea presented in the 1965 Wednesday Play *Up the Junction* is still fresh today partly because of the innovatory use of portable 16mm cameras, this type of one-off drama is not the heart of the televisual local. This lies in serial drama, when production and viewing are themselves repetitious in a manner homologous to the repetition I have been suggesting characterises local London. The fictional worlds of British soap opera have, historically, always been local – *Brookside*, *Coronation Street*, *Emmerdale Farm* – and with *EastEnders* the BBC has invented and sustained a whole east London borough, Walford. But it is not just through soap opera that television has enriched our understanding of the local. *Only Fools and Horses* (BBC, 1981–96), the popular, long-running John Sullivan situation comedy set in Peckham, renders comically the life of south London estates that we find in some of the films discussed above, while *Desmond's* (Channel 4, 1989–94), the situation comedy that starred Norman Beaton as Desmond the barber, included many of the cast of *Playing Away* and offered an often wry sense of Brixton as a local, rather than just an exceptional, place. Euston Films, in the 1970s and 1980s, offered a range of local Londons in series such as *Minder* (1979–94) and *Fox* (1980), while *South of the Border* (1990) grounded its crime fictions in local south London. Any exploration of the local within television fiction would need to address the role of repetition and seriality in creating this sense of space in which there is a certain kind of belonging.

What I have sought to do in this chapter – with all these omissions – is to suggest that very different local Londons can be understood and compared in relation to different structures. One is a topography, the other a process. Thus, first, I have suggested that there has been what we might call a 'space–time triangle' of the local in the cinema, in which the local is constructed – in a manner that is historically variable – through the relationships between the spaces and times of work, home and recreation. Evidently, in cinema, these relationships are constructed through editing. I am not suggesting that the local is a matter of pro-filmic proximity, but that it is significant whether or not that sense of proximity is created, and that it is principally created temporally, rather than spatially. We do not know, in *Dance Hall*, exactly where the girls' homes, work and the Palais are in relation to each other. But the repetition of the locations creates a sense of their proximity. This is the temporal production of space. Similarly, although it presents itself as natural, with all its longueurs, cinematic local time is as much a production as that of an exciting narrative chase. At the beginning of *All or Nothing* the intercutting of Phil's taxi jobs with other scenes produces a sense of repetition and tedium, while this same formal editing strategy could produce other meanings, such as that of suspense. In the Ealing films, the separations between, and the spaces of, and times for, work, home and leisure were clear, and formed part of the moral framework of the films. Only the delinquent read magazines on their beds in daytime. In *Pressure*, these distinctions between work, home and leisure were not available to Tony, although they clearly governed his parents' world and, increasingly and consequently, he finds himself unable to gain legitimate access to inside spaces. I have suggested that one way of understanding historical change is registered across different dispositions of the local 'space–time triangle', and that different groups of people and individuals have different relationships to it. In *Nil By Mouth*, a drama of the post-industrial white working class, the men have left this triangle of work/home/leisure.[68] They live in a perpetual drink- and drug-fuelled present which seems to abolish distinctions between the spaces within which they move. Here the extreme close-ups and the interior location shooting are significant in creating the spatial equivalence of different environments. The women, on the other hand, do have a relationship to the rhythms of work and domestic life and it is they who sustain what sense of the local there is. *All or Nothing*, in which the sites of the local have been reconfigured as jobs in service industries and an estate, presents a family whose world is precipitously balanced. Here, the psychic health of characters is partly figured through their ability to separate the behaviours and temporalities of home, work and leisure and, again, alcohol figures as a blurrer of boundaries. In both films, one of the textual strategies which is used to guarantee authenticity is a soundtrack in which London vernacular speech, particularly of male characters, is dominated by obscenity. The sound of everyday London life is 'fucking this and fucking that'.

Second, I have pointed to the way in which arguments from cultural geography about the interrelation of the local and the global are relevant to an understanding of the cinematic local. It is not just the everyday life of Tony, in *Pressure*, whose parents come from Trinidad, which is subject to the shaping forces of the global. In both *Dance Hall* and *The Blue Lamp* there is a recognisable attention to the influence of US culture, whether in Diana Dors's sweaters or the shiny milk bars of the West End. Within realist fictions, the very details that guarantee authenticity also carry meanings and traces from an extra-cinematic world. The transformations of the iconography of the ordinary in south London, from terrace to estate, from light industry to service industries, from a mainly white working class to an ethnically mixed population, are the very material of the local, but are also the result of complex, extra-cinematic factors both national and international. The drug money to transform the launderette and Billy's smack, just like most of Phil's taxi passengers, come from elsewhere. The local has been, and is being, transformed.

In each of these films, the local is constructed both internally and through comparison with an elsewhere. This elsewhere can be fleeting: the glimpse of a skyline through a dance-hall window, the memory or fantasy of another place, or the constant rhythm of departing jet planes. Or it can be more sustained, forming part of a familiar journey within London films, which will be discussed in greater detail in the next chapter, 'Going Up West', when the contrast between local London and landmark London is staged within the text, as in Raymond's trip to Soho, Phil's fare to the West End and even Riley and Spud's visit to Piccadilly Circus.

In discussing local London, I have also wanted to document the continuous peopling of London that we find in the cinema, and to insist on the importance of everyday local life to cinematic London. I have explored the way in which different films produce ordinary Londons through various, and changing, relationships between the rhythms of the everyday and the repetitions that produce the local as a cinematic place. Here my concerns are to draw attention to what is almost the tenderness with which cinema can render the banality of everyday life, rather than an interest in the glamour of the solitary flâneur who haunts so much city scholarship. Walter Benjamin's writings on Paris have inspired many to imagine the city from the point of view of the flâneur – and indeed to find London lacking in resources and repertoires for this figure.[69] Mazierska and Rascaroli suggest that 'Cinematic London is not a place conducive to strolling',[70] while Patrick Keiller's *London* can be seen as a film that explores the possibility of this relation to the city. I have argued that there is more strolling in cinematic London than may first seem apparent; but more importantly, that there are many other journeys, which are perhaps more significant in shaping the cinematic city, from Dixon's methodical beat to Billy's frantic pacing. While the paradigm of flânerie may be dominant in the study of the city in the cinema, this chapter has explored some of the other lives and times of the cinematic city.

Notes

1. Mikhail Bakhtin, 'Forms of time and chronotope in the novel', in Mikhail Bakhtin, *The Dialogic Imagination* (Austin: University of Texas Press, 1981), p. 247.
2. Ibid., p. 248.
3. See Amy Sargeant, '*Sparrows Can't Sing*: East End kith and kinship in the 1960s', paper to *Designs for Living* conference, Queen Mary University of London, June 2005. See also her *British Cinema* (London: BFI, 2005), pp. 251–3.
4. Dave is referring directly to the prize-winning modernist Alton Estate on the edge of Richmond Park, the 'crumminess' of which, in contrast to Battersea, would be particularly noticeable as Roehampton is both further out of London and notoriously ill-served by public transport.
5. On *Passport to Pimlico*, in addition to Charles Barr, *Ealing Studios* (Newton Abbot: Cameron and Tayleur in association with David and Charles, 1977), see John Ellis, 'Made in Ealing', *Screen* vol. 16 no.1, Spring 1975, pp. 78–127; Tony Williams, 'The repressed fantastic in *Passport to Pimlico*', in Wheeler Winston Dixon (ed.), *Re-viewing British Cinema, 1900–1992* (Albany: State University of New York Press, 1994), pp. 95–106; and Tim Pulleine, 'A song and dance at the local: thoughts on Ealing', in Robert Murphy (ed.), *The British Cinema Book* (London, BFI, 1997), pp. 114–21.
6. Barr, *Ealing Studios*, p. 81.
7. Colin Sorensen provides a series of photographs of the set for *Passport*, which was built on the south bank of the river in Hercules Road, Lambeth. Sorensen, *London on Film* (London: Museum of London, 1996), pp. 112–13.
8. Barr, *Ealing Studios*, p. 98.
9. See also Antonia Lant on wartime dancehalls in *Blackout: Reinventing Women for Wartime British Cinema* (Princeton, NJ: Princeton University Press, 1991), p. 43. *Dance Hall* uses what looks like stock footage of women leaving factory machines for the end of the introductory factory sequence.
10. Pat Kirkham, 'Dress, dance, dreams and desire: fashion and fantasy in *Dance Hall*', *Journal of Design History* vol. 8 no. 3, 1995, pp. 195–214. See also Melinda Mash, 'Stepping out or out of step? Austerity, affluence and femininity in two post-war films', in Christine Gledhill and Gillian Swanson (eds), *Nationalising Femininity: Culture, Sexuality and British Cinema in the Second World War* (Manchester: Manchester University Press, 1996), pp. 257–63.
11. While press books provide evidence of how the film was packaged on release, they are no more reliable than other advertising copy. In relation to the Palais, it states that the set was designed by Norman Arnold: 'after visits to several halls he designed a composite palais typical of many he found throughout the country. Considerable technical assistance was given to him by the Hammersmith Palais, though the hall in the film is in no way meant to be a replica of that famous dance haunt. When built, the set occupied the whole of Ealing's largest sound stage', *Dance Hall* small press book, Balcon Papers, BFI Special Collections, p. 6. It does seem likely that some visits were undertaken, as the Balcon Papers connected with this film include a four-page (folio)

typewritten list of schools of dancing in Britain, and a ten-page list of 'Dance halls in the British Isles', listed by town. This list gives, for example, seven dance halls in Birmingham, four in Brighton and thirty-six in London. Balcon Papers, G/74, BFI Special Collections.

12. *Dance Hall* small press book, 'The Story', p. 2.

13. Alec is referred to as 'a dance hall "wolf"' in the press book. *Dance Hall*, large press book, p. 2. He is the proprietor of a small garage. Kirkham, 'Dress, Dance, Dreams and Desire', points out that Alec's pale suit indicates that he can afford more than one (p. 199).

14. Phillip Gillett discusses the social space of the dance hall in a comparison of this film with other 1940s films in his chapter, 'The Janus faces of the dance hall', in his *The British Working Class in Postwar Film* (Manchester: Manchester University Press, 2003), pp. 136–49.

15. Christine Geraghty, *British Cinema of the Fifties* (London: Routledge, 2000), p. 90.

16. The odd tone of this scene is perhaps explained by the employment of a technical adviser, Richard Hearne, who specialised in slapstick comedy, to work with the inexperienced Natasha Parry (medium press book, p. 6).

17. Anthony Aldgate and Jeffrey Richards, in 'The Thin Blue Line', ch. 8 of *The Best of British* (London: I. B. Tauris, 2002 [1999]), pp. 125–48, give an account of the genesis of the project.

18. Steve Chibnall, 'The teenage trilogy: *The Blue Lamp, I Believe in You* and *Violent Playground*', in Alan Burton, Tim O'Sullivan and Paul Wells (eds), *Liberal Directions: Basil Dearden and Postwar British Film Culture* (Trowbridge: Flicks Books, 1997), p. 137.

19. Susan Sydney Smith discusses the relationship between the film and the subsequent television series in *Beyond Dixon of Dock Green* (London: I. B. Tauris, 2002). She also reads Dixon's death as 'a symbolic fissure with the social contract of reconstructionism. At the instant of the bullet's impact, the image of a certain kind of consensus politics is forever shattered: the moment recalled in an endless "loop", held in the freeze frame of the collective, public memory' (pp. 51–2).

20. The shooting script makes it clear that the transition from 'crime wave' to 'Dixon' was originally intended to include a montage of 'a policeman's lot', with twelve different policemen in different contexts, including stock footage from the General Strike (*The Blue Lamp* Shooting Script, 27 May 1949, BFI Special Collections, pp. 2–4). This was much reduced in the finished film, with three policemen before Dixon, all filmed in the Paddington area.

21. See John Hill, *Sex, Class and Realism: British Cinema 1956–63* (London: BFI, 1986), p. 70.

22. The point is a methodological one. The shooting script identifies their destination as 'up Windmill Street', but this is not evident from the screen, which does not locate the pool room anywhere except as the next place they go to. However, the pool room has an ethnically mixed clientele, which is in sharp contrast to the rest of the film, and it is this diversity that identifies it as Soho. The shooting script account is: 'A remarkable variety of types frequent the place. Wealthy negroes from the night-clubs. Waiters off-duty from nearby restaurants; Odd Bohemian characters. Racing men' (p. 23).

23. See particularly Chibnall, 'The teenage trilogy', pp. 142–3, and Andy Medhurst's account of the allure of Bogarde, 'Dirk Bogarde', in Charles Barr (ed.), *All Our Yesterdays* (London: BFI, 1986), pp. 346–54.

24. Barr, *Ealing Studios*, p. 85.

25. Ibid.

26. The role of the tic-tac men in this purpose clearly excited those writing the notes for exhibitors in the press book. Suggestion 4 reads: 'A greyhound racing track features prominently in the exciting

climax, when the criminal is cornered by messages sent round the various rings by the tic-tac men. This suggests tie-ups with the dog tracks, and for the bolder minded one can visualise tic-tac men mounted on boxes in various parts of the town, tic-taccing messages across the street, with explanatory messages posted on their boxes.' 'Showtalk', medium press book, p. 5.

27. Horace Ové, interview with Clive Hodgson, *Film (BFFS)* no. 64, August 1978, cited by Stephen Bourne in *Black in the British Frame* (London: Cassell, 1998), p. 230.

28. *Pressure* was not released immediately after completion, which leads to some discrepancies in dating. Ové, in 2005, described the film as 'shot in 1973, released in 1975' (Horace Ové, question and answer session after screening of *Pressure* at the Rio, Dalston, 15 October 2005). Pines, the key historian of British Black film-making, dates it as 1974, Jim Pines, 'Black independent film in Britain: an historical overview', in John Twitchin (ed.), *The Black and White Media Book* (Stoke-on-Trent: Trentham, 1988), p. 106. Lola Young, *Fear of the Dark: 'Race', Gender and Sexuality in the Cinema* (London: Routledge, 1996), suggests that political issues led to a delayed release date of 1978 (p. 142). It was shown at the London Film Festival in 1975.

29. See Pearl Jephcott, *A Troubled Area: Notes on Notting Hill* (London: Faber and Faber, 1964); Alison Crawford, *Notting Hill: The History and Development of North Kensington* (London: Ealing College of Art, 1971); Charlie Phillips and Mike Phillips, *Notting Hill in the Sixties* (London: Lawrence and Wishart, 1991).

30. End credits; for a pertinent discussion of the Rillington Place murders within the cultural geographies of post-war London, see Frank Mort, 'Scandalous events: metropolitan culture and Moral Change in Post-Second World War London', *Representations* 93, Winter 2006, pp. 106–37.

31. See Colin MacCabe, *Performance* (London: BFI, 1998), and Paul Dave, *Visions of England* (Oxford: Berg, 2006), pp. 103–13, for the parameters of the discussion of this cult film.

32. *Sammy and Rosie Get Laid* is scripted as set in south London. The wasteland, and some other scenes, were filmed in Notting Hill (Hanif Kureishi, *Sammy and Rosie Get Laid: the Script and the Diary* [London: Faber and Faber, 1988], p. 72).

33. In 2005, Ové reported the BFI contribution as 'about £7,000', stressing that the film was only possible because so many of those involved, including Selvon, worked without pay. For performers and production staff, this included a five-week shoot (Horace Ové, question and answer session after screening of *Pressure* at the Rio, Dalston, 15 October 2005). See also the interview with Ové in Jim Pines (ed.), *Black and White in Colour: Black People in British Television since 1936* (London: BFI, 1992), pp. 123–4. Minutes of the BFI Production Board between 19 December 1973 and 29 April 1976 suggest a figure more like £18,000, with distribution still unresolved in February 1977.

34. Pines, 'Black Independent Film in Britain', p. 107.

35. Kobena Mercer, 'Recoding narratives of race and nation', in Kobena Mercer (ed.), *Black Film/British Cinema* (London: Institute of Contemporary Arts, 1988), p. 10.

36. See Moya Luckett, 'Image and nation in 90s British cinema', in Robert Murphy (ed.), *British Cinema of the 90s* (London: BFI, 2000), pp. 88–99.

37. Young, *Fear of the Dark*, pp. 136–40.

38. In classic cinema geography, this sequence unites more than one location, so that although it finishes in the shadow of the Trellick Tower, it certainly doesn't start there.

39. Young, *Fear in the Dark*, pp. 112–14. *Babylon*, which is set in Brixton and has some similarities with *Pressure*, also features one of these negrophobic white women (played by Maggie Steed), who is the first person in the film to articulate racist abuse.

40. John McLeod, *Postcolonial London: Rewriting the Metropolis* (London: Routledge, 2004), points to the recurrence of the derelict house in post-colonial immigrant fiction, p. 106.

41. On Phillips's London, including some discussion of the screenplay for *Playing Away*, see Sukhev Sandhu, *London Calling* (London: HarperCollins, 2003), pp. 287–302. On the film, see Charles Barr, '*Playing Away*', review, *Monthly Film Bulletin* vol. 54 no. 646, November 1987, p. 342, and, for a context, Karen Alexander, 'Black British Cinema in the 90s: Going Going Gone', in Murphy, *British Cinema of the 90s*, pp. 109–14.

42. Caryl Phillips, 'Introduction', *Playing Away* (London: Faber and Faber, 1987), p. x.

43. Barber's next significant film role is in *The Full Monty* (1997), in which he is also naked. See Richard Dyer, *White* (London: Routledge, 1997), pp. 146–7, on the differential nakedness of 'black' and 'white' bodies.

44. On *Black Joy* see Young, *Fear of the Dark*, pp. 148–52, and Paul Medford in Pines, *Black and White in Colour*, pp. 200–1.

45. *Wonderland*, which has already been discussed in Chapter 1, could be seen as the third member of this fin-de-siècle trilogy. It is further discussed in the final chapter. In Chapter 6 there is a discussion of 'crossing the river'.

46. See Dave, *Visions of England*, pp. 24–6. SW9 is the Brixton postcode.

47. Rob Shields, *Places on the Margin: Alternative Geographies of Modernity* (London and New York: Routledge, 1991), p. 6.

48. Andrew Higson makes a detailed, historically contextualised reading of this film in his *Waving the Flag* (Oxford: Clarendon Press, 1995), pp. 243–62.

49. And often, in the post-war period, a wasteland. For example, *Waterloo Road*, which is set around the station, is notable, apart from being generally regarded as the first 'spiv' film, for the flatness of its bomb-damaged setting. Muriel Box's 1952 film about one family's resistance to the demolition of their shop as part of the Festival of Britain site, *The Happy Family* (1952), also shows a flat and cleared site.

50. Carrie Tarr, '*Sapphire, Darling* and the boundaries of permitted pleasure', *Screen* vol. 26 no. 1, 1985, pp. 50–65; Hill, *Sex, Class and Realism*, pp. 83–9; Raymond Durgnat, 'Two "social problem" films: *Sapphire* and *Victim*', in Alan Burton, Tim O'Sullivan and Paul Wells (eds), *Liberal Directions* (Trowbridge: Flicks Books, 1997), pp. 59–88; Young, *Fear of the Dark*, pp. 95–101.

51. For example, Hill, *Sex, Class and Realism*, pp. 83–9.

52. Bill Schwarz, ' "The only white man in there": The re-racialization of England, 1956–68', *Race and Class* vol. 38 no. 1, 1996, pp. 65–78; 'Reveries of race', in Becky Conekin, Frank Mort and Chris Waters (eds), *Moments of Modernity* (London: Rivers Oram, 1999), p. 206.

53. John Hill, *British Cinema of the 1980s* (Oxford: Clarendon Press, 1999), pp. 205–18; Christine Geraghty, *My Beautiful Laundrette* (London: I. B. Tauris, 2005). See also Timothy Corrigan, *Cinema without Walls: Movies and Culture after Vietnam* (London: Routledge, 1992), pp. 218–32. Directed by Frears, the film is frequently discussed within the oeuvre of its writer, Hanif Kureishi, as in Sandhu, *London Calling*, pp. 230–71. See also Lester Friedman and Scott Stewart, 'Keeping his own voice: an interview with Stephen Frears', in Dixon, *Reviewing British Cinema*, pp. 221–40; and 'Hanif Kureishi on London', in *Critical Quarterly* vol. 41 no. 3, 1999, pp. 37–56.

54. 'At the moment, everything is so horrific that if you wrote straight social realism people wouldn't be able to bear to watch it.' Hanif Kureishi, 'Scenes from a marriage' (Hanif Kureishi talks to Jane Root), *Monthly Film Bulletin* vol. 52 no. 622, 1985, p. 333.

55. See for example, Geoff Eley, '*Distant Voices, Still Lives*. The family is a dangerous place: memory, gender and the image of the working class', in Robert Rosenstone (ed.), *Film and the Construction of a New Past* (Princeton, NJ: Princeton University Press, 1995), pp. 17–43; Sheila Rowbotham and Huw Beynon, *Looking at Class* (London: Rivers Oram, 2001); and Dave Russell, *Looking North: Northern England and the National Imagination* (Manchester: Manchester University Press, 2004).

56. There is, as I discuss in Chapter 5, a strong documentary tradition in relation to the East End, and feature films such as *Bronco Bullfrog* (1970) are set in an East End 'local London'. However, I maintain that there is something about the 'ordinariness' of south London in the cinema that is particularly consonant with 'the local'.

57. Mikhail Bakhtin, 'Forms of time and chronotope in the novel', in Bakhtin, *The Dialogic Imagination*, p. 248.

58. Gary Oldman, '*Nil by Mouth' Shooting Script* (Suffolk: ScreenPress, 1997), Foreword (unpaginated).

59. Doreen Massey, 'A global sense of place', in her *Space, Place and Gender* (Cambridge: Polity, 1994).

60. Nick James, 'Being there: interview with Hugo Luczyc-Wyhowski', *Sight and Sound* vol. 7 no. 10 (NS), October 1997, pp. 6–9.

61. John Orr, 'Traducing realisms', *Journal of Popular British Cinema* no. 5, 2002, p. 108.

62. Glen Creeber, ' "Can't help lovin' dat man": social class and the female voice in *Nil By Mouth*', in Sally Munt (ed.), *Cultural Studies and the Working Class: Subject to Change* (London: Cassell, 2000), pp. 193–205.

63. The exception here is *Naked* (1993), which offers an expressionist 'hell is a city' London, partly realised through the intensity of David Thewlis's performance.

64. John Caughie, 'Mike Leigh', in *The Companion to British and Irish Cinema* (London: Cassell and BFI, 1996), p. 101. Michael Collins, *The Likes of Us* (London: Granta, 2004), p. 209. See also Andy Medhurst, 'Beyond embarrassment', *Sight and Sound* vol. 11 no. 3, 1993, pp. 7–10; Michael Coveney, *The World According to Mike Leigh* (London: HarperCollins, 1996); Ray Carney and Leonard Quart, *The Films of Mike Leigh* (Cambridge: Cambridge University Press, 2000); Garry Watson, *The Cinema of Mike Leigh* (London: Wallflower Press, 2004).

65. Collins, *The Likes of Us*, p. 209.

66. The photographer's studio in *Secrets and Lies* is a similar device, putting before the camera a much greater variety of people than those involved in the narrative, and thus providing an economical, narratively integrated city metonym. In *All or Nothing*, it is also Phil who escapes into a more rural scene with a fare to a cemetery.

67. On *Babymother*'s London (Harlesden), see Rachel Moseley-Wood, '"Colonizin Englan in reverse"', *Visual Culture in Britain* vol. 5 no. 1, 2004, pp. 91–104. On *The Low-Down*'s London (Hackney), see Claire Monk, 'Projecting a New Britain', *Cinéaste* XXVI Contemporary British Cinema Supplement, Autumn 2001, pp. 34–7.

68. An opposite, but related, configuration can be found in Ken Loach's only recent London-set film, *Riff-Raff* (1990). Set on a building site, this film shows a world that is haunted by the older patterning of the local: work, home and leisure. But here all the workers are migrants of one kind or another, and most have no homes of their own to go to.

69. For the relevant literature, see notes 32 and 33 of the Introduction. Benjamin was less grand than some subsequent commentators, observing 'The sandwich-man is the last incarnation of the flâneur', Walter Benjamin, *The Arcades Project* (Cambridge, MA: Harvard University Press, 1999), p. 451.

70. Ewa Mazierska and Laura Rascaroli, *From Moscow to Madrid* (London: I. B. Taurus, 2003), p. 170.

3

Going Up West

Like many Londoners born north of the river, I grew up knowing very little of south London; much of it might have been as remote as the south bank of the Amazon. My thoughts didn't often stray eastwards, either. But the west beckoned, as it says in one of Auden's poems, like a wicked uncle.

From early on, I was fascinated by the idea of the West End. I dreamed of exploring it, of entering into its excitements, of mastering its intricacies. That there were different West Ends packed together, so near and yet so far – that Burlington House, say, was only a short walk from Brewer Street – was all part of the appeal.[1]

Do you think there's any chance of this becoming a trend, Battersea becoming an 'up area', as we say in the property world?

Estate agent to Polly in *Up the Junction* (1967)

Near the beginning of the 1947 East End-set film *It Always Rains on Sunday*, Rose (Googie Withers) remembers the excitement of her romance with the well-dressed criminal, Tommy Swann (John McCallum), while brushing her hair at her dressing table mirror one Sunday morning. Her reverie has been initiated by a small item in the newspaper announcing that Tommy Swann has escaped from prison, and the present-day unmade-up, brunette Rose is replaced in the mirror with the blonde made-up Rose, reflected in the mirroring behind the spirits bottles in the pub where she works. Rose catches sight of Swann as he enters the pub, framed so that we see clearly his slightly waisted jacked, his trilby hat, the handkerchief in his pocket, and begins to fill a glass for him. Music swells with his entrance, and Rose is clearly attracted to this debonair figure, smarter and even taller than the other customers, who are still inhabiting post-war austerity. As he approaches the bar he says 'Two of those', and as he pays he indicates that one of the drinks is for her. Tommy Swann looks Rose up and down carefully and then asks what she does on her nights off. Expressionless, she replies, 'Nothing'. 'Why don't we do nothing together?' he suggests coolly, 'We could go up West.' 'Why don't we?' agrees Rose, matching Tommy's minimal, almost indolent invitation with her laconic answers and a refusal to be flustered by his attention. The silent contract is made as they meet each other's eyes and down their drinks.

The whole of *It Always Rains on Sunday* is set in the East End of London except for the next scene, which is set, not in the West End, but on a hill in the countryside. The editing of Rose's flashback memory jumps from the invitation to go 'up West' to a rural moment where they have been doing nothing together on a picnic rug in the sunshine. The scene shows us that Tommy's invitation has led to an affair, both in the way they lie comfortably together on the rug, and in Tommy's gift of a ring 'for a bad girl'.[2] 'Going up West' is literally absent, but its pleasures and temptations are invoked most poignantly in Rose's wish that 'there was no such place as Bethnal Green'. In Rose's memory, the next scene shows her packing to meet Tommy for their wedding, only to be given the news that he has been arrested for robbery with violence.

So we never actually go up west in *It Always Rains on Sunday*; we never see the bright lights of Piccadilly Circus and Leicester Square. Apart from that one afternoon in the studio-shot countryside, Rose is doomed to spend her whole life in rainy Bethnal Green, and it is in the terraced streets, market and pubs of the East End that the film is set (see Chapter 5). Tommy's invitation is an invitation to escape the East End, to share some of the glamour to which he aspires in the carefully fashionable outfit which enhances his spivvy good looks.[3] And Rose's desire for this other, not ordinary, life is her downfall. The West End, in British cinema, for those who do not live there, who need to 'go up West', is an alluring place which promises an escape from the everyday, the ordinary and the local. This was a geography of pleasure for all classes of people, although some of the attractions were different. Rose and Tommy's West End would be different to that of smart shops found in the 1942 MGM film *Mrs Miniver*, made in support of the British war effort, which represents pre-war Britain through middle-class Mrs Miniver's shopping trip to the West End to buy a hat.[4] The West End, as a cinematic location, recurs throughout the twentieth century, signified through, and signifying, neon, music, clubs, dancing, shopping, gambling, strolling crowds and sex. These attractions appear in both elite and low forms, catering to all sorts of visitors, and often distinguished by what John Gross, in the epigraph, refers to as 'the short walk' between establishment privilege and underworld vice. In some ways, 'going up West', in its promise of an excursion to a special place devoted to entertainment, is a little like going to the cinema. And going up West 'beckons' as an invitation and an excitement throughout twentieth-century British cinema, from E. A. Dupont's 1929 *Piccadilly* to Gillies MacKinnon's *Pure* (2003) and Menhaj Huda's *Kidulthood* (2006).[5]

This chapter is concerned with this journey 'up West' in British cinema and the West End, which is its destination. I discuss five generically contrasted films made between 1947 and 2002 as a way of exploring what I argue to be a central trope in cinematic London, one which recurs as either aspiration or actuality for characters in a large number of London-set films. I suggest that analysis of this journey is one way of understanding cinematic London as a 'biographical city' (as discussed in the Introduction), a city in which individual characters understand their lives partly topographically, through journeys which they do and don't, can and can't aspire to make. However, this journey is also one of the ways in which the cinematic city, imagined through different generic repertoires, gains coherence, through trips

'We could go up West', Tommy Swann (John McCallum) to Rose (Googie Withers) in *It Always Rains on Sunday*

taken and not taken up West, in films as various as *Smashing Time* (1967), *Babylon* (1980) and *Bend it Like Beckham* (2002). For the West End is both singular, as a focus of desire and aspiration, and plural, in the modes, address and diversity of the pleasures offered. It is generically and historically specific (Carnaby Street in *Smashing Time*, the homosexual prostitution of the amusement arcades in *Babylon*) but it also persists as the imaged and imagined entertainment centre of the city. This exploration necessarily includes some consideration of the relationships between genre and geography in the cinema. Erika Rappaport, in her history of shopping and consumption in the West End, quotes Michael Bonavia recalling, 'Going Up West never had any connection with geography; it meant shopping in Oxford Street or visiting a theatre.'[6] Bonavia's middle-class West End is interesting here for his proposition it 'never had any connection with geography'. While this would be a foolish mantra with which to undertake travel in London, with its radial arrangements of most bus and tube routes, it does point to the way in which the journey to the West End is distinguished by a 'going out' and a 'going up' rather than its direction. Banally, this could be argued to be a centre/periphery model, but I want to argue that the 'wicked uncle' of the West End beckons visitors to the 'city of attractions'[7] in a way that, as Bonavia suggests, has little to do with geography. Going 'up West' is a journey in British cinema that has resonances that far exceed physical travel. And as we have seen with *It Always Rains on Sunday*, it is not a journey that necessarily needs to be shown, either as passage or destination, for its meanings to shape the destinies of individual characters.

The contrast between the East and West End is a formative distinction in the historical understanding of London. Asa Briggs, who surveys some of the ways in which this distinction is made in his classic study, *Victorian Cities*, observes: 'The contrast between East End and West End in London ... was the great contrast of the 1880s and 1890s.'[8] This 'great contrast' of Victorian London, which has its own genres and modes, such as 'silver fork' novels of the 1820–40s discussed by Franco Moretti,[9] persists to our period of study, after the Second World War, when the post-war settlement, as one of a range of factors, including the war itself, enabled a limited but distinctive increase in class mobility. I want to explore the persistence and modalities of this contrast through what I see as its constitutive dynamic, the journey to (and from) the West End, often figured as simple journey in search of entertainment 'up West'. In this argument, the West End is constituted both through what it is not: the poverty of the East End; the bowler-hatted uniformity of the City; the uncharted lowlands of south London; the suburbs; 'the country' – and through what these other places are not: the city of attractions. Michael Bonavia's point is that to journey to the West End, in his recollection, is to intend to spend time in certain types of leisure consumption. If, as I have argued in Chapter 2, 'local London' must be understood partly as temporal, rather than a spatial category, then 'going up West' is its constitutive other. It is to go from the everyday world to the world of leisure, from banal time to special time, from work to play, and it is partly the passage itself, from that other London, whether metaphorical or material, that makes the cinematic West End.

Before commencing the detailed analysis of individual films, I want to outline a little more the ideas about the cinematic West End and the journey 'up West' that I am proposing. This will, I hope, make it easier to see the way in which these ideas flicker in and out of the analysis of individual films, and allow me to offer an analysis of each film, which, while organised through attention to its production of the West End, respects its textual integrity, its generic heritage and its historical moment.

The first point, to which I have already alluded, is the hypothesis that the attractions of the cinematic West End can sometimes be read, within an individual film, as a *mise en abyme* of the trip to the cinema. While scholarship on the experience and meanings of cinemagoing has lagged behind attention to the film text, there are now several accounts of going out to the cinema, many of which draw attention to the excitement and the specialness of these outings.[10] If going to London is one of *the* stories of British cinema, just as it has been of English literature, the West End is the destination within cinema that is most like cinema itself: a place of pleasures outside everyday life. Evidently, all meaning in the cinema is created through light, but the West End is particularly dramatically evoked through the allure of light.[11] Neon, shop windows, illuminated displays: all are recruited to mean 'up West', and there is frequently an attention to a restless crowd seeking distraction. The key topos here is Piccadilly Circus, signified through the statue of Eros and the neon display (sometimes with a helpful tube sign in shot), which, as Mark Adams puts it, 'is one of those London sites that crops up regularly in the movies, but usually as a quick background image rather than as an extensively used location'.[12] Piccadilly Circus can be used, in a chain of landmark imagery, to signify 'London', as discussed in Chapter 1, or within a London-set narrative, to signify arrival in the West End.[13] Historically, it is redolent of a democratic London (as opposed to landmarks such as the Tower of London or Buckingham Palace); it is a destination for anyone, a landmark for those mingling in the 'city of attractions'. A trip to the bright lights, which can end in many different ways for characters in a narrative, is, for the cinema audience (another democratic pleasure), a reminder of what they are themselves doing as they sit in the dark and watch the play of light.

The identification of the West End with the cinema is one of the key structures of the 1957 documentary short set in Piccadilly Circus, *Nice Time*, made by Claude Goretta and Alain Tanner with assistance from the British Film Institute's Experimental Film Fund.[14] Shot with concealed 16mm cameras over several months, the film is set on a Saturday night in the West End. Christophe Dupin quotes the film-makers as hoping 'to catch and interpret the responses of the crowd to the fare it is offered'.[15] *Nice Time* opens and closes on the statue of Eros, in between showing a montage of people meeting, talking, queuing, wandering about, buying and selling, intercut with neon signs and shots of merchandise and posters. The central temporal structure of the film is a visit to the cinema, with uniformed commissars organising the cinema queues as a gypsy woman serenades them, singing and selling heather. This temporal arc of an evening out is counterposed with an interest in the juxtaposition of abstracted elements of popular culture, initially manifest in a sound montage, which juxtaposes cinemagoers' 'the film's just starting' with the film soundtrack, 'What else could I do? Marry me, Maria'. Although the camera doesn't enter the cinema, the structure of the performance is retained, with the soundtrack of the National Anthem played at the end of the evening over images of the flashing Coca-Cola advertisement in Piccadilly Circus, followed by shots of streets suddenly crowded with people leaving the cinema.

Within this temporal structure of the evening out watching Hollywood films, montage is also used to convey the variety of attractions and entertainments on sale: hot chestnuts, corsages, balloons, hot dogs, fruit, little wooden snakes, paper flowers in shells, pin-ups, naturist magazines with titles like *La Belle France* and *Nudita*, while a violinist plays. As with the city symphonies of the 1920s, *Man with a Movie Camera* (1929) and *Berlin: Symphony of a Great City* (1927), the cinematic city in *Nice Time* is produced through an articulation of location-shot footage with an extremely elaborate editing structure, which often involves the use of only a few frames from particular sequences. Here, though, the complex soundtrack is used to work with and against the images, and there is no joyous celebration of the modernity of the city. The film-makers seem distanced from the pleasures of the crowd, treating the faces and bodies of individuals as curiosities, as in the long close-up on the ravaged face of a syphilitic newspaper vendor, or as elements in a montage which includes the juxtaposition of shots of bananas followed by images of two black men. However, there are glimpses of people's pleasure, excitement and wonder, as well as their patience in the busy streets. Going up West for 'a nice time' is shown to be a crowded, commercial, tawdry affair, the temporality of the respectable evening out closing down into the night when only streetwalkers and their clients are left out in the streets.

Piccadilly Circus lies at the nexus of John Gross's 'short walk' between Burlington House and Brewer Street, between the Royal Academy and Soho. Ian Nairn, in 1966, suggests, '[t]his really is the centre of London'.[16] It is also, as Mort and Nead point out, 'a site for the uneasy convergence of multiple social relations: of bureaucracy, tourism, consumption and simply a meeting place for friends and strangers. It is at once a site of licit and illicit exchange.'[17] This historical double-faced aspect of the West End is, I suggest, both represented and reconstituted in post-war British cinema through film genre. Mayfair and the 'pleasant London' discussed below in the 1948 film *Spring in Park Lane* is found in musical comedy and romantic comedy. The Hollywood studios, too, are comfortable with this West End, which often extends to include a royal park and Belgravia terraces, as in films like *Mary Poppins* (1964), and it persists, sometimes with a slightly more raffish edge, into later London-set films, such as those of Working Title like *Notting Hill* (1999). Alongside this, there is the West End of thrillers and film noir, a much darker place, in which the façades of Nash's Regent Street are likely to give way to the alleys and courts of Soho as they do in *Noose* (1948) and *The World Ten Times Over* (1963), and the generic drives towards investigation and pursuit often uncover despair and degradation. Soho is the most significant topos of this West End, and is figured as a site of cosmopolitanism (which can be criminal, as noted in *The Blue Lamp* [1950], or sentimental, as in *Miracle in Soho* [1957]), and youthful pleasures (*The Red Shoes* [1948], *Expresso Bongo* [1959]) as well as vice, and is discussed here in the film *Mona Lisa* (1986).[18]

In Tommy's invitation to Rose with which I started, he is speaking literally, 'We could go up West.' We could leave Bethnal Green for the evening and visit the bright lights – this is an attractive invitation to do something special, but delivered in a casual manner so that he doesn't lose his cool by trying too hard. But it is also a metaphorical invitation, as we see from the next scene, when Rose is rewarded for being 'a bad girl', to venture into the exciting and sinful city. The edit between the two scenes of Rose's flashback equates the West End with sex, and the journey 'up West' in the cinema is often a journey 'to' sex, and the display of sexual bodies that are for sale in one way or another. In London as a biographical city, the journey to the West End to sell sex marks a point of degradation for characters from Myra (Vivien Leigh) in *Waterloo Bridge* (1940) to Blue (Brinsley Ford) in *Babylon*. It is within this representational nexus that we frequently find a structuring and generative contrast of 'West End stories', which is the distinction between those who go up West for pleasure, and those workers who provide that pleasure. This aspect of the West End I discuss in relation to *Mona Lisa*. So the West End in the cinema is always bound up with the contrast between the bright and the dark city: either characters come from the dull and dingy everyday and go up West, or, in the West End, there is a distinction drawn between its glittery allure for visitors and its dingy reality for workers.[19] The cinematic West End is structured through display and revelation: the display of goods, riches, art, bodies, and the revelations of the conditions of this display.

If going up West is in some sense a spectacle of cinema, and of sex, it can also be, I want to suggest, a spectacle of class. This can be observed in a scene from a film of the swinging 1960s, the Peter Collinson version of *Up the Junction*. The film structures its narrative through the journey across the river, by chauffeur-driven car, of its wealthy protagonist, Polly (Suzy Kendall), and the friends she makes in working-class Battersea, particularly her boyfriend, Peter (Dennis Waterman). When Polly later brings her luggage to Clapham Junction Station, there is a shot of a sign saying 'Trains to the West End and City', a juxtaposition repeated with a road sign seconds later. Thus Battersea, instead of just 'being there', and being taken for granted, is repeatedly seen through Polly's eyes as somewhere strange.[20] The class gulf between Polly from 'just over the bridge' and Peter, Sylvie (Maureen Lipman) and Rube (Adrienne Posta) from Battersea, is shown to be much wider than a river through differing tastes such as Sylvie and Rube's politely repressed horror at Polly's choice of second-hand furniture, 'something ordinary and plain', in contrast to their own embrace of the modern. These differences are most vividly expressed in relation to notions of 'going out', and particularly Peter's ideas of what is appropriate for a date with a posh girl. His first suggestion is that they should go to the pictures, and when Polly asks where, he says 'Up the West End'. Polly's little moué of disappointment, her unexcited 'Oh', puzzles him. Polly, it turns out, would rather stay in Battersea on Saturday night, despite his dismissive claim that 'it's all just pubs and "Knees up Mother Brown"'. She wants to 'just walk around the streets', and when they do this – Peter still slightly puzzled – she finds the gas-holders, the terraced streets and the railway viaducts 'beautiful', whereas he just sees 'poxy little houses'. 'Going up West' is here matched with another journey, Polly's downwardly mobile pursuit of 'real people'. For Polly, the Junction is a series of spectacles.

This doubling of the spectacle of class mobility is repeated later in the film when Polly does accept an outing, 'Up West, over the water'. 'Oh no, not the West End,' she teases as she climbs on the back of Peter's scooter. The camera cuts to a close-up on the bonnet of a Rolls-Royce, angled to show the stucco buildings and canopied walkway behind. Polly and Peter stay on his scooter, watching, as the rich enter the building. The West End for Peter is a street exterior of luxury cars, canopies in the street and stuccoed house fronts, and he has brought Polly up there to gaze, as he does, at what is unattainable but desirable. On their return to Battersea, they arrive in the middle of a street brawl between one of Polly's new friends and her husband. It is her turn to gaze, but after a while she hides her face in Peter's shoulders, and when they get home he asks her, 'Seen enough?' As with Rose in *It Always Rains on Sunday*, Peter's desire for the West End proves his undoing, just as he too never really gets there. 'Up West' for Peter is an envious gaze across a street, an impossible destiny in his imagined biographical city. The closest he will get to the West End is Polly herself and, by the end of the film, his and Polly's fantasies of class mobility are exposed in a magistrate's court, when Peter is given a prison sentence, while Polly turns out to know one of the lawyers.

This class journey can also be taken in a different way, perhaps most famously by Eliza Doolittle in *My Fair Lady* (1964). In this class journey, going up West is a matter of speech, deportment, costume and manners, rather than geography. Henry Higgins (Rex Harrison) finds Eliza Doolittle selling flowers in Covent Garden. He does not have to go to the East End to find a girl to improve, but finds her instead in one of the historic haunts of prostitutes in central London, hence her constant insistence that she is 'a good girl'. Under Higgins's tutelage, Eliza learns to hold her own with the aristocracy, and she leaves her local geography of the market, with her pitch, and her friends, to move convincingly, if not comfortably, within the virtual geography of the upper-class season, from town house to ballroom to Ascot.[21]

The geographies of the West End, then, are, as many have observed, geographies of desire and aspiration. As an imagined destination, the West End does not need to be shown as a place for it to shape the biographical city inhabited by the characters in a movie, as we have already seen with the examples of Rose and Peter. In this sense, the West End of British cinema can be a little like the Moscow of Chekhov's *Three Sisters*. However, in this chapter, I will concentrate on films that do offer settings in, or excursions to, the West End, juxtaposing the different figuring of these desires and aspirations in the West Ends of romantic comedy and film noir. The point of the juxtapositions is not a comparison in search of a real London, nor a survey of West End-set films, but instead an exploration of the way in which all cinematic geographies are generic. Thus, in some ways the London of *Night and the City* (1950) has more in common with that of *Mona Lisa*, which was made more than thirty years later, than it does with *Spring in Park Lane*, which was made only two years earlier. The 'noirness' of the first two films is more significant than their historical geographical setting, or which, and what, was studio or location shot. However, all the films discussed in this chapter do have some significant West End settings, which have their own historical variants, and it is also possible to trace certain iconographic and landmark elements, as well as tropes, which are cross-generic. It is within this matrix of the generic and the geographical, through the opposition between glitter and 'not glitter', that the dark and bright cinematic West End is created.

The chapter is organised to discuss the bright and dark West Ends with films chosen from the immediate post-war period, the 1980s and the end of the century. I am not trying to offer a history of the cinematic West End, but these three 'moments' – the post-war settlement, its radical 1980s dismantling and what could be called the neo-liberal fin de siècle – are interesting times in this history when considered through the contrasted film genres of romantic comedy and noir-influenced thrillers. From the post-war period, the pleasant London of *Spring in Park Lane*, one of the Herbert Wilcox/Anna Neagle 'Mayfair' films and the most successful British film of 1948,[22] has clear memories of a pre-war London, while the financially rather less successful film noir production *Night and the City* apprehends London partly through the style of the US studios. *Mona Lisa* was made in the middle of the 1979–90 Thatcher government, and is one of a group of 'angry' London films from this time. Picking up some of the themes of Chapter 2, this film has a residual south London/Soho opposition, while also placing a cockney in a post-colonial London, and imagining more than one type of journey up West. There is, however, no pleasant London with which to consider *Mona Lisa*. The cinematic London of the 1980s is a dark London. While there are generically contrasted London-set films from this period with some West End settings, the most interesting of which include *Defence of the Realm* (1985) and *Dance with a Stranger* (1985),[23] there are few pleasant cinematic Londons of the 1980s. As much scholarship on British cinema attests, the significant generic alternative to the expressionist realism of *Mona Lisa* in the 1980s would be heritage cinema, which is in general not an urban genre, although *84 Charing Cross Road* (1987) offers an almost sepia, rationed London, contrasted with the bounteous modernity of New York and its London scenes (shot at Shepperton) are set just over the street from Soho. The final part of the chapter moves to the end of the twentieth century to consider the 'global West End'. Here, I juxtapose the enormously successful transatlantic romance *Notting Hill* with the twenty-first-century below-stairs romance/thriller *Dirty Pretty Things* (2002), set in the world of illegal immigrants in a West End hotel. This comparison takes considerable liberties with the notion of the journey to the West End, and explores the developing iconography of London as a global – as opposed to an imperial, or post-colonial – city.

As will already be evident, it is not just the different West Ends that are, in John Gross's words, packed together. There is a certain 'packing together' in the writing of this chapter as well, as I move between narrow alleys and broader thoroughfares, between darkness and light, using different conceptual paradigms at different points in an attempt to point to significant patterning in the cinematic West End over the second half of the twentieth century, in the context of major changes to London, the film industry, and the ways in which films and cities are thought about. The West End is the glittering heart of London's urban imaginary: it is impossible to do it justice without a certain jostling in crowded, pleasure-seeking streets.

Pleasant London: *Spring in Park Lane*

Spring in Park Lane (1948) was the most successful of the very popular 'West End suite'[24] of films made by Anna Neagle and Herbert Wilcox in the 1940s. Geoffrey MacNab notes that journalists of the time were quick to point out that the film titles in this cycle read like a smart address book: *I Live in Grosvenor Square* (1945), *Piccadilly Incident* (1946), *The Courtneys of Curzon Street* (1947) and *Maytime in Mayfair* (1949).[25] David Thomson recalls being taken to the films as a child and 'being enchanted by such tales of Samarkand on the other side of the river and thinking how long-suffering of my mother to go on living in south London'.[26] C. A. Lejeune reviewed *Spring in Park Lane* as 'a pleasant film with a pleasant name',[27] and it is perhaps this very pleasantness that has told against them. In this, their fate is not unlike the Richard Curtis films made over fifty years later, in which London is also a very pleasant place. In both cases, the perceived femininity of the generic address has counted against critical prestige. In the Mayfair series, Neagle often wears modish and extravagant costumes and *Maytime in Mayfair* casts her as the director of a fashion house. The films themselves have been unfashionable since, and Sarah Street, in her spirited account of Neagle in her 1999 *British National Cinema*, points out that even in the 1940s their popularity was with audiences rather than critics.[28] She discusses Neagle's star image, her patriotic roles and her appeal to women viewers, particularly middle-class women viewers, suggesting that it is her role as a 'lady' that has limited her subsequent appeal.[29] Despite her origins as a chorus-girl, in these films, if Neagle is not playing an aristocrat, she plays a servant who marries into the upper classes. If she is a career woman, her premises are in Park Lane or Mayfair. It's an expensive world, and the films too were not cheap. Produced by MGM in their Elstree studios, the films match their Mayfair lifestyle with quite high production values. So the films neither meet long-standing criteria within British film criticism which valorise realism and authenticity, nor do they fit the revaluation of costume cinema articulated in relation to the 'bodice-rippers' made at Gainsborough Studios. For the critics of the time, their imagination of the upper classes was a little too proletarian, while subsequently, their concerns are perhaps insufficiently so.[30] They remain resolutely British, and middle class, thus also being excluded from the allure and achievements of Hollywood musical comedy. If these Neagle/Wilcox films have proved unpopular with most historians of British cinema,[31] they are no more popular in the London canon. Enthusiasts of the city and the cinema are usually more interested in the labyrinthine metropolis that we find in a film like *Night and the City*, or low-life authenticity – not well-brought-up women in pretty frocks and furs in well-appointed town houses in London's best districts.

The pleasant London of this world is all the more pleasant for being set mainly inside the Park Lane house where Judy (Anna Neagle) works as a secretary for her rich uncle, where the most significant set is the huge, light, spacious marble-floored entrance hall, of which Richard Winnington commented with some asperity: 'That the façade doesn't represent any part of Park Lane that I've seen and the palatial interiors of the houses by some structural magic are about five times the width of the frontages is irrelevant to the pursuit of gay romantic comedy.'[32] It is in this house that the younger son of an impoverished aristocratic family, Richard (Michael Wilding), masquerades as a footman for reasons connected to a sub-plot about the trade in stolen and faked paintings. The film traces the growing attraction between Richard and Judy, the revelation of his identity and the solution of his financial problems. The display here is of wealth and space: there is a picture gallery of old masters in a domestic house and private houses have extensive ballrooms with large balconies which permit the spectacle of a dance by Anna Neagle and Michael Wilding. However, there are traces within the film of a slightly different London, a London of spivs and rackets, and the modernity of the central couple is constructed in relation to this other London. As John Gross observes in the comment at the head of the chapter, these different West Ends are 'packed together – so near and so far'.

Richard, the footman (Michael Wilding) watches Judy (Anna Neagle) in the 'palatial interior' of *Spring in Park Lane*

Richard's class origins are clear from the beginning of the film. He is an inappropriately interventionist footman, and, as Judy observes to her mother, 'He pronounces Marseilles like a Parisian and wears an old Etonian tie like an old Etonian.' Indeed, it is precisely his incompetence as a footman that reassures Judy that he is not, in class terms, behaving inappropriately when he flirts with her. However, the masquerade that he is a footman allows the film, and Judy, to flirt with the idea of cross-class romance, just as his fluency in semi-criminal argot when confronting spiv picture forgers suggests that the war has broadened his class perspectives and competences. By having a wealthy heroine who works, the film shows some sensitivity to changed attitudes to inherited wealth in the post-war period. Similarly, Richard's absurd masquerade is subtended by a post-war familiarity with the modes of the black market and the entrepreneurial working class. The film dips its toes into a world in which class configurations are changing, and to some extent the Judy and Richard couple are marked by modernity through their mobility in relation to the film's topographies.[33] As Leonard Mosley suggested in the *Daily Express*, 'It moves pleasantly and easily from below-stairs to drawing room, from nightclub to palais-de-danse.'[34] In this mobile context it is significant that one of the settings is an airport, in 1948 both modern and exclusive, while Richard is also shown to be familiar with the sea voyage to New York.

The film's title promises a classed topography and the opening shot uses footage of a spring-like Park Lane, with the trees of Hyde Park on one side and an orchestrated version of the folk song 'Early One Morning', played over a busy, but not crowded cityscape: buses, taxis, buildings and a fountain. A cut on a tree in blossom leads us to Judy, who walks jauntily along a row of houses, swinging a couple of neatly wrapped purchases as she walks to her destination, one of the large houses where a tree is also in blossom. Spring in Park Lane clearly means pretty, fashionably dressed maidens ('Early one morning, I heard a maiden singing') and blossom. This is London, but this London, as Robert Murphy has argued of a later group of films, which includes *Notting Hill*, is 'a city of delights'.[35] This tone is maintained throughout the film, partly through the simple device of often opening and closing scenes on flower arrangements and blossom. Richard opens the door to Judy, and the romance begins. The street set is repeated very shortly afterwards, by which point the audience understands something of Richard's masquerade. In this second street sequence, the same street features are shown, as two more women walk along the same stretch of street in the same direction. But these are the cook and the maid, and instead of going in by the front door that Judy used, they must go down the steps to the area below stairs. So the smartness of a Mayfair address in comparison to the rest of London is represented through the micro-topography of above and below stairs, with Cook, Rosie and Perkins based downstairs. Richard's modernity is figured through his mobility. He, alone of all the characters, uses both entrances to the house. And he, through his wartime experience in the Navy, has learnt the language and mores of 'Chatham Dockyard', and is thus more suited to the modern world than his stuffy, old-fashioned brother, who lives in a castle.

Richard and Judy's romance progresses through a series of interactions and outings, but it is an outing to dance at the Lyceum that gives a sense of Richard and Judy as part of a post-war crowd enjoying themselves, while also suggesting their difference. The city of delights offers lovers the willow-fringed pastoral of the Serpentine's boating lake and the crowded excitement of a commercial dance hall where Richard and Judy do their best to jive with the common people, but where she in particular seems very stiff and rigid in comparison with other dancers. This same ambivalence towards popular culture is perceptible in the film's presentation of another of Judy's suitors, Basil, a film star, who is gently mocked throughout for his vanity and inability to differentiate real life from the movies. Unlike Basil, this film knows that its pleasant London is partly make-believe, a post-war imagination of a 1930s Mayfair, or, as Thomson puts it, 'a purple patch in the Monopoly of love and idleness'.[36]

West End Noir 1: *Night and the City*

The pleasant London of *Spring in Park Lane* can be usefully juxtaposed with the noir London of *Night and the City*, a film released two years later, and directed by Jules Dassin, in Britain because of the Hollywood blacklist. Produced by Twentieth Century-Fox, *Night and the City* was one of several films made by the American Majors in London at a time when tax concessions made 'off-shore' productions attractive, and features US stars Richard Widmark and Gene Tierney, along with Googie Withers.[37] *Night and the City* was not much liked by the British critics, and Robert Murphy describes it as provoking 'a string of petulant, small-minded and unfair reviews'.[38] Arguably, these adjectives also describe the lead character, Harry Fabian (Richard Widmark), which, along with the film's lengthy wrestling plot, may go some way to explaining its relative lack of success. However, the film is visually very striking in its presentation of the city at night and Tom Ryall, who has traced the way in which different critics have construed the film as part of different traditions, draws our attention to its significant place within the film noir canon.[39] Colin McArthur's account of the film's London is significant within the film's critical reception: 'The London of *Night and the City* has no temporal or geographical location; it is Thomson's "city of dreadful night", Warshow's "dark, sad city of the imagination". Its underworld is reminiscent of Villon's Paris or Lang's Dusseldorf.'[40] McArthur sees the film as quintessential film noir in which 'the city' is an existential location, rather than a specific place, and shows how others have also understood the film in this way. However, I don't think that the generic noir city is the only city in this film, and want to explore the film in a slightly different way, paying attention not to 'the dark sad city of the imagination', but to the *mise en place* of 'the city is London', which is spoken over a London landmark montage.

My project here, in its attention to the local and the particular, runs rather against a significant trend within 'noir' studies, which emphasises the apprehension of a mood and an attitude towards the city *in general* within film noir. In this scholarship, film noir is the urban genre par excellence, and the one which renders the alienated urban experience of the twentieth century most expressively.[41] This tendency towards the abstraction of the urban experience has been accompanied by an extension of the cultural texts that are considered 'noir'.[42] As James Naremore argues in his demythologising historical study, 'film noir has become one of the dominant intellectual categories of the late twentieth century, operating across the entire cultural arena of art, popular memory and criticism'.[43] Naremore both works with film noir as an extended category, and, at the same time, is concerned to locate historically and materially the particular instances of noir, which he analyses within his larger argument about the liminality that characterises noir. *Night and the City* displays this liminality at many levels, but the one with which I am concerned is the traffic between 'any city' and 'the city is London', a movement which produces a very particular London.

Robert Mighall has argued, in his study of the gothic novel, *A Geography of Victorian Gothic Fiction*, for the importance of a historically contextualised understanding of the use of location within this fiction. His book is partly a polemic addressed to the dominant understanding of the gothic within psychoanalytic terms, in which the repeated tendency is towards the symbolic reading of space. There are connections that can be made between readings of place in the gothic and the city in film noir. While the attention to 'the dark sad city of the imagination' in film noir has been significant for the understanding of some of the reciprocities of the relationship between the cinema and the city, it can usefully be augmented by attention to the historically specific city. This is the achievement of Edward Dimendberg in his *Film Noir and the Spaces of Modernity*, who argues '[T]reating the city as an expression of some underlying myth, theme, or vision has tended to stifle the study of spatiality in film noir as a historical *content* as significant as its more commonly studied formal and narrative features.'[44] Thus, while *Night and the City* does, particularly in its closing sequences, present an abstract, hostile, labyrinthine nightmare city, it also shows, quite precisely, the double-faced West End centred on Piccadilly Circus, which is the concern of this chapter, and which has been a very strong tradition in the historical representation of London. There are two Londons in this film, and the way in which they are mapped over each other makes it impossible, by the end of the film, to see the first London, a public, tourist, landmark West End London, without understanding the way in which it is subtended by another London, one of graft, pay-offs and the hierarchies of the underworld.

The titles of the film, with words spelt out in light-bulbs, are run over a series of classic landmark London shots of the embankment, Westminster and Tower Bridge (see Chapter 1). The imbrication of the two Londons begins as the film opens with the narration running over landmark shots of London, which, once location has been established, are narrativised by a shot of a man running desperately, pursued across the screen. Although Harry runs through to a carefully framed view of St Paul's, this repertoire of landmark London is made strange through the shooting of the dark, deserted streets and bombed wasteland through which he is chased. This is a noir London. Harry too is an unusual figure for landmark London, running, and dressed in a loud checked jacket, which, with the pale belt and the correspondents' shoes, which he wears throughout, signify his professional Americanism. Here though, in the opening sequence, the key indicator of Harry's character, of his vanity and the significance of appearances, is the way in which – while being chased – he stoops to retrieve a carnation that has fallen from his buttonhole.

Harry Fabian is a club tout who repeatedly loses money – generally other people's and particularly his girlfriend Mary's – through investing in dead certs such as a football pool or a dog track in Birmingham because he is ambitious to make it big and 'just want[s] to be somebody'. The film follows Harry's most ambitious and final scheme, when he tries to wrest the control of London's wrestling from the Greek entrepreneur Kristo (Herbert Lom) through manipulatively befriending Kristo's visiting father, a former wrestler in the Greco-Roman style. Harry raises money for this scheme with the duplicitous help of Helen (Googie Withers), wife of the proprietor of the Silver Fox club in the West End, but Nosseros (Francis L. Sullivan) secretly deals with Kristo to bring about Harry's downfall. Throughout the film Harry's ambitious, irresponsible, untrustworthy, American criminality is contrasted with honest British graft. Harry is all dreams and schemes, an American fly-by-night, willing, at both the beginning and end of the film, to steal from his girlfriend, while British criminality is shown to be a skilled trade across a range of swindles.

Harry's appearance is important because his mode of operation as a tout is to exploit his nationality to befriend visiting American businessmen in London. The film shows his scam in careful detail at the beginning. After leaving the Silver Fox in the backstreets of St Martin's Lane, Harry is shown framed in the doorway of the The American Bar. The sign for the bar is made of neon lights, and Harry stands beneath this lights, staring across the street at the similarly bright Café de l'Europe, looking for custom. These brightly lit bars and the crowds on the far pavement place the location as the West End, which is confirmed as a taxi draws up to disgorge Harry's prey. Through deals with taxi-drivers, barmen and the doorman of The American Bar, Harry works a routine round the finding of a money-filled wallet, which allows him to impress his honesty on his naive, but suspicious, touring compatriots. Honest Harry appears to be merely taking the pity of a man of the world on some anxious mid-Westerners when, about to leave, he remembers that he does 'know of a place – a bit naughty, but great fun'. This sequence, which is shown in great detail up to the moment when Harry leaves The American Bar, paying off the doorman as he leaves, shortly to be followed by his three dupes on their way to the Silver Fox, establishes the double space of the film, the shiny West End fronting something 'a bit naughty'.

Harry is shown throughout to be a confidence trickster and chancer whose dreams exceed his potential and position. This contrasts thoroughly with the mores of the British underworld, which is consistently shown to work harder and to know its place. British criminality is shown as requiring dedication and labour, rather than the pursuit of 'a life of ease and plenty'. This contrast is developed most systematically in Harry's tour through the obscurely lit British underworld to raise money for his new wrestling scheme. First, he visits Figler (James Hayter) who runs a *Beggar's Opera/Threepenny Opera*-type operation, while he arranges the disabilities of those he is sending out to beg, 'Strap this on you, you look a good type for a stump'. Figler refuses Harry money but offers to set him up with 'a few good beggars', offering him all the supplies he would need, 'legs, eyes, stumps'. Harry encounters the same judicious self-limiting generosity with the forger, Googan (Gibb McLaughlin), who offers passports, birth certificates and medical licences, but observes, of the issue of giving Harry money, that 'if you ain't got socks, you can't pull them up'. Anna O'Leary (Maureen Delany), a riverwoman whose cargoes include nylons and cigarettes, also resists Harry's suggestion that she must be tired of 'living like this, shady deals, a life on the river', claiming that she is a 'hard-working, hard-headed business woman'. By the time we get to Harry's final putative backer, the owner of a drinking dive, Harry's own pitch has been eliminated by the film, and we hear only the refusal of the industrious and realistic British criminal, 'No, I don't want a life of ease and plenty, take your drink and drink it quietly and don't mess about with my customers.'

This sequence of scenes is an instance of the creation of place through situated performance. Robert Murphy, who discusses *Night and the City* within a chapter on 'the spiv

The American noir hero, Harry Fabian (Richard Widmark) in the West End/landmark London in *Night and the City*

cycle' in his book about 1940s British cinema, argues that the film 'brought more of London to the screen than any other before the "Swinging London" films of the 1960s', and draws particular attention to the performances of the British actors.[45] The low-key, assured professionalism of McLaughlin, Hayter and Delany, their absorption in their tasks – none stop working while they talk to Harry – and their willingness to help through work, is contrasted with a much shriller performance from Widmark who is, throughout, given star lighting, which contrasts with the dinginess of his hosts' quarters. But this dinginess and, indeed, the criminal trades of the Londoners – begging, forgery and smuggling rendered with such careful detail – also point to the way in which criminal London, in this film, is to some extent a Victorian city. The old city, with its courts and alleyways, its flower-sellers and street hustlers, conceals itself from the neon of The American Bar and the Café de l'Europe. And this is perhaps the complication of 'noir London': the Victorian London that lurks behind it, which, through media other than cinema, as well as the many Dickens adaptations, subtends the post-war city. If film noir, as Dimendberg and others have argued of Hollywood, is marked most strongly by an engagement with the spaces of modernity, London noir, if it exists, is inextricably caught up in the Victorian city.[46]

With scenes in Trafalgar Square, Piccadilly Circus, Regent Street and the Embankment, the film repeatedly grounds its action in landmark London, while in fact mainly setting it in back-alleys, glistening wet flights of stairs and sordid interiors. The dominance of underworld London is such that even a location-shot Trafalgar Square is rendered suspicious, and rightly so, for this clever scene uses daylight in Trafalgar Square for the final stitch-up of Fabian. The fountains and the lions are used as a set, a familiar tourist backdrop to Fabian's over-confidence. The carefully planned betrayal, in which Nosseros coaxes Harry into catastrophe, is set in full view of the crowds and the pigeons in one of the most landmark of landmark locations. This has the effect of making Trafalgar Square seem almost unnaturally bright: landmark London has been made strange. The imbrication of these two Londons, the West End with its underworld, is made plain towards the end of the film when word is put out by Kristo (who runs the wrestling racket) that he will offer a reward of £1,000 for Harry Fabian, whom he blames for his father's death. A henchman of Kristo's leaves the gym to spread the word and goes first to Piccadilly Circus to tell a newspaper vendor. Driving round the lights of the West End, his first set of messengers are all already on the streets plying legitimate trades in tourist London. As more than one character has already told Harry, he is a dead man, and we the audience understand this because we see that there is no part of London which is not part of the underworld. This vision of a doubled London is embodied in the central shot of this sequence, the most flamboyant of the film, when the camera seems to pan 180 degrees, while actually being driven round Piccadilly Circus, offering, dizzyingly, both the familiar lights of tourist London and the ubiquity of the underworld. While other characters, without ambition, have been content to remain within their particular milieu, the Fiddler in his den, Helen hoping only for another nightclub, Anna on her barge, with only Nosseros, who outwits Harry, venturing into Trafalgar Square and public London, Harry has wanted to make it big, to be recognised in the West End as well as the underworld. It is his ambition – and refusal of honest toil – that both articulates these two Londons together, and makes of them an inescapable trap for himself. Kristo's word is spread from Piccadilly Circus to the docks, the dogs and the drinking dives. These final montage sequences tell both a general city story about organised crime, and, in the particular locations, tell a London story. Harry Fabian is chased, caught and killed; and thrown into the river without ceremony.[47]

The centrality of Richard Widmark's performance to *Night and the City* has contributed to the understanding of the film within the paradigm of 'the dark sad city of the imagination'. What I have tried to demonstrate is the way in which the darkness of this city is at least partly the darkness of a Victorian London still present in the mid-twentieth century. Harry Fabian, like the tourists he fleeces, is seduced by the bright lights of the West End, unable to grasp the relationship between this brightness and the surrounding shadows.

West End Noir 2: *Mona Lisa*

The West End as a place of display and revelation dominates the topography of *Mona Lisa* (Neil Jordan, 1986). 'Up West' is comprised of luxury hotels and sleazy sex clubs at night, while south of the river, ordinary people live in terraced streets in daytime. Made in the mid-1980s, the film has some continuities with a group of London films from the Thatcher period, including *My Beautiful Laundrette* (1985), *The Last of England* (1987), *Empire State* (1987) and

Sammy and Rosie Get Laid (1987), which have attracted considerable critical attention, functioning metonymically in a debate about what a British national cinema should be.[48] While *Mona Lisa*, which was produced by HandMade Films, has a slightly different genealogy to the other, mainly Channel 4- and BFI-funded London films in this group, its portrait of London is clearly contemporary, while its aspiration towards Hollywood generic pleasures recasts the debate about a British national cinema in a familiar direction.

Mona Lisa was widely recognised as a significant London film on its first release. For example, Peter Ackroyd's review commences,

> This is a film about London, and in the first few moments we are presented with some of that city's principal landmarks – among them the sturdy figure of Bob Hoskins, who is rapidly taking the place of Tommy Trinder as everyone's idea of a Londoner.[49]

Ackroyd's comment nicely condenses two propositions: that London landmarks must be understood to include more than buildings, rivers and bridges, and can include personae such as the cockney, and that these representative London figures have histories often associated with particularly performers.[50] *Mona Lisa* stars Hoskins (who won best actor at Cannes) as a small-time crook, George, who had 'taken the rap' for his employer, Mortwell (Michael Caine), seven years earlier, and now, on his release from prison, is given a job chauffeuring a prostitute, Simone (Cathy Tyson), who works the exclusive West End hotels such as the Ritz. The film traces George's passionate involvement with Simone, from dislike through curiosity to love, and his attempts at a rapprochement with the daughter he hardly knows. There is passion too in Simone's initial furious dislike of George, but her subsequent feelings are more opaque as he helps her to track down a former workmate, Cathy, a teenage girl with whom she used to work the meat-rack of King's Cross. George realises too late that Simone loves Cathy and there is a bloody shoot-out in Brighton when the pimps track them down. George is still alive at the end of the film, and the film closes with him, his daughter and his friend Thomas (Robbie Coltrane) together back in south London.

In *Mona Lisa* George discovers that Simone is not what she seems. The film too is deceptive, as is its London, while in its unfolding, George, its hero, must learn to seem what he is not. These deceptive symmetries give the film a certain elegance which is embodied, at key points, by Simone. The London revealed in *Mona Lisa* is the 'hellish city' which has a very long literary and filmic genealogy: the city as the consumer of innocents, the perverter of desires, the ruin of hope and aspiration. This London is discovered through one of the stock city narratives, the arrival of the stranger in town. However, here the innocent stranger has not come from the country, but from a prison term of a peculiar temporality discussed in more detail below. George (Hoskins), the native Londoner who has 'been away' for some years, is here the innocent who comes to the city, a city that the film suggests he finds transformed. This transformation is first marked as the visible presence of black British citizens 'who live here' and which includes Simone. Since George has been away, crime has become technologised, and he is now expected to wear a bleeper. Through his involvement with Simone, George explores the *topoi* of the London vice industry, Soho and King's Cross. The city here is an infernal one, run by evil men, mobsters and villains, who cater to the perverse tastes of the anonymous crowd and are themselves mainly shadowy presences in the background. This city will devour young girls like George's daughter, and put them on the meat-rack of King's Cross, drug-addled, able to eat only ice cream, unless he prevents it.[51] This hellish expressionist London was frequently attributed in reviews to Neil Jordan's vision and Philip French captures the film's peculiar mixture of infernal city and cockney 'naif-in-the-city' in his comment,

> The film's London is a nightmare world, as unnaturalistic as the heroine's dreams in Jordan's last picture, *Company of Wolves*. It's as if the Soho of Frank Norman's 'Fings Aint Wot They Used To Be' has been re-worked in the style of Scorsese's *Taxi Driver*.[52]

This comment, as well as wittily identifying two of the contrasted urban imaginaries that shape this film, also points to the issue of the temporality of the figure of the cockney, which I will discuss below. The production design of the film was consciously non-realist for the King's Cross sequences, which were shot on location near Liverpool Street Station. In an interview, Neil Jordan is quoted:

> 'Some of the locations we treated in a special way', says Jordan. 'For example, we removed half the panelling on the bridge where the prostitutes gather so that the lights of the city would shine through – and we lit fires beyond it. It was deliberately over the top, meant to be like hell.'[53]

This image of King's Cross flickers throughout the film, the girls on the meat-rack like lost souls, human urban debris.

This archetypal city story 'takes place' in a specifically 1980s London in which another familiar story is told: the old values of working-class criminality have been replaced by a greedier, more perverted exploitation. This story is carried by character types: the cockney, the black prostitute, the black pimp, the white master-criminal, the rich Arab. The film puns on a noir narrative with a central black protagonist in the role of the enigmatic woman. In this context, the film's central narrative thread is the relationship between George and Simone, in which each learns to see beyond each other's stereotypicality. Simone's dislike of George's vulgarity is matched with his prejudice towards her, and their identity as an unlikely couple is repeatedly stressed within the film by their physical difference, he, short, stout and white, she a 'thin black tart'. While critical commentary on the film has drawn attention to the way in which it is the sexuality of the black woman that is its object of investigation,[54] I want to inflect this argument and suggest that, in different ways, both George and Simone embody the West End and the journey 'up West'. I also want draw attention to these characters' embodiment of different temporalities of London as an imperial and post-imperial city, and their negotiation of coexistence in this city.

Mona Lisa opens with a 'landmark London' sequence at dawn: a long shot of a bridge over which a double-decker bus passes in the opposite direction to a walking man, and then a cut to a tracking shot of George walking over the bridge, clutching the paper package which signifies the belongings of a released prisoner. The view from Waterloo Bridge, with St Paul's in the background, is laid out for both the spectator and George, who looks around him as the

Simone (Cathy Tyson) and George (Bob Hoskins) in *Mona Lisa*

sky brightens and others pass him, seeing the river and the city beautiful in the morning light of this Waterloo sunrise. This mood continues as he sits on a bench in a park, the sun beginning to burn off the mist as he waits for it to be late enough to arrive. 'Outside' is manifestly strange to George, used to confinement and routine. But outside has also changed while he has been inside, the film is at pains to establish, and his south London street now includes black residents, perfectly at home, fixing cars, and asking him if he is going to clear up after he throws a dustbin in his doorstep row with his wife. George is abusive and out of control, nearly getting into a row with these neighbours. 'Where did they all come from?' he asks his friend Thomas, who is trying to calm him down and excuse him to the crowd. 'The man's upset, that's all, just upset.' In his 'just upset' lies the recognition that George's anger could be interpreted differently. 'They live here,' responds Thomas.

In a discussion of the opening of the film in terms of its representation of 'race', Lola Young draws attention to a brief encounter in the credit sequence when George does a double-take as he passes a black stranger. She comments, 'He has been in prison for seven years. Logically, having lived in a working class district of South London and been in prison, it is highly unlikely that George would be seeing a black person for the first time.' Young continues, 'The grossness of his initial reaction seems to be intended as a contrast with his attitude to Simone as the narrative develops.'[55] She is surely right about the establishment of this contrast. But I want to spend a moment on her argument and the question of the 'seven years' of George's absence in relation to images of London. My question is what is served, or enabled, by what I agree is the anachronistic suggestion that Commonwealth immigration took place in a distinctive and noticeable fashion only recently to the film's present day?[56] The revelation of the length of George's prison term is not made until after this initial sequence. Taken on its own terms, the opening sequence suggests that George has been away for much longer, although it would have to have been very long indeed, as Young points out, for him to be surprised at seeing black people in London. The revelation that it is only seven years is a shock after this opening. But by bringing together these two different times rather anachronistically, the film can use the also rather anachronistic figure of the cockney more straightforwardly than would otherwise be possible. Here, I need to take a detour through Gareth Stedman-Jones's influential analysis of the discursive history of the cockney.[57] His study traces the meanings, temporality and topography of the cockney, concluding that the end of Empire also led to the end of the 'cockney'. He suggests that one of the reasons 'why the word cannot now be employed without embarrassment or anxiety' is that 'The "cockney" has no legitimate place in the declassed and multi-racial society that post-imperial Britain has officially become.'[58] In *Mona Lisa*, the device of the very long seven years permits George both to notice difference, but to do so in what is proposed – initially through Thomas's intervention 'he's just upset' – in an 'innocently' racist manner. George can be a cockney, can embody a certain taken-for-granted imperial sensibility, without, in Stedman-Jones's terms, 'embarrassment or anxiety' because his prison term, the seven years that have lasted from the late 1940s to Mrs Thatcher's Britain, has kept him away from negotiations of citizenship in post-imperial London.

The most widely circulated images from the film show Simone with her body swathed in a long, expensive grey coat.[59] Underneath the coat she wears her working clothes: silk under-wear. Thin and tall, in high heels, with her hair swept up, Simone possesses a certain hauteur, wrapped in her luxurious coat, as she walks through the lobbies of West End hotels, daring the managers to challenge her. To work for Simone successfully, to pass as a guest in the lobbies of the West End hotels in which he waits for her, George too must pay attention to his appearance. Simone, rather than George, understands that George's job as her chauffeur requires him to masquerade successfully as accustomed to these hotels. He must go 'up West' sartorially, so that he looks as if he belongs there, rather than as if he has just come from over the river. George's sartorial journey demonstrates the way in which going 'up West' can be a class journey as well as a geographical one, a journey involving costume, deportment and etiquette, and is dealt with by the film in some detail. On his first trip to meet Simone the hotel doorman glances over George's outfit with an undisguised contempt that finishes on his shoes. When George enters hotels at the beginning of the film, he doesn't understand how to order drinks, or how and when to tip. Conscious that he is out of place, George is easily offended and irascible, drawing attention to himself rather than blending in. Simone gives him money to buy clothes, which he is reluctant to accept. 'You don't even like me,' he protests. 'I can claim it,' she replies, unanswerably. The outfit he chooses would appear like revenge were he not so simply proud of his shiny orangey leather blouson jacket, tropical print shirt and pale trousers. George's purchased outfit is at the top end of his class taste code: it is loud, casual, flamboyant and, to Simone's ridicule, also includes a medallion. George looks like a pimp who is doing well out of his business.

Simone's response, which marks a mellowing in their relationship, is to take George shopping to a men's outfitters in the Burlington Arcade: classic posh West End. This is the moment – in daylight, in the Burlington Arcade – that the film offers a London that is both post-imperial and Thatcherite. An exclusive West End shop is patronised by a black prostitute and her white petty criminal minder. The flat lighting of the scene, its difference from the expressionist noir city that surrounds it in the film, confirms its ordinariness. George is at first mystified by their purpose in the shop, evidently prepared to have his sexual horizons further broadened by the tastes of Simone's clients, but is without hesitation in his appreciation of the quality of the merchandise, 'Pure silk, that is', 'classy'. Simone selects an outfit which turns out to be for him: discreet, formal and expensive. She admires an overcoat while he is changing into the suit, and drapes it round his shoulders with some tenderness, and appreciation of what she has bought, as he looks in the mirror. While short, white, fat George may still *be* 'cheap', the outfit purchased for him by the 'lady' Simone makes him look much classier. The film reverses the 'tart made good' trope by showing Simone dress George so that he too will fit in the West End. And George is shown learning the class lesson that it is not ostentatious display, but instead discreet quality, that will allow him to pass in this version of the West End.

Simone's transformation of George is just one instance of the film's repeated concern with appearances. Simone describes the pimp Anderson as 'flash cars and paraffin heaters', whereas she herself, for much of the film, wears a cashmere coat over underwear. She may now work the West End hotels, but this luxury is rendered tawdry through George's investigation of the lower depths of the sex trade on her behalf. This takes us, once again, to John Gross's perception of the proximity of 'Brewer Street and Burlington House', the doubling of vice and respectability, the bright and dark city, which structures so many imaginations of the West End. The luxury hotels, where even the waiters are snooty, are only the cashmere coat of a world that runs on the selling of young girls, the blackmailing of clients – and Simone's bondage wear. It is this dark West End George explores when he enters into a hellish pilgrimage through 'Brewer Street', a cinematically familiar Soho of neon lights, bead curtains, and promises of 'Girls, Girls, Girls'. This iconographic familiarity, the trip to the display of the sexual, is, however, given an investigative narrative motivation; because George is only there on behalf of someone else, these sights can be scrutinised without moral contamination. They are presented through a semi-backstage *mise en scène* which renders the attractions seedy and emphasises the labours of the sex industry workers. Display and revelation. Thus George's scrutiny of a peep show is filmed from the dancer's side of the apertures, and, after paying for the compulsory bottle of champagne, in a move that confirms both location and character, George tries to wangle a cup of tea out of one of the dismissive strippers. While other punters might just see the show, George turns up when the door handles are being sprayed with disinfectant.

The *mise en scène* of George's Soho quest, its backstage, out-of-hours quality, and the use of angles and points of view that are not those of the punter, is a familiar cinematic strategy to render the treatment of performances (theatrical, musical, sexual) as both display and revelation. George's Soho appals and shocks him: but we still get to see the displays. George goes up West, and George learns what lies behind its attractions. His innocence is our passport.

This ambivalence, this alibied voyeurism, is absent from a later, 1997 version of the Soho 'up West' trope, in *Nil By Mouth*, when Raymond, Jamie and Billy take a trip to Soho quite early in the film, before the relentless damage to the family of alcoholism and drug addiction have become fully apparent (see Chapter 2). Soho is treated differently here, without the distancing of George's awkwardness, but Soho too is different after lap-dancing has become mainstream. They are lads on a night out: spruced up and coked up, leaving Val, Raymond's wife, behind, stuck in the flat with their daughter. It is the men's prerogative to take their pleasure where they wish, and this turns out to be Soho, with an establishing shot of the Piccadilly Circus neon display and Tony Christie singing 'Las Vegas' as the camera cuts to the neon hoarding of a strip joint called 'Las Vegas' advertising 'Adult Entertainment'. The three men wander the streets, half-purposeful, in search of pleasure, passing Japanese tourists, gaming arcades and signs for 'sexy girls'. The space of Soho is not directionally or geographically coherent. Instead, it is a temporal space: time off. But it is also a gendered cinematic space of sensation and attractions. The woman left behind in the home, drab, naturalist, fully clothed Val, is the counterpoint to writhing, nearly naked, anonymous, glittery body parts. Dark neon-lit Soho is a space of display for masculine pleasures.[60] And partly what is attractive is the excessive availability of different modes of consumption. The spatial incoherence is necessary to construct the multiplicity of choices. Everywhere the men look is an invitation.

In a gaming arcade, the men become very involved in a racing game in which each player has a mechanical camel mounted by an Arab. Their concentration on the game is intense. They are more focused than we have seen them before. The surrealism of the little camels is both noted and ignored by the camera movement – as with *Nice Time*, the icons of popular culture are, for a moment, isolated from their context and presented as instances of what Peter Wollen, in a discussion of settings such as amusement arcades and fairgrounds, has called 'the vernacular fantastic'.[61] 'Come on, my son,' shouts Jamie at his little camel, and the camera pauses on the exotic brightly coloured models of Arab 'sheikhs' on camels. In a strip joint, they move along with the women, ogling and fondling them, and above all, signalling to each other what a good time they are having. And all the time they are drinking, have taken cocaine and are smoking joints in the car. Their bodies too are sites of excessive merchandising.

This trip to Soho, the only time when any characters are filmed outside south London, works to confirm the dreariness of Deptford in the manner I have suggested is characteristic of the trip 'up West'. However, its use of close-up, and the extreme proximity of the men's faces to the womens' naked bodies in the club scenes, also serves as a reminder of the way in which Soho as a cinematic location is partly produced through changing regimes of film censorship. The significant liberalisation of British cinema censorship regulation since the 1960s, particularly in relation to sex, is an important determinant in understanding the difference between the cinematic Sohos of, say, *Noose* in 1948, *Peeping Tom* in 1960, *The Spy Who Came in from the Cold* in 1965 and that of *Mona Lisa* and *Nil By Mouth*, while there have also been very substantial shifts in the modes and sites of the commodification of sex in the period.[62] In *Nil By Mouth*, though, while Soho does still serve as the site of the cinematic 'city of attractions', this sequence also shows something of an erosion of its specialness as a place of pleasure by the end of the twentieth century. For the men carry their heady, pleasure-seeking disorientation with them; they inhabit their daily lives of 'not Soho' in the same way as they inhabit Soho: out of their heads. The men have been shown lurching their sweaty way through the pleasures of the night-time streets. But Soho and home are blurred together in the same haze of drink and drugs. Raymond and Billy are never straight. None of the men work. They are permanently 'up West'.

The Global West End: The Film Star and the Refugee

In the last section of the chapter, I look at two cinematic West Ends from the turn of the twentieth century in *Notting Hill* and *Dirty Pretty Things*. In contrast to the journey up West in *Nil By Mouth*, which juxtaposes blurry naturalist south London with a gaudy sleazy Soho, I want to draw attention to the way in which the clean, attractive London of romantic comedy in *Notting Hill* also owes something to an opposition between its 'village of Notting Hill' and the West End, although here, the West End is mainly the luxury hotels suitable for a major US movie star. The chapter concludes with an analysis of the London of *Dirty Pretty Things*, which offers a generically contrasted view of the London luxury hotel trade, and explicitly engages with London as a city of migrants.[63] The trope of the trip up West, with its geographies of desire and aspiration, and its relation to the city of attractions and the trip to the cinema, are still discernible in each film, but my choice to discuss *Dirty Pretty Things* involves what could be seen as a sleight of hand, whereby the local London journey to the West End becomes an international journey to a city in the West. The motivation for this move will, I hope, be made clear in what follows.

These films are considered together because each registers a sense of London, at the end of the twentieth century, as a global city. While there is an international aspect to the West End in each of the other films discussed in this chapter, it has been the genealogy of Empire that has been the most discernible thread of internationalism in London. In *Spring in Park Lane* Judy's uncle made his money mining in South Africa. The London George finds when he comes out of prison in *Mona Lisa* is one in which he must learn about the end of Empire. 'Global London', or London as 'world city', implies a different mode of internationalism, a shift traced indicatively by Anthony D. King in his analysis of the shifting frequency of terms such as 'Empire', 'International', 'Euro-', 'World' and 'Global' in the names of organisations listed in the London directories between 1920 and 1987.[64] I am not suggesting that suddenly, at the end of the twentieth century, London in the cinema has 'gone global', but I am proposing that the complex debate about how to understand what are called 'global' or 'world' cities of the late twentieth century, in which London figures repeatedly as a significant example, has some relevance to cinematic London, and that one way of thinking of London in the cinema of the 1990s is as a 'global' city.[65] So what follows is informed, on the one hand, by the claim that London, in the latter part of the twentieth century, because of the heritage of Empire, may have become *differently* rather than *more* international and, on the other, that some of the characteristics of what is being debated as 'the global city' are very suggestive in an approach to some of the London-set films of the turn of the twentieth century.

The first aspect of the characterisation of the global city that is relevant concerns shifts in what I will call the 'representational terrain' of the city. Before I briefly summarise these tendencies, I must stress that my argument is not that changes in patterns of employment, investment, industry, infrastructure and residence in London find direct expression or reflection in the cinema; it is that these changes, attested to by a range of sources, although frequently interpreted and evaluated differently, provide some of the imaginative contours and discursive contexts for the apprehension, as plausible, of the cinematic city in *Notting Hill* and *Dirty Pretty Things*. My concern here is not to compare generically different films in terms of the truth of their representation of London (a truth determined extra-textually by reference to a real of the global economic), a project which all too often, tautologically, concludes that romantic comedy is less realistic than social realism, but to pay attention to the co-existence of such dramatically different cinematic Londons. The bright and dark Londons of these fin-de-siècle films can be seen in relation to a long tradition of cinematic West Ends which I have begun to sketch in this chapter. Both the continuities, and the differences, are significant.

There are three ways in which notions of the global city are suggestive. First, all investigations of London as global city, as well as all histories of London in the later twentieth century, see it as characterised by a continuing expansion in financial and associated service industries, and the decline in manufacturing and light industry. New structures of economic activity have brought about changes in the organisation of work and a shift to increased polarisation in income and occupational distribution. Sassen points out that jobs in what she calls the 'producer services' are concentrated at the very top and bottom of the scale, rather than the wider distribution across 'the middle' characteristic of manufacturing.[66] This social polarisation is accentuated by the demands for low-wage jobs to support the high-income gentrification, both residential and commercial, of the spaces occupied by highly paid workers. Exaggeratedly, this could be translated into a city peopled by fund managers and cleaners, in some cases, international executives and illegal immigrants – a very different social repertoire to that of post-war London. Banally, in the registers of everyday life, these changes are experienced through continuing house-price inflation and the 'pricing-out' of key workers and most young people from house purchase in the capital. I will explore below whether these social changes consequent upon the increased dominance of international capital in the city might render particular generic modes and character types, such as the melodramatic, increasingly attractive to film-makers.

Second, as will be discussed in more detail in Chapter 7 in relation to the transformation of the London Docks into Dockland, the material fabric of the city has, since the 1980s, undergone changes which are at least as significant to its look as the post-1957 office-building boom.[67] These have significantly affected the London skyline – important in the cinema – so that previous landmarks such as St Paul's are now dwarfed by buildings like the Swiss Re Building (the Gherkin) and No. 1 Canada Square.[68] These buildings, and others such as the Lloyd's Building, London Bridge City, the stations of the Jubilee Line extension – most of which are significantly east of the West End, and some of which also mark the 'opening-up' of the South Bank – could be seen, along with attractions such as Tate Modern and the Millenium Wheel, as the landmarks of London as a global city.[69] That is, London as a global city draws on a slightly different iconographic landmark repertoire while also rearticulating familiar landmarks such as Tower Bridge, red buses or the Ritz in Piccadilly.

Finally, there is the role of cinema itself within the constitution of the global city, and the contribution of films such as *Four Weddings and a Funeral* (1994), *Sliding Doors* (1997), *Notting Hill, Love Actually* (2003), *Closer* (2004), *Wimbledon* (2004) and *Match Point* (2005), with their judicious mixes of British and American casting and finance, in creating the image of London as a world city.[70] In this context, David Martin-Jones's analysis of the London of *Sliding Doors* should be noted. His argument is that the split-time narrative of *Sliding Doors*, with its doubled Gwyneth Paltrow roles, shows different options for living in a global city, one right, one wrong. He suggests that in the 'right' life,

> the film goes out of its way to choose locations that demonstrate the overhaul that occurred in London during the 1980s and 90s. From its expensive restaurants to its converted waterfront warehouse bars, the film reassures the international viewer, there are as many amenities here as can be found in any other global city.[71]

Not dissimilar to Robert Murphy's notion of London as a 'city of delight' in 1990s romantic comedies,[72] Martin-Jones's argument begins to recast the city of attractions into a global frame. This attention to a global frame is also pursued by Paul Dave in his 'tracking of the contemporary metamorphoses of capitalism' in an analysis which characterises films such as *Notting Hill* as involving 'an *idyllic* denial of the logic of capitalism as a social form'.[73] It is not so much 'the West End' that constitutes the city of attractions in these films, but a more radically post-geographical, eclectic city in which elements of the West End (like the theatre or opera) are combined with the authenticity of street markets and subcultural sites to make a kind of 'ancient and modern' London, with, as we see in *Closer*, a combination of twenty-first-century modern (offices, converted warehouse apartments) and unique, place-specific vintage features, such as the memorials in Postman's Park.[74] However, this version of the city of attractions also has its dark side, and it is this juxtaposition, which is again cross-generic, that the final section of the chapter explores.

Notting Hill is Working Title's extremely successful follow-up to *Four Weddings and a Funeral*, which was also written by Richard Curtis and produced by Duncan Kenworthy. The plot of the film, the romance between someone who lives in Notting Hill and a film star who lives in Beverly Hills, explicitly addresses both the film's own conditions of production and a series of issues about national cinemas, fame, and types of film-making. It is a film which has spawned a 'Rough Guide' to Notting Hill Gate, and some quite angry reviews about the way in which the area is represented. I wish to consider the way in which the film's central conceit, *rus in urbe* (the country in the city), is developed through the metaphor of Notting Hill as a village in contrast to the West End, and the type of space that the West End is in this film.

The opening titles of *Notting Hill* juxtapose the two worlds of the film. First, a montage of images which establish the beauty and fame of the Hollywood star, Anna Scott (Julia Roberts), to the strains of Charles Aznavour's 'She'.[75] At photo-shoots, on film sets, at press conferences, on red carpets: there is a multitude of images of Anna Scott breaking into her wide smile. She is everywhere, but nowhere in particular, other than movie-land, a location confirmed by a repeated camera movement from close-up outwards. It seems as if the movement will locate her, but, each time, the location of the image turns out to be a magazine cover. The film's other world is introduced by the voice-over narration of William Thacker (Hugh Grant) as he walks down Portobello Road, telling the audience conversationally about the 'small village' in the centre of London where he lives. William's commentary also introduces one of the tones of the film, a wry self-deprecation which underplays both inheritance and effort ('a lot of friends have ended up here', 'a house I bought with my wife before she left me for a man who looked like Harrison Ford'). William's London, his local sense of place, is counter-posed to Anna's global fame, although the film is very clear to demonstrate, in these opening moments, that where William lives is hospitable to American visitors. Thus two of the features of his locality use icons of US popular culture: the radical hairdressers 'where everyone ends up looking like the cookie monster', and as an example of 'not so genuine' antiques, stained-glass panels of Beavis and Butthead. Even at this introductory moment of 'locality', William's world is penetrated by US media characters, and William's commentary, which makes no comment on the origin of these characters, involves a disavowal that lies at the heart of the film. Phillip Drummond describes the juxtaposition of these two worlds of the film as follows:

> For William, London is a city of particulars, the affectionately rendered district favoured by the title of the film. His bookshop is an emblem of an older, disappearing form of local business, even if its speciality – travel books – points to the wider world of modern, international travel. It is into this locality that Anna intrudes – apparently in search of a travel guide to Turkey, but, in truth, in pursuit of the very 'hereness' offered by the 'world' of William's Notting Hill.[76]

The romance of the film is pursued across these two different worlds. To see William, Anna must enter the local, meet his friends, use his un-luxurious bathroom, and, late in the film, try to convince him that she is 'just a girl'. To see Anna, William must go up to the West End, where he must enter the world of luxury hotels (the Ritz and the Savoy), false names (Anna always travels as a cartoon character), film publicity, press conferences and Anna's abominable Hollywood actor-boyfriend (William Baldwin). The West End in this film is landmark London, but there is no need for Tower Bridge or Piccadilly Circus to mark arrival: William can take a red double-decker bus to the Ritz he lives so close. William does not so much go to the West End to go to the cinema: he goes to the West End to fall in love with a film star, and then subsequently must go to the cinema to trace her career and to torment his broken heart. However, if the West End, with its demands that William must always pretend to be someone else – a reporter, a waiter – to remain in Anna's presence, is identified with international celebrity space, from which Anna, to some extent, seeks an escape, its opposite, William's Notting Hill, is not as innocent as first seems. Indeed, the process of the film could be seen as a recruitment of Notting Hill, signified by Portobello Road, into landmark London, rather in the manner of a boutique hotel. As most commentators note, the crucial space here is the private Notting Hill communal garden into which Anna first coaxes William on their first date, and in which we see them get married and then passing time in her pregnancy at the end of the film. When they first come across the garden, with its discreet locked gate, Anna needs to have its design principle explained to her. Although William doesn't put it like this, describing the garden and its surrounding houses as being like a village, it is a gated community without the grossness of gates, for the houses of the Ladbroke Estate themselves form the boundaries of the gardens, which are enclosed between the crescents and terraces. While Anna's move, at the end of the film, may be from international movie space to London, William's move is from his narrow house with a roof terrace to legitimate occupation of this private garden.

The setting of *Notting Hill* has attracted more critical attention than is often the case with romantic comedy because its title promises an engagement with the former rather rackety area of west London, North Kensington, which is the poorest part of the Royal Borough of Kensington and Chelsea. *Pressure* (1974) and *Performance* (1970) were both set in Notting Hill. Bordering Kensington Gardens (Diana-land – part of Hyde Park) in the south – and on the hill – North Kensington stretches down northwards into the lowlands of the historically poorer Notting Dale. North Kensington has a long history of social deprivation and unrest, and parts of the area have always seen their rather grand nineteenth-century housing devoted to multi-occupancy rented tenancy. The Ladbroke Estate, the early Victorian development of crescents and squares with privately accessed communal gardens, which is an important location of the film, was designed with barrier crescents of houses to the north-west to mini-mise communication with the poorer areas.[77] Portobello Road, imaged as the heart of the film's London, runs from the posh white antiquey end right down into the Dale of what has historically been one of the 'front lines' of British black communities. Notting Hill was the site of the Rachman scandal (following the decontrol of private rents in 1957), involving extortion and the threatening of private tenants, and leading eventually to increased legal protection for tenants. It was to North Kensington that Irish and then Commonwealth immigrants came in search of work in the last century, and, as discussed in the last chapter, Notting Hill has been the setting for significant works about the West Indian and British black experience. The Notting Hill Carnival, a West London version of Caribbean carnival, which attracts about a million revellers to the streets of Notting Hill every August, figures in films from the Spanish *El efecto Mariposa* (1995) to the avant-garde British short *Territories* (1984).

In this context, even the most conservative of British film reviewers commented that there was something funny about a Notting Hill with no black people. While most of Notting Hill is now so expensive that only the rich can afford to live there, there is a provoca-tion in the way in which the film represents 'this small village in the middle of the city'. This provocation is accentuated by its title with its claim to say something about a part of London that has been extremely significant both historically and cinematically in the devel-opment and representation of British black cultures. However, this representational choice is only an aspect of the film's contribution to the well-documented phenomenon of gentri-fication. Thus, rather than pursue an argument about whether Notting Hill is or isn't like this, my question is 'what does this representation of Notting Hill do?' I think what it does, in the very moment of the erasure of the history of North Kensington, is add a formerly 'edgy' area to the repertoire of the city of attractions. Just like the planners of the Ladbroke

Estate where it is set, the film opens access in the south-east, to Piccadilly and the Strand, but otherwise excludes the history and the cinehistory of the area. In doing this, the film uses the now familiar opposition between the glitter of the West End and the authenticity of the local, but everyone concerned has moved up several income brackets. The West End is recruited to international celebrity space, manifest primarily as the Ritz and the Savoy, with a quick glimpse of Trafalgar Square and the National Gallery, while the local is home to lawyers, stockbrokers and architects-turned-restaurateurs. The much noted lack of success of William's friends should be seen as a trope of 'the local': a manifestation of authentic Britishness, rather than an indication of their actual financial position. Nick James suggests that Curtis and Kenworthy are 'in some respects telling the story of the second phase of gentrification, of the gradual stop-start take-over of a street economy by restaurants and estate agents'.[78] Here, Robert Murphy's grouping of the film with other London-set romantic comedies of the 1990s such as *Sliding Doors, Jack and Sarah* (1995) and *Martha – Meet Frank, Daniel and Laurence* (1998), which he describes as showing 'life in Britain as exciting, glamorous and full of romantic possibilities', is useful, in that it draws attention to the generic qualities of the film.[79] Murphy considers these films as 'urban fairytales' of post-Thatcher Britain, suggesting that they express a yearning for social cohesion and harmony. Paul Dave's judgment is rather harsher. He analyses the world of *Notting Hill* using the Bakhtinian concept of the 'chronotope' (a narrative time and place that has particular features, characters and in which certain events take place), suggesting that it is the 'idyllic' chronotope that governs the world of Notting Hill. This chronotope is formed within the tradition of the urban pastoral, and Dave emphasises the significance of the 'littleness' of the narrative world of the film. However, he points to the way in which the film, in its repeated, incidental invocation of trauma and difficulty outside the 'little world' of the film, such as 'third world debt', displays anxiety about its privilege, which he argues functions to demonstrate the 'charitable subjectivity' of its inhabitants.[80]

All commentators on this film agree on the privilege of the world depicted, while the critical disdain it has attracted recalls the response to *Spring in Park Lane*, the film with which this chapter commenced. The move from Mayfair to Notting Hill, with the hero pretending to be a journalist instead of a footman, offer details in the changing modalities of post-war privilege and the plausible personae and locations of romantic comedy. There was no going 'up West' in *Spring in Park Lane* – although there was an outing into the popular culture of The Lyceum – because the wealthy characters already lived in the West End. In *Notting Hill*, the West End has gone 'celebrity global': it is occupied by movie stars and press conferences. The rich must cultivate their gardens further north-west. *Notting Hill* is an exemplary 'global London' text. The city that, in a complaint revisited in the film, can never provide iced water for Americans, is shown to offer the lure of the safe, secure village in the city. The quintessence of this safe, exclusive localness is the magical private garden in which the film concludes, and for which, as both Drummond and Dave discuss, the most interesting camerawork of the film – a long, elaborate crane shot – is reserved.

From *Notting Hill* to *Dirty Pretty Things* is a move from a London of luxury hotels, private gardens, charming street markets and 'boutique locality' to a London of rubbish-strewn alleys and 'non-places', although this too features a luxury hotel and a street market. *Dirty*

Pretty Things begins and ends in an airport, a location that is a classic example of Marc Augé's idea of the 'non-place'.[81] At the beginning of the film, its hero, Okwe (Chiwetel Ejiofor), is discreetly and illegally touting for minicab passengers, offering a ride back into London 'for those that the system has let down'. Okwe is an illegal immigrant from Nigeria, a former doctor, who is now holding down jobs as a minicab driver and a hotel receptionist, chewing khat constantly to keep awake. At the end of the film, in another airport, Okwe is seeing another immigrant, Senay (Audrey Tautou), off to New York, himself returning to Africa. She is Turkish and Muslim, and had come to Britain because she 'did not want to be like my mother'. She is leaving on a fake passport, which is part of the trade-off in the main plot of the film, which is a semi-thriller about the illegal trade in bodily organs. Okwe and Senay have fallen in love, but their insecure immigrant status forbids a romance, and by the end of the film it turns out that for both of them their stay in London, this dirty city where 'nothing works', was temporary.

Dirty Pretty Things was a return to a London topic for Stephen Frears, whose 1985 film *My Beautiful Laundrette* has proved such a significant south London story. If *My Beautiful Laundrette* imagined a post-imperial London in which the inheritors of Empire jostle up against each other, *Dirty Pretty Things*, made nearly twenty years later, brings to visibility the underside of life in London as a global city. *Dirty Pretty Things* is set mainly in the Baltic Hotel,[82] another non-place, with its marble and leather lobby, uniformed staff and its international display of clocks showing the time in New York, Delhi and Tokyo.[83] Hugo Luczyc-Wyhowski, production designer for this film (as well as *Laundrette*), and a significant shaper of cinematic Londons, has produced a dark London unified by an underlying thread of red – the colour of the hotel's carpets, of the fire in the hospital furnace and, finally, the blood of the organs and organ donors – which points to its nature. For this is an infernal London, an underworld, in which lost souls barter body parts and identities are traded. The expressionist use of red, as well as its hellish London, are among the several qualities that the film shares with *Mona Lisa*. Both films too are characterised by generic hybridity, with Nick Roddick describing *Dirty Pretty Things* as 'a black comedy/thriller about a sinister illegal trade in organs, with a few flinch-inducing close-ups of the surgical procedures involved; and a touching but impossible love affair'.[84]

Dirty Pretty Things confirms that a new character has appeared in the London version of the ancient narrative of the arrival of the stranger in the city. This figure is the global migrant: the asylum seeker, the refugee, 'the illegal', and is found simultaneously in films such as Jasmin Dizdar's *Beautiful People* (1999), Michael Winterbottom's *In This World* (2002) and Pawel Pawlikowski's *The Last Resort* (2000).[85] That it is London in which this traveller arrives – and not Rome, or Barcelona, or Marseilles – is both significant and not significant. In the repertoire of the 'migrant cycle', emergent also in other European cinemas, London is a global city of the West. It is a destination of otherness, just as the West End has been in the history of British cinema. Here though, the journey is not from the suburbs, but from wars, persecution, drought, poverty and famine. There is a residual use of landmark imagery, but only to disavow it – yes this is London, but it's not like you see it in the movies. The global London of *Dirty Pretty Things* is a debased city of attractions, a twenty-first-century version of the dark London already discussed in various forms in this chapter.

My hypothesis here, which is generated from the encounter between accounts of the changing social structure of the global city and the fictional world of *Dirty Pretty Things*, is that the strong contrasts in play suggest a representational terrain which offers a predisposition towards the melodramatic. This would be reinforced if one of Sassen's arguments is correct, that, in the global cities themselves – as opposed to the former manufacturing cities – the 'downgrading of the manufacturing sector' is characterised by the energy of growth rather than the desperate, impotent lassitude of decline. This contrast would be helpful in an understanding of contrasts between cinematic Sheffield and London. The implications, for the representation of London, would be that we might expect a renewed vigour in the Victorian/Dickensian repertoire for the twenty-first century – what, to tinker with a phrase of Raphael Samuel's, could be thought of as Oliver Twist in Docklands,[86] or what John Orr has called 'a neo-Dickensian art of the city'.[87] Certainly, in *Dirty Pretty Things*, there is a Manichean simplicity of virtue and vice in relation to character. This simplicity of character in the film, its melodramatic clarity (Okwe, Senay and their friends are good; Sneaky, the buyers of organs and the immigration officers are bad), must be considered alongside its treatment of identity. In post-imperial London films, however angry they are, there is a narrative of entitlement, as discussed in Chapter 2. There is no narrative of entitlement in a 'global London' film such as *Dirty Pretty Things* and, in many ways, there is no coherent or progressive narrative of identity. Identity in these films is not an attribute from which characters start. It is something they have left behind – as Okwe says, of the events that brought him to Britain as an illegal immigrant, 'It is an African story'. Identity is left behind – but it is also bought, traded and assumed. It is fragmentary, transitory and pragmatic. Identity is a piece of paper with stamps, it is the inaccurate transliteration of a name by an immigration official, it is a passport traded for a kidney: identity here is a forgery, a commodity to be bought and sold – and the one thing these characters fear, above all, is recognition. This theme of the mobility of identity is introduced immediately the film opens as Okwe touts for custom at the airport, in which he declares himself, if not the person sent to meet particular travellers, willing to act in that capacity. When he arrives back at the cab office, he removes his cab-driver identity card, passing it on, with the car keys, to another driver. This man has a large gold crucifix hanging round his neck, and Okwe laughs at him, telling him to put it away as his name – pointing to the identity card – is now Mohammed. This first introduction to the flexibility of identities in this film is then followed by seeing Okwe, introduced as a cab-driver, asked to diagnose his employer's rash – as someone, apparently, with medical knowledge – and then go to work as the night receptionist in a hotel. Identities are both mobile and elusive – as Juliette (Sophie Okonedo), the woman who works the hotel as a call-girl, explains, 'I don't exist' – and subject to scrutiny, with one of the film's repeated tropes being the hotel night cleaners raising their faces to the CCTV cameras as they start their shifts.

If individual characters with origins in former British colonies, such as Tony and his family in *Pressure*, seek recognition as citizens 'living here', as Thomas tells George in *Mona Lisa*, in the global London of *Dirty Pretty Things*, recognition must be avoided at all costs.

In this film, Okwe knows that the game is up when he is hailed by his full name and quali-fications in the presence of witnesses. In the only use of the main hotel staircase in the film, Okwe is confronted by the Spanish manager of the hotel, who runs both the 'dirty' and the 'pretty' sides of the business, and the witnesses are otherwise unseen guests. To be known as who you are in this London is both dangerous and irrecoverable. As Guo Ki (Benedict Wong), Okwe's friend who works as a porter between the rubbish chutes, incinerator and dead bodies of a hospital morgue, observes, 'This is a weird city. I don't ask questions after eleven years here – and I'm a certified refugee. You're an illegal.'

These people without identities work, and struggle to evade detection, in a London of back doors, of fire escapes, of underground car parks – and of CCTV cameras. A London of 'out the back', 'round the side', 'in the basement' and 'through the shop'. Exterior shots are closely cropped and there is a rigorous exclusion of landmark imagery: a bus in a City street after Senay has lost her job providing an unaccustomed glimpse of a wider London, peopled by commuters and office workers. The only substantial, repeated London setting outside the hotel is Ridley Road Market, which is where Senay has her flat and Okwe buys his khat. Of this setting, Iain Sinclair observed, 'It may be fresher to dig out Ridley Road Market for your establishing shots, in preference to the derided red bus, Nelson's column, Tower Bridge routines. But is it any more honest?'[88] In the context of this book, the question is not one of honesty, but of effect. This choice of Ridley Road Market, a market with a very strong West Indian, African and Turkish presence, draws attention to the many migrations to London. It contextualises the stories of Senay and Okwe within many lives and many settlements in London. The liveliness of the market scenes also provides a contrast with some of the non-spaces of the film such as the hotel lobby and the car park, and works to confirm the film's potentially melodramatic spatiality, in which immigrant London is colourful and authentic, while the London 'above ground' of the rich is dead and empty. Apart from the Ridley Road scenes and one scene in Bunhill Fields, the spatial emphasis of the film is internal and arti-ficially lit, the entrails of the city: cab offices under railway bridges, hospital basements, the hotel kitchen, corridors and underground car park. It is a *mise en scène* suffused with rubbish and bodily organs and functions. Early in the film Okwe has to inspect the penises of his fellow workers, who have all caught venereal disease; the organ trade plot is inaugurated by his discovery of a human heart in a hotel lavatory; the suppurating flesh of a Somali who has sold a kidney is juxtaposed with, from their council flat in Tower Hamlets, the glittering river of Docklands far below. And in this filthy city, Okwe and Senay constantly struggle to keep clean. She bathes, bleaches her hair, attempts to defend her virginity; he demands soap in the cab office, uses a spotless handkerchief, irons his clothes and transforms a hotel bed-room into a sterile, white environment. The West End does not really exist for these charac-ters, for the rubbish and dirt of one global city is much like the rubbish and dirt of another. Their sights are set much lower than the dome of St Paul's or even Piccadilly Circus, on the endeavour to find a bed (not a couch, or a hospital trolley) to sleep on, and to assemble together hot water, soap and a towel for their own use.

Okwe (Chiwetel Ejiofor) in the non-place of the airport in *Dirty Pretty Things*

In juxtaposing the rather different films discussed in this chapter, I wanted to give a sense of the generic variety of the West End of London in the cinema, while also pointing to the persistence of certain sites and tropes. Although the expression 'going up West' has become dated, characters are still doing it in twenty-first-century movies, and personae too persist, so that the hostesses of *Night and the City* are replaced by the call-girls of *Mona Lisa* and *Dirty Pretty Things*. The glittery attractions of the West End of London – like those of comparable districts in many other world cities – still combine sex, cinema, sensation and consumption.

Evidently, there is a structural suggestion that *Spring in Park Lane* is to *Night and the City* as *Notting Hill* is to *Dirty Pretty Things*, with the rather more obscure couple of *Mona Lisa* and, say, *Howards End* (1991) making some of the same contrasts in the 1980s. This comparison is one that I wanted to suggest as an historical counter to the idea that it is only in the later period that strikingly different Londons are to be found in the cinema. There have always been generically contrasted Londons, although it is significant that romantic comedy Londons were hard to find in the 1980s. However, while suggesting that generically contrasted Londons are a feature of most periods of film-making, there are also aspects of each film's London that demand further investigation synchronically. The fantasies of, and aspirations to, class mobility in *Spring in Park Lane* do bear comparison with other Neagle/Wilcox films, but also with a range of other post-war films which are marked by the new experience of Britishness of the war years. This post-war vision of possibility is articulated across a range of texts of the period, as other scholars have investigated, and can be compared with what Paul Dave has identified as the 'retreat' of films from the end of the century like *Notting Hill*. Similarly, the particularity of immigrant 'low-life' in films such as *Dirty Pretty Things* or *Breaking and Entering* (2006) is quite different to the low-life of *Night and the City* or *It Always Rains on Sunday*, even though each, as I have suggested, recalls Victorian London. *Breaking and Entering*,

Anthony Minghella's film set in King's Cross, is, in this context, interesting for the way in which it combines these different pleasant and low-life Londons. The hell that is the King's Cross of *Mona Lisa* is, in *Breaking and Entering*, being redeveloped to provide a plausible meeting place for liberal gentrifiers and illegal immigrants, and their different generic worlds grind uncomfortably together in a 'neo-Dickensian' building site, as I discuss in the Afterword.

Notes

1. John Gross, *Double Thread: A Childhoood in Mile End and Beyond* (London: Vintage, 2002 [2001]), p. 137. The W. H. Auden poem he refers to is 'The Capital'.

2. The shooting script, which specifies two versions of this scene, suggests that for the American release, this implication of sex was removed, and the ring was given as a present for 'a good girl'. Shooting script, *It Always Rains on Sunday*, p. 15, A63. The script also suggests that there were plans to include a Soho scene in 'a little drinking club of the Rupert Street type' (p. 14).

3. David Hughes suggests that post-war, 'it was the spiv that stood for London … as flashy as neon, as exaggerated as the cut of their suits … against the scarred hungry background of a city down on its uppers'. 'The Spivs', in Michael Sissons and Philip French (eds), *The Age of Austerity, 1945–51* (Oxford: Oxford University Press, 1986), p. 77.

4. Christopher Breward compares the ways in which Mrs Miniver and Mrs Dalloway move through the West End in a discussion of the different fashionable wares available to suit the middle- and upper-middle-class woman, *Fashioning London* (Oxford: Berg, 2004), pp. 97–9; Mark Glancy discusses the class nuances of the Miniver family in his *When Hollywood Loved Britain* (Manchester: Manchester University Press, 1999), pp. 144–54.

5. The diversity of the cinematic West End as a marketplace of legitimate and illegitimate pleasures could be exemplified through many films, but junkie Louise's invitation to ten-year-old Paul in *Pure*, invoking the very skills of the Artful Dodger in *Oliver Twist*, must suffice to represent its persistence: 'Fancy going up West for a bit of late night dipping and lifting? Come on, I'll show you how to do it.'

6. Michael Bonavia, *London Before I Forget* (Upton-upon-Severn: Self-publishing Association, 1990), p. 71, cited by Erika Rappaport, *Shopping for Pleasure* (Princeton, NJ: Princeton University Press, 2000), p. 183.

7. 'City of attractions' is Ben Highmore's phrase from *Cityscapes* (Basingstoke: Palgrave Macmillan, 2005), p. 49. His account of its genealogy cites Tom Gunning's 1986 essay 'The cinema of attractions: early film, its spectator and the avant-garde', *Early Cinema: Space, Frame, Narrative* (London: BFI, 1990).

8. Asa Briggs, *Victorian Cities* (Harmondsworth: Penguin, 1990 [1963]), p. 314.

9. Franco Moretti prints a map of the locations for these novels written between 1812 and 1840, showing all locations west of Regent Street. He argues, 'in order to make London legible, silver-fork novels must amputate it, erecting a (symbolic) wall that cuts it in halves, from Regent's Park down to Piccadilly. And quite a few readers must have said to themselves: the West End, lovely. But the rest of London? What is there, what *kind of stories* are there, east of Regent Street?' *Atlas of the European Novel 1800–1900* (London: Verso, 1998), pp. 79–83. See also Christine Gledhill on the city geography of 1920s British cinema, *Reframing British Cinema 1918–28* (London: BFI, 2003), p. 24.

10. Ray Winstone recalls being taken to the cinema in the West End in the 1960s by his father: 'We went locally too, but the West End was Cinemascope, see. We saw *Zulu* there, *Lawrence of Arabia*, *How the West was Won* …' Brian Viner, 'The hard man: profile of Ray Winstone', *The Independent*, 6 May 2006, p. 40. Most research on British cinemagoing addresses the period preceding my study:

Jeffrey Richards and Dorothy Sheridan, *Mass Observation at the Movies* (London: Routledge, 1987); Annette Kuhn, *An Everyday Magic* (London: I. B. Tauris, 2002); but see also Christine Geraghty, *British Cinema in the Fifties* (London: Routledge, 2000), ch. 1, and Mark Jancovich and Lucy Faire, with Sarah Stubbings, *The Place of the Audience* (London: BFI, 2003).

11. See Wolfgang Schivelbusch, *Disenchanted Night* (Berkeley: University of California Press, 1995 [1983]), for a discussion of light in the city, particularly chapters on 'The Street' and 'Night Life', and Joachim Schlör, *Nights in the Big City* (London: Reaktion, 1998 [1991]), which uses a 1934 Felix Mann photograph of a policeman in Piccadilly Circus for the cover of the English edition.

12. Mark Adams, *Location London* (London: New Holland, 2003), pp. 33–4.

13. Listing shots of Piccadilly Circus in films is not my object here, but two contrasting usages, from different ends of the study period, which demonstrate the persistence of the site as landmark, are found in, first *The October Man* (Roy Ward Baker, 1947), in which the high point of the romance between the John Mills and Joan Greenwood characters is a trip to town in which, in a two-shot sequence, we see the couple in front of a Piccadilly Circus backdrop while he buys her flowers from another, now archaic, landmark, a London 'flowergirl', and then there is a cut to the gleaming aluminium of the statue of Eros. In the 2001 *Bridget Jones's Diary* (Sharon Maguire), one of the sites of Bridget's intimate thoughts is the display neon at Piccadilly Circus, which records her intake of alcohol and cigarettes. Its absence within landmark syntagms is also significant: thus the London sequence at the end of *Appointment in London* (1953) (an RAF war film which is dedicated to those who cannot, because of death, meet their 'appointment in London' to receive military honours), which finishes on Buckingham Palace, includes Admiralty Arch and the Mall, but not Piccadilly Circus, which was presumably thought to be tasteless for a film with such a sombre final dedication.

14. *Nice Time* was screened in the Third Free Cinema programme in May 1957. Christophe Dupin, *Free Cinema* booklet to accompany BFI 50th Anniversary DVD of *Nice Time* (London: BFI, 2006), booklet unpaginated [p. 16].

15. Ibid. [p. 18].

16. Nairn continues, 'But why: What makes it the focus of everyone's night out; why, when you stand under Eros, with the traffic swirling endlessly round, does it suddenly feel as though the whole enormous city is in the palm of your hand?' *Nairn's London* (Pleasantville, NY: The Akadine Press, 2002 [1966]), p. 75.

17. Frank Mort and Lynda Nead, 'Introduction', *New Formations* no. 39, 'Sexual Geographies', 1999, p. 5.

18. Soho in British films and television deserves a book of its own, and I can only touch on it here. John Oliver lists 137 feature films and television dramas with scenes set in Soho between 1905 and 2003 (John Oliver, 'Soho Feature Films and Television Fiction', unpublished document, BFI Cataloguing Departmen, n.d.). A sense of Soho's cinematic range can be seen by comparing Emeric Pressburger's *Miracle in Soho* (1957), which presents Soho as the 'continental quarter' of London, with his co-worker's *Peeping Tom* (Michael Powell, 1960), made three years later, which opens with the murder of a prostitute and a shop selling pornography. On Soho see Frank Mort, 'Mapping sexual London: The Wolfenden Committee on Homosexual Offences and Prostitution 1954–57', *New Formations* no. 37, Spring 1999, pp. 92–113, and John Eade, *Placing London* (Oxford and New York: Berghahn, 2000), pp. 49–84.

19. This structure is frequently manifest in sets, such as the concealed door in the post-Wolfenden *Passport to Shame* (1959), which separates the stucco town house from the whore house, or the town house/mews house pairing of *The Informers* (1963).

20. In contrast to the Loach/Garnett version, in which there is no inaugural journey over the bridge, and the class contrasts are not emphasised as a matter of gazing at the other. See Jacob Leigh, *The Cinema of Ken Loach* (London: Wallflower Press, 2002), pp. 26–38.

21. See Rachel Moseley, *Growing Up with Audrey Hepburn* (Manchester: Manchester University Press, 2002), for discussion of the class mobility of *My Fair Lady*, particularly pp. 139–45.

22. Phil Wickham and Matt Ker have recently suggested that it is actually the most successful British film of all time, '*Spring in Park Lane*', in Ryan Gilbey (ed.), *The Ultimate Film* (London: BFI, 2005), pp. 24–9 (no author specified for entry).

23. Both discussed by John Hill in his *British Cinema in the 1980s* (Oxford: Clarendon Press, 1999).

24. Campbell Dixon, 'Mr Wilcox's best film', *Daily Telegraph*, 29 March 1948, n.p.

25. Geoffrey MacNab, *Searching for Stars* (London: Cassell, 2000), p. 73.

26. David Thomson, *A Biographical Dictionary of Cinema* (London: Secker and Warburg, 1980 [1975]), p. 429, cited by Andy Medhurst in 'Myths of consensus and fables of escape', in Jim Fyrth (ed.), *Labour's Promised Land* (London: Lawrence and Wishart, 1995), p. 299.

27. C. A. Lejeune, Review of *Spring in Park Lane*, 28 March 1948, in Anthony Lejeune (ed.), *The C. A. Lejeune Film Reader* (Manchester: Carcanet, 1991), p. 226.

28. Sarah Street, *British National Cinema* (London: Routledge, 1997), pp. 124–34.

29. Ibid., p. 134.

30. 'Some may still sigh over the childishness of the great British public whose proletarianized soul still hankers, apparently, after a peer in the pantry, his marquis brother at the ancestral lettuce-patch and a Cinderella who carefully both earns and inherits her privileged position in Park Lane as niece and secretary to that wealthy art collector', *Time and Tide*, 3 April 1948, n.p.

31. Most historians of British cinema prefer to concentrate on Neagle's very successful 1930s historical films such as *Nell Gwyn* (1934) and *Victoria the Great* (1938), but see MacNab, *Searching for Stars*, pp. 67–73; Marcia Landy, *British Genres* (Princeton, NJ: Princeton University Press, 1991), pp. 69–70, 313, and Street, *British National Cinema*.

32. Richard Winnington, '"Coo", said the Duchess', *News Chronicle*, 27 March 1948.

33. Sue Harper claims, 'It purported to be about cross-class marriage, but was in fact about the difficulties of the post-war settlement', *Women in British Cinema* (London: Continuum, 2000), p. 55.

34. Leonard Mosley, 'Soft lights in a harsh world', *Daily Express*, 28 March 1948, n.p.

35. Robert Murphy, 'Citylife: urban fairytales in late 90s British cinema', in Robert Murphy (ed.), *The British Cinema Book* (London: BFI, 2001), p. 296.

36. Thomson, *A Biographical Dictionary of Cinema*, p. 430.

37. Separate versions were made for US and British markets. Sue Harper and Vincent Porter, *British Cinema of the 1950s* (Oxford: Oxford University Press, 2003), p. 124. I have worked with the US version throughout, which is understood to be closer to Dassin's preferences. Dassin quotes Zanuck on the beginning of the project: 'Get out. Get out fast. Here's a book. You're going to London. Get a screenplay as fast as you can, and start shooting the most expensive scenes. Then they might let you finish' in '"I'll always be an American": Jules Dassin interviewed', *Film Comment*, November–December 1996, p. 40. The 2005 Criterion Collection DVD of *Night and the City* provides documentation of the film's production and versions, although some of its geography is dodgy. Thanks to Tom Ryall for recommending it.

38. Robert Murphy, *Realism and Tinsel* (London: Routledge, 1989), p. 163. For example, Audrey Leonard observed that 'there is too much London and too little story' ('London is not as bad as this', *Sunday*

Graphic, 18 June 1950, n.p.), while the review in the *Sunday Chronicle* asks of the Richard Widmark character, 'Can his hell, perhaps, be Jules Dassin's London, which is certainly not the London which belongs to you and me?' (P.D., 18 June 1950, n.p.). Roy Nash's review in the *Star* is headed, 'This film insults London' (13 June 1950, n.p.), while the *Daily Herald* review commences, 'Poor London. She suffered from a bombing and now she suffers from a gross misunderstanding. In one way the latter is worse' (P.H., 16 June 1950, n.p.)

39. Tom Ryall, 'American Runaway Productions', paper given at the University of Warwick, 18 January 2006.

40. Colin McArthur, *Underworld USA* (London: Secker and Warburg, 1972), p. 98.

41. Alain Silver and James Ursini (eds), *Film Noir Reader* (New York: Limelight, 1996 [1970]), reprints many of the defining articles in the constitution of the category film noir. See also E. Ann Kaplan, *Women and Film Noir* (London: BFI, 1998 [1978]); Frank Krutnik, *In a Lonely Street* (London: Routledge, 1991); Ian Cameron (ed.), *The Movie Book of Film Noir* (London: Studio Vista, 1992); Joan Copjec (ed.), *Shades of Noir* (London: Verso, 1993); and *Iris: European Precursors of Film Noir* no. 21, Spring 1996.

42. See, for example, Paula Rabinowitz, *Black and White Noir* (New York: Columbia University Press, 2002), which 'interrogates *noir* sensibility', p. xi.

43. James Naremore, *More than Night* (Berkeley and Los Angeles: University of California Press, 1998). See also Robert Murphy, 'Dark shadows around Pinewood and Ealing', for an argument for historical specificity in relation to British film noir, *Film International* vol. 2 no. 7, January 2004, pp. 29–35.

44. Edward Dimendberg, *Film Noir and the Spaces of Modernity* (Cambridge, MA: Harvard University Press, 2004), p. 9.

45. Murphy, *Realism and Tinsel*, pp. 163–4.

46. There is a developing debate about film noir in British cinema. See Raymond Durgnat, *A Mirror for England* (London: Faber and Faber, 1970), and 'Some lines of inquiry into post-war British crimes', in Robert Murphy (ed.), *The British Cinema Book* (London: BFI, 1997 [2001]), pp. 135–45; William Everson, 'British film noir', *Films in Review* vol. 38 no. 5, 1987, pp. 285–9 and vol. 38 no. 6, 1987, pp. 341–7; Raphael Samuel, *Theatres of Memory* (London: Verso, 1994), part VI; Laurence Miller, 'Evidence for a British film noir cycle', in Wheeler Winston Dixon, *Reviewing British Cinema 1990–1992* (Albany: State University of New York Press, 1994); Steve Chibnall and Robert Murphy (eds), *British Crime Cinema* (London: Routledge, 1999); Murphy, 'Dark shadows' and *Shadows are my Friends: British Film Noir* (forthcoming, BFI). Andrew Spicer, *Film Noir* (Harlow: Longman, 2002), provides a bibliography of the debate in relation to British cinema (and a filmography), which is indicative of the expansion of the field.

47. It is the US version that finishes most brutally with Fabian's death. In the British version, Mary is not left without comfort as her long-term admirer is present at the end.

48. A debate partly initiated by Norman Stone in 1988 with his *Sunday Times* article, 'Through a lens darkly', 10 January 1988, C1–2, in which he attacked six recent British films: *My Beautiful Laundrette*, *The Last of England, Empire State, Eat the Rich, Business as Usual* and *Sammy and Rosie Get Laid* (not *Mona Lisa*), calling them, among many other insults, 'rancidly provincial' (C2). *Business as Usual* was set in Liverpool. See also Hanif Kureishi, 'England, bloody England', *The Guardian*, 15 January 1988, p. 19, and Kobena Mercer, *Welcome to the Jungle* (London: Routledge, 1994). See Hill, *British Cinema in the 1980s*, ch. 7, for further discussion of what he calls 'the state of the nation' films.

49. Peter Ackroyd, 'London pride', *The Spectator*, 13 September 1986, p. 37. See also, for example, Adam Mars-Jones's review, *New Statesman*, 12 September 1986, pp. 23–4, and Charles Clover's 'British brilliance', *Daily Telegraph*, 5 September 1986, p. 14.

50. For those familiar with Trinder in films like *The Foreman Went to France* (1942) and *The Bells Go Down* (1943), Ackroyd also seems to be suggesting that the Londoner has a sort of naive innocence, which is certainly an attribute of Hoskins in this film.

51. The physical similarity between George's daughter and the young women he encounters in his quest is noted by several critics: Lola Young, *Fear of the Dark* (London: Routledge, 1996), pp. 170–1; Joy James, 'Black femmes fatales and sexual abuse in progressive "white" cinema: Neil Jordan's *Mona Lisa* and *The Crying Game*', *Camera Obscura* no. 36, September 1995, pp. 33–47. As George tells Simone, on one of their King's Cross expeditions, 'I've got a daughter that age.'

52. Philip French, 'The lady is a tart', *The Observer*, 7 September 1986, p. 25.

53. Graham Fuller, 'How to get a hot time in the old town', *The Guardian*, 28 August 1986, p. 21.

54. See Young, *Fear of the Dark*, p. 169, and James, 'Black femmes fatales'. Also on the film, Geoff Eley, '*Distant Voices, Still Lives*. The family is a dangerous place: memory, gender and the image of the working class', in Robert A. Rosenstone (ed.), *Film and the Construction of a New Past* (Princeton, NJ: Princeton University Press, 1995), pp. 17–43.

55. Young, *Fear of the Dark*, p. 167.

56. The shooting script reverses the bridge and the park, opening with George sitting in the park while 'Opposite him is a Pakistani man on a tattered straw mat. He is kneeling, his forehead bowing low to the grass. The man smiles at George' (Neil Jordan and David Leland, *Mona Lisa* [London: Faber and Faber, 1986], p. 1). Although this scene doesn't appear, it does suggest that there was a clear interest in establishing a multi-cultural London as a *changed* context at the opening of the film.

57. Gareth Stedman-Jones, 'The "cockney" and the nation, 1780–1988', in David Feldman and Gareth Stedman-Jones (eds), *Metropolis – London* (London: Routledge, 1989), pp. 272–324.

58. Ibid., p. 273.

59. For example, Russell Campbell's survey of prostitution in the cinema uses this image of Simone on its cover, despite spending only two paragraphs on the film, *Marked Women: Prostitutes and Prostitution in the Cinema* (Madison: University of Wisconsin Press, 2006), pp. 337–8.

60. John Orr describes the trip as 'drug-fuelled male hedonism wearing its cliché on its lapel', observing that 'the spectacle is both ugly and poetic at the same time', *The Art and Politics of Film* (Edinburgh: Edinburgh University Press, 2000), p. 144.

61. Peter Wollen, 'Riff-raff realism', in his *Paris Hollywood: Writings on Film* (London: Verso, 2002), p. 187.

62. Anthony Aldgate, *Censorship and the Permissive Society* (Oxford: Clarendon Press, 1995), and James C. Robertson, *The Hidden Cinema* (London: Routledge, 1989).

63. Phillip Drummond discusses each of these films as migrant narratives in 'London, fortress europe and the cinema of migration', paper to SCMS Conference, London, 2005.

64. Anthony D. King, *Global Cities* (London: Routledge, 1990), pp. 83–7.

65. My account draws on King; Saskia Sassen, *The Global City: New York, London, Tokyo* (Princeton, NJ: Princeton University Press, 1991); Sharon Zukin, *Landscapes of Power* (Berkeley and Los Angeles: University of California Press, 1991); John Eade, *Living the Global City* (London: Routledge, 1997) and *Placing London*; Linda Krause and Patrice Petro (eds), *Global Cities* (New Brunswick: Rutgers University Press, 2003); Chris Hamnett, *Unequal City* (London: Routledge, 2003). Within the context of British cinema, the decline of former manufacturing cities such as Sheffield has provided a rich representational terrain in films such as *The Full Monty* (1997). 'The North' has been cinematically identifiable as the site of de-industrialisation and the local consequences of neo-liberal policies in

the context of globalisation, and commentary includes John Hill, 'Failure and utopianism: representations of the working class in British cinema of the 1990s', in Robert Murphy (ed.), *British Cinema of the 90s* (London: BFI, 2000), Claire Monk 'Underbelly UK', in Justine Ashby and Andrew Higson (eds), *British Cinema: Past and Present* (London: Routledge, 2000), pp. 274–87, Paul Marris 'Northern realism: an exhausted tradition?' *Cinéaste* XXVI no. 4, 2001, pp. 47–50, and Paul Dave, *Visions of England* (Oxford: Berg, 2006). Less identifiable as a grouping are films that work over, or are formed within, concurrent transitions in the capital city London, which, in my view, includes both films discussed here.

66. Sassen, *The Global City*, pp. 5–6.

67. Christopher Booker claims that Richard Seifert (architect of Centre Point and the National Westminster Tower, among many others) 'had more influence on the London skyline than anyone since Wren', quoted by Stephen Inwood, *A History of London* (London: Macmillan, 1988), p. 843. On the first post-war office-building boom see Ibid., pp. 842–50, and Oliver Marriott, *The Property Boom* (London: Pan Books, 1969 [1967]); on the 1990s see Hamnett, *Unequal City*, pp. 211–48.

68. King quotes the *Financial Times* (4 July 1986), 'American conglomerates moving into London have little interest in rabbit warren Victorian blocks or older glass towers, but rather want layers of dealing floors buried in wide efficient structures', King, *Global Cities*, p. 98.

69. The history of each of these 'global London' landmarks, in which I would also include, for example, the reconstructed Globe Theatre in Southwark, long campaigned for by the actor Sam Wanamaker, is quite different. My point is not that they were brought into being with a single aim, but rather that they now provide the repertoire through which global London is articulated. See David Morley and Kevin Robins, *Spaces of Identity* (London: Routledge, 1995), pp. 105–24, on the competitive marketing of cities in the global context.

70. The production company Working Title is particularly significant (*Four Weddings*, *Notting Hill*, *Love Actually*, *Wimbledon* and *Bridget Jones*), but the role of the agency Film London would also repay further research.

71. David Martin-Jones, 'Two stories, one right, one wrong. narrative, national identity and globalization in *Sliding Doors*', *CinéAction!* no. 64, 2004, p. 24.

72. Murphy, 'City Life', p. 296.

73. Dave, *Visions of England*, p. xiv. Italics in original.

74. *Closer* has a 'Movie Map' as part of the Film London website: <www.filmlondon.org.uk/moviemaps>. The use of Postman's Park in this film, where it is integral to the final plot revelation, is an example of the use of a non-landmark 'secret', but eminently visitable, London location as a guarantee of the authenticity of the film's London.

75. Sung by Elvis Costello for the UK and Europe, by Charles Aznavour for all other territories (*Notting Hill* credits, *Sight and Sound* vol. 9 no. 6, 9 June 1999, p. 49).

76. Drummond, 'London, Fortress Europe', p. 11.

77. Alison Crawford, *Notting Hill: The History and Development of North Kensington* (London: Ealing College of Art, 1971).

78. Nick James, 'Farewell to Napoli', *Sight and Sound* vol. 9 no. 5 (NS), May 1999, p. 21. See also Frank Mort, 'Scandalous Events: Metropolitan Culture and Moral Change in Post-Second World War London', *Representations* 93, 2006, pp. 106–37, for an account of the North Kensington/West End juxtaposition in the urban imaginary on the cusp of the first wave of gentrification.

79. Murphy, 'City Life', p. 292.

80. Dave, *Visions of England*, pp. 50–2.

81. Marc Augé, *Non-Places: Introduction to an Anthropology of Super-modernity* (London: Verso, 1995 [1992]).

82. The location of the Baltic Hotel is never specified, partly because the film is rigorous in its avoidance of London landmarks. The proportions and cleanliness of the street suggests central London. Tony Reeves cites Whitehall Court, Horseguards Avenue, as the exterior, and Wandsworth Town Hall as the hotel lobby, *Worldwide Guide to Movie Locations Presents London* (London: Titan, 2003), pp. 38 and 128.

83. Douglas Tallack discusses the hotel lobby as a narrative space in '"Waiting, waiting": the hotel lobby in the modern city', reprinted in Neil Leach (ed.), *The Hieroglyphics of Space* (London: Routledge, 2002), pp. 139–51.

84. Nick Roddick, '*Dirty Pretty Things*', *Sight & Sound* vol. 12 no. 12, December 2002, p. 45.

85. See Drummond, 'London, Fortress Europe', for a discussion of these films, and papers given at the Fortress Europe and its Others conference at London University, March 2005.

86. Samuel's essays 'Docklands Dickens' and 'Who calls so loud?', *Theatres of Memory*, pp. 401–25. See also James Donald's comments on Dickens and Docklands, *Imagining the Modern City* (London: Athlone Press, 1999), pp. 176–7.

87. John Orr, 'Traducing Realisms', *Journal of Popular British Cinema* no. 5, 2002, p. 104. See also Grahame Smith, *Dickens and the Dream of Cinema* (Manchester: Manchester University Press, 2003).

88. Iain Sinclair, 'Heartsnatch Hotel', *Sight & Sound* vol. 12 no. 12 (NS), December 2002, p. 34.

4

The London Underground

The 1997 film *The Wings of the Dove* opens, unlike the 1902 Henry James novel on which it is based, with a scene set in the London Underground.[1] The dancing reflected lights of the titles resolve themselves into the headlights of a tube entering an Underground station. Kate Croy (Helena Bonham Carter), wearing a large-brimmed, becoming hat, sits waiting for the train, which she then boards. The train is crowded, mainly but not exclusively with middle-class men, and Kate initially does not find a seat, strap-hanging as she gazes down the compartment. Her gaze meets that of the seated Merton Densher (Linus Roache), who rises from his seat, indicating with a meaningfully directed gaze that she should accept it. She moves down the carriage and brushes close to him as she accepts his seat, over which he stands. Their proximity permits a comparison of their status. In addition to her grand hat, trimmed spectacularly with blue ostrich feathers, she has a fur trimming to her costume and a silver fox around her neck. He wears a thin jacket, not a coat, and his shirt collar is a little threadbare. Because she is sitting and he is standing over her, his jacket flaps at the level of her face. With the very slightest of movement – slowly shutting her eyes – and facial expression, she seems almost to swoon into the flapping jacket.

In the next shot, she has left the train and walks along a crowded platform, looking back to him, whom we see following, some way back. As she turns a corner to ascend stairs, she looks back again, her face framed by the curve of rounded tunnel. They mount stairs in tiled underground corridors, and, against the stream of other passengers, find their way to an empty lift, which Merton – as far as we know, a stranger – closes. Here the punctuating device of a frontal shot of the two strangers standing in the lift is used, the doors in front of them reading 'Stand Clear of the Doors'. Until this point, the camera's viewpoint has been naturalistic, the camera too waiting for the train, in the carriage and back on the platform. Now its viewpoint is more obviously privileged, the lift rising through several floors to give an intermittent image of the couple in the lift, just like the strip of images on a piece of film. First they stand unmoving, then he takes off his hat, and then, when the next floor passes, we discover them kissing passionately. He embraces her strongly and sexually, pulling her to him, his hand caressing her body: 'Kate.' She stops him with an abrupt 'Merton, no'.

In this powerful, erotic opening to the film, the two central characters are, as we later learn, meeting each other for the first time after a period of enforced separation. The eroticism lies in the absolute contrast between the two modes of behaviour shown. The rigorous observance of the codes of silence on the tube followed by the wordless, passionate embrace in the temporarily private space of the lift is shocking in a way that is accentuated by the use of a period setting. At the same time, we are sufficiently familiar with wordless, frantic sex in the grinding lifts up to New York loft apartments in films like *Fatal Attraction* (1987) to believe in sex-in-lifts. The Victorian space left behind, still present in costume, reminds us constantly that they are behaving deeply scandalously in a private space that is really still a public space.

The film was shot at Shepperton Studios, where the train lines for this carefully researched opening scene were laid out into the car park.[2] On close – perhaps pedantic – examination, the scene has its own historical implausibilities. It is unlikely that Kate would have had to stand for long if gentlemen were sitting – she would not have needed to wait for Merton to give her a seat.[3] Then, as now, the chances of being in a lift alone are slight and, certainly, managing to negotiate a lift without an operator while everyone else is being directed to a different lift, unlikely. These elements, though, are the very stuff of the encounter between Kate and Merton in which the private drama is played out in public. The accomplishment of the scene, the way in which we the audience are also rendered slightly breathless in the lift, lies in the shift in point of view. We are initially placed just as an observant fellow traveller, except that we see, through the camerawork and editing, the exchange of looks, the slight gesture of the offered seat, and Kate's almost imperceptible swoon into Merton's jacket. It is the last moment, above all, which is comprehensible only retrospectively. Only after our viewpoint is radically shifted to that of privileged voyeur through the lift grille do we reconsider the scene of the seat-giving. Kate and Merton may be breathing hard with passion – but for the audience, it is the revelation that they are not strangers at all which causes the gasp.

The verisimilitude of the scene is sufficient – the 1910 train, the colouring and texture of the interior and the upholstery, the patterning and shade of the tiling, the proportions of the tunnels, passages and steps, the use of costume with its own class-specific nuances – to allow us to ask the more significant critical question, how does this scene work dramatically in relation to the rest of the film? What is gained by the Underground setting? First, we learn, immediately, about the material circumstances of the two central characters. We see, through the physical proximity of their costume and skin, that she is rich and he is poor. We also see that she is modern. She may be wealthy, but she is on the tube, not in a carriage, and on the tube by herself. And we see that their relationship is one of sexual passion – so she is modern in this sense too, despite being thoroughly encumbered by her costume. Through the masquerade of public and private that the scene enacts, we are also introduced to one of the central themes of the film, the gap between appearance and desire, and perhaps more specifically, the masking of desire in the public world. This is achieved more elegantly through an Underground setting than it would be in a more select semi-public setting such as a ball or pleasure garden, for Merton and Kate, initially introduced to the viewer as strangers, have, in these first moments, an equality as fellow travellers which they could not be shown, plausibly, to possess in a less functional setting.

The Wings of the Dove: the offer of a seat …

… the ascent in the lift

This scene enacts many of the features that Wolfgang Schivelbusch has taught us to understand as historically specific in his study of the railway journey.[4] We see the close physical proximity of the passengers juxtaposed with the necessity of ignoring each other, and the use of reading newspapers as a way of dealing with this peculiar space. However, on the Underground there is no external panorama at which to gaze. Space is not made panoramic, as Schivelbusch shows us with the train journey, but abolished, turned into time, the time it takes for the tube to pass through the dark tunnels to the illuminated, but spatially abstract, platforms of the stations. Narratively, this absence of panorama makes the space more immanent – space in which something is going to happen – and the patterning of movement and glances in this scene that we can make sense of only retrospectively is that happening.

Generically, though, the film is doing something else, and is offering us an unusual representation of the London Underground for the late twentieth century. For *The Wings of the Dove* is costume drama, and rather exquisitely costumed drama at that. The representational terrain of this genre is country houses, large estates, coaches and carriages and women in long dresses. It may extend to steam trains and chirpy cockneys, but does not generally include the Underground. The critic Nigel Floyd made the point economically when discussing this scene. Acknowledging its power, he said that, nevertheless, what had struck him most was Helena Bonham Carter's costume. We are, of course, accustomed to seeing her in Victorian and Edwardian costume, as a stalwart of heritage cinema, but seeing her dressed like this on the tube, he found himself thinking 'It the tube really that old? Has the London Underground been with us since the period when women wore full-length dresses?'[5] Floyd's question points to the way in which the Underground, in origin a Victorian space, is used here to signify the modernity of the young lovers in 1910 and their lack of access to any private space which would be sanctioned for their meeting. They have to make the public private because they have no permitted, shared, private space.

This dramatically powerful use of a London Underground setting employs many of the characteristics of the metro setting which recur in the cinema: an iconographically identifiable location, constrained sculptural spaces, temporal rhythms independent of character action, anonymous crowds and sudden solitude – and a chance meeting. These are not characteristics of the *London* Underground alone, and have been explored by film-makers all over the world working in a range of genres. However, the 'lift' part of this sequence, in its camerawork and editing, also images, at a meta-level, the question of the suggestive relationship between Underground space and cinematic space. In the shots from outside the lift doors in which the strangers reveal themselves to be on kissing terms, Iain Softley makes a vertical visual analogy between Kate and Merton's ascent in the lift and a strip of film (see p. 129). But this affinity between the Underground and the cinema can also be apprehended in other ways, such as in the horizontal alternation of the dark tunnels with the bright stations, and the transformation of space into time, as explored in Amil Naderi's 2002 New York-set film, *Marathon*, which consists mainly of the heroine travelling the subways, doing crosswords in an attempt to beat her own marathon record. One of my interests in this chapter is the sympathy, or resonance, between these temporal journeys in the dark which makes the Underground a seductive setting for the cinema.[6] Perhaps sometimes too seductive, as Luc Besson observed wryly in discussing his use of the French métro in *Subway*: 'j'avais une

idée forte: le métro. Mais je n'arrivais pas à trouver une histoire aussi forte que ce décor.'
('I had a strong idea: the métro. But I couldn't find a story as strong as this setting.')[7]

I will suggest in this chapter that what might be called the 'strong stories' of the spaces of the Underground are mainly about time. But there is also, as I hope to show, a surprising persistence within the cinema of an aspect of the London Underground that we find in *The Wings of the Dove,* its role as a paradoxically private space. It is this 'public privacy' that is also relevant in the context of the Underground and the cinema. Here, Marc Augé's ethnography of the 'social phenomenon of the métro' in which he observes that, 'for those who take it everyday, the prosaic definition of the métro: [is] collectivity without festival and solitude without isolation',[8] is useful, and I will return to his analysis of the role of solitary reverie and memory later in the chapter.

If these aspects of the London Underground as a cinematic setting are not specific to London, they are always mobilised within the particular historical context of the London Underground and its history as the oldest of the world's subway systems. It is this that Nigel Floyd's question about the age of the tube in *The Wings of the Dove* points to, and some preliminary, partially generic periodisation is possible. The Victorian infrastructure of the Underground may signify modernity – as recreated in *The Wings of the Dove* – in the early part of the twentieth century, with film plots exploring its potential for the promiscuous mixing of the classes as in *Underground* or the opening of Alfred Hitchcock's 1932 *Rich and Strange.* However, the modernity of the Underground vanished for ever after the use of the stations as shelters during the Second World War (discussed below), to be succeeded, in the second part of the century, by a rather more banal Underground, used often in ways related to the use of the London bus discussed in Chapter 1. It is the banal Underground on which the citizens of Pimlico try to police their borders in *Passport to Pimlico* (1949), or on which, alternating with buses, Billy Savage (Richard Attenborough) attempts to avoid detection in *Seance on a Wet Afternoon* (1964).[9] But the banal Underground, particularly after the relaxation of censorship in the 1960s, is matched by another more spatially and temporally complex one, in which the dark spaces of the Underground return as a space of horror. The Underground as location for psychic or temporal disruption and horror is found in films such as Hammer's 1967 *Quatermass and the Pit,* the 1972 cult classic *Deathline,* with its 2004 descendant, the very bloody *Creep,* and the 'tourist horror' of *An American Werewolf in London* (1979). In these films, the age of the Underground is recruited to the horror genre in a way that would support the suggestion that London, as a cinematic city, may be significantly shaped by this genre. Christopher Smith, the director of *Creep,* made this point explicitly when he refers to the Underground as 'the veins of yesterday', suggesting that 'everything that's happened in London since the days of Jack the Ripper is kind of embodied in the Underground'.[10] Alongside this archaic cinematic Underground, there is also a documentary tradition which portrays the Underground as a contemporary place of labour in which it can be a surprisingly private place. The documentary Underground is usually included within one of two documentary Londons, 'London at night' and 'Subterranean London', which are identifiable London sub-genres, the latter in particular enormously generative across a range of texts, sites and practices.[11] In this chapter I will analyse the cinematic Underground as a place of horror and a place of labour, paying particular attention to the complex temporalities of the space and the way in which interiority, privacy and public life are articulated. However, before doing this, I need to pay some attention to perhaps the most famous versions of the London Underground, Harry Beck's 1933 map and the use of the tube as bomb shelters in the Second World War.

Mr Beck and Gert and Daisy

It is impossible to think about the type of narrative space the London Underground is in the cinema without first paying attention to the most distinguished and influential representation of the Underground, Harry Beck's 1933 diagram of the network. The peculiarity of the London Underground as a space is that, in a sense, it has no outside. Of course, several lines, particularly outside central London, run overground, but the core London Underground is just that: underground. Station buildings and the bar and circle roundel signify its presence in the city; lifts, stairs and escalators lead to it; but once inside we can only know it internally – and through our imagination and maps like Beck's. Beck's diagram is an iconic image of twentieth-century London and, along with the Underground roundel ('the bullseye'), frequently functions as a location-setting landmark in the cinema. Enormously influential internationally in the mapping of underground railways, the diagram is a key landmark image of London, as well as shaping people's understanding of the spatial relations of the city.[12] Its popularity is such that the bookshop at the London Transport Museum offers versions of the map on posters, postcards, place-mats, T-shirts, fridge-magnets, coffee cups, mouse-mats and carrier bags, while Ken Garland's loving account, *Mr Beck's Underground Map*, first published in 1994, has been twice reprinted.[13] Both the diagram and the space of the Underground have inspired and occasioned artworks, while London Transport itself had a long and honourable history both in relation to design and as an art patron. David Pike's discussion of the map places it convincingly within what he characterises as a modernist conception of space, and he explores the paradoxes of the temporalities and spatialities of the Tube in a comparison of the map and the Underground:

> As a material space, the tube is not unified at all; it is quite literally Victorian, modernist, and post-war, all at the same time … Aboveground, its colors and lines continue to exude the utopian modernism of its abstract, controlled and rationally organized space; below, its cramped conditions and tiny tunnels recall not the utopian Underground, but the subterranean space from which it has always striven so strenuously to escape.[14]

This vision of the Underground as partaking of different temporalities is illuminating, and can be further explored in relation to the cinema. Pike's own concern is partly to explain the endurance and popularity of Beck's map; however, he is also concerned to explore other artistic engagements with the Underground, such as the work of Simon Patterson, which 'discover what its [Beck's map] efficiency has occluded',[15] and in this too, the cinema may prove interesting. The Underground map, as well as making spaces, is also itself placed within spaces in the cinema. As the London Transport Film Office explains on its website, 'filmmakers often use the tube to show they are in London'.[16] Tube iconography can be deployed in different ways to signify location, sometimes as part of a string of landmark icons along with Big Ben or the Houses of Parliament, sometimes, particularly in social realist cinema, as the only landmark icon, perhaps, with the flash of a red bus, used to indicate more than local location. For example, *Nil By Mouth*, discussed in Chapter 2, has a sequence in which heroin addict Billy (Charlie Creed-Miles) is waiting to score outside the Elephant and Castle tube station. The film is shot in a very limited colour palette, with the dim lighting of the Underground tunnels and escalator echoing the grim corridors of the block of flats in which Billy seeks drugs. In this scene, which takes place about halfway through the film, when the audience is beginning to grasp the remorselessness of the repetitions within the family, Billy emerges from the tube and is trying to use a phone box outside Elephant and Castle Station to make his connection. The phone box is busy, and Billy paces agitatedly up and down the pavement, passing the posters around the station entrance. The diegetic soundtrack to this scene is supplied by a busker outside the station, a young black man playing classical violin. Billy crosses and recrosses the Underground map displayed outside the station, pausing by a poster exhorting the regular traveller to 'save your one day travel cards and collect dramatic savings'. Here Beck's 1930s map finds itself part of a different temporality to those Pike discusses. This is scuzzy, down-at-heel, post-colonial south London, where the unemployed – and unemployable – white working class frenziedly pursues oblivion. The map and the poster also function directly as ironic *mise en scène*, in that there is no one in the film less likely than Billy, with his £60-a-day habit, to go anywhere using the 'Journey Planner' as the map is now called, just as he will never 'collect dramatic savings' by saving his old tickets. The map and the poster both ground the film in late-twentieth-century London and remind the audience, but not Billy, that there are other ways of living and other journeys.

If Beck's map, as Pike argues, represents one vision of a utopian Underground, then the Second World War occasions another vision, this time of an heroic communality when Underground stations were used as bomb shelters. The shelter of the Tubes is one of the privileged tropes of London's war and is also a key moment in the script of the London Underground as part of the living city. Pierre Nora has developed the concept of the 'Lieu de mémoire' to signify sites through which memory is made material and public.[17] To propose that tube station shelters constitute British 'lieux de mémoire' is obviously complicated by their number, but their representation as affective spaces within the national imaginary is striking. The best-known representations of Londoners sheltering in the Tube are Henry Moore's shelter drawings and Bill Brandt's photographs, originally published together in the magazine *Lilliput* in 1942,[18] and most documentaries about the London Underground include some reference to Henry Moore's shelter drawings and his account of his accidental discovery of the shelterers in the Tube, after a dinner in town.[19] In Jill Craigie's 1944 film about the flourishing of art in London during the war, *Out of Chaos*, Moore is represented 'wandering about' among the sleepers on the platform, taking notes and later making images. Moore has drawn attention to the relations between the 'rounded perspective of the tube' and the 'rows and rows of reclining figures, which has always been a favourite subject of mine',[20] and it is the combination of the vulnerability of the (private) sleeping bodies with their massing in dramatically lit and shaped public space that is so powerful. This is an exceptional version of the public/private paradox of the Underground.

This story is not always told in the same tone though. Craigie's film, setting out to raise morale, documents a democratic art of the people and the work of the war artists' committee: Moore's work treated alongside that of firemen artists and a civil defence exhibition. It is Moore who is the agent, observing the passive sleepers. This perspective is reversed in the 1943 comedy *Gert and Daisy's Weekend*, starring Elsie and Doris Waters, which has an early scene set in a station shelter, although most of the film follows Gert and Daisy as they care for a group of East End children evacuated to a large county house. The film is essentially a comedy of class manners, contrasting the pragmatic, earthy communality of the London shelterers with the excluding snobberies and dishonesties of those gathered at 'the Hall'. This contrast is principally established through the forms of entertainment in each milieu. As Gert and Daisy shelter, sitting on a bench in front of a Goodge Street sign, a group of people in evening dress dismount from a train, just like Moore and his companions return- ing from an evening out, and proceed to make their way through the shelterers, as Daisy says, 'Gert, look at this' and Gert responds, 'Oh blimey, posh'. However, this evening-dressed party turns out to comprise 'some West End stage stars' who have come to entertain the shelterers. This develops into a full-scale singalong, with Gert and Daisy leading a rendition of 'Won't We Have a Party When It's Over' and everyone on the platform dancing. The excep- tional circumstances of the war are shown here, remembering Augé's terms, to create not just a collectivity, but communal festivity under duress, and this is contrasted, later in the film, with an evening of music and song at the Hall. Here, the songs come from opera, and are presented as affected and screechy. Gert and Daisy don't enjoy the recital and try to get things going by offering 'She's a Lily, but Only by Name', a monologue with choruses. The country house guests, though, are too stuffy to join in. At the end of the film, having helped to foil a jewellery theft, Gert and Daisy can't wait to get back to London and the Blitz – and we see exactly why they'd rather be sleeping in a tube station. The alienation of the city of strangers and the barriers of class division are abolished in these images of London- ers singing and lying down together, and the London Blitz is figured as an opportunity for courage and conviviality, a transformation of the city into a community.[21] There is a strong contrast between the corporeality of the shelterers' Tube and its diagrammatic presence in Beck's map, but together they show the way in which this Underground network is made and remade in the visual imagination, providing more than one instance of a privileged national image of London and Londoners.

The Strong Stories of the Underground

The story of the London Underground during the Blitz could be seen as 'a strong story' of the Underground. The transformation of the city that it effects, the exceptional imagery of recumbent bodies on the platforms, the conviviality represented in films such as *Gert and Daisy's Weekend* and Arthur Askey's *I Thank You* (1941), all point to 'an idea as strong as the set- ting'. More commonly though, the Underground appears in the cinema in two types of stories, both of which privilege time in this constrained space. One, which I will discuss below in both feature and documentary versions, is a story about something forgotten, repressed or unknown emerging from the dark tunnels underground. The second, often rather literal, and perhaps, as Besson recognised, sometimes overly seductive for the film-maker, is a set of urban narratives structured through the 'too late' of closing doors, ticket barriers and just- missed trains. Cities worldwide have underground transport systems, and their use as cinematic location provides both local specificity and an easy and plausible setting for chance encounters, pursuits and chases. Many a villain or intended victim, in films set all over the world, has tried to escape by running through subways and up and down stairs, endeavouring to leap on a train just before the doors close, from Regina Lambert (Audrey Hepburn) in Paris in *Charade* (1966) to Spiderman in Manhattan in *Spiderman II* (2004). Death through electrocution by the live rail also enlivens film climaxes, such at that in *Piccadilly Third Stop* (1960). Romances and romantic encounters too are enabled and impeded by just catching or just missing trains, as in *Sliding Doors*, which used the device of 'the train not taken' to elaborate a double 'what if' time scheme for the whole film. The attractions of the underground for a film-maker are many, providing both movement (the train, the passengers, the escalators) and a visually distinctive environment (the tunnels, carriage or platform), identifiable locations which can be specific but also generic, and an impersonal, *deus ex machina* temporality, a world of 'just in time' and 'just too late'. Like the bus, the underground train can represent the city in miniature, and it would be possible to spend a whole chapter on 'just-missed' and 'just-caught' (and 'just killed by') underground trains in the cinema. Instead, I want to look in some detail at two contrasted British films of the mid-1960s that feature the London Underground. The first, *Quatermass and the Pit* (1967), is an example not of the chase, but of the other type of 'strong story', in which the underground reveals something of what lurks in its depths. This colour feature film from one of the most distinctive British studios opens with a group of workmen labouring at a major excavation in a fictional London Underground station. The second, *The Irishmen* (1965), made for the BBC, is a black-and-white documentary which includes footage of Irish labourers working on the tunnels of the Victoria Line. In each film, the Underground proves to be a complex temporal space, while in *The Irishmen* it is constructed as a more subjective and private space than might be generically anticipated. Rosalind Williams, in her book on the imagery of the Underground, observes that:

> Both Marx and Freud depend so much upon subterranean imagery that it is now virtually impossible to read a text about the underworld without filtering it through a Marxist or Freudian interpretation – without reading the buried world as the subconscious, or the working class, or both.[22]

The cinematic imaginary too tends to people the Underground with the repressed or the oppressed, and each of the films I will discuss could be seen to enact the topography that Williams describes. However, 'what lies beneath' is always articulated in particular historical forms, and that is one of my interests here, along with an exploration of the way in which this iconic London space contains and condenses other times and places.

Quatermass and the Pit is the third of the Hammer films based on the BBC *Quatermass* serials and was also scripted by Nigel Kneale.[23] As the particular horror unearthed in the pit of the Underground excavation is a Martian spaceship, generically the film is usually seen as science fiction. However, its topography is gothic, and the aliens are Martians 5 million years old. The film, set in the present day, is located in and around a fictional London Underground station, Hobbs End. Hobbs End Station is introduced in the opening sequence as a police constable, on his night rounds, pauses to investigate the partially open station gates, pausing to read a London Transport notice about the regretted inconvenience caused by the current extension to the Central Line. The unclosed gate – a pantograph grille not fully expanded – detains this guardian of order for a moment or two, and introduces the next scene for the viewers, when, with a sharp cut, we descend into the tube station to see the work that is being undertaken on the extension. But this shot of the three-quarters-closed pantograph gate to the Underground, very early in the film, also condenses what will become its key narrative, the wilful human disturbance of the boundary between the over-ground and the underground.

The second scene in the film shows the labouring navvies excavating the tunnel extension. Their labour is shown to be hard and heavy, hewing out with pickaxes great chunks of rock and clay, which are then carried away from the excavation on a motorised belt. There are clear affinities here with the representational terrain of the *The Irishmen*, which I discuss below, and indeed the name of the Irish construction firm, Balfour Beatty, is discernible on the sides of the conveyor belt being used in Hobbs End tube station. However, although the referent – the tunnel-digging labour – may be the same, the construction of narrative space is quite different. In *Quatermass and the Pit* the construction of the underground set is dominated by the necessity for it to be clear, narratively, where people are. This means the set is also rather abbreviated because it needs to contain both the relative safety of the station platform and the excavation site, which eventually becomes filled with the mystery spaceship. *Quatermass and the Pit* is an instructive example of the aesthetic of the Underground as a gothic place in that it displays the two key structuring oppositions of this aesthetic within seconds of its beginning: the over-ground/underground opposition and that between the platform and the tunnels. As is generically predictable, we do not spend long with the workers digging the extension before one of the lumps of rubble sent up the moving belt turns out to be something horrible – in this case, a skull, which is then followed by more skeletal remains. Although the workmen make the find, their role is limited to strong emotional responses and uninformed speculation: the generic struggle of the film, to understand the significance of the discovery, is entrusted to others.

Throughout the film, what is found in the excavation at Hobbs End is subject to competing explanations, each associated with key characters. A palaeontologist, Dr Roney (James Donald), is at first convinced that the skull is 'pre-pre-historic'; his assistant, Miss Judd (Barbara Shelley), recruits Professor Quatermass (Andrew Keir) to her investigation of a history of trouble, horror and apparition at the site, seemingly connected to 'the disturbance of the earth' through activities such as tree-felling and well-boring; while the Army are convinced that it is German military propaganda from the last war. The older folk knowledge investigated by Professor Quatermass and Miss Judd is the most resonant, but does not fully explain what is found in the tunnel. What first seems to be an unexploded bomb is excavated to reveal a futuristic spaceship-type pod which is made of a substance unknown to man and contains a hidden compartment. This vehicle embodies the generic hybridity of the film – buried deep below ground, it nevertheless seems to have come from outer space. The horror of the film lies in the eruption of an archaic future – the awakening of a former invasion from Mars – and it is the disturbance of the earth in the proposed extension of the Underground that excites these hidden temporalities.

In a metonymic scene, which condenses the spatial relations of the film, the space pod is revealed to be a bad and powerful place when entered, after hours, by a workman returning to collect his tools. The workman, who had previously been employed to (unsuccessfully) drill through the impregnable secret compartment, has been shown to be a cheery, competent fellow who boasts how much better he feels knowing that he has insurance. In his second scene he enters the deserted station insouciantly, joking, as the lights go out, 'Where was Moses when the lights went out?' and answering himself, 'In the dark.' He tries drilling again inside the pod but it seems to become sentient and angry, shaking and rumbling. The workman, his tools and other bits of equipment inside the pod are tossed around, looking partly as if they are in the gravity-less atmosphere of outer space. He part flies, part tumbles, is part tossed out of the pod, and, with other debris, is swept up onto the platform – just as rubbish can be by an approaching train. He is thrown out of the station gates, past the waiting watchman and Miss Judd and is accompanied by exactly the sort of animated litter that flaps against tube station gates. The empirical detail of his possession is precisely the detritus of everyday tube travel: great gusts of litter made animate by approaching trains.

Possessed, or, as Professor Quatermass theorises, with an archaic part of himself reawakened, the workman crashes into a tea kiosk. Bad space has emerged from the Underground somehow in his body, and as soon as he touches the stall, cups and plates are swept off their hooks and shelves. It is both hurricane and a very contemporary imagery of gravity-less movement. He is swept on to a churchyard, grabbing at gravestones and, finally, coming to rest on asphalt. But the disturbance in the Underground has abolished the distinction between above and below ground and the very ground on which he is lying begins to ripple.

Peter Hutchings, who discusses *Quatermass and the Pit* in the context of 1950s and 1960s invasion fantasies in film and television, points out that this 1967 film is 'something of an anachronism'[24] when compared to both the earlier BBC *Quatermass* serials and Hammer films. 'Quatermass's Britain is visibly weak and vulnerable, caught as it is in a kind of collective post-war doze.'[25] The film does, however, offer three interesting 1960s contemporary referents in addition to the references to space travel. The first is the significant, 1960s presentation of the female lead, Miss Judd (Barbara Shelley), who, while she still wears gloves with her short-skirted Chanel-style pink suit, also wears smart, fashionable boots and a cape. Miss Judd, although always an assistant, is evidently extremely competent and can be relied on not to succumb to horror or fear at the discoveries made in the pit (although she does prove particularly sensitive to Martian life). In many ways she takes the interpretative initiative as it is she who mediates between Roney and Quatermass in researching the history of the area. She is very much a modern, mobile 1960s woman, both in this mediation, and in the way in which she races about the set.[26] The second 1960s referent, rather literally, is the relevance of London Underground expansion, as this film was made during the excavation and building of the first post-war Tube line, the Victoria Line.[27] The third contemporary referent, which is much more developed in the earlier BBC version, and here persists only in a residual manner, is the oblique address to Commonwealth immigration in the inclusion of a black workman in the labourers' team.[28] In the Hammer version, in the film's climax, some humans attempt to kill others 'just because they are different'. In the television version, made shortly after the Notting Hill 'race riots' of 1958, there is explicit reference to a 'race war' between Martians and humans and a rather more explicit analogy. So the film's narrative space and time is complex, combining as it does the vocabularies of alien invasion and gravity-less space travel with modern young women, architectural finds, a changing London and the drilling and boring of the expanding space of the Underground. Excavating the Underground does not just send workmen mad. It muddles time, producing a space which is past and future, contemporary and archaic.

While films such as *Quatermass and the Pit, Deathline* or the later *An American Werewolf in London* show or refer to labour in the Underground, they do so generally within an aesthetic informed by key oppositions between the surface and the underground, and, symmetrically, once underground, between the safe, illuminated platforms and the dark gaping tunnels. One of the narrative tensions in *Quatermass* is the question of whether it is safe to go down to the excavation and whether the public can be allowed in. There is an anxiety, throughout the film, about going too far, crossing an unseen frontier, either underground or in space. Similarly, the most dangerous activity in *Deathline* is standing on the edge of the station platform and peering into the tunnel.[29] This perilous topography is replicated in the 2004 *Creep*, in which the doors of tube trains also, scarily, open in tunnels, abolishing the distinction between the bright capsule and the dark outside.[30] The horror genre does penetrate the tunnels, but only to discover horror. In *Deathline* we do enter the dark, dank lair, decorated with suspended human limbs, where the last survivors of a nineteenth-century engineering accident have lived, just as, in *Quatermass*, people who return to the spaceship in the tunnel become possessed. In documentary, the tunnels are treated differently, not as places of horror, but as places of labour. I want to discuss this in relation to a 1965 film, *The Irishmen* (produced and directed by Philip Donnellan, shot by Michael Williams), made during the building of the Victoria Line, and in relation to a group of workers known as 'fluffers' who appear in glimpses in several documentaries about underground London.

The Tunnel Tigers and the Good Fairies of the Underground

The Irishmen: an impression of exile is about the lives of the Irish emigrants who came over to Britain to work as labourers after the Second World War. It is one of a group of films Philip Donnellan made in the 1960s on aspects of contemporary life, the best known of which is *The Colony* (1964) about Birmingham, also made in collaboration with Charles Parker. *The Irishmen* was made in 1965 for the BBC, although it was never shown.[31] The immigrants are shown working on two major projects, one of which is the M1 and the other the Victoria Line, London's first post-war Tube line.[32] Both were built using a labour contract system called the Lump – which is non-unionised casual labour – and the film starts with men waiting to be picked up for jobs in Camden Town,[33] and then interweaves work and leisure sequences, with one of its concerns to show the relative isolation of the labourers outside their work companionship. The canteen-like bar on site in which they are shown to drink after work in one scene is thus contrasted with the family life left behind in Ireland, while at the same time, the inevitability of exile for the young is set up early on, with a young man, Josie McDonagh, whose journey we follow, musing, 'What's it to be, England or America?' The film has several simultaneous temporal structures: the working day (finishing with a drink), the working week (including hurling at Wembley on a Saturday), generational migration from Ireland to England and the particular journey of this one young man who arrives at a London terminal as the film finishes. The four-and-a-half-minute sequence I want to analyse juxtaposes McDonagh's ferry trip across the Irish Sea with the labour of tunnelling under London. As with much of the film, Donnellan and Charles Parker (the radio producer, credited as tape editor) use song as soundtrack. In this sequence, the song is not diegetic, but is used to structure both space and exposition. The intro of the fiddle begins as the traveller is shown on the deck of the ferry with the seagulls circling. This is the song of the 'London Clay', a traditional melody arranged by Ewan MacColl and Peggy Seeger, which has lyrics that counterpose the beauty and freedom of country rhythms in Ireland, the trout, the salmon and the wild geese, with the team commands of the labourers, 'Up with the shield, jack it, ram it, driving a tunnel through the London clay'.[34] The juxtaposition is one of loss, the loss of the life of the countryman: the hares run free and the curragh rots because no one is there to trap and fish, to live off the land, because the men have gone to London. The song is precise in its invocation of both the plenitude of the Irish country and the locations from which the emigrants leave – Connemara, the Wicklow mountains, Armagh – offering possibilities of identification for any migrant listener and creates an elegiac narrative space to which the first two minutes of the sequence are cut. The montage juxtaposes the emigrant on the boat with increasing flashes of tunnel labour contrasted with seagulls, mountains, fishing boats and an abandoned curragh. While it is the space of the man's journey, it is more significantly a space of exilic consciousness; the labour of the tunnelling overwhelming rural origins, while the flight of the wild geese is recalled while underground. The song is absent for the second part of the sequence, which is all underground with the harsh diegetic sound of tunnelling. The cramped, quick shots to which we have been introduced earlier are now sustained in a way that emphasises the constriction and heat and dirt of the labour. We see a section of tunnel roof being installed, the men working alongside the mighty shield, their sweaty skin and the whites of their eyes the lightest part of the image. The melody returns more urgently as the sequence concludes with the spoil being carried out of the excavation on a conveyor belt, and now that we understand the labour that awaits our traveller, we return to the ferry.

So what does this sequence of film document? It shows us something of the building of the Victoria Line; that it was built by Irish immigrants, and how very hard this was, both physically and psychically. The cutting of the sequence, partly to the song, allows us to apprehend the rhythms of repetitive labour. This is combined with quite detailed documentary footage of tunnelling, of the underground as a place of work, which is woven into an evocation of consciousness. Thus, we have both a strong sense of physical labour and of the memories and desires – and home – of the workers. This is clearly an example of the exilic consciousness that Hamid Naficy[35] has shown has its own internal elsewhere, but it is also an instance of the way in which the very cramped nature of the dark tunnels of the Underground, even as they are being built, offers the privacy Augé refers to. Just as Kate and Merton found, in the Underground, somewhere to embrace, Donnellan chooses to use the Underground sequence to evoke the exilic yearning of individual labourers.

Donnellan's concern, in *The Irishmen*, is not with the Underground as such, although the building of the Victoria Line does provide the film with its most memorable imagery, and he

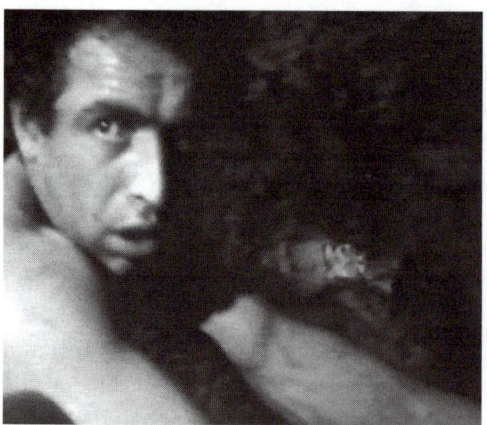

The labourer in the tunnel (*The Irishmen*)

A seagull following the boat from Ireland
(*The Irishmen*)

uses the visual contrast between the dark tunnels, the sea and deserted rural Ireland to evoke the felt meaning of exile. He records that he chose the Cavendish Square excavation site for the Victoria Line because 'the contrasts were sharpest: the shifts of diggers, nearly all Irish, in ragged trousers stained with London clay, would come up from the tunnels in the dawn or evening straight into the glare and glitz of the West End'.[36] His skill as a documentarist lies in the way in which he combines film footage, recorded speech, sound and song to reveal not only what the work and the life was like, but what it felt like. In this, he makes an unusual representation of manual labour entailing feelings as well as strength. The other times and places of memory can be summoned to fill the dark tunnels, and, within the cinema, perhaps surprisingly, underground spaces can be particularly amenable to the project of suggesting interiority.

More commonly, the London Underground features in documentary film in two formats: the 'London under London', in which the Underground is featured alongside underground sites such as sewers, government bunkers, wine cellars and silver vaults; and 'London at Night', in which the focus is on the work conducted by postmen, underground cleaners and musicians while the city sleeps. The world of each type of film is a man's world – only men are found working and it is men who act as guides to the documentarists – with two exceptions.[37] Women working as prostitutes figure briefly – but repeatedly – sometimes just through shots of a swishing skirt above some idling high-heeled feet. Claude Goretta and Alain Tanner's 1957 short film about a night out in London, *Nice Time*, concludes with the key tropes of the 'London at Night' group of films: the tube closing down, the barrow boys wheeling away their barrows and only the police, some sailors and 'the ladies of the night' left in Piccadilly Circus. Donovan Winter's *The Awakening Hour* (1957) also features a prostitute and then porters in Covent Garden as typical workers of the night. *City After Dark* (1955) has a two-shot prostitute sequence, the first shot of a high-heeled woman, standing against a shop window, tapping her foot, framed from just below her shoulders, the second of a man's legs and feet apparently approaching her. But there is also another group of women who can be found in several post-war underground documentaries, and they too have a curiously transgressive presence.

Fluffers were maintenance workers who cleaned the Tube lines during its night-time closures, and can be found in films of each type. They used knives, dusters, brushes and any other suitable implements to clean, particularly, the rails and the 'chairs' in which they are set, of dust, human hair, rat excrement and other litter. The most interesting discussion of the fluffers is given in an anonymous personal account of going out with the night-time crews written in the 1940s, 'London's Underground Army: Laying and Maintaining the Tracks':

> These pleasant happy-looking women work in pairs, collecting the dust into heaps which are shovelled into containers and taken away by a special train … Work in the transport service often seems to run in families. One of the women told me her brother-in-law had been a bus-driver for fifteen years; another had her sister working there with her … And all of them, of course, have domestic responsibilities. Most of them have young children. When they get home from the night's work, they have breakfast to cook, housework to do, shopping to get in. They go to bed after lunch, for before they leave home for their night's work, they have more meals to get, the children, perhaps, to put to bed, and all the small things to do which make up the housewife's round. They all seemed particularly cheerful, and there was a fine team spirit. We left these good fairies of the Underground, singing at their work.[38]

The fluffers can also be found in *Under Night Streets* (1958), a twenty-minute British Transport film which has been selected by London's Transport Museum[39] as one of the films available to the public on its website; it concentrates on showing the myriad safety activities going on in the Underground 'while you're pressing the mattress'. Workers are shown climbing and cleaning the ventilator shafts under a deserted Piccadilly Circus Station, and then the 'big gang boys' undress on the platform to go down into the tunnel. The camera then switches to a group of women in overalls on the platform, and introduces them saying, 'Fluffers, that's what they're called. They're VIPs, they are, for this is fire prevention work', as the women move down into the tunnels to start work. There is a hint here, in both the tone and vocabulary of this introduction, of a difficulty about the status of, and attitudes to, the fluffers.[40] When the women are shown working in the tunnels, in the next scene, they are represented in the tradition of the representation of working-class women doing manual jobs as jolly, cheeky and potentially bawdy. This is achieved through the interaction between the working women and their foreman/boss who rides past them on a strange tricycle-like vehicle adapted to run along the train rails. As he glides past the women who are brushing and scraping, he greets them familiarly and they quip back. The introduction, though, tries to set up the fluffers slightly differently. Referring to the women as 'VIPs', and specifying that their labour is 'fire-prevention work' (which it undoubtedly is), insists on both status and the significance of the labour in a way that amounts to a disavowal. The tone of the narrator argues against dismissing the women as insignificant, but to call them VIPs inscribes within the narration the very opposite: that these were extremely poorly paid women, working night shifts in filthy and dangerous conditions, who presumably only took the work because they also had households and families to run – and possibly day jobs.

The fluffers also appear in *City After Dark* (Ian K. Barnes), a nineteen-minute film that deals with 'another world' which lies 'beneath the quiet paving stones of the city'. Once again starting with Piccadilly Circus, this film shows night-life closing down and then goes underground to reveal the labour of the sewage workers, underground maintenance, post-office sorters and the BBC. This film is keen to stress the precision of the timing and execution of underground maintenance work, showing the last Bakerloo Tube leaving Piccadilly Circus, observing:

> A dead city needs no transport. The time is 1.32am. But by 1.52am, the night gangs have taken over. Every foot of every mile must be checked. The Tubes never rest. Every night when the last train has passed, the ghostly tunnels witness men, and women too, checking, cleaning, tightening.

'And women too' recognises that the employment of women in this type of work may surprise an audience, just as 'the ghostly tunnels' suggests that a gothic topography haunts documentary as much as fiction film. The women are shown wearing dark overalls with their hair tied up in pale headscarves. With their sleeves rolled up to show bare arms, the women also wear earrings visible under their headscarves. Holding lamps, they wield a variety of implements to scrape and brush the line.

This film, then, gives us a very unusual representation of the Underground through camera placement and movement. A shot of the women working in the dark of the tunnels, the only lighting visible their individually held lamps, transforms into a very eerie view of the platform as the camera, without a cut, pans right, away from the fluffers and up to the brightly lit, deserted station platform. The shot becomes eerie because of the revelation of concealed space and depth. While we are with the fluffers in the tunnel, the camera is appropriately placed to allow us to observe their work. Only with the pan and tilt is the height of the platform – and our own lowly position – revealed. While in horror films, the horror lurks in the tunnels, in this documentary it is the light, bright, deserted and elevated platform that seems uncanny.

The fluffers transform underground space again in Molly Dineen's 1989 television documentary *The Heart of the Angel*, which was made at the Islington tube station, Angel, before it was redeveloped.[41] The Angel is the deepest station on the London Underground, and was built with the two lines running on either side of a central platform island, rather than in separate tunnels, which means that the underground part of the station is a unified space. The film follows a fairly standard 'day in the life' structure, with a central fourteen minutes concerned with the invisible, underground, night-time work. It is a poignant portrait of an enclosed world, the first outside shot occurring nineteen minutes in. The workers at the station are demoralised by their deteriorating working conditions and the film opens with the clearly regular failure of the lifts and the streams of commuters labouring their way up the long stairs. The staff's inability to give the travelling public a satisfactory service is just one element in their low-grade dissatisfaction and dreams of elsewhere. These are differently expressed by different workers, from the hard-line 'I hate work' of the man in the ticket shop, to the lift operator who would rather try farming, to the man who would rather return to

Yorkshire and observes that 'It's not the same, London'. The topography of the film emphasises the verticalness of life in the station, the same faces going up and down, with nothing of the Islington outside. However, there is a horizontal dimension to space, but only deep underground. The linesmen appear on the platform from the tunnels and Dineen asks, 'How far have you just walked?' 'From Camden Town', comes the reply, and they are going on to Bank. But it is, once again, the fluffers whose use of space is most transformative. Unlike the 1950s representations of these workers, where we see them already in the overalls and ready to work, here Dineen films the women as they prepare for work, and interviews them directly. What we learn poses the question of where the women in *Under Night Streets* or *City After Dark* changed – and suggests one of the sources of the awkwardness of tone in which these workers are discussed – for in *The Heart of the Angel*, in 1989, the women change on the platform. Indeed, we first see the fluffers as they start to change on the deserted station platforms, performing for the camera as they strip to their underwear to put on their overalls, using the benches daily sat on by commuters to store their clothes. In a reversal of the public and private space staged in *The Wings of the Dove* with which we started, here the wooden benches polished and worn by millions of commuting bottoms are used like bedroom chairs or dressing-table stools. The empty public space of the station is rendered both intimate and unfamiliar. Their clothes neatly folded on the benches, the women climb down onto the tracks and enter the tunnels with their dusters and scrapers.

It is clearly still a filthy job – possibly filthier in 1989 than it was in 1958 – and there is still something that is both incongruous and shocking about the labour of these women in the tunnels, on foot, performing a hidden, public housework.[42] And that is perhaps the scandal, the awkwardness of the references to these workers, for the work has all the attributes of housework: invisible, repetitive, directed at maintenance not production, dealing with the detritus of everyday lives – and is, like housework, unrecognised. But it is also conducted in the middle of the night in dark tunnels, with women working in gangs, and both maintains and makes strange the spaces of the London Underground. The scandal in 2006, with a 'private finance initiative' in place, is the possibility that there is no one in the tunnels doing the dirty work.

These documentary films, revealing the hidden labour that has built and maintains the London Underground, provide a kind of negative of the 'strong story' of what lurks in the tunnel. It is not horror, or monsters, but labour that is realised very precisely through the way in which underground space is rendered in these films. *Deathline* recognises this relationship, for the cannibals who haunt the tunnels are the descendants of nineteenth-century labourers, abandoned by the entrepreneurs financing the building of the Underground after a fatal accident, but the spaces and labour of the fluffers are perhaps stranger because they are less generically familiar.

So the cinematic space of the London Underground is both a surprisingly bodily space and also a space to which the lack of an outside or a view lends a curious privacy. It is an internationally recognisable national space that signifies London, but also an international narrative space that prefers certain kinds of stories about the forgotten, the repressed, pursuit and chases. It is a space that is constantly made and remade in different times, and stories, and films. If the strong stories of the Underground are all about time, and space transformed into time, just like the cinema, we can also find there surprising intimacies.

Notes

1. The film is set in 1910. Peter Matthews observes 'The film-makers have updated the story to 1910, presumably to take advantage of the lifting of Victorian repression', Review, *The Wings of the Dove*, *Sight and Sound* vol.8 no. 1, January 1998, pp. 55–6. In the novel, Kate and Merton have a significant second meeting on the Underground, which is described as an accident that 'had been as natural as anything in London ever is', Henry James, *The Wings of the Dove* (Harmondsworth: Penguin, 1974 [1902]), p. 38.

2. Advice was taken from the London Transport Museum curators and archives about the Underground set and scenes. Thanks to Simon Murphy, Film and Photography Curator, London's Transport Museum, 11 December 2003.

3. The 1928 film *Underground* (Anthony Asquith) opens and closes with play generated by the offers of seats to women on the Tube. On this film see Tom Ryall, *Anthony Asquith* (Manchester: Manchester University Press, 2005), pp. 35–8, and Amy Sargeant, *British Cinema* (London: BFI, 2005), pp. 98–9.

4. Wolfgang Schivelbusch, *The Railway Journey* (Berkeley: University of California Press, 1986).

5. Nigel Floyd, interviewed on *Back Row*, BBC Radio 4, 14 March 2003.

6. See Lynne Kirby for a discussion of early cinema and the railway journey, *Parallel Tracks: The Railroad and Silent Cinema* (Durham, NC: Duke University Press, 1997). Kirby argues that early cinema and the railway both produce the modern subjectivity of 'spectator-passenger'. The underground railway can offer no analogy of panorama, view and screen because of its very undergroundness. Indeed, the carriages on one of the early London lines were known as 'padded cells', carpeted on floor and walls, with their tiny windows too high up to be seen through. Stephen Halliday, *Underground to Everywhere* (Stroud: Sutton, 2001), pp. 46–7.

7. Luc Besson in *Film Français* no. 2029, March 1985, p. 8, quoted by David Berry in 'Underground cinema: French visions of the Métro', in Myrto Konstantarakos (ed.), *Spaces in European Cinema* (Exeter: Intellect, 2000), p. 21.

8. Marc Augé, *In the Metro* (Minneapolis: University of Minnesota Press, 2002), p. 30.

9. Although this film does have an unusual, narratively unmotivated shot of tunnel and approaching platform from the driver's cab.

10. Christopher Smith, 'The making of *Creep*', *Creep* DVD (2004, Pathé Distribution).

11. Underground London (in general, not just the Underground) attracts passion which is manifest in clubs, tours, books, films and television series, and could be seen to be similar to some forms of film-buffery, such as horror film fandom. Trench and Hillman's 1984 study, *London Under London* (London: Murray, 1993 [1984]), is a significant exploration, while recently, Stephen Smith, in *Underground London* (London: Little, Brown, 2004), is ironically defensive in his anticipation of being chastised by 'my fellow underground explorers' for any inaccuracies in his book: 'they're completists, they're hair-splitters. In their view, no-one ever gets anything entirely right about what's underground, not even each other' (p. 31). Among the television series are *Under London Expedition* (*World About Us*, 7 November 1971) and *Underground London* (Granite for Carlton, weekly, 10 April 2001–1 May 2001).

12. Mark Ovenden, *Metro Maps of the World* (Harrow Weald: Capital Transport, 2003).

13. Ken Garland, *Mr Beck's Underground Map* (Harrow Weald: Capital Transport, 1994). Reprinted 1998 and 2003, selling 17,000. Ken Garland points out that 'Though not strictly speaking a map, this term is almost universally used by people referring to the London Underground diagram, hence the title of this book' (p. 3). Sales figures courtesy of Capital Transport Publishing, 5 December 2003.

14. David Pike, 'Modernist space and the transformation of underground London', in Pamela K. Gilbert, (ed.), *Imagined Londons* (Albany: State University of New York Press, 2002), p. 112. See also John A. Walker, 'The London Underground Diagram', in Teal Triggs (ed.), *Communicating Design: Essays in Visual Communication* (London: Batsford, 1995); Christian Wolmar, *The Subterranean Railway* (London: Atlantic, 2005 [2004]), pp. 274–7.

15. Simon Patterson, 'The Great Bear', 1992; Pike, 'Modernist space', p. 116.

16. Transport for London website <www.tfl.gov.uk>, accessed 21 May 2004.

17. Pierre Nora, 'Between memory and history: *Les Lieux de mémoire*', *Representations* no. 26, 1989, pp. 7–25.

18. *Lilliput*, 11 June 1942, pp. 472–82.

19. London Transport's celebratory *One Hundred Years Underground* (directed and narrated by John Rowdon, produced by Edgar Anstey and John Shearman). Julian Andrews, *London's War* (Aldershot: Lund Humphries, 2002), pp. 36–40. Andrews suggests that there is controversy about whether Moore sketched when actually in the shelters. In Craigie's film, Moore is shown using a notebook, but the framing is so tight that it is impossible to see whether he is in the presence of shelterers. See also John Gregg, *The Shelter of the Tubes* (Harrow: Capital Transport, 2001), p. 64; Imperial War Museum, *Henry Moore: War and Utility* (London: Imperial War Museum, 2006).

20. Henry Moore, interview in *Out of Chaos*.

21. Angus Calder's *The Myth of the Blitz* does not discuss this particular film, but his account provides a genealogy for this view of the London Blitz (London: Pimlico, 1992 [1991]). See also Wolmar, *The Subterranean Railway*, pp. 278–91.

22. Rosalind Williams, *Notes on the Underground* (Cambridge, MA: MIT Press, 1990), p. 48.

23. The 1959 BBC serial (written by Nigel Kneale, who also wrote the screenplay for Hammer), which opens on the street sign for Hobbs Lane, with the earlier, differently spelt sign visible underneath, does not use an Underground setting. The excavation is, instead, of an office development in Knightsbridge.

24. Peter Hutchings, '"We're the martians now"', in I. Q. Hunter, *British Science Fiction Cinema* (London: Routledge, 1999), p. 46.

25. Ibid., p. 41.

26. See Moya Luckett, 'Travel and mobility: femininity and national identity in Swinging London films', in Justine Ashby and Andrew Higson (eds), *British Cinema: Past and Present* (London, Routledge, 2000), pp. 233–46.

27. Trench and Hillman observe that during the excavation for the Victoria Line, 'Six fossil nautiloids, fifty million years old, were discovered near Victoria, and a plague pit was discovered near Victoria when a drum-digger began to churn up ground bones.' Trench and Hillman, *London Under London*, p. 159.

28. Played in the BBC version by the film-maker Lionel Ngakane.

29. On *Deathline*, regarded by some as a neglected classic, see Marcelle Perks, 'A descent into the underworld: *Deathline*', in Steve Chibnall and Julian Petley (eds), *British Horror Cinema* (London: Routledge, 2002), pp. 145–55, and Nick Freeman, 'London kills me: the English metropolis in British horror films of the 1970s', in Xavier Mendik (ed.), *Shocking Cinema of the Seventies* (Hereford: Noir, 2002), pp. 193–210.

30. *Creep* has a more inclusive understanding of underground London, starting in sewers and extending to nameless storage bunkers. Kim Newman discusses the relationship between *Creep* and *Deathline* in his review of *Creep*, *Sight & Sound* vol. 15 no. 2 (NS), February 2005, pp. 47–8.

31. Lance Pettit discusses the film at more length in *Screening Ireland* (Manchester: Manchester University Press, 2000), pp. 85–8, and 'Philip Donnellan, Ireland and dissident documentary', *Historical Journal of Film, Radio and Television* vol. 20 no. 3, 2000, pp. 352–65. In his unpublished autobiography, Philip Donnellan relates the refusal to show the film both to institutional changes at the BBC and to English hostility to the Irish. *We Were the BBC: An alternative view of a producer's responsibility 1948–84*, ch. 11.

32. These Irish workers are part of a long tradition: the majority of labourers on Brunel's tunnel under the Thames (1825–43), the first subacqueous tunnel, were Irish. Benson Bobrick, *Labyrinths of Iron* (New York: Newsweek Books, 1981), p. 59.

33. In the almost contemporary *Smashing Time* (1967), northerners Rita Tushingham and Lynn Redgrave arrive in London at St Pancras and naively ask a drunken Irishman for directions to Carnaby Street. He is picked up for work and they end up in Camden Street with other Lump workers.

34. The songs are credited to MacColl and Seeger as 'songs to traditional Irish melodies'. The credited singers are Paul Lennihan and Joe Heaney, although many individuals are featured singing diegetically. Other non-diegetic songs used include 'The Rambler from Clare' and 'Jack of all Trades', both of which share precise reference to the different parts of Ireland, which might have been home to the singers or the audience.

35. Hamid Naficy, *An Accented Cinema* (Princeton, NJ: Princeton University Press, 2001).

36. Donnellan, *We Were the BBC*, p. 152.

37. Smith, *Underground London*, is wryly self-conscious about 'a stripe of men – and they were predominantly men – who had a fascination with what was underground' (p. 22).

38. London Transport Museum Library, Document 001355 18R6, p. 3.

39. Directed by Ralph Keene, produced by Edgar Anstey for British Transport Films. The film was given a theatrical release in the West End in 1958, and the *London Transport Magazine* publicised it as 'A Film You Should See', observing 'The content of facts and figures has been judged well. Not too much to overwhelm the general cinemagoer, but sufficient to hold the interest of the transport man himself', *London Transport Magazine* vol. 12 no. 5, August 1958, p. 16.

40. This difficulty of tone is also apparent in Trench and Hillman's classic study, where they refer to 'that esoteric body of workers in the Underground: the fluffers. The fluffers are a small group of stalwart ladies who work in the tunnels in the small hours …', Trench and Hillman, *London Under London*, p. 130. See also Smith, *Underground London*, p. 274.

41. *The Heart of the Angel*, an Allegra Film for the BBC. Camera, editing and producer: Molly Dineen. Producer for the BBC: Caroline Pick. Transmitted in the *40 Minutes* slot, BBC2, 26 November 1989. See Stella Bruzzi on this film, in *New Documentary: A Critical Introduction* (London: Routledge, 2000), pp. 164–7.

42. Halliday, *Underground to Everywhere*, suggests that the fluffers were mainly replaced in the 1970s by the 'big yellow duster', a five-car cleaning train (p. 195). Clearly not at the Angel. London Transport records on this group of workers appear almost non-existent.

5

The Gangster, the Ripper and the Housewife

Foreigners somehow expect the squares of London to be fog-wreathed, full of hansom cabs and littered with ripped whores.

Pub conversation: Frenzy (Alfred Hitchcock, 1972)

The East End was emphatically not the same thing as East London. Outsiders might mix up the two terms, but no Guermantes ever distinguished himself more jealously from a Courvoisier than a true East Ender did from an East Londoner. But what exactly was the true East End? Here there was ample room for disagreement.

John Gross[1]

Most writers who have concerned themselves with East London are motivated by ethnic or family connections, by a spirit of adventure, or by political zeal.

Dick Hobbs[2]

When planning the structure of this book and puzzling over the arrangement of different kinds of cinematic London, the East End was always going to be included. Other topics and chapters – Swinging London films, Victorian London, heritage London, the suburbs, Michael Caine, Soho films, London musicals – have waxed and waned, but it has always been clear that a book on London in the cinema should consider the cinematic East End. This is because the East End of London, in ways I shall explore, exists as a strongly generic space. In the East End, certain characters can be found and certain narratives take place. In addition to Tower Bridge, St Paul's and the Palace of Westminster, the mean and sometimes misty streets of the East End are among the most internationally resonant images of London. What Rob Shields has called 'the place image' of the East End is of the terraced streets, overcrowded courts and dingy alleys, where poor people and immigrants live, and the stories that take place there are set in poverty and deprivation.[3] In Chapter 2, on 'Local London', I discussed several different cinematic Londons, in which 'the local' was constructed as the space and time of everyday life for working-class people. This local ordinary London can also be found set in the East End, in films such as *It Always Rains on Sunday* (1947) and *Sparrows Can't Sing* (1963). However, I will explore the ways in which the cinematic East End, while it can be staged as a 'local London', is more commonly imagined as a dark place where 'the poor' live. The poverty of the East End has proved fascinatingly 'other', not ordinary at all, and its cinematic repertoire is dominated by the strong generic markings of horror, melodrama and gangster films. This is not an argument that the local and ordinary east London produced through realist, naturalist and sub-naturalist codes, its personae the cockney and the matriarch (this is, after all, where *EastEnders* is set), is not also a generic London. But it is a suggestion that the complex cultural matrix that is 'the East End' is most easily recognised in the cinema through heightened, non-naturalistic, generic marking. The point was nicely made by Rachel Neale, who was the production manager on the Phil Collins vehicle *Buster* (1988), a film based on the involvement of the south London criminal Buster Edwards in the 1963 'Great Train Robbery'. Neale, discussing the choice of locations for shooting, commented: 'We use Hackney [east London] in *Buster* because it had the right seedy, slightly dodgy feel. And it seemed appropriate as the film had wide release in the America, where they seem to assume that Buster was from the East End.'[4] The image of the London East End, particularly the late-nineteenth-century London East End, has an international currency, and has historically attracted a gaze which is both fascinated and horrified. This gaze, from Victorian philanthropists, novelists, journalists and revolutionaries, from Berlin, New York, Paris and the West End and City of London, has created an image of the East End as darkest London which pre-dates cinema, but which is endlessly revisited and recreated by the cinema.

There are, in the cinematic East End, three story sites which are particularly generative, and which engender their own, familiar, protagonists: the Whitechapel murders of the 1880s (Jack the Ripper); the 'cosmopolitan' East End, particularly the Jewish East End and 'Chinese' Limehouse;[5] and the story of the stalwart East End community: cheery heroic cockneys and ruthless gangsters who 'look after their own'. There is also a fourth story, which I can't discuss here, but which must be acknowledged, as much of the notable growth of writing about the East End in the 1980s and 1990s, such as that of Patrick Wright and Iain Sinclair, is related to this tradition, which has inaugural texts in the work of those nineteenth-century pioneers, such as Henry Mayhew and Charles Booth, who explored the East End. This is the story of the documentarist: the film-maker who travels to the East End (rarely a native), and reports back on his findings, often with a view to improvement. Edgar Anstey's *Housing Problems* (1935), in a revolutionary technique for the time, used interviews with East End slum-dwellers to report on housing conditions,[6] and there are several 1940s documentaries, most notably *Land of Promise* (Paul Rotha, 1945) and *Neighbourhood 15* (1948 about West Ham), which address the problem of post-war reconstruction with particular reference to East London.[7] Lorenza Mazzetti's fiction *Together* (1956), about two deaf-mute dock-labourers, shown in the first Free Cinema programme, is part of this tradition. The device of the deaf-mute central characters (played by Michael Andrews and Edward Paolozzi) both permits and makes strange the location-shot everyday East End life, just as the soundtrack moves between the everyday and silence. Following their daily routines demands a practice of documentary on the part of the viewer. The provenance of this type of work begins to change in the latter part of the twentieth century, as changing patterns of gentrification lead to a greater concentration of 'cultural workers' in the East End, who are involved in witnessing and documenting the changes of which they are themselves the avant-garde.[8] The building of Docklands, the widening of the A13 and the site-clearing for the 2012 Olympics have provoked film work such as William Raban's A13 (1994) and Emily Richardson's *Transit* (2006), which is often elegiac in its documentation of the transformation of the East End, just as *The Vanishing Street* was in 1962.[9]

It is through these stories that I have structured this chapter, starting with a recent version of the Whitechapel murders, *From Hell* (2001). The cinematic Limehouse of films such as E. A. Dupont's *Piccadilly* (1929) and D. W. Griffith's *Broken Blossoms* (1919) deserves much more substantial study than I can give it here, rooted as it is in silent cinema and the early part of the twentieth century. Colin McArthur has pointed to its importance in shaping cinematic London in sequences such as the 'Limehouse Blues' section of the 1946 Hollywood film *Ziegfeld Follies*,[10] and it was to be found in the twenty-first century on British television in a new Sherlock Holmes story starring Rupert Everett, *Sherlock Holmes and the Case of the Silk Stocking* (2004).[11] In this version, Holmes smoked opium in Limehouse, and the patronising relationship between Holmes and Watson was given a new twist through Holmes's ability to speak Chinese to café/den owners. In this chapter, I can only note that the Johnny Depp character in *From Hell* begins and ends the film (and his life) in an opium den, and does so glamorously in a way that mobilises his earlier, decadent, star persona.

The central protagonists of these East End stories are usually men, and the East End could be characterised as the terrain of serial killers, detectives, opium dealers, gangsters, spivs and dockers. It is certainly in this guise that it enjoyed a revival in the 1990s as a homosocial world of 'diamond geezers' and hard men in the mainly London-set gangster cycle, which includes films such as *Lock, Stock and Two Smoking Barrels* (1998) and *Gangster No. 1* (2000), wittily discussed by Steve Chibnall as gangster 'light' and 'heavy'.[12] But there are women in the East End too, and I suggest that there is shadow story to these macho exploits, which can be traced within and across these East End films. The woman's East End story is an old story too, figured through the familiar opposition of the mother and the whore, although here good women wear a patterned pinny or a Salvation Army uniform, and bad girls can come to very nasty ends indeed.

While I have been preparing this book, the US crime novelist Patricia Cornwell has spent huge amounts of money trying to prove the identity of Jack the Ripper as the painter Walter Sickert, paying for full-page advertisements in the British newspapers to support her theories.[13] This is just one of the more recent instances of the fascination with this figure and his crimes that seems to stalk the East End. Rather like the London Underground, as discussed in Chapter 4, Jack attracts fans and fanatics: he is a cult text, and so is his London. I cannot match this expertise, nor do I care who Jack the Ripper was, but note that the continuing uncertainty legitimates the obsessive return to the scenes of the crime in a type of murder tourism. In particular, the speculation of the involvement of 'a gentleman', or one of higher rank, renders this tourism as another variant of the journey from the bourgeois West End to investigate the 'darkest East' which has characterised so much scholarship on the East End. However, in relation to London in the cinema, Jack is inescapable, and so I have chosen to discuss him here in the 2001 Hughes Brothers film *From Hell*. This film was studio-shot in Prague, and is the latest in a long line of internationally produced London East Ends, thus raising some interesting questions for the study as a whole.

In a survey of the historical development of the 'spatial idea' of the East End across litera-ture, film and television, Paul Newland has argued that the East End is 'an essentially pre-modern spatial idea', a necessary 'low Other' to the construction of middle-class London identities further west, with its apotheosis in the late nineteenth century.[14] Newland explores the persistence and transformations of the late-Victorian East End across the twen-tieth century, arguing that by the end of the twentieth century 'the generic spatial idea of the East End continues to function in representations of London',[15] and showing how it is dif-ferently inflected in different kinds of film-making and writing, ranging from the work of Iain Sinclair and Monica Ali to Kaurismäki's *I Hired a Contract Killer* (1990) and David Cronenberg's *Spider* (2002). Newland's account is illuminating in its tracing of the persistence of the 'chronotope' of the Victorian East End, so evidently with us still in the cult of Jack the Ripper, and impressive in its scope. My account is inflected towards the representation of com-munity – for which the Second World War is particularly significant – within the cinematic East End and, more generally, to the question of the gendering of the place image of the East End.

The devastating damage caused to the East End and the Docks during the Second World War was followed by large-scale redevelopment and the movement of populations out to new towns and suburban development. These upheavals, in the context of the slow decline of the Docks, which is addressed in the following chapter, the changing patterns of immi-gration into, and emigration from, the East End and the further casualisation of the labour market, meant that for the second half of the twentieth century, the East End was charac-terised by change as brutal as the original upheavals of the building of the Docks in the nine-teenth century. In this context, I discuss two tales of crime in the working-class community of the 'old' East End, the first, *It Always Rains on Sunday*, a post-war Ealing film centred on Pet-ticoat Lane market, made at the beginning of the study period; the second, *The Krays* (1990), made towards the end, but looking back to mid-century and pre-dating the laddish 1990s British gangster cycle. Each of these films gives a central role to an active East End woman, and through this, disturbs some of the patterns of representation of a generic, criminal East End with its tired imagination privileging the murdered prostitute as the figure of the femi-nine. Violet Kray (Billie Whitelaw) and Rose Sandigate (Googie Withers) are each in their own ways struggling hard to gain and retain the status that distinguishes the respectable from the 'rough' working class. This respectability is signified most frequently and economically in the cinema through a detail of costume: wearing a pinny. This garment, an overall worn over everyday clothes to protect them while cleaning and cooking, has a symbolic resonance throughout these East End films, in both its presence and its absence.

I draw attention to this detail of costume for two reasons. First, it is an example of the way in which place, in the cinema, is signified through details such as costume. While this might seem an obvious point, I stress it because some writing about the city and the cinema addresses only the spaces of the streets, buildings and architecture. A woman standing on her doorstep wearing a pinny signifies one type of working-class area – in these films the East End – just as a woman wearing a bedraggled bustle, bonnet and shawl in a foggy street

Rose Sandigate (Googie Withers) in a pinny in *It Always Rains on Sunday*

The Krays: Violet Kray (Billie Whitelaw) wearing a pinny to clean her front doorstep at the beginning of the film

signifies another, and each will stimulate generic expectations. Second, while in some ways the figure of the working-class matriarch is as stereotypical as that of the murdered whore – and here Sinclair demonstrates his characteristic attention to detail in pointing out that offence was taken on behalf of Violet Kray because of the way in which her 'smartness' was betrayed in *The Krays*[16] – there is something about the banality of a pinny that is not quite assimilable to the cultish imaginary of the East End. The patterned fabric of the pinny, its repeated, busy designs repelling attention from any dirt or stains, reminds us of other stories than those of sexual murder in those mean streets. The pinny is a garment that testifies to an everyday life of undramatic labour, of clothes and parlours kept for best. Of a local London persisting in the macho imagination of the East End.

London Horror: Murderous Places

From Hell is a recent version of one of the most resonant London stories, that of the 1880s Whitechapel murders, usually known through their unidentified perpetrator, Jack the Ripper. There are hundreds of versions of this story, which has been retold across many media and contributes strongly to an image of London as a perpetually Victorian city where murder is committed in labyrinthine alleyways. The fog of Jack the Ripper's East End makes of London a murderous place. The international currency of this London is directly, and rather archly, referenced at the beginning of Alfred Hitchcock's 1972 return to serial-killer London, *Frenzy*. As one gentleman observes to another in a Covent Garden pub after the reporting of another 'neck tie murder', 'good juicy sex crimes' are 'so good for the tourist trade', continuing, as cited at the opening of this chapter, 'Foreigners somehow expect the squares of London to be fog-wreathed, full of hansom cabs and littered with ripped whores'.[17] Judith Walkowitz commences her scholarly investigation of the contexts of the Whitechapel murders by reporting on the 1980 installation of a 'Ripper Street' at Madame Tussaud's in London in response to public demand for horror greater than that offered by Tussaud's 'Chamber of Horrors'.[18] 'Ripper Street' is just one variant of a cross-media cultural phenomenon which, partly because the case has no closure, has proved both resilient and generative. There are post-cards, maps, tea-towels, comic books, graphic novels, scholarly articles, books, television pro-grammes and films. Kim Newman, in a survey of Ripper films, suggests that 'The case at once embodies a melodramatic vision of the Victorian era (gaslight, fog, Sherlock Holmes, gin-swilling drabs) and sets the agenda (forensic medicine, gutter journalism, criminal psychology) for the supposedly twentieth century phenomenon of the serial killer.'[19] The story of the Whitechapel murders and Jack the Ripper is told and retold across many sites, with many different kinds of participation by tellers and audiences. There were once street ballads, and now there are walking tours and websites. This is a story that is told about the East End of London, but that, in its endless retelling, makes and remakes London as a city within which certain types of stories take place. The filmic collocation of the 1880s and 'Whitechapel' or 'London's East End' signifies a place of sexual murder. I will look at the filmic presentation of this place of murder in relation to a studio-shot US film. I am interested in the resonance of the cultural meanings of 1880s Whitechapel, and the way in which, here, 'place' is most evidently constructed through generic narrative and iconography. Jack's Whitechapel, I will argue, is a unique narrative place or topos, in which certain events must take place. The variations in *how* they take place, and how these variations might be understood, is dealt with only briefly here, through a comparison with an earlier German version of Jack's story from G. W. Pabst's *Pandora's Box* (1929).

From Hell was shot in Prague, using, mainly, a specially built set, and was made by two film-makers, Albert and Allen Hughes, known for their representation of the African Ameri-can city space, 'the hood', in *Menace II Society* (1993) and *Dead Presidents* (1995). The Hughes Brothers are quoted as saying that they regarded *From Hell* as a 'ghetto film',[20] and its sym-pathies lie, if not exactly with the poor, certainly not with the hypocritical British establish-ment. It is based on the graphic novel of the same name by Alan Moore and Eddie Campbell, which is told from the point of view of Queen Victoria's physician, Sir William Gull, who is, from the beginning, revealed as the murderer. The film withholds the identity of the mur-derer, offering instead a series of red herrings, which are investigated by the sympathetic Inspector Abberline (Johnny Depp), a man who, in his mourning for the death of his wife in childbirth, takes refuge in opium dens. There are echoes of the Holmes/Watson partnership in Abberline's relationship with his sergeant, Godley (Robbie Coltrane), while the Abberline character is also familiar from television cop shows as the under-appreciated, put-upon policeman getting his job done despite his superiors.[21] The film creates an immediately recognisable London ghetto location for the telling of a well-known London story, but its pro-duction had little to do with London, apart from the employment of some British actors. Newman refers to the perpetuation of 'a timeless Ripper-and-fog-blighted London', in dis-cussion of the cycle of 1960s German Ripper films, and *From Hell* partakes of and contributes to this London, in ways that are also, as I suggest below, historically specific.[22]

Location is immediately established at the opening of *From Hell* through the use of titles. Opening with 'London, 1888', the film's graphic novel origins can be discerned in the silhou-

ndon skyline, with the dome of St Paul's prominent under a red sky. This is landmark a view of a Victorian city, presented under a twenty-first-century CGI sky promising

There is a cut to a contrasted view, a closer shot of the upper floors of residential houses and second title, 'Whitechapel District'. The camera tilts down the houses, showing them to be multi-occupied, with people and families in every room, until it reaches the street. The palette has become drab, the grey-brown of poverty, and it is only when the camera reaches two women standing opposite the Ten Bells public house that there is bright colour again, this time in the red hair of the woman we soon learn is Mary Kelly. These are, initially, the two locations of this film: 'London' and the slum that is 'Whitechapel District', where the non-native usage, 'Whitechapel District', is a trace of the film's origins, but also testifies to the international currency of Jack the Ripper. 'London' in the film has a few West End locations: the offices of the Special Branch, Cleopatra's Needle, Buckingham Palace and some interiors; but mainly it appears as a variant of this initial silhouette of the St Paul's skyline to signify 'London: not the East End'. This is most pronounced when the River Thames is included in the landmark imagery, as it is when we see the killer's coach rattling over Westminster Bridge or heading east along the Embankment with the river and Westminster in the background. This is a good example of cinematic geography, for in each case, what we see is a transition from the West End to the East End which is made more striking by the inclusion of water in the passage. This is an aesthetic choice that privileges the representation of the significance of this journey over its geography – Whitechapel is not south of the river, nor would this be an imaginable route. The point is the separation between the two Londons.

Pandora's Box is set mainly in Berlin, where its beautiful heroine, Lulu (Louise Brooks), blithely lives off men, tormenting, in particular, a father and son, and only moves to the East End of London for its last twenty minutes. Structurally, the shift to the East End is rather odd and abrupt, unanticipated in the earlier narrative, although it is clear that Berlin has become a little too hot for Lulu. As Mary Ann Doane puts it, 'In Pabst's film there is no preparation

From Hell: a landmark London skyline

whatsoever for the appearance of Jack the Ripper.'[23] Despite the presence of Jack the Ripper at the end, this is not, as a whole, a Ripper film. However, the use of the Whitechapel location and the Jack the Ripper character is illuminating for the argument that I wish to pursue in relation to cinematic London. Throughout the film, Lulu has created havoc through the desire she inspires in both men and women. It seems that no one can resist her, particularly when she tilts her head and smiles, so that light seems to shine from her black shiny hair, her eyes and her teeth. Lulu is uncontrollable, and those involved with her lose control of their own destinies. The awkwardness of the move to the East End thus has a meta-narrative logic in the recruitment of Jack the Ripper to put an end to Lulu's story. It is as if Lulu's seductive presence can only be controlled through what amounts to a *deus ex machina*, an almost extra-textual killing agent. The film moves Lulu to a location that signifies the killing of prostitutes. The *mise en scène* is economical. A lonely figure in overcoat and hat wanders the misty streets: excluded and isolated, he peers through the brightly lit windows at Christmas trees. This is a sad Jack (not yet identified as such), already in the East End, himself too one of the poor. A Salvation Army band plays, and Jack's neediness is recognised by a uniformed Sally Army lass – her uniform protecting her from being mistaken for a bad girl on the streets – who offers him mistletoe and a cup of tea.[24] The fog is thick, obscuring most of the street scene. Only when we learn that Lulu, to provide food for her companions, is preparing to leave their shared garret to solicit do we see a notice warning 'Women of London' of four successful murders. Lulu's destiny is clear, although her death is delayed by Jack's attempts to resist his urges and his confession that he has no money. Lulu does, most literally, ask for it, as she persuades him to come upstairs even without money. In two sequences, visual equivalences are established between bright shiny Lulu, light reflecting off her hair and her eyes, and a knife, its blade caught in the light. Finally, Lulu's bright, shiny life-force is extinguished by a knife which catches Jack's eye as it gleams in the guttering candle. Outside in the fog, no one knows what has happened.

In the east London ending to *Pandora's Box* we find an elegant condensation – designed by Andrei Andreiev – of the *mise en scène* of the Ripper myth in the cinema: the mist, the cobbled streets, the dim gas lights, the contrast between the good Salvation Army girl and the prostitute, the poverty and wretchedness, the dark entrances and the pub. There is in this version no aristocrat summoning poor women into his coach and no other victims, so Lulu's fate seems more her own – paradoxically, for a woman who has lived on her sexual allure, the consequences of not charging for sex. However, the structure of the film, the unanticipated transition to London, even the very sympathy of the portrayal of the murderer, thus reveals something of the Ripper's East End as a narrative topos. It is a place where women of a certain type, who are unprotected by uniform or pinny, will meet their death.

Seventy years later, this same killing place is staged in *From Hell*, a colour film which was made with quite different technological resources and generic affiliations. The vast set of *From Hell*, the use of garish colour for the women's clothing and blood, the use of CGI, particularly for the rendering of Christchurch Spitalfields, and the invoked heritage of graphic novels and a century of Ripperania, means that the look of *From Hell* is quite different to that of *Pandora's Box*. There is more attention to the rendering of three-dimensional spaces, rather than the idea of the East End perceived through fog. However, as a generic destiny for women, the cinematic place remains recognisably the same. Lulu's murder in *Pandora's Box* is formally rather beautiful, with the candlelight moving from Lulu to the blade of murder weapon. The chiaroscuro lighting illuminates tenderness in both Lulu and Jack's faces before he becomes gripped by mania. The death itself is shown merely by Lulu's slackening hand, and finishes a story that began and mainly takes place elsewhere. *From Hell* is, self-consciously, another version of a familiar story, with its own hypothesis about the identity of Jack the Ripper, and an attractive and fallible detective hero played by Johnny Depp. Peter Hutchings suggests that the version of the Ripper story found in *From Hell* was a 'rather worn-out conspiracy narrative', originating in the 1970s, a decade rich in political conspiracy thrillers. He argues that the existence of the many different versions of the Ripper narrative points to its historical mutability, the way in which it changes over time in response to its broader contexts.[25] Thus, in *From Hell* there is both the political conspiracy narrative and a more contemporary nostalgia for 1970s horror also apparent in other recent horror re-makes. The East End here is understood through late-twentieth-century understandings of the social context of 'the ghetto' and post-feminist female solidarity, which affects both the portrayal of the women, but also the fates of the two central male protagonists. The elaborate East End set is not, it seems to me, realised in the detail of the simulacrum because of anything to do with place, but as a kind of aesthetic *quid pro quo* for more highly elaborated and visceral portrayals of the murders.

The first murder takes place within ten minutes of the film opening. As Inspector Abberline 'sees' the murders in his opium dreams – flashed, bloody visions – the audience is offered a double access to them. There is Abberline's apprehension of them, which is offered as a subjective vision, and there is the murder itself. This device in part responds to one of the difficulties of retelling this well-known story in the twenty-first century. Every audience member must know that this is a film about killing women, and some at least will know the names of the victims and the whereabouts of their murders. Abberline's psychic responsiveness to the murders is like an internalised generic knowledge. In bloody glimpses he sees knives, cut throats, dress fabric, mutilated bodies: the generic iconography of Jack the Ripper, and what an audience too will anticipate. In a similar strategy, twentieth-century theories about ritual in serial killing are embodied in the narrative of the film by the shots of significant place names 'Millers Court', 'Mitre Square', which cue the fan to what is about to take place, allowing them to participate in the ritual at a narrative level, a participation that is developed in the interplay between Abberline and Godley as they examine the clues on each body.

The murders in the film are progressively more detailed and explicit. The horror of the mutilations is both flaunted and withheld. The police surgeon and his assistant are overcome with nausea and revulsion during the first autopsy, the surgeon declaring that he should not have to work with 'this degradation' – and it is not quite clear whether he means the bodies of whores or the mess that has been made of them. The most extended blood sequence intercuts Gull's removal of a human heart during a medical/scientific demonstration in a lecture theatre with the killing of the final victim. He is seen wrestling with the muscularity of the bloody organ as he tries to remove it from the body cavity: the strenuousness of 'good' scientific organ removal standing in for the frenzied evisceration of the murder victims. However, even this gory struggle is insufficient, and the film augments its depiction of sexual murder with two other forms of body horror. One of these, the display of John Merrick (Anthony Parker), 'the Elephant Man', to a fund-raising gathering of the great and the good, was evidently meant to condemn high society for its voyeurism on the less fortunate.[26] A careful distinction is made, within the scene, between the expressions on the faces of those in evening dress and that of Inspector Abberline, in day clothes. Abberline averts his gaze slightly, and an expression of discomfort registers. More integrated within the narrative, and thus more significant, is the administration of a lobotomy on Annie, the prostitute unfortunate enough to have secretly married the Duke of Clarence and borne him a child – and imagined that she has thus gained respectability. This scene, and its sequels, is arguably more horrifying than the murders. It extends the depicted mutilations of the female body through a planned and deliberately undertaken operation which is performed before an audience – and filmed with close-ups of the whirring metal drill which will be driven through Annie's frontal lobes after she has been tied down and chloroformed.[27] The sequence does two things. First, it is clearly part of an argument, which also includes the Elephant Man sequence, which seeks to indict the upper classes in their attitude to the bodies of the poor. But, second, it provides an unexpected – extra-generic – form of female mutilation for its audience, which is matched, in a twenty-first-century equal opportunity fantasy at the end of the film, with a similar operation performed on Dr Gull. Arguably, this 'equal opportunities' generic variation is also to be found in relation to death at the ending of the film, when it is the Johnny Depp character, Inspector Abberline, who dies (beautifully, suicidally, peacefully), and the last of the Ripper's victims Mary Kelly, who, through his solicitude, is alive. Without wishing to enter the back-alleys of Ripper scholarship about the fate of Mary Kelly, *From Hell*'s version could be seen to offer a twenty-first-century transposition of the death of film's major star with the life of the last victim, who is shown in a country cottage wearing white, with the hint of a clean pinny.

Newman suggests that the Jack the Ripper narrative combines a melodramatic vision of Victorian London with the more twentieth-century agenda associated with serial killing. *From Hell* conforms to this description with its iconography of the Victorian slum, its emphasis on press photography and its knowing attitude to 'the destruction of evidence' in the case of the removal of graffiti. Inspector Abberline understands the ritual elements of serial killing, and has an involuntary capacity to apprehend the murders in vivid, blood-soaked dreams. However, the film also offers a radically republican retrospective on the social relations of the 1880s, recasting the narrative as one in which royal peccadilloes are concealed by a racist and snobbish establishment against the valiant efforts of the 'common' Inspector Abberline and his staff and the whores whom they seek to protect. The hell that is the East End in this film is shown to be both contained and preyed upon by the upper-class establishment. It is their ruthless protection of their own power that leads to the murders and Annie's lobotomy, and against their established might, Abberline and trusty Sergeant Godley are honest but impotent. So although the East End is portrayed as a lower depths clustered around Christchurch in Spitalfields, the world of the ruling class is finally shown to lie even deeper below the surface of the city. The downward camera movement that first introduced Whitechapel, in contrast to the West End, is repeated to make this point, showing that underneath the city lie the catacombs of class conspiracy. A daytime view of the City of London, with a railway viaduct and a view of St Paul's giving depth in the background to the street scene in the foreground, is transformed as the camera pans down, through a cross-section of the cobbled street. This first pan down is then matched with a second, which reveals, after following the movement of Special Branch Commander Sidney through an underground passage, a huge, subterranean Masonic temple. Here, all the key players of the conspiracy can be found, participating in the initiation of the lobotomist surgeon into their ranks. So the two worlds of the film are shown to be maintained by underground conspiracy and murder. The murders may take place in the netherworld of the East End, but they are planned and executed in the underworld that subtends the Establishment of the West.

Newland's discussion of the film places its recreation of 'pre-modern' space within his broader argument that the East End of London persists within the cultural imaginary as 'a spatial idea' onto which are cathected 'continuing anxieties concerning material progress and modernity, rationality and irrationality, ethnicity and Otherness, class and its related systems of behaviour, violence, crime and sexuality'.[28] In the context of this argument, the Hughes Brothers' choice to make this 'ghetto' film can be interestingly aligned both with the history of the representation of the African American 'hood' in the cinema and with the contemporaneity of some elements of From Hell. Most bizarre of these, now that the first stage of the redevelopment of the former Spitalfields Market has been completed, is that the huge set of From Hell seems now to prefigure the simulation of Spitalfields that has been built and preserved in the East End. Raphael Samuel has pointed out,

> It is the pathos of conservation, even where, as in Spitalfields, it is carried out under expert guidance, that it produces the opposite of its intended effect. Returning buildings to their original condition (or attempting to do so) robs them of the very quality for which they are prized – *oldness* … Fetishizing period, it freezes the building at a point where history has not yet happened to it.[29]

Newland carefully traces some of the differences between the London district of Spitalfields and the set of From Hell.[30] In a Baudrillardian cycle, it seems now that the 'pre-modern' idea of the East End finds itself manifest as a quaint postmodern shopping opportunity.

In relation to London and the cinema, a simpler point related to Franco Moretti's notion that 'different forms inhabit different spaces' can be also made.[31] In the cinema 'Whitechapel, 1880s' makes a generic promise, and gives a place and time for the sexual murder of women. While there are many cinematic spaces that are dangerous for female characters in gothic, thriller and horror genres, such as upstairs rooms, cellars, locked rooms, dark alleys, deserted buildings, sheds, empty streets, 'Whitechapel, 1880s' is unique.[32] These other locations are made threatening cinematically, through the generic and diegetic construction of space. The upstairs room is scary when the woman goes up there alone after the electricity has failed and she has dropped the torch. This scary room can be created anywhere, in any house, in any country. Whitechapel, 1880s, is both geographically and temporally specified – this area of London at this historical time – and can be staged through the most minimal – or the most extravagant – of sets. All that is required is a little mist, some cobblestones, a gas street light, a knife, some alleyways – and some victims. The international meaning of this East End of London is that it is a narrative place in which unspeakably horrible things will happen to women.

For London in the cinema, the power and international resonance of these stories means that the East End of London acts as the horror 'other' to landmark icons such as Big Ben and red buses. The redness of blood is more vividly present in the iconography of the city than a concentration on buses, post-boxes and telephone kiosks might at first suggest, lending weight to suggestions about the significance of the horror genre to cinematic London.

East End Noir

> It was a Sunday afternoon, wet and cheerless: and a duller spectacle this earth of ours has not
> to show than a rainy Sunday in London.
> > Thomas de Quincey, *Confessions of an Opium Eater*, 1821, Penguin, 2003, p. 43

> *Notes to Departments*: The indication (*RAIN*) in heading of scene means rain certainly required;
> (?RAIN) means rain may be required, depending on set-up. Absence of indication means rain
> not required.
> In all non-rain sequences where exteriors are seen (even through windows and doors) some
> degree of post-rain wetness will probably be required.
> > Shooting script, *It Always Rains on Sunday*, 24 January 1947, p. ii. London,
> > British Film Institute Library

It Always Rains on Sunday is one of Ealing Studios' rare excursions to the East End of London. Like the earlier Ealing film set among the recruits to the Auxiliary Fire Service, *The Bells Go Down* (Basil Dearden, 1943), the film offers the ancient street market of Petticoat Lane as an identifying landmark for the district, although in *It Always Rains on Sunday* Petticoat Lane is more central to the action. Both films are set east of the City but they have very different tones, and invoke different Londons. Evidently, this is partly attributable to their different relation to the war. *The Bells Go Down*, made during the war, is distinguished by the violent coexistence of the comic and the heroic, both embodied by the comedian Tommy Trinder who is killed in a burning building at the end of the film while rescuing his chief. Despite this tragedy, the film works to maintain the sense of an optimistic and unified community, working together and overcoming differences amid a London in flames. *It Always Rains on Sunday*, made two years after the end of the war, is, as its title suggests, rather more downbeat in mood. The theft from the Docks of individual barrels of Guinness by one fireman in *The Bells Go Down* is here extended to the involvement of many characters in deception, theft, robbery, bet-fixing and a range of under-the-counter deals. As Barr has observed, there is very little sense of a community except as a pressure on the individual,[33] although the film does present the area as teeming – to use a word often used about the East End[34] – with enterprise and character. This is achieved through the detail of plot and performance, from the would-be spivs' theft of 'a gross of children's roller-skates' to Hermione Baddeley's magnificent dismissal of Jack Warner's CID man by scratching her bottom as she turns away from him. The tone of the London in *It Always Rains on Sunday*, though, is one which would be recognisable to Thomas de Quincey writing more than a century earlier about London further West: 'wet and cheerless', in which different individuals' dreams of escape from Bethnal Green end in disappointment.

I want to look at this 'dull spectacle' of the East End in relation to some key personae of post-war London, the spiv, the cockney and the housewife, and the different generic contexts these personae demand. I also want to explore the extent to which the film represents the East End as a Jewish East End, a topic that attracted some fierce commentary when the film was first released but which has been rarely mentioned since.[35]

It Always Rains on Sunday is set in and around Petticoat Lane and Bethnal Green. Within a realist 'day in the life' structure, which opens and closes with old newspapers blowing against the closed gates of Whitechapel tube station, the film contains a generically more melodramatic story about the dreams and dilemmas of a former barmaid, Rose Sandigate (Googie Withers), who is now married with stepchildren. This story is contextualised within the area through a range of sub-plots, several of which are criminal or semi-criminal. The Sandigate family live in a small terraced house near Petticoat Lane, and the film deals with the disruptions to their normal routine on a wet and rainy Sunday. The principal – but not the only – disruption is that caused by the sudden reappearance of Rose's former lover, Tommy Swann (John McCallum), on the run after escaping from Dartmoor, and the final part of the film is a long location-shot chase sequence in a railway marshalling yard.

The film's East End is staged with the familiar iconographic elements of 1940s working-class London: terraced housing, a pub, the Salvation Army and a street market with its soundtrack of traders' cries. These elements are found in other 1940s films set in working-class areas, such as the earlier Ealing film *The Bells Go Down*, which includes the cranes of the Docks, and the south London-set *Waterloo Road* (1945), which depicts the area around the railway station. The specificity of the East End is suggested here by the significant role of a Jewish family (with the Yiddish Theatre actor Meier Tzelniker as patriarch), amateur boxing and the identification of the market as Petticoat Lane. The East End setting, and particularly the use of Petticoat Lane, was seen to offer a distinctive authenticity when the film was released, with critics suggesting, for example, that 'the film could be subtitled "A Day in the Life of an East-End Street"' (Fred Majdalany, *Daily Mail*, 28 November 1947), or that Robert Hamer 'has handled this Cockney mosaic with all the skill of a first-class documentary' (Harold Conway, *Evening Standard*, 28 November 1947). In this, the critics were following the lead of the studio, which claimed in the press book that 'most of the picture was actually filmed in the East End itself',[36] and 'London's famous Petticoat Lane Market was so faithfully rebuilt that it is impossible to distinguish between the real and the prop sets in the finished picture'.[37] The studio's claims were exaggerated, but there was some location shooting in the Commercial Road, Silvertown and in a marshalling yard for the final chase sequence.[38]

Margaret Butler, in her review of contemporary critical responses to the film, points out that several critics were disturbed by the way in which the film seemed to privilege 'the spiv' over 'the cockney' in its representation of working-class London, citing the *Monthly Film Bulletin*:

> It is perhaps a pity that thousands of honest cheerful citizens of Bethnal Green could not have had a stronger representation, but for those who like serious portrayal of a section – a very minor section – of East End life it can be recommended.[39]

Here, the cockney is summoned in the description of the 'honest cheerful citizens of Bethnal Green', which is contrasted with a 'minor section of East End life'. In her discussion of the representation of community in British and French films in the middle of the twentieth century, Butler uses Gareth Stedman-Jones's historical analysis of the cockney and Robert Murphy's discussion of spiv films to develop an analysis of some 1940s British films, particularly *Waterloo Road* and *The Bells Go Down*, in terms of the relative significance and treatment of these two personae, the spiv and the cockney.[40] She suggests that

> In wartime, when the nation centred on London, the cockney became both indispensable to and representative of the British character. *The Bells Go Down* uses the mildly anarchic character of Tommy Turk (Trinder) to demonstrate the diverse but ultimately unified nature of the community and of Britain.[41]

It is this analysis that underpins her reading of the critical reception of *It Always Rains on Sunday*, which can be further developed by using the notion of cinematic genre. Stedman-Jones's argument about the cockney is that 'as an emblem of London life … the "cockney" is a figure successively constructed and reconstructed by different types of discourse'.[42] He traces the changing representations and meanings of the cockney from the eighteenth century through to its 'Indian summer' of the 1940s.[43] In the much shorter durée of cinema, the point is crisper: the cockney is generally a comic character and is thus at home in certain cinematic genres and not others. *It Always Rains on Sunday*, although it comes from Ealing Studios, is not a comedy. It is generically a very mixed film, drawing on traditions of British realism, melodrama and film noir. While the central family in *It Always Rains on Sunday*, the Sandigates, could be considered cockneys, this is not the role that the film calls on them to perform – unlike Tommy Trinder in *The Bells Go Down* (see also the discussion of *Mona Lisa* in Chapter 3). Instead, different characters, at different points, behave in relation to different generic norms and, as we shall see, occupy different generic spaces.

Within the East End, *It Always Rains on Sunday* is mainly set in the Sandigate household in Coronet Grove.[44] The film is punctuated with shots of Coronet Grove throughout the Sunday of its action – always the same view of the terraced street, the railway bridge at the end and St Saviour's church beyond. Rose Sandigate lives with her middle-aged husband, their son and his two daughters, Vi and Doris, from his previous marriage. The Sandigate family are central to the film, with each of its female members spending the Sunday caught up in romance and fantasy, all, in different ways, rained on – and off. Rose finds her everyday life overturned by the sudden, clandestine arrival of her former lover. Her anxious bad temper affects the rest of the family all day and his dripping clothes drying by the fire nearly lead to his discovery. Blonde Vi (Susan Shaw) starts the day hung-over, after her night out with a married man, Morry Hyams (Sydney Tafler), and spends the day discovering that maybe he doesn't feel true love. Brunette Doris, sensible and kind, rows with her boyfriend over a job offer from the local Mr Fixit, and they both get very wet indeed before they make up. The Sandigates are the central family of the film, but they are matched by another family, the Hyams. While the Sandigates are firmly located within Coronet Grove, and indeed Rose only leaves it in an ambulance after her suicide attempt at the end of the film, the Hyams are more dispersed, to be found individually in many of the public spaces of the film. If the Sandigates are the family to whom things happen in this film, in a way, the Hyams, or at least the two brothers, Lou and Morry, are what happen. It is Morry Hyams with whom Vi is infatuated, and it is Lou Hyams (John Slater) who offers Doris a job, much to her boyfriend Ted's (Nigel Stock) disgust. The Hyams are both agents and context. If Rose Sandigate spends the film confined to her terraced house, one or other of the Hyams family is shown in nearly every other set of the film. Alfie Sandigate (David Lines) does a paper round for Morry and Lou's father, Solly Hyams (Meier Lieibovitch); Doris and Ted go to the church youth club where Bessie Hyam (Jane Hylton) works; Morry Hyams is the bandleader at the Palais and runs a music shop on the Lane; Lou Hyams controls an arcade and is involved in running and fixing boxing matches. Even the nearly comic story line about the three petty criminals and their stolen batch of children's roller-skates, which forms a counter point to the story of Tommy Swann's escape from Dartmoor, is, like all other stories in the film, eventually connected to the Hyams family. The Hyams family, in a way, are the East End in which the Sandigates live. And the Hyams, in a film made just after the Second World War, are Jewish.

The Jewishness of the Hyams is presented differently for each character, and suggests different degrees of orthodoxy and observance. The father, Solly, wears a skullcap and a beard. He is immediately identifiable as Jewish. His son, Morry, on the other hand, when first introduced playing saxophone in front of the band, displays no such signs, and the relationship between Solly and his sons must be deduced over the progress of the film. It is only later, when we see Morry in his music shop, where he is visited by his brother Lou who brings him some pickled herrings and uses Yiddish words, and where he is later reprimanded by his wife Sadie (Betty-Ann Davies) for his carrying-on with his 'shiksas', that the relationships become clear. Lou is played as a spiv-like entrepreneur of the East End, a man who wears gloves and well-cut clothes and arranges for boxing matches to be thrown. Morry's wife Sadie is a respectable housewife and mother who wears a small scarf over her hair. Their sister Bessie works closely with the vicar at the local youth club. Made in 1947, this film clearly intends a portrayal of the East End of London as an area with a large, integrated Jewish population in which individual Jews are differently observant and live in ways that are more or less assimilated. This is, at least in part, a representation of the East End as a Jewish East End, although the dispersal of this community is strongly voiced in the film by Lou's urgings to his father and sister to leave the East End ('it stinks') for Stamford Hill.

The inclusion of clearly identified Jewish characters, some of whom are involved in legally dubious activity, occasioned some comment when the film was first released. Leonard Mosley commented in the *Daily Express*, 'Incidentally, there is a Jewish family in this film which is hardly surprising in a story about the East End. At the showing I attended, some people started complaining that the film had been given an anti-Semitic flavour,' continuing, 'As one who vehemently hates racial prejudices, I still maintain that there is absolutely nothing to complain about in this film.'[45] This critical debate is interestingly developed in a series of letters from a Reverend L. Shaposnick of Whitechapel sent to Michael Balcon (the head of Ealing Studios) in December 1947 after the film's release.[46] Although Balcon terminated the correspondence before the end of the year, after three letters each, concluding that they 'could only agree to differ' (16 December 1947), and Shaposnick's letters are not themselves very illuminating, Balcon's replies provide a most unusual statement of purpose in relation to Jewish representation in the film. Shaposnick's first letter upbraids Balcon as a traitor, 'that you, a member of the Jewish Faith should be associated with so perverted a film is strange and inconceivable', continuing, 'the film depicted your Mr Hyams as gay philanderer, black-marketeer and mean racket-driver' (3 December 1947). Balcon takes Shaposnick's comments seriously, and points out in his reply that, of the film's production personnel, it is not only he (the producer) who is Jewish, but also the associate producer and the author, and proceeds,

> when we decided to make a film set in the East End of London, I was very conscious of the possible pitfalls. The worst would have been to present the Jewish element in an entirely favourable light. This would have been seized on by anti-semites.
>
> (5 December 1947)

Balcon's comments suggest that the decision to make a film of Arthur La Bern's East End novel so shortly after the Second World War was consciously informed by a desire to represent East End Jews as various, while a later letter suggests a desire to separate East End ethnicities from East End criminality: 'The point is not that the character of Mr Hyams Senior appears briefly, but that in a picture dealing with the disreputable element of the East End, only the minority are shown to be Jews' (10 December 1947). In this context, the very wide range of petty crime in the film and the rather 'un-Ealing' preference for the spiv over the cockney, can be understood within a drive to locate the chicanery of Lou Hyams as part of an urban culture which is also home to real villains such as Tommy Swann and the suddenly violent Whitey (Jimmy Hanley). At the same time, Balcon was determined not to erase the Jewish character of the East End:

> had I refused to make a film of the East End because of the possible snags, I should have subscribed to the most defeatist theory that the very existence of Jews should be hushed up in case anybody reads anything 'anti-Semitic' in what I have done.
>
> (10 December 1947)

Balcon's robust defence of his film, and his determination to represent Jews as part of the East End, and, like the East End, both good and bad, anticipates by several decades the now better-known debates about the representation of black and Asian Londoners.[47] In particular, this correspondence, and the tone of the Reverend Shaposnick, recalls the public castigation of Hanif Kureishi following the success of *My Beautiful Laundrette*, and the exasperated cry of Uncle Nasser within the film, 'I am a professional businessman, not a professional Pakistani.' A similar debate about the characterisation of the East End has already been joined in relation to the filming of Monica Ali's novel *Brick Lane*, in which Ruby Films gave up location filming in Brick Lane in response to organised protest in July 2006.[48] This form of censorship at the production stage offers a very depressing contrast to the debate occasioned by the exhibition of *It Always Rains on Sunday* in 1947. However, as I have argued throughout this book, cinematic place has no necessary relationship to location shooting, although location shooting, as I will discuss further in the next chapter, may offer particular qualities to the *mise en scène* of a London-set film. *Brick Lane* filmed away from Brick Lane may be more interesting as a cinematic space than any location-shot version. Where something is shot is not, in the end, necessarily what matters in the cinema in relation to setting. What matters is how cinematography, *mise en scène* and editing are mobilised together to present the illusion of a narrative space – a setting, which is then available to both audience and critic for pleasure, escape and critical analysis.

It is within a realist project, signified most strongly by the unremitting rain of *It Always Rains on Sunday*, that the dramatic narrative of Tommy Swann's escape, refuge with Rose and eventual recapture, introduces different generic elements. Tommy is first introduced as a fugitive, crossing railway cuttings, running through the rainy streets and sheltering in a church porch. His progress is intercut with the day beginning for other characters, most particularly the Sandigates. We are properly introduced to Tommy through Rose's romantic memories of him which are sparked by her middle-aged husband reading the news of his escape from the newspaper, as discussed in the opening of Chapter 3. Dreamily brushing her dark hair in the dressing-table mirror, Rose is transported through a dissolve back to another mirror, that of the pub where she worked when her hair was blonde. This sequence is clearly marked as Rose's memory as Tommy appears in the pub, and the detail of his appearance and the self-assurance with which he buys her a drink both grounds him in the realist discourse of the film and shows him to be a romantic and exciting, if dangerous, prospect.

This remembered encounter shows Tommy in local – if romanticised – space, a point confirmed both by the musical score of the pub scene and the *mise en scène* of their day 'doing nothing together', when the symmetrically framed studio countryside emphasises the fantasy of Rose's desire that there was 'no such place as Bethnal Green'. Blonde Rose's understanding of Tommy is informed by romantic fiction and film: her desires are brightly lit, a world of glances meeting across crowded rooms, low-cut dresses and engagement rings. But she has got the genre wrong, as we see from the lighting as soon as Tommy reappears in the present day, hiding in the bomb shelter in the garden, catching Rose by surprise as she goes in there to find some old blackout material to mend a broken door pane.

In the Anderson shelter, Rose and Tommy are lit and shot differently to each other. Rose is framed with the oblong of daylight from the shelter doorway behind her. Through this doorway lies her everyday life, her family, her husband and the Sunday joint: her respectable, pinny-wearing life as a brunette. The framing reminds us of Rose's obligations and commitments; it shows us a character grounded in an east London space. In contrast, Tommy is shot against a dark, featureless background. In realist terms, this is the dark interior of the Anderson shelter where he has been hiding. But in its very featurelessness it is also abstracted from the east London milieu. Tommy, his grimy, sweaty face shining in the dark, is in some ways in a generic, rather than a realist, space. He is the con on the run, but also the insistent, demanding, physical representation of another way of making movies. This contrast is further explored in the bedroom where Rose is hiding Tommy later in the day. This second scene of Rose and Tommy together, when he is actually present in the bedroom, balances her earlier memory. Then, she remembered the detail of his appearance on his first entry to the The Compasses. In the bedroom, Tommy is stripped of his finery, wearing only a shapeless jacket and trousers, his bare chest both vulnerable and shocking. Tommy's almost abstract physicality, accentuated by framing which makes him appear naked, is balanced by the naturalistic detail of the room, with Rose framed against floral curtains wearing a patterned pinny. These two spaces are then brought together with Tommy lying in the marital bed, the shiny eiderdown pulled up to his naked chest and grimy jacket. In the last part of the film, however, when Tommy is on the run, these details diminish in significance, and he is chased through a recognisably noirish space, under bridges and over the rail tracks. Suddenly, the movie is not 'the day in the life of an East End street', but something much more internationally generic, evoking other meaner streets, and certainly severing all connections with pinnies, floral curtains, eiderdowns and 'haddock for breakfast'.

It Always Rains on Sunday was the most profitable Ealing film of 1947, and Gillett reports that it did particularly well in south-east Essex, 'probably because of the large number of former East End residents who lived there'.[49] In the 1970s and 1980s, through the work

It Always Rains on Sunday: Tommy (John McCallum) in the marital bed

of critics such as Sheila Whitaker, the film attracted renewed interest from critics for its representation of a disturbance in the sphere of sexuality, with Tommy Swann's eruption into the Sandigate household a reminder of the sexual passion that the characteristic Ealing making-do and making the best of things must repress.[50] More recently, the film has been repositioned within traditions of British low-life cinema and within the oeuvre of the director Robert Hamer.[51] What I have explored here is the relationship between the film's generic hybridity and the representation of the East End. It is the very complexity of the film's generic inheritance that is both its strength and its weakness. At a meta-level, it is the film's generic hybridity that offers a reflection of its treatment of the East End: the film itself is crowded with generic conventions of different types, both permitting and preventing engagement with its different characters and stories. The invisibility of the film's attention to the Jewishness of the East End after its first release raises germane questions about noticing and not-noticing ethnic difference which are relevant today in the East End and further afield. Rose's story, in which her present-day uniform of dressing gown and pinny is contrasted with her earlier, blonde self, dramatises the costs and benefits of respectability for working-class women, a story that is also played out in the next generation through the contrast in her stepdaughters. Rose's story both structures the film, and is almost invisible within it, closed up, like Rose, in the achieved respectability of Number 26, Coronet Grove.

Performing the Old East End: *The Krays*

The 1990 film *The Krays*, directed by Peter Medak from a script by Philip Ridley, is set in the East End of London from the 1930s, through the war, to the 1960s. Apparently made with the co-operation of the family,[52] and serving as a vehicle for two brothers, Martin and Gary Kemp, from the New Romantic pop group Spandau Ballet, the film creates, at the end of the 1979–90 Thatcher government, a nearly fondly remembered image of family and violent criminality in the old East End. The film stages the key iconographic elements of this East End: the terraced streets, the close-knit community, the resilience under the Blitz, as a background for a tale of a mother who loves too much and her monstrous sons. Gangsters recur as metaphors within the cinema of late Thatcherism, but here the emphasis of the story is shifted through a concentration on Violet (Billie Whitelaw), the twins' mother, which complicates the film's generic heritage.[53] There is arguably a discernible disappointment in some responses to *The Krays*, a disappointment that can be attributed to its determined location of its sadistic heroes in the domestic, in thrall to their mother. Thus, Steve Chibnall and Robert Murphy, editors of the genre-defining *British Crime Cinema*, declare that '*The Krays* (Peter Medak, 1990) is more of a family melodrama than a gangster film'.[54]

The bloody violence of the film – and there is plenty, with James Robertson reporting that a shot of a man with a bloody 'smile' administered by Ronnie Kray with a sabre was censored from the rough cut – is never quite permitted to be free of its psychic causations and casualties.[55] For example, quite early in the film, there is a raid on the Royal Oak pub when the brothers spray the bar with machine guns. Here, there is a spectacle of violence in the shattering of frosted glass, mirrors, bottles and glasses, but the brothers are actually discussing whether Reg will get married as they enter the pub, and the scene cuts immediately to the wedding and then back to their mother's home and a passionate speech from their Aunt

Rose (Susan Fleetwood) about the violence of women's lives during the war. The Kray twins are never, in this account of their lives, far from pathological, and the final blood-soaked killing seems to support Kim Newman's judgment that

> The direction does not flinch, as do most other crime-class-nostalgia movies, from graphic violence, making it impossible to read this film as a wistful lament like *Buster* for a never-never time when crime was simpler and nobody really got hurt.[56]

The Krays is one of a group of late-twentieth-century British films that look back to the 1950s and 1960s. There has been some critical discussion about the extent to which films such as *Dance with a Stranger* (1985), *Wish You Were Here* (1987), *Absolute Beginners* (1986), *Scandal* (1988) and Medak's own, later, *Let Him Have It* (1991) should be understood as nostalgic texts.[57] While Newman's argument that the violence of *The Krays* prevents a reading of the film as nostalgic certainly works in contrast to films like *Buster*, I wonder whether he underestimates the role of this cinematic violence in providing generic pleasures which are in their own way equally powerful in celebrating the Krays. For the visceral quality of the violence could be seen, in precisely the moment when blood spurts, to guarantee that this is not a sentimental vision. In this way, the film's presentation of familiar tropes of the East End – to which the violence of the Krays, in turn, belongs – solicits recognition from the viewer of both a familiar East End and of the wider, transatlantic generic ambitions of 'heritage gangsters' found in films such as *Scarface* (1983) and *The Untouchables* (1987).

For our purposes, then, the film is of interest because of the way in which it braids together different tales of the East End, and because of the question of its tone. A recognisable international hybrid genre, 'gangster heritage', is made to 'take place' in a part of London famed for its working-class community, but also notorious for sadistic sexual murder. The strong mother of the traditional working class is shown to produce her narcissistic, pathological sons through her contempt for men and her intense love of her boys. And arguably, through the mediating term of Violet and her boys, a key trope of British national identity, cockney defiance towards Hitler, is remobilised, into a Thatcherite 'Bollocks to society'.

The film follows a straightforward chronological structure, using dates on screen to trace key moments in the Kray twins' lives, commencing with their birth in 1934. The Kray twins were both still alive when the film was made, although they had been imprisoned since 1969, and Ronnie Kray was held in Broadmoor (the high-security prison for the criminally insane). Their story, however, was already mythologised, its key elements circulating within British popular culture: the brothers' violent control of criminal activity in the East End of London and the cross-class glamour of their empire in the 1960s; their devotion to their mother; the murder of Jack 'the Hat' McVitie; their loyalty to 'their own people'.[58] The story had its own topography: Vallance Road, the Knightsbridge club Esmeralda's Barn, the Blind Beggar public house and the business excursions 'up West' to join the Swinging Sixties. It also had its own iconography, with David Bailey's photographs of the Krays circulating as one of the iconic images of the 1960s, in which working-class London lads such as Bailey himself, Michael Caine, Terence Stamp, Terence Donovan and Ronnie and Reg, in professions of glamour and violence, mixed with the Establishment to form the new glitterati. Several earlier films had engaged with the story, including *Villain* (1971), in which Richard Burton had played the mother-loving, homosexual gangster Vic Dakin, and the 1970 cult film from the druggy, bohemian end of 'Swinging London', *Performance*, of which Colin MacCabe observed, 'In *Performance* we hear the authentic twentieth-century tones of the Krays: the language of capitalist enterprise conjugated with euphemisms for violence to produce the industry of protection.'[59]

The narrative terrain of *The Krays* is thus already known, just as the iconography of the old East End is familiar. Violet Kray had died only eight years before the film was premiered, and there had been substantial press coverage of her sons' compassionate release to attend the funeral. Comparisons between Mrs Kray and Mrs Thatcher have proved attractive. Mary Desjardins has argued that '[I]n many ways, Violet allies herself with the Thatcher philosophy that respects and gives Spartan nurturing to those who succeed through individual initiative.'[60] Perhaps this analogy overlooks a more contradictory aspect of the film's staging of the 'old East End', a violent working-class revenge. The depiction of 'the industry of protection', a tale of the 1950s and 1960s told in the 1990s, in which fierce working-class familial and territorial loyalties are violently maintained, was perhaps both appalling and attractive at the end of the decade that saw the substantial defeat of the trade unions in the 1984–5 coal strike, the move of national newspapers from Fleet Street to Wapping and the end of the 'the Print' as well as the transformation of the Docks into Docklands. In *The Krays* working-class men control their neighbourhood, get to be snappy dressers and repay their mother with everything she could want. They may also be shown to be psychotic, but the casting of Martin and Gary Kemp from Spandau Ballet is significant here. Robert Elms, who was associated with the brothers in the early days of the New Romantics – a moment in popular music culture distinguished by its commitment to sartorial spectacle – describes them as 'a pair of preening council estate coxcombs who'd always walked that walk'.[61] This casting, then, reinscribes 1960s sartorial detail on the bodies of 1980s working-class pop stars. In this context, the graphic violence of the film is both generically gratifying and a spectacular exercise of power.

The film explicitly uses allegory and symbolism, opening with a dream and using a recurrent motif of the 'monster' in relation to both the twins and their mother's love. These textual features encourage a reading of the film partly within the codes of art cinema, as does a certain thinness of texture, which could be read as an explicit engagement with the Krays as myth and a retelling of their tale with an elegant simplicity: an explicit recognition that the film offers the East End as a performance. This is most noticeable in its rendition of Bethnal Green, both indoors and out: a couple of terraced streets with a view of a power station (shot on location in Greenwich), physically cramped interiors which are rather minimally dressed, some pubs, a wrecker's yard, a music-hall turn by a veteran. There is no attempt to render the depicted world as complex, although the motif of the monster – a monstrous birth, an exhibited 'two-headed boy', a fondness for crocodiles, Ron's pet snake – is used in an attempt to give symbolic depth to the twins. Although there are some scenes with large casts, such as a fairground, a boxing match and the opening of their first club, and there are two scenes featuring local people patiently queuing, there is significantly no street market and little sense of an East End separate from the brothers. This East End is not teeming. Instead, the Krays' East End upbringing is offered as a set of vignettes, which recruit tropes of the East End to the telling of their particular story. Thus the first scene after the twins' birth and christening combines the 'poor but house-proud' trope of the representation of the respectable working class with a depiction of the power of gossip in a closely self-monitoring community. Under a title '1936', the establishing shot of industrial chimneys overlooking a terraced street pans round to the trundling movement of coal merchant's horse and cart to then follow a postman wheeling his bike. The movement in this shot, in which the camera seems motivated by first the coal merchant and then the postman who greets Mrs Kray by name, gives a sense of a limited locality in which our eyes are led towards Violet Kray washing her front step as her twin sons play in the street. This initially established space, traversed by men who service it, is then revealed as one which is closely monitored by its inhabitants. A close-up on Violet shows her notice a neighbour on the other side of the street also beginning to clean her front step. This is a task which the neighbour has clearly neglected, as other front doors open and Violet's siblings and her mother all come to discuss the fact 'she' is finally cleaning her front step.[62] The shared judgment of the respectable, pinny-clad Kray women is that their neighbour had 'let herself go' and the scene establishes that the Kray women may be poor, but they keep their houses and their bodies clean, unlike their neighbour who is a 'dirty cow', and, in a detail calculated to revolt a modern audience, between whose teeth you can see bits of toast, the grandmother claims.

This is the third scene of the film, and confirms the dominance of the Kray women within it and their world. Men appear here in bit parts: the driver of the horse and cart and the postman, but it is women who monitor the neighbourhood, women who set the standards. The dominance of matriarchy in the birth scenes is conventional, but this brief street scene works to stage the power of these East End women outside the birthing room. Nothing in the street passes unnoticed – and of signal importance is keeping up a good front with a cleaned and leaded doorstep. This power is confirmed in the following scene when we witness Violet Kray and her sisters in conflict with a middle-class doctor who is looking after Ron – who has diphtheria – in a very cold hospital. Not only do the Kray women set the tone in their own neighbourhood. They are shown to be impossible to intimidate in an institutional setting, insisting that Ron comes home with them, teasing the doctor about his age, and then, finally, Rose pushing him to the floor. The fresh-faced doctor, who is, as he tells them, 'nearly twenty-four', is no match for the group of tough women determined to look after their own.

These two scenes use long-established images of working-class mothers – 'Mam' as Richard Hoggart called her, writing of his upbringing in Hunslet (Leeds), 'Mum' as Young and Willmott call her in their classic study of the East End – both to represent the East End and to contextualise and give an origin to the twins' later behaviour.[63] The street scene shows the maintenance of standards through observation and gossip; the hospital scene pits the real knowledge of working-class women against the class-privilege and book-learning of inexperienced middle-class doctors. However, there is a brutality in the women's conduct that begins to establish the grounds for a comparison with Thatcher. 'Don't tempt me, there's a good boy,' mutters Rose as she clutches the doctor by his collar before tossing him to the floor, anticipating the twins' similar inability to resist temptation twenty years later. 'Bollocks to the lot of you,' shouts Violet as they leave the hospital, and the sound of air-raid sirens signals the Second World War.

The East End is thus created at the beginning of the film through a combination of setting and culture: the terraced houses and the matriarchy. This is then immediately matched by the incorporation of two other East End tales: the Blitz and Jack the Ripper. Again, the material is so readily available within British culture that the film-makers need few preliminaries to the invocation of sheltering in Bethnal Green tube station during an air raid. As discussed in Chapter 4, the image of the cockney resistance to the Blitz in the Underground stations is one of the most significant images of British national identity in the period. The iconic status of this image is acknowledged in the scene's relatively elaborate opening shot, in which the camera first moves down the crowded station steps to pivot on the platform and then moves slowly through the crowds, gradually revealing the numbers of the shelterers, to rest on the face of the twins' grandfather (Jimmy Jewel) recounting a sighting of Jack the Ripper, and the bloodstains that still persist on the paverments of the East End. Violet sits darning on the crowded platform, but the boys, and other children, are entranced by the story their grandfather is telling. This story is being told to entertain the shelterers, and dramatic embellishments such as 'teeth like little razors' and red-glowing eyes augment its thrill. As it is told, Violet and her sisters and mother raise their eyebrows at each other in a 'men will be boys' gesture which both recognises and denigrates the skill of the performance. The film's explicit linking of these different East End tales: the cheery cockney tube-shelterers and the Whitechapel murders in a biography of the Kray Brothers, superintended by unimpressionable East End women, produces the East End, in 1990, as a narrative space in which all its stories run into each other. This performance of the old East End by Jewel, a music-hall veteran, filmed in a way that emphasises the performance, is confined underground. Above the heads of his cockney audience, the East End is being 'opened up', to City money and tourism. Robert Mighall has traced the expansion of the East End crime trails in guidebooks to London in the period 1979–2001, showing how east London is increasingly present in guidebooks, and arguing, with due acknowledgment to Ackroyd and Sinclair, that there is a complicity between gentrification and the valorisation of London's 'dark heritage'. As he puts it: 'a spoonful of Ripper or Ronnie helps the loft price go up'.[64] The 'studied anachronism' which he characterises as the dominant trait of this representational field – all too evident in the many British gangster films that follow *The Krays* – has a long and complex history in the British cinema, as consideration of, for example, *They Made Me a Fugitive* (1947), with its post-war Victorianism, would confirm. What I hope to have demonstrated here is the complexity of the tone in which *The Krays* self-consciously contributes to this.

Coda: 'Fashion Street'

> Petticoat Lane is a far cry from Berlin or Vienna ... but London's own streets contain characters even more fabulous and exciting than those which made Reed's *The Third Man* and *The Man Between* landmarks in screen history.[65]

I want to finish the chapter by looking briefly at a mid-century East End film *A Kid for Two Farthings*, Carol Reed's 1955 film of Wolf Mankowitz's novel. This story of a little boy who believes that a one-horned kid he has bought is a unicorn, and will thus grant the wishes of his family and neighbours in 'Fashion Street', is frequently dismissed as sentimental. It certainly has as much potential as many a child-centred film for sentimentality, and does have a couple of mawkish moments.[66] However, something more than an aesthetic judgment about the manner of a film's solicitation of an emotional response is going on in comments such as the following from Tony Reeves, an author of a well-researched book about London film locations when he observes: 'a colourful and sentimental fable set in the old Jewish East End, with Jonathan Ashmore convinced his one-horned goat is a unicorn. Enough of this softie stuff.'[67]

The film is set in the East End in 'Fashion Street', a street market dominated by Jewish tailors and finishers, dry cleaners and fabric shops. This fictional Petticoat Lane, which is repeatedly filmed with the dome of St Paul's visible at one end of the street, is the setting for all of the action with the interiors of Mr Kandinsky's tailoring shop, Madame Rita's fabric emporium and Blackie's Gym all opening from the street. However, the film opens by locating Fashion Street within landmark London, using the flight of a pigeon to demonstrate the proximity – six shots – of the East and West Ends of London. This is an elegant little sequence, which I want to give in detail because it displays two significant ways of representing the East End of London. The first, establishing, shot is of Trafalgar Square, a familiar landmark site with people and pigeons clustered round Nelson's Column. The camera tilts upward to focus on a single pigeon perched on a lamp-post, and then cuts to follow it on an eastward journey down the Strand, Aldwych and to St Paul's, where, after a cut from the dome to close-up, it perches on a statue. With the pigeon perched up high, the next shot is a pigeon point of view, a high angle of a busy street market, with a sign reading 'Petti.' visible. The final shot shows that the east has been reached as we see St Paul's again, but now it is a reverse angle looking west, in the background, as the pigeon comes to its final resting point on the sign of a pub called the Unicorn. This last shot is composed to show the dome of St Paul's in the background, with the horned head of unicorn and a painted sign in the foreground. The pigeon perches on the unicorn's horn, and the image condenses some of the film's concerns: a London caught between the prosaic and fantastic worlds of the pigeon and the unicorn.

The most obvious feature of this sequence is the use of St Paul's to signify the heart of London. The pre-eminent landmark for centuries, the cathedral is shown here facing both west and east, a landmark within the familiar tourist grammar of Trafalgar Square and Nelson's Column, but also introduced from outside the city walls to the east. The second notable feature of the sequence is the attempt to connect 'Fashion Street' with the West End. As the pigeon flies, the street market is shown to be close to broader, less crowded boulevards. The viewer is led from a familiar West End London sight to what is suggested as a less familiar – but equally London – sight. The sequence suggests both proximity and difference: it is a little cinema geography riff on an establishing shot. St Paul's from the west and from the east. Many reviewers commented, sometimes with some asperity, on the appearance of St Paul's at the end of Petticoat Lane;[68] the more interesting question is how this recurrent image works. For either as the end of the Lane, or as a view from the back garden, or through the repetition of the 'pigeon/unicorn/St Paul's' shot discussed above, these shots of St Paul's are reminders of location, and, only ten years after the end of the war, of national identity.

A Kid for Two Farthings: the pigeon and the unicorn

This is London, these shots insist. And it is this axis of proximity and difference that is a recurrent feature of the cinematic East End. It is both a real London, and a London quite different to the West End, the City and the suburbs.

Shot in Technicolor, the film also offers a strong visual account of the impact of American imagery on post-war British culture, with its illuminated red Coca-Cola sign opposite the tailor's shop where Joe and his mother live, Diana Dors's platinum hair and hourglass figure and her bodybuilder boyfriend's narcissistic devotion to the perfection of his image. Richard Hamilton's contemporary collage, 'Just what is it that makes today's homes so different, so appealing?', first shown the following year, works with almost exactly the same visual register.[69] This is an East End in which Pop Art is imaginable, in which the lure of the apparently classless USA, as Dick Hebdige has shown, was so attractive to working-class Britons.[70] As Peter Evans has commented, Fashion Street itself brings together a diverse and hybrid community, including orthodox Jews, an Irish tramp, a Sikh perfume seller and an Italian wrestler,[71] but it is the interplay of this with an emergent American iconography that is the dominant visual note of the film. This traditional, multi-cultural home of buying and selling in working-class London is shown on the cusp of an engagement with a different kind of consumerism, an intoxication with the bright shiny commodities of the American dream.

The problem with this film, the way in which it is repudiated as 'softie stuff', is not really to do with whether or not St Paul's can be seen from the end of Petticoat Lane, or whether Joe and his mother would have the accents they do. It is made quite clear that they are not from the East End. As Peter Evans argues, it is characteristic of the work of Carol Reed in many ways, particularly in the focus on the experience of a child, which we see in such different forms in the earlier *The Fallen Idol* (1948) and later *Oliver!* (1968). The trouble is that the film breaches the dominant representational codes of the cinematic East End already explored in this chapter, the canon of dark murderous streets, relentless poverty and macho gangsters.[72] In this, the key aesthetic choice, as Reed was well aware, was the move away from black-and-white film:

> The East End of London is not a good setting in black and white for what is really a kind of fairy story. A tragedy or drama might well be photographed so against its crowded streets, its war-damaged buildings and its grimy arches. A fantasy such as Wolf Mankowitz's delightful book needs colour.[73]

The film offers neither ripper, nor gangsters, nor, in the mid-1950s, the kitchen sink realism of the angry young men. Set in one of the key East End iconographic sites, the street market, the film is vivid and lustrous, and is much occupied with the very materiality of Fashion Street. Colourful, patterned dresses hang from the shop front and great rolls of shiny, bright-coloured fabrics dominate the screen in several scenes set in Madame Rita's. Sonia (Diana Dors), who spends most of the film trying to get her boyfriend to commit to their marriage, drapes herself in fabric and wanders about while imagining her wedding dress. The petty bitching and sniping from other girls in the shop is delivered in a manner nuanced by the appearance and costume of each co-worker. Set in 'Fashion Street', the film pays attention to fashion as both an aspect of character and a field of pleasurable consumption. As Madame

Rita (Sydney Tafler) proclaims, 'You've heard of Christian Dior, well I'm Yiddisher Dior.' The film delights in the displays of the market – carefully erected piles of glassware, pyramids of fruit and vegetables, and hucksters proclaiming their wares – while the adjacent shops are full of goods newly available to working-class people. Sonia is excited at the prospect of buying new modern bedroom furniture – unimaginable to earlier generations. On a wasteland with the illuminated Fashion Street signs of 'Cleaners' and 'SILKS' as background, she fantasises about a bathroom with 'a pink WC and black marble wallpaper' that 'doesn't come off in the steam'. These colourful and alluring opportunities for new, 1950s consumption are juxtaposed with older, traditional market figures: the woman plucking chickens in the door of the shop, the tailor, the prophet with his wind-up gramophone. Among the male characters, there are some familiar types: the Jewish tailor, the dim muscle-bound wrestler, the entrepreneur and the huckster. But there is also Sam (Joe Robinson), Sonia's intended, clad only in a leopard-skin posing pouch for some of the film and displaying his rippling muscles hanging from beams in the shop when he is not working at his sewing machine. This is a sensuous, vital world in which consumption is recognised as a significant social motor, with the role of women's desires in transforming traditional culture explicitly recognised.

This is an East End on the cusp of modernity, with a story line dominated by solicitude for the dreams of others, rather than murder, in which American film culture, and what Richard Hoggart called the 'sex in shiny packets' of the 'newer mass art', is beginning to shape desire.[74] Sonia is a new type of woman for the East End.[75] Modelled on the 1950s Hollywood sex goddesses ('Marilyn Monroe is coming out like a rash,' comments a romantic rival), she nevertheless dreams of bathroom suites and an engagement ring. Joe's mother wears a pinny, but Sonia doesn't, and while she is clearly sexy, she also aspires to respectability: she represents the beginning of the aspiration to a 'post-pinny' femininity. The East End here is being gendered in a different way. Sentimental the film may be, but it also suggests a different cinematic future for female characters in the East End, the possibility of transcending the Victorian for the modern, of moving through the streets without either dispensing charity, wearing a Salvation Army uniform or a pinny, or being murdered. When Reeves declares, however ironically, 'Enough of this softie stuff', he is making a comment about the place of women in the streets of the cinematic East End.

Notes

1. John Gross, *Double Thread: A Childhood in Mile End and Beyond* (London: Vintage, 2002 [2001]), p. 116.

2. Dick Hobbs, *Doing the Business* (Oxford: Oxford University Press, 1992 [1988]), p. 85.

3. Rob Shields, *Places on the Margin* (London and New York: Routledge, 1991), pp. 6–7. Shields does not discuss the East End in particular: his concern is with 'marginal places' and 'peripheral sites and regions', p. 3.

4. Quoted in Lloyd Bradley, 'What's wrong with this picture?' *Empire*, June–July 1989, p. 67.

5. Farrukh Dhondy's television serial, *King of the Ghetto* (BBC2, directed by Roy Battersby, 1, 8, 15, 22 May 1986) is one of the relatively few dramas of the Bengali East End. See also the pilot detective series, *Chopratown* (Hat Trick BBC1, 19 December 2005), and the themed BBC2 evening, 'A Night on Brick Lane', 24 March 2006.

6. See John Corner, *The Art of Record* (Manchester: Manchester University Press, 1996), pp. 63–71.

7. *Land of Promise* refers to the views of 1930s tenants' associations in Stepney on pre-war conditions and then offers a contrast between 'Homes as they are' and 'Homes as they might be'. This film, and *Neighbourhood 15*, which focuses on post-war life for a young boy, 'Harry Jackson', imaged among bombsites, are very careful to explain what 'planning' is. On these films see: John R. Gold and Stephen V. Ward, 'Of plans and planners: documentary film and the challenge of the urban future, 1935–52,' in David B. Clarke, *The Cinematic City* (London, Routledge, 1997); Nicholas Bullock, 'Imagining the post-war world: Architecture, Reconstruction and the British Documentary Film Movement', in Francois Penz and Maureen Thomas (eds), *Cinema and Architecture* (London: BFI, 1997), pp. 52–61; Toby Haggith, '"Castles in the Air": British film and the Reconstruction of the Built Environment 1939–51', PhD thesis, University of Warwick, 1998. On the post-war planning of London, see Frank Mort, 'Fantasies of metropolitan life', *Journal of British Studies* 43, January 2004, pp. 120–51.

8. On the role of cultural workers in redevelopment, see Sharon Zukin, *Loft Living* (London: Radius, 1988 [1982]). On the East End in particular, see Raphael Samuel, 'The pathos of conservation', in Mark Girouard, Dan Cruikshank, Raphael Samuel and others, *The Saving of Spitalfields* (London: Spitalfields Historic Buildings Trust, 1989), pp. 135–71; Jane M. Jacobs, *The Edge of Empire* (London: Routledge, 1996), pp. 70–102; and Geoff Dench, Kate Gauron and Michael Young, *The New East End* (London: Profile Books, 2006).

9. *The Vanishing Street* (Robert Vas, 1962) was part-funded by the *Jewish Chronicle* and documented Hessell Street, with its Jewish shops and market traders, just before its demolition.

10. Colin McArthur, 'Chinese boxes and Russian dolls', in Clarke, *The Cinematic City*, pp. 34–5.

11. Screenplay: Alan Cubitt; director: Simon Cellan Jones; Tiger Aspect Productions, 26 December 2004.

12. Steve Chibnall, 'Travels in ladland', in Robert Murphy (ed.), *The British Cinema Book* (London: BFI, 2nd edn, 2001), pp. 281–91. See also Claire Monk, 'Men in the 90s', in Robert Murphy (ed.), *British Cinema of the 90s* (London: BFI, 2000), pp. 156–66.

13. For example, 'Patricia Cornwell and the Jack the Ripper investigation', full-page statement by Cornwell, *The Independent*, 27 August 2005, p. 3.

14. Paul Newland, 'A Howling Sea of Human Wreckage: the Discursive Construction of the East End of London', PhD thesis, University of Exeter, 2005, pp. 57 and 17.

15. Ibid., p. 287.

16. 'Violet was a very smart woman … she used to love Tricosa and other makes from the White House in Bond Street.' Shirley Pitts, quoted by Iain Sinclair, 'Smart Guys' *Sight and Sound* vol. 6 no. 8 (NS), August 1996, p. 22.

17. Peter Hutchings discusses the resonance of London as a city of 'ripped whores' in '*Frenzy*: Return to Britain', in Charles Barr (ed.), *All Our Yesterdays* (London: BFI, 1986), pp. 368–74.

18. Judith R. Walkowitz, *City of Dreadful Delight* (London: Virago, 1992), p. 1.

19. Kim Newman, 'Jack the Ripper', in Phil Hardy (ed.), *The BFI Companion to Crime* (London: BFI, 1997), p. 183. See also Denis Meikle, *Jack the Ripper: the Murders and the Movies* (London: Reynolds and Hearn, 2002).

20. Andy Richards, '*From Hell*', *Sight and Sound* vol. 12 no. 3 (NS), March 2002, p. 45. See also Paula J. Massood, 'City spaces and city times', in Mark Shiel and Tony Fitzmaurice (eds), *Screening the City* (London: Verso, 2003), pp. 200–15, on 'hood' films.

21. Holmes himself investigates the Ripper case in *A Study in Terror* (1965) (released in the USA as *Fog*) and *Murder By Decree* (1971), and *From Hell* has clear affinities with *Murder by Decree*.

22. Newman, 'Jack the Ripper', p. 184.

23. Mary Ann Doane, *Femmes Fatales* (London: Routledge, 1991), p. 162. Thomas Elsaesser suggests that Jack, like other men in the film, is a stand-in for the spectator, 'Lulu and the Meter Man', *Screen* vol. 24 nos. 4–5, October 1983, p. 33.

24. See Judith Walkowitz for discussion of the type of female presence in the streets represented by the 'Sally Army lasses', *City of Dreadful Night*, pp. 73–6.

25. Peter Hutchings, private correspondence, 30 March 2006.

26. *From Hell* DVD, directors' commentary (2005, Twentieth-Century Fox)

27. See Giuliana Bruno's discussion of 'The "analytic" spectacle of the female body as the shared territory of film and psychoanalysis' in the early twentieth century, *Streetwalking on a Ruined Map* (Princeton, NJ: Princeton University Press, 1993), pp. 69–76.

28. Newland, 'A Howling Sea', p. 300.

29. Samuel, 'The pathos of conservation', p. 164. See also John Eade on Spitalfields in *Placing London* (Oxford and New York: Berghahn Books, 2000).

30. Newland, 'A Howling Sea', pp. 298–9.

31. Franco Moretti, *Atlas of the European Novel 1800–1900* (London: Verso, 1998), p. 34.

32. Transylvania is a related, but less gendered, cinematic topos. See Peter Hutchings on *Dracula* as a geography lesson in his *Dracula* (London: I. B. Tauris, 2003), pp. 61–2.

33. Charles Barr, *Ealing Studios* (Newton Abbot: Cameron and Tayleur in association with David and Charles, 1977), p. 70.

34. For example, the medium press book for the film: 'London's East End is teeming with drama' (p. 10), or contemporary reviewer Elspeth Grant, 'The setting is London's East End, with its drab slatternly streets teeming with vulgar, vigorous life', ('Teems with rain – and real life', *Daily Graphic*, 28 November 1947).

35. Philip Gillett's detailed reading of the film refers only to the market, 'A Yiddish voice is a reminder of the area's large Jewish population – and why a street market is held on a Sunday' (p. 41); Gillett, *The British Working Class in Postwar Film* (Manchester: Manchester University Press, 2003), pp. 39–45. See also Kevin Gough-Yates, 'Jews and exiles in British cinema', *Leo Baeck Yearbook* no. xxxvii (1992), pp. 538–9. John Gross, recounting a Jewish East End childhood, refers to it as 'the only film I have seen which captures the genuine feel of the East End of the period', *Double Thread*, p. 121.

36. *It Always Rains on Sunday*, medium press book, p. 14.

37. Ibid.

38. Shooting script, 24 January 1947, BFI Library. While the designation 'location' in a shooting script is no guarantee that a scene was shot on location, these locations do seem to have been used. Pierre Sorlin, in contrast to the press book, claims that the film was completely studio shot, which gives some indication of the amount of studio work. Pierre Sorlin, *European Cinemas, European Societies 1939–90* (London: Routledge, 1991), p. 112. Googie Withers told Brian McFarlane that Hamer said, '"I want to do this out in the streets where it all happens", so there was very little studio work.' Brian McFarlane, *Sixty Voices* (London: BFI, 1992), p. 235.

39. 'It Always Rains on Sunday', *Monthly Film Bulletin*, December 1947, n.p., cited in Margaret Butler, *Film and Community in Britain and France* (London: I. B. Tauris, 2004), p. 92.

40. Gareth Stedman-Jones, 'The "cockney" and the nation, 1780–1988', in David Feldman and Gareth Stedman-Jones (eds), *Metropolis – London* (London: Routledge, 1989), pp. 272–324. Robert Murphy, 'The spiv cycle', in his *Realism and Tinsel* (London: Routledge, 1989), pp. 146–67.

41. Butler, *Film and Community in Britain and France*, p. 58.

42. Stedman-Jones, 'The "cockney" and the nation', pp. 274–5.

43. Ibid., p. 315.

44. Sorlin suggests that Coronet Grove is in the suburbs (Sorlin, *European Cinemas*, p. 113); however, Rose sends Doris 'up to the Lane' to pick up the cheese ration when she wants to get her out of the house.

45. Leonard Mosley, 'Googie is a joy to behold', *Daily Express*, 28 November 1947, n.p. See also Gough-Yates, 'Jews and exiles in British cinema', pp. 538–9.

46. Letters between Reverend L. Shaposnick and Michael Balcon, 3–16 December 1947, Balcon Collection, British Film Institute, MEB G -/71.

47. The selected articles collected in 'Critical Voices', in Kobena Mercer (ed.), *Black Film/British Cinema* (London: Institute of Contemporary Arts, 1988), pp. 16–25, are indicative here.

48. See for example the letters by Salman Rushdie and others, 'Brickbats fly over Brick Lane', *The Guardian*, 29 July 2006, p. 41.

49. Gillett, *The British Working Class in Postwar Film*, p. 43.

50. The classic account is Barr, *Ealing Studios*, pp. 68–70; see also Gerry Turvey, 'The moment of *It Always Rains on Sunday*', and Sheila Whitaker, '*It Always Rains on Sunday* part ii', both in *Framework* 9, 1978/9, pp. 13–26.

51. Philip Kemp, 'The long shadow: Robert Hamer after Ealing', *Film Comment* vol. 31 no. 3, May–June 1995, pp. 71–8; Robert Murphy, '*The Long Memory*', in Brian McFarlane (ed.), *The Cinema of Britain and Ireland* (London: Wallflower, 2005), pp. 85–93.

52. Hugo Davenport, 'Soft-pedalling the violence', *Daily Telegraph*, 26 April 1990, p. 21; Philip Ridley, 'Keeping it in the family', *What's On*, 9 May 1990, p. 63; Debbie Kruger, 'Miramax nabs Brit "Krays", about real-life murderers', *Variety*, 16 May 1990, p. 21; John Pearson, *The Profession of Violence*, 4th edn (London: HarperCollins, 1995), p. 319.

53. John Hill, 'Allegorising the nation', in Steve Chibnall and Robert Murphy (eds), *British Crime Cinema* (London: Routledge, 1999), pp. 160–71. See also, from this book, Claire Monk, 'From underworld to underclass', pp. 172–88.

54. Chibnall and Murphy, *British Crime Cinema*, p. 4.

55. James Robertson, 'The censors and British gangland', in Ibid., p. 25.

56. Kim Newman, '*The Krays*', *Monthly Film Bulletin* vol. 57 no. 675, April 1990, p. 111.

57. John Hill, 'Remembering the 1950s', in his *British Cinema in the 1980s* (Oxford: Clarendon Press, 1999) pp. 124–6. See also Sarah Street, *British National Cinema* (London: Routledge, 1997), pp. 100–6; Amy Sargeant, 'The Content and the form', in Claire Monk and Amy Sargeant (eds), *British Historical Cinema* (London: Routledge, 2002), pp. 199–215; Anthony Aldgate and Jeffrey Richards, *The Best of British* (London: I. B. Tauris, 2002 [1999]), p. 146.

58. Pearson, *The Profession of Violence*.

59. Colin MacCabe, *Performance* (London: BFI, 1998), p. 43.

60. Mary Desjardins, '"Free from the apron strings"', in Lester Friedman (ed.), *British Cinema and Thatcherism* (London: UCL Press, 1993), p. 139.

61. Robert Elms, *The Way We Wore: A Life in Threads* (London: Picador, 2006 [2005]), p. 199.

62. The cleaning of front steps was one of the indicators that Charles Booth used, along with lace curtains, hanging birdcages and closed front doors, to indicate the distinction between 'rough' and 'respectable' working-class neighbourhoods in his survey of London, cited by Judith Walkowitz, *City of Dreadful Delight*, p. 35.

63. Richard Hoggart, *The Uses of Literacy* (Harmondsworth: Penguin, 1958 [1957]); Michael Young and Peter Wilmott, *Family and Kinship in East London* (London: Routledge and Kegan Paul, 1957).

64. Robert Mighall, 'Crime and memory in the capital', in Joe Kerr and Andrew Gibson (eds), *London from Punk to Blair* (London: Reaktion, 2003), p. 374. See also John Eade's interviews with estate agents in 'Reconstructing places: changing images of locality in Docklands and Spitalfields' in John Eade (ed.), *Living the Global City* (London: Routledge, 1997), pp. 134–5.

65. Caption for still BB1/1, p. 60. *A Kid For Two Farthings* Information Pack 1955, Carol Reed Collection, British Film Institute.

66. *Sunday Express*, 15 May 1955, commented, 'This is the latest combination of Sir Carol Reed with Small Boy, a film which audiences will either love or loathe', n.p.

67. Tony Reeves, *The Worldwide Guide to Movie Locations Presents London* (London: Titan, 2003), p. 116.

68. The *Evening News*: 'Sir Carol Reed went riding out from Mayfair one day, setting his face to the East. Up the hill from Fleet-street he passed the great dome of St Paul's and so, in due time, he found himself in a place of strange tongues, noisy markets, drab homes and garish jazz haunts where the courage and despair of displaced peoples go hand in hand./The sights he saw fascinated him and he returned with the idea that St Paul's is just at the end of Petticoat-lane. Perhaps it was a very fast car he rode in.' 'Sir Carol Rides East', 12 May 1955, n.a.; n.p.

69. See David Robbins (ed.), *The Independent Group: Postwar Britain and the Aesthetics of Plenty* (Cambridge, MA, and London: MIT Press, 1990).

70. Dick Hebdige, 'Towards a cartography of taste', in his *Hiding in the Light* (London: Comedia, 1988).

71. Peter Evans, *Carol Reed* (Manchester: Manchester University Press, 2005), pp. 130–5.

72. Although Iain Sinclair does conclude his article on screen gangsters with the film, 'Smart Guys', pp. 22–4, and includes a discussion of the film between Tony Lambrianou and Robin Cook in the Carpenters' Arms (a former Krays' pub), 'Every day above ground is a good day', in *London: City of Disappearances* (London: Hamish Hamilton, 2006), pp. 256–7.

73. *A Kid for Two Farthings* Information Folder, p. 14. Cited in many of the contemporary press reviews, such as *East End News*, 24 May 1955.

74. Hoggart, *The Uses of Literacy*, pp. 246–72.

75. She was also, evidently, seen as a new type of actor for Carol Reed. For example, Ken Sherry, 'I bet this shook the boys' (on the teaming of Reed and Dors), *PictureGoer*, 25 September 1954. *A Kid* cuttings scrapbook, Carol Reed Collection, British Film Institute.

6

Thames Tales

From the *Pool of London* to the 'Pont de la Tour'

In *Wonderland* (1999), when Eddie (John Simm) has, without warning or reflection, walked out of his job as a kitchen salesman, he goes to Southwark Bridge and, leaning on the parapet, looks unseeingly in the water as he rehearses what he will say to his very pregnant wife when he tells her the news. The scene is shot in the evening, so the river is mostly a dark invisible presence, with occasional flashes of reflected lights from the offices on its banks. Eddie isn't really looking at the river as he stands, imagining, on the bridge, but being on the bridge provides a temporary refuge for him before he enters the maelstrom of consequences that his action will provoke. As traffic rushes past him, he stands above the water that pays him no heed and considers his future.

More than thirty years before, Alfie Roberts (Michael Caine) had stood on the Victoria Embankment to consider his prospects at the end of the film *Alfie* (1966). This final scene starts with a shot of the rejected bunch of carnations Alfie throws in the dark river. He had broken his rule of never giving women flowers only to discover that the intended recipient, Ruby (Shelley Winters), has a younger man in her bed. His way with girls seems to have deserted him, and in the concluding sequences of the film Alfie has seen his former lovers choosing other, less exciting men, for greater security – or, most painfully, for younger sexual prowess – than Alfie offers. As Alfie moves on to Waterloo Bridge he is framed by the iconography of landmark London as he too meditates on his future as he looks at the river. It is night in the city, and it is overlooking the river that Alfie meditates, and the theme song of the film rises, 'What's it all about?'

These are instances of what can be called 'subjective river' in the cinema. In these scenes, the River Thames has no plot role or necessity. Eddie and Alfie could have reflected on the meaning of life in other locations, although few are as rich and resonant. The river here, perhaps to the extent that it exceeds the control of a set designer, provides an appropriate setting for this meditation. This is a recognised attribute of 'large water' in both the cinema and life. The river into which Eddie and Alfie stare gives solace in a general, watery way, as do other rivers and the sea, with their constant motion and neglect of human concerns. However, the river into which Eddie and Alfie gaze is also a very particular London river, and each film ensures that it is recognised as such through the inclusion of location-identifying landmarks such as Tower Bridge, the Festival Hall and the distinctive lamp-posts of the Victoria Embankment.[1]

This final chapter is about the cinematic River Thames, perhaps the most generative of London landmarks. Tidal inland to the west of London at Teddington, the River Thames is the subject, occasion and inspiration for many artworks. Stephen Daniels has suggested that the River Thames is '[t]he thread which has traditionally held London together as a visible city',[2] but it has also figured in, and shaped, the city's literary and musical history, inspiring a canon which ranges from Edmund Spenser to Benjamin Zephaniah, from Handel to Ray Davies. The river and its bridges have provided a vantage point from which to apprehend the city, while Charles Dickens's description, in *Our Mutual Friend*, of Gaffer Hexham hauling dead bodies from the water provides an image of the Victorian Thames that resonates still. Iain Sinclair has called the Thames 'the great London referent: metaphor and fact'[3] and continues, 'Riverside subjects are borrowed, never owned'. In this chapter, I want to look at 'river subjects', and my suggestion will be that although, at one level, there are few new river stories in the cinema, at another, the way in which the River Thames is found and used in film is of interest in two different ways. First, it provides a beautiful and troublesome focus for some of the methodological and theoretical issues in the analysis of the city in the cinema. Second, in the 'Thames Tales' of the second half of the twentieth century, we find a significant set of stories about Britain's imperial decline and her reinvention as a different kind of global player under the Thatcher government.

Geoffrey Nowell-Smith, writing about the city and the cinema, proposes that some films 'yield up a sense of place that would have been impossible without the ontological link between nominal setting and actual location'.[4] In his use of the phrase 'ontological link', Nowell-Smith is explicitly referring to André Bazin's famous essay, 'The ontology of the photographic image', and, thus, one of the founding debates of cinema studies.[5] Without entering this debate about the photographic image as such, I want to use Nowell-Smith's claim as a basis for exploring 'the sense of place' that some – only some – location-shot films evoke. I have argued, throughout this book, that place in the cinema cannot be understood through attention solely to location. The setting of a film – the London of a film – is constructed through the complex, designed, interaction of the many elements of film-making, from performance to costume, from narrative to sound stage. But, in this final chapter, I want to explore Nowell-Smith's proposition, for I think that a river setting may sometimes provide a privileged instance of what he refers to as a 'recalcitrance', an 'inability [of the city] to be subordinated to the demands of the narrative'.[6] This is not just because water, despite the many achievements of film technicians, remains one of the most difficult effects to fake. It is also the very qualities of rivers that make the Thames attractive to both Eddie and Alfie in the two scenes with which I started the chapter. While what is on the banks – indeed the very banks themselves – and the bridges that cross that river may burn down and be built up, changing how we see the river and what is reflected in it, up till now, in the words of a famous song about another river, 'It just keeps rolling along'. Rivers are privileged metaphors of change in many art forms, and cinematic rivers in films such as

Jean Renoir's *The River* (1951) or Werner Herzog's *Aguirre, Wrath of God* (1972) provide a rich cinematic context for the exploration of the metaphor. In relation to a particular cinematic river, the Thames, what may be a metaphor for change in any one film, becomes, over a series of films, a history of it. The cinematic river is both unimaginable without the cultural history of previous rivers Thames, and also, simultaneously, through the 'ontological link' of which Nowell-Smith writes, however this is theorised, always new. The 'sense of place' of which Nowell-Smith writes seems to me, in the case of the river, to sometimes exceed the narrative world of the film, and to invite the audience to pay the screen a different kind of attention. This, in the context of this book, I would call a 'documentary gaze', which can be related to Thom Andersen's notion of the 'voluntary attention' that must be paid to fiction film in order to think about place.[7]

MGM's Culver City-shot *Waterloo Bridge* (1940) was surely not the considerable success it was for its 'sense of place', although its wartime London narrative concerning the desperate plight of a young woman, Myra (Vivien Leigh), who resorts firstly to prostitution and then to suicide, is a familiar river tale, and points to a consistent gendering of the figure of 'subjective river'. While male characters may gaze at the water in existential crisis, female characters rarely have this freedom. This film is partly structured through the alternating gaze into the river of its romantic leads. However, while the Clark Gable character relives poignant memories in this act – remembers the film, in fact, as it is structured through flashback – Myra's gaze into the river is associated only with degradation and death. Her most extended 'subjective river' sequence is concluded by the evident decision – conveyed through the parting of her lips and a near head-tossing gesture – to enter prostitution. The subsequent subjective river sequence leads to her suicide. The river, created mainly through reflected light, with some water visible at points, and a view of a St Paul's skyline, is the film's most disappointing setting, despite the promise of the title; a disappointment that is registered in the decision that Myra's suicide be effected under the wheels of traffic, rather than in the river. In contrast, films such as *Pool of London* (1950) and *Four in the Morning* (1965), discussed below, could be seen as aesthetically rather patchier, but they do 'yield up a sense of place', and this place is the river. Arguably, as I will explore, it is precisely the failure to fully integrate performance, narrative and setting, and the relative weakness of aspects of the former in relation to setting, that makes the locations in these films more available for scrutiny by a documentary gaze. However, other films discussed in this chapter, such as *The Long Good Friday* (1979) and *Thames Film* (1984–6), could be seen to be primarily, and evocatively, concerned with this 'sense of place', and so I am not suggesting that it is merely a consequence of aesthetic failure. In different ways, and to different extents, each film chosen for discussion here renders something of the river that exceeds its role within the fiction as a setting for narrative events. And this is what may be troublesome for some in my argument, for I propose that this is a matter of judgment. In each case, though, the river seen is one at which we can never gaze afresh without its other manifestations haunting and shaping the vision.

In the context of a loose, preliminary taxonomy of the cinematic river, I will concentrate on four 'river films', *Pool of London* (Basil Dearden, 1950), *The Long Good Friday* (John Mackenzie, 1979), *Four in the Morning* (Anthony Simmons, 1965) and *Thames Film* (William Raban,

1984–6), which each, in their own way, document the changing river as well as making stories from it. These are mostly downriver tales, and so this chapter is also a companion to the discussion of the East End in the previous chapter, for east London would not be the East End without the Docks. The traffic, the commerce, the pollution, the industry – and for many years, the stink – of the city itself divides the river between the Arcadian and the industrial. Indeed, the art of the Thames can be seen to condense the imagery of the country and the city, which, as Raymond Williams has shown, has always been a story of class and labour, a story about the production of nature and, frequently, the concealment of labour.[8] In Peter Ackroyd's 2006 exhibition about the Thames on the Millennium Bridge, the exhibit was organised so that east-facing images documented the 'River of the Dead' and the 'River of Money', while upriver, to the source, it was the 'River of pleasure and spectacle'.[9] The representational repertoire of the River Thames west of London is created most seductively in John Boorman's autobiographical film about the Second World War, Hope and Glory (1987), when Billy and his family are forced to evacuate upriver to his grandfather's. On this island in the Thames, Billy's life becomes river-ruled and joyous – and fish literally fall from the sky to feed the family when a bomb is dropped. Upriver tropes are those of rowing boats, swans, fishermen, weeping willows and a rural imagination of England, as we see in both Hope and Glory and Close My Eyes (1991). Downriver, though, the river has always been a working river, and the story I will trace is the story of the replacement of the arduous manual labour of the dockers and the boatmen with the electronic labour of the financial markets and its associated global workforce. So while, on the one hand, this chapter partners the previous one on the East End, it also returns to the 'world city' London introduced in the last part of 'Going Up West'.

For London as a lived city, the River Thames is most significant as the border between 'north' and 'south' London. Many films mobilise the cultural significance of 'crossing the water' to demonstrate the exceptional nature of an expedition for an individual character. The journey across the river is symbolically significant in several of the films already discussed in this book. Up the Junction (1967) commences with Polly being chauffeured across the bridge from Chelsea to explore life in working-class Battersea, a class journey echoed by the Prime Minister's chauffeured journey, across the Albert Bridge, to the home of his former aide in Love Actually (2003). In Mona Lisa (1986), George's journey 'home' is over Waterloo Bridge from north to south. In All or Nothing (2002), Phil escapes south London with a fare to central London through the Blackwall Tunnel. Joe Kerr, in a comparison of the way in which the 'north/south' border in London is maintained through maps such as the tube map and the map of London postal districts, has wittily pointed out how much of 'south London' is further north than the London on the other side of the Thames, and how much of the Thames doesn't flow east–west.[10] This doesn't alter the significance of the distinction within London as a biographical city, as I have already discussed in relation to 'south London' and 'going up West'. Hanif Kureishi has described the meaning of this journey, in his case from the suburbs: 'And for us the important place, really, was the river. And when you got on a train and you crossed the river, at that moment there was an incredible sense that you were entering another kind of world.'[11] The scale of the distinction, in a journey in the opposite direction, is nicely captured in a novel by Atima Srivastava in the reaction of a young north

Londoner's response to a suggestion to visit the (south London) Vauxhall Arts Centre, 'South London, I thought. Abroad.'[12]

The most cinematically conventionalised use of the River Thames is as an establishing shot, a postcard shot meaning 'This is London', as discussed in Chapter 1. There are two main variants, the most common being the view of the Palace of Westminster from the south bank of the Thames, or Lambeth or Westminster Bridges, with the river in the foreground. This view has recently been altered by the addition of the London Eye, as Jonathan Coe puts it, 'transforming the whole cityscape with casual impudence'.[13] The second variant relies on Tower Bridge, rather than the Houses of Parliament and Big Ben, to identify the city, and is generally shot downriver. This is a slightly less official version, identifying London but avoiding the seat of government, substituting boring parliament with a bridge that opens. These historic landmark 'river views' have been inflected, since the 1990s, by the redevelopment of the South Bank between Waterloo and Tower Bridge, and the modernity signified by the Millennium Bridge. The point about these views, apart from their very substantial extra-cinematic history, is that the river acts as foreground and frame for an identifying London landmark, permitting compositions that set off Victorian Gothic – and later additions – with water and sky. Just water would be no landmark at all. The river here, though still beautiful, is usually inert, not called upon, not addressed, not imagined – in a way, almost not seen.

What the subjective river and the postcard river often have in common is that neither river image proposes the river itself for further contemplation. When characters stare into the river to think about their lives, it is, exactly, their lives, and not the river on which they reflect, and the camera usually stays focused on their faces, rather than on the river. Similarly, the landmark river is a view already known, asking only recognition, not interrogation. The opposite of a landmark river view is what I am calling a 'river tale'. This is an enormous category which precedes cinema by centuries, but which takes the river as both setting and story. The river is rich with story, and offers its own structure of the journey up- or downriver very readily. Just as there are many written accounts of journeys up, down and through the history of the Thames, so too are there many film and television documentaries tracing these journeys.[14] Most notable here, apart from Gavin Weightman's 1990 series, *The River Thames*, and Patrick White's 1999 series, *The River*, which fall outside the terms of this book, are the Mark Harrison/Fred D'Aguiar film poem *Sweet Thames* (1992), which uses the river as the focus of a lyrical exploration of black metropolitan history and is discussed in detail by Sukhdev Sandhu, and William Raban's *Thames Film*, which I discuss below.[15]

If the journey through space from source to sea is the most obvious river tale, that through time from the original settlements on the banks of the Thames, through to the Imperial port, is the other.[16] The second half of the twentieth century, however, has generated a new river story which is told across both space and time: the decline of the working river and, particularly, of the *Port* of London, and a gradual shift eastwards, downriver, in the city's centre of gravity. By the end of the twentieth century, it has its own landmark view, its own establishing shot. Instead of looking downriver to Tower Bridge, so that the bridge gives London a type of closure, punctuating the river, distinguishing 'London's river' from the easterly river outside the city walls, this new establishing shot is taken from the east, often by helicopter, as in *StormBreaker* (2006). This London commences with the glittering towers of

Docklands, and then proceeds upriver: Shanghai-on-Thames dwarfing the fake gothic of Tower Bridge, a view anticipated with characteristic perversity by Alfred Hitchcock in *Frenzy* (1972), when the aerial shot of Tower Bridge concludes with the discovery of a woman's body. This story of the River Thames is arguably the London story of the second half of the twentieth century, for the changes to the river and its banks provide both material and symbolic imaging of the end of Empire and the commitment to finance capital. The transformation of the Docks into Docklands is, to rephrase Sinclair, 'both metaphor and fact'.

There is an upbeat version of this story, found in wildlife and nature programming on television, of the River Thames as an increasingly hospitable habitat for the full range of native species. The underlying narrative is that of the increased cleanliness of the river waters and the consequent return of fish to the river.[17] In this version, the decline of the working river is understood through a notion of the return of the natural river. A piquant anecdotal contribution is given in the episode of *Joe Brown's East End* (16 December 1988) dealing with the Docks, when it is averred that Dr David Owen, the SDP politician also known for (being middle class and) living in Wapping, used to live on a houseboat there when a medical student, and would pump the stomachs of anyone unlucky enough to fall in the river. Now, he swims regularly off Wapping pier. The benefits of being an early gentrifier made manifest in both a beautiful house and a tidal exercise pool.

The return of the natural river, though, is a minor story compared to the decline of the working river and the transformation of the Docks. This story of decline is both articulated within individual films and can, with a documentary gaze, be traced across films ranging from *The Horse's Mouth* (1959) to *The World is Not Enough* (1999). Stephen Poliakoff's television film *Close My Eyes* mobilises traditional distinctions between up- and downriver, through a contrast between a progressive architectural practice in Docklands, fighting to retain local people's rights, and the glorious luxury of a sunlit riverside family house upriver. Subsidiary characters in films, and their homes and occupations, often tell tales neglected by the main thrust of a narrative. Barge-dwellers like Anna O'Leary (Maureen Delaney) in *Night and the City* (1950) work both within the film – where she rents out boats and deals in contraband nylons and cigarettes – and outside it, where, along with the marsh dwellers in, for example, *The Long Memory* (1952), she testifies to a way of life, and a riverscape, long gone. The increased use of riverside and dockland apartments as settings in films ranging from *A Fish Called Wanda* (1988) to *Love Actually* gives mute witness to the material transformation of the city.

Buildings and locations are documented through transitions, and can be dressed to tell yet other stories. In relation to the Docks, an exemplary site is Shad Thames, a narrow thoroughfare between warehouses on the South Bank of the Thames just east of Tower Bridge, behind Butler's Wharf. This cobbled way, rendered steep and dark by the warehouse walls and dramatic by the high footbridges, features in *The Long Memory* as part of a contemporary working wharf. In 1980, Shad Thames was dressed even more darkly for the nineteenth century of *The Elephant Man* (1980), where the location is almost obscured in smoke and mist. At the turn of the twentieth century, it has become a plausible location for a date between Hugh Grant and an American actress playing a British woman in *Bridget Jones's Diary* (2001), where it is notably brightly lit as a street of restaurants and bars. These appearances of Shad Thames condense the a-chronological cinematic history of the docks across three films.

The intrinsic qualities of the location, the steep warehouse walls, the limited light, the striking footbridges, the cobblestones and the proximity of the river offer a material memory of the heyday of the Port of London as the centre of the British Empire. This texture of 'the old' makes Shad Thames irresistibly authentic *both* for the cinematic recreation of Victorian London and the well-lit postmodern playground of Working Title's London. The 'ontological link between nominal setting and actual location', while it may, in some films, yield up a sense of place, does not determine how this sense of place is apprehended.

So my procedure in this chapter will be to look in some detail at individual, generically contrasted films with significant river settings, thinking about their evocation of 'a sense of place' and the extent to which this sense of place contributes to, and exceeds, cinematic narrative. On the one hand, I want to argue that these films' sense of place enables us to read them, at a meta-level, as a series of contributions to a story the main vectors of which lie outside the cinema, in patterns of world trade, of containerisation, in shifting patterns of global power and the waxing and waning of empires. I read fiction film in a realist manner as documenting a changing river in a changing city, even when that is not part of the film's project. On the other hand, I want to insist on the aesthetic 'wroughtness' of the films that I read in this manner. Each of the films tells stories in which the river plays its part. These stories mobilise diverse spaces to render a believable cinematic world that has its own logics and plausibilities, which are governed internally through cinematic codes and generic convention, not through a relation to the real. Their location shooting is governed by cinematic geography. Thus I spend some time on each film as a whole, because I do not want to rip the river from the movie in order to illustrate a thesis. I'm interested, precisely, in the tension between these different modalities of the cinematic river.

The Spaces of Empire: *Pool of London*

Pool of London, an Ealing film, was set in the Port of London over a weekend, and follows the adventures of a merchant ship's crew from their arrival in London to their departure on the Monday morning. Through ensemble playing the film shows many different reactions to the weekend in port, including the chief officer's, who stays in his cabin to read poetry and drink brandy, quoting lines on the disparity between the allure of distant London and its actuality; different types of smuggling, some played for humour, some part of the crime plot; and the complicated love lives of sailors. Canadian Dan (Bonar Colleano) and Jamaican Johnny (Earl Cameron) are friends and shipmates, and the presence of 'social problem' concerns within the narrative is established when we learn that Dan once defended Johnny from racial abuse. The film uses location shooting for the Pool (the River Thames between, roughly, London Bridge and Wapping, bifurcated by Tower Bridge), parts of London, and a later downriver sequence. The river spectacle is matched, within the film, with two other significant spectacles, that of Greenwich Park with the Royal Naval College and that of an audacious diamond robbery in the City of London and the consequent pursuit and later Rotherhithe Tunnel chase. The friendship between Dan and Johnny unites the diverse narrative threads which include the crime plot (mainly Dan) and Johnny's tentative relationship with Susan Shaw's 'Pat', 'the screen's typical London girl'.[18]

Pool of London, which premiered in February 1950, went into production not long after the 1948 Nationality Act, which granted United Kingdom citizenship to citizens of Britain's colonies and former colonies, and the arrival at Tilbury in June 1948, in what has been cast as the inaugural moment of West Indian immigration, of the *Empire Windrush* carrying immigrants from Jamaica.[19] In this context, the film, with its story of a young, lonely Jamaican merchant sailor in London for the weekend, wears its intentions on its sleeve. Johnny, in Earl Cameron's first feature film role, is vulnerable to both abuse and exploitation, but is shown to be both gentle and forgiving. The London of the film is both laid out for him, as a series of spectacles and views, and – perhaps inadvertently – shown as a London that he cannot inhabit. This, as I explore below, is achieved through the interplay of a landmark London inflected as the centre of a maritime empire, with which he is familiar, with the everyday London, which is sometimes hostile and strange. However, Johnny's story, which can be seen as a way of imagining what the post-imperial city might be like, is only one of several stories in a film that Ealing, perhaps over-optimistically, labelled 'Britain's "Naked City"'.[20]

Andrew Higson opens his analysis of *Pool of London* with the description offered by the production company, 'a drama of the River underworld', and then points to the generic hybridity of the film by describing it as 'a noirish crime thriller embedded in an Ealing story documentary-cum-soap opera, saturated with picturesque location photography of London's streets and docklands, with a story-line about race relations thrown in for good measure'.[21] Higson shows how these contrasted generic modes construct the spaces of the film in different ways, while also demonstrating how the different elements and modes of the film provide different satisfactions for different contemporary critics, some lauding the blending of documentary, social problem film and thriller, some disliking it. My interest lies in the juxtaposition, within the film, of several generically different Londons, each with its own kind of spectacle, and, fifty years after it was made, the changed valency of the film's location shooting. So I am concerned to show the ways in which the film renders London spectacular, but I am also interested in how some of the aesthetic difficulties of the film – its ambitious generic mix, the relationship between character and setting – make it more amenable, now in the twenty-first century, to a reading in terms of a meta-narrative of the cinematic Thames.

Pool of London yields up a sense of London as a place perhaps more strongly than its narrative coheres, but also, in this, demonstrates the complex relationship between cinematic space and location shooting. The film opens, in a pre-title sequence, with a shot of HMS *Dunbar*, a large merchant ship, moving through an unidentifiable wide open estuary. When hailed from a Port of London (PLA) tug, the captain gives her destination as 'the Pool', 'out of Rotterdam', and she is given permission to move on to her berth. Only then, after the setting has been identified as the Thames, does the film title appear, and the *Dunbar* moves upriver to the Pool under the credits, making her entry to London up a river busy with craft of different shapes and sizes. The arrival into the Port uses a montage of shots of Tower Bridge, including overhead shots of the opening bridge, and a policeman directing motor traffic which must wait for the ship. The musical soundtrack, jaunty and military, divests the arrival of particularity, showing instead the general and repeated spectacle of the arrival of a ship into the Pool. This ritual is countered, in a very Ealing manner, by the introduction of the ensemble of port, ship and river workers, whose lives are governed by 'same old bus route' of regular sea traffic, the shooting and editing brisk and business-like. Sally (Renée

Asherson), working in a riverside office, looks wistfully out of the window at the sound of the ship's horn when she is told the *Dunbar* is in. 'Never seen a ship before, Sally?' she is asked briskly by a fellow worker, who knows she is ill-advisedly in love with a *Dunbar* seaman. 'How's that boy of yours?' the ship's captain asks the customs officer. 'Still want to go to sea?' 'No fool like a young fool,' he is answered with a wry smile, the attractions of the busy river all around. This river is peopled, and the film succeeds in giving a sense of these people and crafts, including those not involved in the particular narrative of the film, but still governed by the rhythms of the river. However, the sense of the river here has a studio specificity. This is an Ealing Studios River Thames, with its valorisation of generally unobtrusive cinematography, its commitment to the real, and its peopling of London with small, interdependent communities. Except for the opening and a sequence towards the end of the film, the river is staged through a series of human contacts, little worlds in which characters know and remember each other's business and character. It is useful to recall the discussion of local London in Chapter 2, for this River Thames is, in some ways, a local river, despite a narrative set when the British Empire goes into freefall, its story of visiting North American and Jamaican sailors, and its presentation of a London both Imperial and war-ravaged.

Johnny (Earl Cameron) at home, on board, framed against Tower Bridge in *Pool of London*

The working river, as the film's title indicates, is the core of the film, and was clearly envisioned by the film-makers as worthy of attention in itself.[22] The final shooting script pays considerable attention to the appearance of the river. The opening of the second day of the action is described as follows,

> Saturday: A fine promising day. The Pool is at its busiest. On either bank, the cranes wing to and fro, loading and unloading the ships that crowd the wharves. A weekend holiday crowd sets sail on the *Golden Eagle* from Tower Pier, destination Dreamland or Margate beach. A river bus sails upstream to Westminster.[23]

But the visual fascination of the Pool is invoked not just as setting, but as revelatory of character. Following the direction 'Dan walks across Bridge', there is the following comment:

> The whole busy scene of the Pool forms a panorama now behind him. On a fine busy morning, with the tide running high, as now, this can be one of the sights of London … Dan does not pause to admire it.[24]

Dan is in a hurry – but he is also not a man to waste time looking at the river, at what 'can be one of the sights of London'. It is only towards the end of the film, when Dan is fleeing London and must choose whether or not to betray his friend Johnny, that he has time for the reflection associated with gazing at the river.

The film's topography is centred on the *Dunbar*, at anchor in the Pool, a location that is produced and reproduced within the film either through static framing, which includes Tower Bridge or the Tower of London, or through the mobility of smaller boats – customs and police launches, which approach the *Dunbar*, revealing its proximity to these landmark icons. The location shooting of the river setting gains its authenticity partly through these repetitions, which themselves have a 'cinematic geography'. Thus it would be difficult to map these different approaches to the ship coherently: their point is to insist on the reality of the river and the Tower Bridge location of the *Dunbar*. As complement, the landward approach to the *Dunbar* is filmed as a narrow, warehouse-lined street, which acts as a transition between the Pool and 'London'. This street, like Shad Thames, is typical of the alleys between the dock warehouses, with high walls, walkways and cobbles, and is used both to signify a dockland location and for several encounters for the ship's crew.[25] It is in this setting in which an attempt is made to render Johnny's feelings expressively through the way in which he kicks an empty tin can on two successive nights after his meetings with Pat, and it is also here that Dan is ambushed within the crime drama. As a transition between the river and the city, the dramatic, place-specific (the Docks) look of the lane reminds the audience of the proximity of the Pool in this 'drama of the river underworld', while also giving the film-makers much more flexibility in the use of space than that afforded by the ship at anchor. As a location which is used more than once, at different times of day, for different story lines, it also provides an interesting instance of the way in which location and genre work simultaneously to 'render up a sense of place'. For while the space is always architecturally distinctive, it is in the crime story segments that it is most expressive: a material place which

Battlebridge Lane at night: the London Docks as noir setting in *Pool of London*

is generically recognisable both as 'real place' and as a narrative space in which certain things are likely to happen.

Beyond the Pool there are busy location-shot London streets, buses and trams, and a group of public places – principally a music hall, a dance hall and a pub – to which both Dan and Johnny go and where they interact with many different Londoners. Dan is noticeably mobile through these different spaces, and is also the only character who enters other's private places, the homes of bad girl Maisie (Moira Lister) and good girl Sally, both of which, as Higson points out, are constructed through the codes of soap-opera and melodrama. Johnny, however, who visits public spaces unhindered when he is with Dan, and later Pat, is subjected to racial abuse and trickery as soon as he is alone. Pat too is abused for 'going with him' at the dance hall, when Maisie learns that the remaining pair of smuggled nylons is within Johnny's gift. There is no entry into the private, nor much mobility in public spaces for Johnny. When he tries to surprise Pat 'at the Palais' he is framed, like a film spectator, in a space quite separate to hers, standing in the shadow, his face lit by what he watches, seeing her greeting all her other friends, and retreats unnoticed, ending up in a criminal drinking den. There is a topography of race within the film in which Johnny's mobility is dependent on white companions. Dan (mainly) and Pat are benign towards Johnny, while his final guide, an Irishman, picks him up with evil intent when he spots the sailor's wages and takes him to a drinking den, where a wide-angle lens and low-angle shots indicate that the documentary world of the Pool has been left behind, and he is fleeced, abused and thrown out to sleep in the streets. So if Moretti is correct that each space encourages its own kind of story, one aspect of this is the way in which certain characters can move between spaces while others are spatially constricted.

However, this restriction of Johnny was not limited to the film's London. It was also a feature of the advertising of the film, as exemplified in the International Campaign Sheet of poster formats offered to exhibitors. Credits and posters confirm five starring roles, Bonar Colleano (Dan), Susan Shaw (Pat), Renée Asherson (Sally), Moira Lister (Maisie) and Earl Cameron (Johnny).[26] These names appear on all available poster formats offered to exhibitors in the International Campaign Sheet. However, on the twenty-two different poster formats available, there is no image of Cameron, most focusing on Colleano and Shaw. While Colleano and Shaw were better known, the complete absence of an image of Cameron is striking, and suggests that, despite the clearly liberal intentions of the film's 'colour prejudice' story, in film exhibition a 'coloured' actor could not even go out in white company.

The working London of the river, which draws on documentary traditions within both Ealing and British cinema, is juxtaposed with another London, documentary in its own way, the landmark London that Pat shows Johnny on the Sunday. In this London, there are sights and views displayed for both tourist and cinemagoer. Johnny and Pat climb up to the dome of St Paul's, from where, as Johnny observes, they can see the whole of the Pool, and then take a river-boat to Greenwich. The choice of Greenwich and the Maritime Museum is appropriate for the characters, but also displays London as the capital of a seafaring nation which once held such dominion, that, as Johnny explains when he and Pat struggle to understand longitude at the Greenwich meridian, 'everything starts from here'. The film is self-consciously inscribing the history of the British Empire, attempting to find, for Johnny, a place in which he can speak. Higson points out that these scenes, in contrast to the 'crime thriller discourse', are within 'the discourse of the social problem picture' where 'vital information is conveyed orally'.[27] Certainly, this tourist Imperial London, the splendid view of Greenwich from the Observatory down to the river, is curiously flat and uninteresting, lit brightly and flatly, as an illustrative backdrop to the heart of a maritime empire. This tourist excursion explains Johnny's presence within the fiction, and provides somewhere away from the ship for him to express feelings; but the cinematic language seems to have difficulty in integrating him into these spaces outside the ship.

The ambitions of this film, its desire to document 'one of the sights of London', as well as thrillingly entertain its audience and explore the question of racial prejudice, means that the different kinds of generic spaces these different types of story require have to be woven together. This, as Higson shows, is only intermittently successful. There is a notable moment of strain in the filming of the key jump of the heist sequence (an ambitious roof-top jump). Here, the use of painted sets for the landing space draws our attention to the way in which the crime narrative requires a different kind of cinematic space, one which can be more flexibly manipulated to meet narrative demands, than the documentary spaces which authenticate the setting as the city. This difficulty is articulated within the film in an earlier moment in which Pat, in the gallery of St Paul's, cries out, 'Look, isn't that a man climbing on that roof?' but Johnny can't see him – a moment that expresses both the desire to integrate the two narrative threads, and its difficulty. The paradoxical consequence of these strains and difficulties in the integration of the film's narrative spaces is the resonance of some of the location shooting in documenting post-war London. In a process that is the obverse of the 'narrativising of space' seen as characteristic of the feature film, certain spaces of this film persist as just that, spaces. The film lingers in the memory through individual images and scenes rather than any sense of a whole; its Londons don't quite cohere. But its river persists, perhaps most notably in the later sequences of the film, when Dan is fleeing downriver on a sailing barge. In these very beautiful sequences when the barge sails through the low-lying desolate marshes of the estuary by the light of the moon, Dan has nothing to do but contemplate his surroundings and the consequences of his actions. The dark folds of sail billow over his head, and the river, on its way to the sea, fills the image. This sequence, towards the end of the film, is an instance of 'subjective river', although it is at the dark sails above him, rather than the water, that Dan gazes as they move downriver and he confronts his moral responsibilities. However, the austere, empty images persist in a different way when we recall, fifty years later, that these waters run past the projected site of the Thames Gateway development.

The Temporalities of *The Long Good Friday*

Although *Pool of London* is so firmly located within the Thames as a working river, the docks themselves are closed to the film. The high dock walls, more prominently visible in *To Sir, With Love* (1967) or Lorenza Mazzetti's *Together* (1956), keep the actual space of the docks away from the cinema.[28] The nearest we get is when Johnny meets some dockers walking away from the wharf as he returns to ship on Sunday night. Their brief dialogue condenses a set of assumptions about the dock labour force, which had a reputation for militancy, as Johnny asks if they are striking and is laughed at for suggesting they'd go out on a

Sunday: 'Sunday, double time, not likely'. By the time of the James Bond film *The World is Not Enough* (discussed below), the docks and the dockers are gone, and the Isle of Dogs, an area dominated by the dock walls of Millwall and West India Docks, excluding all but those with business or labour within, has been penetrated by finance, rather than merchant capital.

The key transitional film here, in this move from Docks to Docklands, from unloading sugar to eating profiteroles, is *The Long Good Friday*. The move east is anticipated here both in the substance of the narrative, the proposed redevelopment of derelict London docks, and in the mooring of the central protagonist's boat downriver from Tower Bridge throughout the film. The distance between the mooring of the *Dunbar* (*Pool of London*), just west of Tower Bridge, on the south bank and the mooring of Harold Shand's (Bob Hoskins) boat in *The Long Good Friday*, just east on the north, is one of those very short distances which has a symbolic significance beyond metres or miles. *The Long Good Friday* is a film which is explicitly about transitions, but, retrospectively, can also be positioned in transition. It shows a London caught between its imperial past and 'global' future. A London in which there is the imagination of a shift eastwards, away from the old money of the City to different, post-imperial partnerships. The director, John Mackenzie, in his 2002 DVD commentary, describes his film as aiming for a new representation of London:

> I wanted to change the image of 60s London. I do try not to show the red buses or the square taxi cabs or all the things that one associates with films set in London. I just try to bring it more up to date than hitherto it had been seen.

If cinematic London in the 1970s was, with some exceptions, often dull, televisual London was quite exciting, particularly in the grounded, local products of Euston Films like *The Sweeney* (series one, 1975), *Out* (1978) and *Fox* (1980).[29] *The Long Good Friday* is also transitional in this sense, in that it draws strongly on televisual criminality in 1970s London, and so is stylistically caught between British television crime drama and US crime cinema.[30] The explicit aim of the writer Barrie Keefe was to write, with the encouragement of the producer, Barry Hanson, 'an American gangster film set in the East End'.[31] It is a film that is explicitly about the future – will Britain go with Europe or the US? What will happen after the end of Empire? Will the Irish war ever end? – and that chooses to explore the future through the literal question of the rebuilding of the capital city. Mackenzie's desire to be 'more up to date', and Keefe's commitment to showing something of the east and south-east London he knew, proved so successfully realised that the film has been hailed as 'perhaps the quintessential London film'.[32] It is also a film that is often discussed in a rather strange tense, and it is partly on this that my analysis will concentrate.

The Long Good Friday is an ambitious film which takes London as its topic, is concerned with the future of London, uses stock London characters, such as the cockney, and is location shot there.[33] It is also a film that has a significant place in several different British narratives. The most obvious of these is the story of the British gangster film, in which it is frequently paired with Mike Hodges's 1971 Newcastle-set thriller *Get Carter*, while also being understood as part of a longer tradition of 'social critique through criminality' in British cinema.[34] But the film can also be related to broader, non-film-specific stories, as does Angus Calder, in his influential account of the British Second World War, *The Myth of the Blitz*. Calder sees a place for Harold Shand within this narrative of Britishness:

> Harold, as representative Cockney, has survived into a situation where wisecracks, sentiment and a sense of History cannot save him. As played by Hoskins, he is not 'tragic' but sympathetically comic, in spite of his propensity to bully and torture. He is a monster spawned in the ruins of blitzed Stepney, who finds that the Americans are no longer admiring and patient and the Celts can no longer be overawed. His only interest in 'Europe' is in leading it. In terminal crisis, the Dunkirk spirit is the talisman by which he preserves self-esteem. His type, he believes, are never really beaten. He's wrong.[35]

The story I want to place this film within is that of London's river, where, along with *Close My Eyes* and *Empire State* (1987), it can be seen as a film which directly addresses the changing status of the London Docks and the city as a no-longer-Imperial port. Because the transformation of the London Docks into Dockland in the 1980s was such as privileged policy of the Thatcher government, this transformation has in turn come to signify 'Thatcherism', accompanied as it was by the radical deregulation of enterprise zones, sustained industrial unrest and the aggressive gentrification of parts of the Isle of Dogs. The Canary Wharf tower, One Canada Square, opened in 1991, has come to symbolise both an attitude and an era. *The Long Good Friday*, made in 1979, but not released until 1981,[36] which deals directly and purposefully with the question of the redevelopment of the Docks, has become entangled in this matrix of subsequent meanings, and is often discussed in a curious tense, as if Harold Shand knew what was going to happen. While the 1979 election of the Thatcher government led to a very rapid acceleration of the processes which would lead to the creation of the London Docklands Development Corporation in 1981, and the creation of the 'Wild West' of the Development Zone,[37] the subsequent symbolic resonance of Canary Wharf sometimes seems to obscure the distinctive feature of the dockscapes in *The Long Good Friday*: their emptiness.

Early in *The Long Good Friday*, at the reception that Harold Shand (Bob Hoskins) is holding for the American gangsters whom he is hoping to persuade to invest in his London project, we are shown a small-scale architect's model of a redeveloped London Dock basin. The model, in one of the cabins on Harold's yacht where he is hosting the reception, stands between Harold and his main lieutenant, Jeff (Derek Thompson), as they discuss the plans for the afternoon. The model, initially, is not shown in close-up, but instead rests between the men, lit through a porthole, and functions to explain Harold's project to the audience through providing a perfect miniature replica of what could be. White buildings cluster round the water of a marina with moorings for small pleasure boats and yachts, rather than ocean-going merchant ships. The model, with its spaces for pleasure craft, echoes both the redeveloped St Katharine's Dock that we have already been shown and Harold's yacht itself, on which it is displayed. The new Docklands will harbour yachts not freight-liners. One of the model buildings, we can infer, is the casino which figures centrally in Harold Shand's plans for the transformation of the area into what Barrie Keefe has called 'the Las Vegas of Europe'. The casino is the centre of the deal, which 'the Yanks' have been invited to join, enticed with promises of 'instant planning permission'. The brief meeting between Harold and Jeff, in which they allocate responsibility for the Americans, and the various corrupt councillors and policemen that they have on board, concludes with a close-up on the model of the redevelopment.

Harold's model of future possibility recalls another model at the beginning of a British film set in London, that made by Mr Pemberton (Stanley Holloway) in the post-war Ealing comedy *Passport to Pimlico* (1949). Mr Pemberton is shown working late at night to craft a model, for the Council meeting, of the recreation area 'for the kiddies' that he sees as the best use of bombed wasteland in the centre of the London village of Pimlico. Charles Barr has shown how the conflict over Mr Pemberton's model in the film can be seen to represent key debates about the direction of post-war Britain and the relative attention due to communal projects and individual enterprise.[38] In *Passport to Pimlico*, Mr Pemberton loses the vote at the Council meeting, and his main antagonist, Mr Wix (Raymond Huntley), flicks cigarette ash onto his playground model. However, the rest of the film explores the conflict between these different valuations of community, and by the end, we know that Mr Pemberton's recreation ground will be built, even though, outside Ealing, Mr Wix could be seen to have his way with the election of the 1951 Conservative government. In *The Long Good Friday*, the display of the

The party on Harold's yacht to welcome the Mafia: Charlie (Eddie Constantine), Victoria (Helen Mirren) and Harold (Bob Hoskins) with Tower Bridge in the background (*The Long Good Friday*)

model on the yacht at the reception is the closest Harold comes to his dream, and the film anatomises the unravelling of his power as a London gangland boss by what turns out to be the IRA and the speedy retreat of the American mafia from bomb-strewn London. Harold may not realise his dream, but his vision of the transformation of the empty, disused London docks, expounded in his celebrated 'Tower Bridge' speech, proved prophetic in a way that has enhanced the reputation of the film.

Barry Keefe gives a passionate retrospective view, which partly uses the tense of hindsight, when he describes the origin of the story in a 1996 article:

> So Barry [Hanson] and I were going to make this gangster film. The only problem was – we didn't have a story. I've sweated and panicked often on the endurance of a long project; funny thing about LGF was, it fell into place so easily. This has never happened to me since. I took a Saturday morning drive round the East End, looking at the developing Docklands on what I still prefer to call the Isle of Dogs. This hideous memorial to Thatcherism: Canary Wharf, the biggest and tallest tower building in Europe. Heck, is that something to be proud of? I live in Greenwich, South East London. Used to have the beautiful view from the hills in the Royal park of Hampstead Heath across the river. Now obliterated by Thatcher's memorial tower. I hate Docklands, maybe because I remember with emotion what a spunky and vibrant village it used to be before the men in striped shirts and flash Porsches moved in. A kind of Cockney genocide. Here, out of a sort of anger, came the first seeds of the story. What if an unscrupulous person tried to move in? Harold Shand, the central character, began to be born. Forty minutes by plane from the continent – could Docklands, with all its millions, become the Las Vegas of Europe?[39]

This tense is evident too in John Mackenzie's director's commentary which was included on the 2002 DVD release of the film:

> I wanted to try and bring out the opulence of Harold's lifestyle, you know, the glitz – the glitz which reflected his own taste really but which also was a reflection of the opulence of the times that were coming.

The film gives a sense of 'the opulence of the times that were coming' with considerable economy, moving between old and new London locations, evoking past and future. The key contrast is between the luxury of Harold's yacht and the empty docks, but the deserted docks are also contrasted with a street in Brixton, where a young British black man works on his car and a crowd of children gather round Harold's car (see Chapter 2). Traditional landmark London, in the form of Tower Bridge and St Paul's Cathedral, is juxtaposed with the vulgarity of the yacht and the mirrored restaurant where the Americans are taken when Harold's pub, the Lion and Unicorn, is blown up by the IRA. Harold's wealth has permitted him to penetrate the topography of the Establishment: he has a club in Mayfair, he visits the Americans at the Savoy, he has married an upper-middle-class woman who went to school with Princess Anne, but the yacht and the flat, his two homes, although expensive, are clearly signalled as vulgar through design details like the 'HS' monogram on the yacht carpet. If the Canary Wharf tower has become the architectural symbol of Thatcherism, Harold's combination of brutality, ambition, drive and vulgarity has come to epitomise its sensibility, and is remobilised ten years later in Peter Greenaway's film *The Cook, the Thief, his Wife and her Lover* (1989). This too features a powerful gangster figure Spica (Michael Gambon), also married to a posh woman played by Helen Mirren. However, in the *The Cook*, the vulgar brutality of Spica is rendered as decadent. Harold, in contrast, is thrusting and eager in his acquisitions and consumption, still hungry for greater profits and legitimacy.[40]

The Long Good Friday attempts to ground a gangster story which would attract audiences on both sides of the Atlantic in a location-shot late 1970s London. Parky (Dave King), the corrupt detective inspector, observes to Harold, after the bombings start: 'It's been calm for ten years, Harold, and that's all down to you.' Parky is referring to Harold's supremacy in London gangland and, while the 1970s might have been quiet on Parky's beat, for most other people in Britain they were pretty turbulent, with continual industrial action, the Irish war and a mainland IRA bombing campaign, States of Emergency, rising unemployment as post-industrialisation begins to bite, the entry into the European Economic Community and an alternation of crisis-driven Conservative and Labour governments. *The Long Good Friday* condenses these turbulent years within its plot: the derelict docks, the corrupt councillor who pays to avoid industrial action ('He's got a hundred Micks working on his sites – haven't you ever wondered why he's got no strikes?'), the IRA bombs, and an increasingly multi-cultural Britain. But through Harold's vision, and his search for partners to invest capital in his scheme for the casino in the Docks, it also poses the political question of future British alliances, and the choice between the USA and Europe. Harold's first choice, which is a generically natural one, is to go to the 'Yanks'. His desperate bid for modernity at the end of the film when they have rejected him, is to declare that he'll go to the 'Krauts – yes the Krauts'.

Harold wants to build to a casino in the Docks, and he knows that he'll need foreign money to do it. When the Dockland Development Corporation came into being in 1981, one of its difficulties was attracting British investment. It was, Foster argues, the Americans and the Germans who saw the site as near the City and full of potential. British firms, initially, wanted nothing to do with the East End.[41] When the deregulation of the London Stock Exchange in 1986 ('Big Bang') produced a need for computerised trading floors on a scale that could not be met in the City, Docklands as a financial centre, home to foreign banks, was born. In a sense, Harold got his casino. One of the sources of the film's power lies in the way in which the precision of Harold's situation and plans is matched by – juxtaposed with, embodied in – the extraordinary spectacle of the empty docks. As Harold plots and organises, for example, when he stands on the yacht watching the sentinel cranes just after the Americans have arrived, or as he walks with Parky in the long tracking shot in George V Dock, the water lies quiet, reflecting its surroundings, empty, vacant – both ghostly and immanent. The location shooting of the film, as it was intended to, renders up 'a sense of place' and this, particularly in this long tracking shot, or the derelict warehouses of the crucifixion scene, is intensified because the narrative of the film is about this place. The question of the future is spatialised in the quiet water and the empty warehouses.

To see *The Long Good Friday* any time since the building of Docklands is to know that the warehouses, if still standing, are now 'stunning apartments', and that the waters are permanently quiet and decorative. These cinematic images in a fiction film offer testimony to

The emptiness of the Docks: Harold and Parky (Dave King) in George V Dock (*The Long Good Friday*)

a 'before' when the present was still the future, and the 1980s had not, by most people, been imagined. In Nowell-Smith's terms, the 'ontological link between nominal setting and actual location' contributes to the power of place within the film, 'saying: this is how things were'.[42] The Docks are not like that any more, and this explains the complicated tenses people use about the film. John Mackenzie's DVD commentary exemplifies the resonance of place in the film. When he is not discussing how scenes were shot, he is mainly concerned to move explicitly between past and future in his commentaries on the use of the locations, offering very precise comments, such as this when Victoria (Helen Mirren) and Harold are leaving the yacht with their guests to go to one of Harold's pubs: 'Right outside that window you would now see Heron Dock … Round about here, to the left, would be the big skyscraper of Canary Wharf.' He is also very sensitive to the way in which old features of the working dock have been incorporated into Docklands, as he shows in his discussion of the long tracking shot past the still water and motionless cranes of George V Dock as Harold and Parky discuss the bombings: 'Here we are on George V dock which is now a built-up area, full of posh houses – still keep the cranes in there, they're like decorative pieces between the houses, like sculptures.' This careful observation about the cranes condenses, in an image, many accounts of the way in which former industrial landscapes have been transformed into leisure sites,[43] and also shows that it is partly Mackenzie's own sensitivity to place which explains something of the subsequent resonance of his film. The tenses that people use to discuss this film can be attributed to the way in which the setting of the deserted docks exceeds the narrative demands of the film, producing, through its desolate beauty, images that can't be reduced to Harold's vision. In this, there are similarities with some of the city- and riverscapes in *Pool of London*. However, in *The Long Good Friday*, because the narrative of the film is *about* the future of these images, this 'excess', this 'sense of place' can, in subsequent viewings, be mobilised back into the narrative to authenticate Harold's dream. In Nowell-Smith's terms, it is to the extent that we can read these images as saying 'this is how things were' that the film seems prophetic.

The ghostly presence of past riverscapes is something to which I will return at the end of the chapter, but before that I want to discuss another kind of cinematic river, the river of dead people.

The River of Dead People and the River of Ghosts

The most famous instance of the Thames as a river of dead people is pre-cinematic. It is the opening of *Our Mutual Friend*, when Gaffer Hexham pulls out of the dark waters of the Thames the body whose identity will affect so many fates within the novel. The finding of this body, part of Gaffer Hexham's fluvial harvest, inaugurates the narrative. This Thames tale has a long history across many media. Lynda Nead has shown the importance of this river through the recurrence of a watery grave in narratives of the fallen woman in nineteenth-century painting and visual culture, where a voluntary surrender to the waters is shown as the only imaginable destiny for the prostitute: the logical conclusion to the feminine version of 'subjective river'.[44] Television documentaries on the river, or the river police, repeatedly deploy the trope of the recovered corpse in a narrative that commences with the establishment of the River Police at Wapping prior to any other police force.[45] In the cinema, the trope of the body in the river is a story that recurs as both the beginning and end of cinematic narratives, producing an endless circle of missing identities. Alfred Hitchcock's 1972 film *Frenzy* opens with the discovery of a naked woman in the river, set up as a macabre counterpoint to a politician's riverside speech about the ending of river pollution. The 1965 film *Four in the Morning* starts with the discovery of a female body, *Night in the City* ends with the consigning of a body to the water. In the former, her identity is the object of speculation throughout the film; in the latter, a confidence trickster is seen to deserve the anonymity and lack of ceremony of a watery grave.

Four in the Morning (Anthony Simmons) uses the Thames to relate its three unconnected, episodic stories to each other. Each story is that of a young woman, and through each story runs the Thames. The framing story, which remains mainly within a documentary mode, is the discovery of the body of a young woman in the Thames.[46] Found downriver, she is brought back up to Wapping, the police station on the river used for these cases. The body story in *Four in the Morning* juxtaposes the contained spaces of the launches, the station and the mortuary with the tidal, lapping, protean river; the banal loquacity of the police in contrast to the silence of the unidentified corpse. The men who find this body are pragmatic and unemotional. 'What have we got this morning?' 'A dead 'un.' They are not without pity, but

The river of dead people: the body on the shore in *Four in the Morning*

their initial concern is all for the mechanics of the recovery, 'Got it', and the transfer of the body from the shore, to the river, to the launch, to the jetty and then to the mortuary, referring all the time to the body as 'it'.

The body is wearing a pale trench coat, and through editing and close-ups on this fashionable garment, connections are drawn between each of the female protagonists: a young mother (Judi Dench), with a sleepless baby and a still laddish husband, and a nightclub singer (Ann Lynn), who finishes work in the early hours. Sue Harper hails the film as 'feminist art' 'enunciat[ing] the traps in which women are caught'.[47] The river threads through each of the women's lives, and the unidentified body, dealt with so prosaically, 'nice appendix scar, that's narrowed down the field a bit', recurs as a possible destiny for each of the despairing women characters. Katherine Shonfield singles out this film for its representation of London because of the centrality of the Thames to the film's structure and the extended central section of a speedboat river trip.[48] She suggests that

The core of *Four in the Morning* London is entirely unofficial. It is uncategorised: neither road, square, building, house nor park. The sense is that the speedboat charts the very heart of the city for the first time. The river suddenly, unpredictably, reveals itself working as a formal centre: looking from its own centre, the monumental buildings of London are presented anew.[49]

Although phrased differently, this is an account of film yielding up 'a sense of place', and one which renders the city afresh. The new, unpredictable vantage point of the speedboat, its fluidity of movement enacting the river, reveals that the river is the heart of the city.

Gavin Weightman's television series *The River Thames* (1990) mourns the working river and remembers the days when 'everything [was] geared to up with the flood, down with the ebb' (ep. 1, 28 October 1990), and features former dockers and river-men as powerful witnesses, 'now there's nothing, nothing, nowadays, it's so sad, it's dead, the whole place is dead'. To these former river workers, it is the river itself that is now dead, and I want to explore this through an analysis of a chase scene from a Pierce Brosnan James Bond film, *The World is Not Enough*, which could be seen to render this 'dead place' spectacular. Unlike the motorboat sequence from *Four in the Morning*, the extended chase from the pre-title sequence of *The World is Not Enough* does not render up a sense of place, and notably fails to make the city anew, even though it includes the new landmarks of Docklands and Dome. This downriver chase, in which Bond appropriates a prototype amphibian vehicle, is the second part of the title sequence, with the first part set in Bilbao, with establishing shots of the new icons of post-industrial Bilbao, the Gehry Guggenheim Museum and the Jeff Koons puppy outside the museum, and its London is similarly postmodern. The establishing shot of Vauxhall Cross, labelled as 'M16 Headquarters London', is a prelude to a landmark London sequence, which is narrativised by the chase downriver. In this, the leisure waterways of Docklands and the architectural volume of the Dome feature as three-dimensional, tactile spaces, while older landmarks, like the Houses of Parliament and Tower Bridge, figure simply as images, part of the spectacular themed racetrack, the River Thames. The chase is filmed by alternating close-ups of the two participants, becoming increasingly drenched with water, in their vehicles, with aerial shots of the Thames. The use of aerial photography, in itself spectacular, and the way in which the River Thames is, through this photography, laid out flat as a gleaming, seductive racecourse, provides an appropriate context for display of the 'boys' toys' spectacle of Bond's vehicle. The sequence neatly condenses Bond's relationship to the British Establishment (he takes the high-tech vehicle without consent, he bursts through the walls of MI6, he speeds past the seat of government without a glance), all in pursuit of a beautiful woman. The slight anachronism of the spy with playboy tastes is then brought into the twenty-first century as he speeds east through Tower Bridge to penetrate Docklands, with high-tech mapping of the redesigned area showing through-routes where none seemed visible. The river sequence is noticeable for the emptiness of the waters, which is accentuated by the aerial shots. The river's gleaming beauty is free of river traffic with the exception of one tourist boat, and it is only when his quarry crashes into a River Police launch that Bond encounters the residual working population of the river, before moving to the new sites of the redeveloped docks, where people sit eating breadsticks, by displays of profiteroles, in waterside restaurants.

Generically, James Bond films are partly identified by the use of high-tech gadgetry and spectacle, and this sequence condenses the generic promises of the film. The use of the river is part of this promise. In a manner that has some similarities with the London montage in *Trainspotting* (1995), discussed in Chapter 1, this sequence mobilises a landmark London repertoire – there is even a Routemaster bus in some narrow streets towards the end of the chase – and, in the way in which the images are combined, suggests that the film's own attitude to London will be more modern and disrespectful. The most obvious aspect of this is the careless audacity of Bond's pursuit downriver, the Palace of Westminster both present and ignored. In contrast, east of Tower Bridge, there is a high-tech Docklands and the then not-yet-devalued Millenium Dome, conveniently situated for a sudden, involuntary landing from a hot-air balloon; the new leisure waters of Docklands and the very fabric of the Dome are the London for this hero. So in terms of the cinematic river, there are at least two different things going on. On the one hand, in a film type identified by its tendency to spectacle, the River Thames is rendered spectacular. Bond's Thames is a generic river. On the other hand, the way in which this is done, from the helicopter shots to the stretch of the river that is seen as significant, is historically specific. Bond's Thames is a late-twentieth-century river.[50] Its traditional landmarks are significantly subordinated both to the narrative chase and to more recent, easterly, landmarks. This is partly achieved, and achievable, through and because of the emptiness of the river.

This sequence, if juxtaposed with the opening of *Pool of London*, could be seen to confirm an argument about the transformation of the cinematic river, in the second half of the twentieth century, from a 'place' to a 'spectacle'. This, in a way, is the argument that John Mackenzie summarises so succinctly when he comments on the way in which the cranes have been retained 'like sculptures' in the redeveloped George V Dock. It has an attractive clarity, but it seems too simple. I have shown that the Thames is spectacular in each of these films, and that in each case the spectacle is both historical and generic. Historically, the River Thames is one of London's great spectacles, and the decision by film-makers to include the Thames in a London-set film is often a choice to engage with the spectacular potential of the medium and city, as costume films like *Orlando* (1993) and *Shakespeare in Love* (1998) testify.[51] However, even if the transformations are from one kind of spectacle to another, from one type of place to another, films such as *Pool of London*, *Four in the Morning* and *The Long Good Friday*, with all their generic particularity, can also be read with a documentary gaze. Through this double reading, together, they give a sense of the river as both persistent and changing. In this 'co-existence of persistence and change', as Raymond Williams puts it when discussing the ideas of the 'country' and the 'city', the cinematic river can be read not just as a metaphor for change within individual films, or as offering a history of change across many films, but also as concentrating many of the ideas about the relationship between the cinema and the city explored in this book. To quote Williams more fully:

> it is the co-existence of persistence and change which is really striking and interesting, and which we have to account for without reducing either fact to a form of the other. Or to put it more theoretically, we have to be able to explain, in related terms, both the persistence and historicity of concepts.[52]

So finally, I want to suggest that whenever we meet the River Thames in the cinema, it is a river of ghosts. These ghosts are of different types, and include the many former workers on the river who people the narratives, the merchant seamen like Johnny and Dan in *Pool of London*, the prostitutes, the dockers, the river police, the crane-operators; and those who open and close narratives by dying there, like the suicides and the murdered. But these ghosts also include ways of seeing the river, the resonance of former views and spectacles. This is explored directly in William Raban's *Thames Film*, which was made between 1984 and 1986. The impact of the redevelopment of the former docks was already very evident in the skyline and waterfront of the river, and these were the most gung-ho days of the London Docklands Development Corporation. Raban chooses to address the changes to the river obliquely through a double strategy of historical exploration and contemporary documentation.

The film places itself within the very rich history of Thames art through its inclusion of extracts from T. S. Eliot reading 'The Four Quartets' (the river as a 'strong brown god'), while its tone is set through repeated references to the Hieronymus Bosch painting *The Triumph of Death*. In some senses a *vanitas*, the film's acceptance of mutability greets the new buildings under construction with a long memory of past riverside splendour. The main body of the film is a journey downriver from Temple Stairs to the Estuary 'on the ebb flow', 'looking for the signs of increase, production, exploration and empire'. This journey, which commences on 7 May 1984, is modelled on the earlier journey by Thomas Pennant, taken on 7 May 1787, and recorded in a manuscript volume now held by the Port of London Authority. Much of the soundtrack of the film – which is dominated by the lapping river water – consists of extracts from Pennant's account of his 1787 journey read over old engravings, photographs and film of the river, which are inserted into footage from the 1984 journey. *Thames Film* is a very beautiful film. It is in some ways elegiac for the changing waterfront, but because of its long historical view, it establishes that there has always been change on the river. There is a precision and a literalness to this sense of a historical view, for many of the key sequences of the film involve attempts to replicate historical views accurately, juxtaposing archive images of, say, Greenwich or Millwall, with current views. This historical perspective is matched by a very close attention to the filming of the river now. Here, Raban's background in the London Filmmakers' Co-operative is evident, manifest in the concern with the materiality of film and the purity of the concentration on the river, with a minimal journey structure, rendering the river almost abstractly. One strategy is the use of close-up on the water, so that the whole frame is filled with the moving patterns of light, shade and reflection, drawing attention both to the constant movement of the water surface and the flatness of the film screen. The dominant strategy, though, is the use of long shots focused on the passing banks. On land, this type of shooting, working from a moving vehicle, would be a tracking shot, but here, with the camera on a small boat drifting downriver on the ebb tide, the 'tracking' is manifest, and interrogated, at several levels. For the film tracks the river and its banks on the journey to the estuary, the camera itself partaking of the journey, low in the water, intercut with historical images which track the river through time. The film tells both types of Thames tale, that through space and that through time. The most striking shots are early morning shots when mist occludes the shoreline, and so the frame is divided horizontally between sky and river, with mist at their meeting. Often the image is symmetrical, with the bankside and its reflection captured on the horizontal axis.

Like the water close-ups, these long shots propose both the medium and the matter for attention. The rectangular frame is divided, in different shots in different ratios, drawing attention to the shape of both frame and screen, while, through its drifting, horizontal

Thames Film: the symmetry of the reflected image

motion, the frame both shows the river in movement and draws our attention to the way in which the river will always exceed the limits of the frame.

Thames Film is the longest piece in a series of Raban's films which address Docklands and the Isle of Dogs in the late twentieth century. His 'Under the Tower' trilogy, *Sundial* (1992), *A13* (1994) and *An Island Race* (1996), are all filmed in the vicinity of the Canary Wharf tower. *Sundial* majestically montages seventy-one shots of the tower overshadowing seventy-one different locations in a minute. For *Thames Film*, Raban posed himself the challenge of making 'a film about London, as it were, from the point of view of the River itself ... The obvious way it seemed to me of doing that was to drift, on the river, in a small boat, as close to the water surface as possible and record what happens on the banks.'[53] The ontology of the photographic image is here addressed in a different way to that of the other films discussed in this chapter. While, on the one hand, there is the employment of the documentary register of 'being there' – 'as close to the water surface as possible', on the other, the film has some formation within the aesthetic history recounted by Peter Wollen in his discussion of modernism and avant-garde film strategies, 'Ontology and Materialism in Film'.[54] There is a discernible 'muting or exclusion of the non-cinematic codes' – not completely, there is still the narration and there is a significant commitment to intertextual references. There is also, in the constant concern with film as a medium, a medium in which images are made

Derelict cranes in *The Long Good Friday*

through the photochemical registering of light on celluloid, the memory of a more austere mode of film-making in which, as Wollen puts it, 'light is no longer seen as the means by which the pro-filmic event is registered on film, but as the pro-filmic event itself'.[55]

Raban's film imbues contemporary footage from 'as close to the water surface as possible', river *actualité*, with a consciousness of rivers past: the ghostly river. It provides a way of looking again at the complex temporalities of *The Long Good Friday* and, for example, the sensibility of John Mackenzie commenting on what now seems a melancholy prescience in *The Long Good Friday*, 'Of course this is all built up now with those rather ritzy buildings of Canada Water but in those days it was just falling to bits.' Former views of the river – old Limehouse, the cranes of the docks – haunt current sights, such as Canary Wharf, while passing technologies – like photographic images recorded on celluloid and projected at twenty-four frames a second – are themselves becoming ghostly as we watch.

Notes

1. For a discussion of the Manhattan waterfront as a place of meditation, see James Saunders, *Celluloid Skyline* (London: Bloomsbury, 2002 [2001]), p. 270.
2. Stephen Daniels, 'Paris envy: Patrick Keiller's *London*', *History Workshop Journal* no. 40, Autumn 1995, p. 222.
3. Iain Sinclair, 'Paint me a river', *The Guardian Review*, 5 February 2005, pp. 16–17.
4. Geoffrey Nowell-Smith, 'Cities real and imagined', in Mark Shiel and Tony Fitzmaurice (eds), *Cinema and the City* (Oxford: Blackwell, 2001), p. 103.
5. André Bazin, 'The ontology of the photographic image', in *What Is Cinema?*, vol. 1, translated by Hugh Gray (Berkeley: University of California Press, 1967), pp. 9–16.
6. Nowell-Smith, 'Cities real and imagined', p. 104.

7. *Los Angeles Plays Itself* (Thom Andersen, 2003). See the discussion in Chapter 1.

8. Raymond Williams, *The Country and the City* (London: Chatto and Windus, 1973). See also Sarah Monks on the imaging of the downriver Thames: 'The visual economies of the downriver Thames in eighteenth-century British art', *Visual Culture in Britain* vol. 7 no. 1, 2006, pp. 1–20.

9. 'Peter Ackroyd's Thames, Millennium Bridge, London SE1, 16–25 June 2006.

10. Joe Kerr, 'North/South', paper to Tate Britain Day Event, *The Thames: History, context, representation*, 6 May 2005.

11. Colin MacCabe, 'Interview: Hanif Kureishi on London', *Critical Quarterly* vol. 41 no. 3, Autumn 1999, p. 37.

12. Atima Srivastava, *Transmission* (London: Serpent's Tail, 1992), p. 19, quoted by Sukhdev Sandhu, *London Calling* (London: HarperCollins, 2003), p. 272.

13. Jonathan Coe, *The Closed Circle* (London: Penguin, 2005 [2004]), p. 56.

14. Including *London and the Thames* (15 September 1977, written by Mervyn Levy, BBC); *Literary Island: 'Thames'* (6 August 1991, directed and produced by Frances Dickenson, LWT for Channel 4); and 'Barnes to the Barrier: a journey down the Thames', *Metroland 5* (2 December 1997, Hawkshead for Carlton, directed by Patrick O Grady).

15. *The River Thames* (28 October 1990, 4 November 1990, 11 November 1990, written, produced, directed and narrated by Gavin Weightman, LWT). *The River* (30 October 1999, 5 November 1999, 12 November 1999, 10 November 1999, produced by James Runcie; directed by James Runcie, Nicky Pattison and Adam Low, written and presented by Patrick Wright, BBC2). *Sweet Thames* (directed by Mark Harrison, made for BBC2's *Words on Film* series), discussed by Sukhev Sandhu in *London Calling*, pp. 311–28.

16. Patrick Wright argues that the Thames has two sources, 'the physical one may lie upstream, but the 'economic, cultural and historical one surely lies in the sea, which has determined so much of what the country has become', *The River* (London: BBC Books, 1999), p. 93.

17. For example, *The Thames through Time* (23 December 2004, Mosaic/ITV), which concentrates on the current fate of salmon and sea trout, which have returned to the river since the 1960s.

18. *Pool of London*, Information Folder, BFI Balcon Collection.

19. There are many accounts of a pre-*Windrush* black presence in Britain. See for example, Peter Fryer, *Staying Power* (London: Pluto Press, 1984), and, on the *Empire Windrush*, Mike and Trevor Phillips, *Windrush: The Irresistible Rise of Multi-Racial Britain* (London: HarperCollins, 1998).

20. From 'Slogans', in 'International Campaign Sheet', *Pool of London*, Balcon Collection, BFI.

21. Andrew Higson, '*Pool of London*', in Alan Burton, Tim O'Sullivan and Paul Wells (eds), *Liberal Directions* (Trowbridge: Flicks Books, 1997), p. 162.

22. The river sequences of the film were location shot, and the press book informs us that the production had to be structured round the fortnightly trips of the MS *Czech* (the *Dunbar*) between Gdynia and London, permitting four days' shooting when the ship was in dock. An old warehouse in Bermondsey was used as a temporary interior studio and, for scenes on the boat deck, filming on board was not meant to disrupt normal working.

23. *Pool of London*, Shooting Script, BFI, Balcon Collection, p. 25.

24. Ibid.

25. The location used for shooting was Battlebridge Lane, which runs from the river down to Tooley Street and is now part-demolished adjacent to the Hays Galleria development.

26. Film print; credit titles, no. 3, 10 January 1951, Balcon Collection, Item G/77.

27. Higson, 'Pool of London', p. 169.

28. There are a large number of short films, some produced by the Port of London Authority (in various guises and co-productions), which document the working of the Docks, including Basil Wright's *The Waters of Time* (1951), *Port of London* (1959), *Faces in a Crowd* (1969) and *Thames Port* (1974). Archive footage of the Docks (along with new footage of the City) is used to incite reflection on London in transition in *Twilight City*, (directed by Reece Auguiste, BAFC and Channel Four, 1989), a film that testifies to the complex imbrication of migration and memory in the city.

29. But see Leon Hunt, *British Low Culture* (London: Routledge, 1998), for a spirited defence of 1970s cinema, and, on Euston Films, Manuel Alvarado and John Stewart (eds), *Made for Television* (London: BFI, 1985).

30. Institutionally the film owed much to television. Barry Hanson, its producer, worked for Thames Television in the 1970s, and primary funding came from Lew Grade's ITC Films through its subsidiary Black Lion Films.

31. Barrie Keefe in *Cast and Crew: The Long Good Friday* (IWCMedia for BBC, 31 August 2005, BBC4).

32. Luke McKernan, 'London on film', in Brian McFarlane (ed.), *The Encyclopaedia of British Film* (London: Methuen and BFI, 2003), pp. 403–4.

33. John Mackenzie confirms that, partly to keep costs down, the film did not use studios. Some sets, such as the pub, the Lion and the Unicorn, were built on location, and Harold and Victoria's flat had to be redressed for different scenes. 'Director's commentary', DVD *The Long Good Friday* (HandMade Films, 2002).

34. See the careful placing of *The Long Good Friday* by Steve Chibnall and Robert Murphy in 'Parole overdue', the introduction to *British Crime Cinema* (London: Routledge, 1999), pp. 1–15, and also Andrew Spicer's discussion of British noir in his *Film Noir* (Harlow: Longman, 2002), p. 196.

35. Angus Calder, *The Myth of the Blitz* (London, Pimlico, 1992 [1991]), pp. 268–9. The film is cited in a range of other 'non-film' texts, such as Murray Fraser's essay on London architecture since the late 1970s, 'Architecture's urban shine and brutal reality', in Joe Kerr and Andrew Gibson (eds), *London from Punk to Blair* (London: Reaktion, 2003), p. 265.

36. While the production of *The Long Good Friday*, before Mrs Thatcher's May 1979 election victory, was straightforward, there were considerable difficulties about the film's release. Evidently the IRA references were unacceptable to the Grade organisation, the main funder, which demanded cuts. Protracted negotiations, including a threat to sue from Hoskins (for the dubbing of his voice), culminated in the purchase of the film by HandMade Films and its subsequent release in 1981. See 'Bob sues to get his voice back', *Daily Mirror*, 18 November 1980, p. 10; David Robinson, 'Cinematic vigour to be wasted on television' (a campaigning review after a London Film Festival screening), *The Times*, 21 November 1980; 'Britishers Bring "Friday" to NY; Face Vex of "Accents" and "Irony"', *Variety*, 21 April 1982; *Cast and Crew: The Long Good Friday* (31 August 2005, BBC4).

37. One of Foster's interviewees makes the 'Wild West' comparison: Janet Foster, *Docklands: Cultures in Conflict, Worlds in Collision* (London: Routledge, 2003 [1999]), p. 135. See also John Eade's discussion of the 'wild frontier' of the East End in LDDC material, 'Reconstructing places', in *Living the Global City* (London: Routledge, 1997), p. 132.

38. See Charles Barr's analysis of Mr Pemberton's model, *Ealing Studios* (Newton Abbot: Cameron and Tayleur in association with David and Charles, 1977), pp. 80–1, 100.

39. Barry Keefe, 'Haunting Friday', *Sight and Sound* vol. 6 no. 8, August 1996, p. 20.

40. See John Hill, 'Allegorising the nation: British gangster films of the 1980s', in Chibnall and Murphy, *British Crime Cinema*, pp.160–71, for a discussion of the gangster metaphor (and more detailed discussion of the IRA in this film); and Michael Collins, *The Likes of Us: A Biography of the White Working Class* (London: Granta, 2004), pp. 208–9, on the snobbery of the metaphor.

41. Foster, *Docklands*, pp. 131–9.

42. Nowell-Smith, 'Cities real and imagined', p. 105.

43. See for example, Sharon Zukin, *Landscapes of Power* (Berkeley and Los Angeles: University of California Press, 1991).

44. Lynda Nead, 'The river and the fallen woman', paper to *The Thames: Context, History and Representation*, Tate Britain, 6 May 2005.

45. For example, 'River Cops' episode of *First Edition* (18 August 1998, directed by Sophie Goodhart), *Joe Brown's East End* gave the derivation of 'whopper' as the blown-up corpses landed at Wapping (16 December 1988, Thames Television).

46. Simmons originally received NFFC funding for a sixty-minute film without dialogue which was planned as the suicide story. 'Four in the Morning', *Sight and Sound* vol. 34 no. 3, Summer 1965, p. 140. Review, *Monthly Film Bulletin* vol. 33 no. 385, February 1966, p. 15.

47. Sue Harper, *Women in British Cinema* (London: Continuum, 2000), p. 122.

48. Katherine Shonfield, *Walls Have Feelings* (London: Routledge, 2000), pp. 147–50.

49. Ibid., p. 148.

50. The Bond chase can be compared with a spectacular river/land chase from the other end of the century, Maurice Elvey's version of *The Sign of Four* (1923), which features a long river journey from Twickenham right through London to the Estuary, when the bridges are given titles to enable identification as the boat speeds past. The chase in this film is one of its spectacular attractions, and glimpses of the landmarks, as these titles suggest, are seen to augment this. The river gets busier as the boat travels eastwards, with sooty tugs and sailing barges in the Estuary. Christine Gledhill discusses Elvey's conscious use of landmarks in *Reframing British Cinema 1918–28* (London: BFI, 2003), p. 101.

51. The frost-fair on the river in *Orlando* could, of course, be seen to testify to the film's complex, international co-production funding: UK, Russia, France, Italy, Netherlands, shot as it was in St Petersburg. Pat Dowell, 'Demystifying traditional notions of gender: interview with Sally Potter', *Cinéaste* vol. 20 no. 1, 1993, pp. 16–17.

52. Williams, *The Country and the City*, p. 348.

53. 'theFrame – William Raban', Artists' Films, *William Raban* DVD, BFI/Illuminations, 2004.

54. Peter Wollen, 'Ontology and materialism in film', *Screen* vol. 17 no. 1, 1976, pp. 7–25.

55. Ibid., p. 14.

Afterword: The Poignancy of Place

Up Midland Road to the traffic lights, turn right under the railway bridges; then in Goods Way, the gasholders come back, a cascade of intersecting circles, a shout of joy from the most unlikely place. All of them come to the party equipped with classical columns, simple Doric and a kind of gasholder Composite. The nineteenth-century equivalent of a Baroque angel is not a Victorian angel but a Baroque gasworks.

The whole of this place at the back of St Pancras is incredibly moving: tunnels, perspectives, trains on the skyline, roads going all ways. If you get nothing from it at first, stay there until something happens: it is really worth the effort.[1]

Three Forms of Melancholy

Paul Gilroy has written of the 'post-colonial melancholia' that he sees afflicting the British.[2] He argues that the repeated return, within British culture, to the Second World War, screens a failure to come to terms with the loss of Empire in the post-war period. 'Plucky little Britain' can be remembered so much less painfully than Partition, Suez, the Mau-Mau, Rhodesian UDI and apartheid South Africa. In London-set cinema, the lure of the war is incontestable, and its imagery and metaphor return as familiar, and sometimes even comforting, in films as diverse as *V for Vendetta* (2006), *Mrs Henderson Presents* (2005) and *The Chronicles of Narnia: the Lion, the Witch and the Wardrobe* (2006), to take only recent examples. London has a particular role in this imaginary: the Palace of Westminster with its clock-tower sentinel against air attacks, search-lights in the sky, the silvery reflective surface of the river, smoke obscuring the dome of St Paul's, air-raid sirens, the camaraderie of the shelter, the attempt to maintain everyday life among the ruins. The Second World War rendered this imagery heroic.[3] The landmarks of a national capital and an imperial city were inscribed into a broader international story as beleaguered but defiant. The post-war London with which I have been concerned is being remade in the shadow of this history – and 'post-war' is a long period in British history. Its cinematic bombsites, whether location or studio, in films like *Hue and Cry* (1947), *Mandy* (1952) and *Hope and Glory* (1987), were often exciting places, in contrast to the tragic bombsites of mainland Europe in films such as *Germania, Anno Zero* (1947), *The Man Between* (1953) or *The Pianist* (2003); its communities united round a single purpose, a fantasy revisited so often in British films.[4] I think it arguable that British cinema has not subsequently found an iconographic repertoire that matches that of wartime London, although, from about the mid-1980s, there appeared, across a range of films, following the utopian moments in *My Beautiful Laundrette* (1985) and *Territories* (1984), a discernible trope of 'multi-culturalism'. Thus, for example, the final dance in *Beautiful Thing* (1995) and the victory celebrations in *Fever Pitch* (1997) work to dispel momentarily the melancholy of which Gilroy speaks in a carnivalesque coming to terms with Empire. Despite these moments of conviviality, also, consciously, manifest in a quieter moments like the final cricket game in *Bend it Like Beckham* (2002), London remains, within the cinematic imaginary, most familiar as a city obscured in Victorian fog or caught in Second World War search-lights.

Cinema studies, too, has been suffering from its own melancholia at the turn of the celluloid century. Cinephilia has become a favoured topic as the move to digital technologies renders films shot and edited on celluloid a diminishing proportion of the audiovisual 'content' available across an expanding number of platforms.[5] While the new digital technologies offer extraordinary and socially extensive opportunities to see again films that were once available only to specialists, there is a discernible melancholy in the writing of some twentieth-century film scholars. The new possibilities of 'home textual analysis', freeze framing and re-viewing at will are counterposed to the loss of the photographic image's indexical qualities. Laura Mulvey's exploration of the way in which 'video and digital media have opened up new ways of seeing old movies',[6] while determinedly welcoming to new possibilities, is, as the title of her book suggests (*Death at 24x a Second*), haunted by mutability and intimations of mortality. In her discussion of the different modalities of the stilled, stopped and reviewed image, Mulvey is concerned with the poignancy of the revelation, through these processes, of the 'there-ness and then-ness of the film's original moment'.[7] While Mulvey's concerns are more with the orchestration of performance and stars, actors and ordinary people, her observations can also give insight into a poignancy of place, my third form of melancholy.

This third form of melancholy has a long history, which could perhaps be indicated by the formation, in 1875, of the Society for Photographing Old London in response to demolitions.[8] The role of cinema in relation to vanishing buildings and landmarks has been discussed by Wim Wenders in the context of his work in Berlin. Wenders has spoken about his 1987 film *Wings of Desire* in 1997, after the 'fall of the wall' and the reunification of East and West Germany. The film was explicitly concerned with Berlin as a site of memory, history and story-telling, and Wenders discusses his choice of location as follows:

> The fact that something is due to go is always a good reason to include it in a scene. *Wings of Desire* is full of examples. Almost none of our locations exist any more. Starting with the bridge where the motorcyclist dies. That's gone. The place where we had the circus is now a park. No need to mention *Potsdamer Platz*, or the Wall either. The whole film suddenly turned into an archive for things that aren't around any more. Films that don't call themselves documentaries, feature films, do that to an amazing degree.[9]

Despite his deliberate strategy, Wenders could hardly have anticipated the radical transformation of Berlin after he made the film. In his use of word 'suddenly' – 'the whole film *suddenly turned into an archive for things that aren't around any more*' – Wenders struggles to express the transformation of a film text by its historical context of viewing, a transformation he consciously solicited ('The fact that something is due to go …'). The film he has made is still the same, structured through the same drama of the angel Damiel's decision to descend to mortality, but it is also, inexorably – suddenly – a different kind of drama, a drama about the disappearance, not just of the old Potsdamer Platz for which Homer searches in the film, but also, subsequently, of the very ruin and wasteland in which he searches.[10] In the twenty-first century, the film offers documentary traces which almost overpower Damiel's drama and the images of places that no longer exist transforms the significance of the *mise en scène*.

This recalls *Los Angeles Plays Itself*, and Thom Andersen's comment in relation to vanished Los Angeles landmarks and neighbourhoods: 'Images of things that aren't there any more mean a lot to those of us who live in Los Angeles, and almost nothing to everyone else.' This melancholy lament of the film city historian is continued over images of the different filmic incarnations of the Pan-Pacific Auditorium, including a final humiliating appearance as a roller disco, as the narrator asks 'who remembers?' and 'who mourns the Pan-Pacific Auditorium?' The neighbourhood of Bunker Hill receives sustained attention in the film because Andersen is both attracted by the diversity of the historical community, and can argue, over a range of clips, that 'The movies unwittingly documented its destruction', finally suggesting that (over an extract from *The Exiles*) 'It proves there once was a city here, before they pulled it down and built a simulacrum.' Andersen's project is revealed as more ambitious than his original desire (discussed in my introduction) to trace the presence of Los Angeles in the movies. For through this montage history, he gathers the fragments of evidence that will support a critique of what has been done to the city.

When I began this project, I was committed to avoiding two tendencies. I didn't want to become a location bore, endlessly informing companions where scenes were actually shot, scrutinising the image for signs of place, puzzling over the geography of an edit: in short, obsessed with a fantasy cinema of geographical veracity. Nor did I want to become one of those people who observes, over many a cinematic image, 'Of course, that's all gone now', as if the value of cinema resided solely in its ability to present us with long-vanished locations.[11]

I have been unsuccessful in both ambitions. While I still think that film-makers must work with whatever seems appropriate to achieve the desired effect, and that part of the joy of cinematic geography is its impossibility (the kino-eye can surpass the human eye), I have pursued the dullest British films for London settings and glimpses of London locations. I wish there was a way in which I could distil this really useless knowledge into this book, but I have become all too aware that many scholars of London start out trying to write about ideas in relation to London, and end up writing lists. And I have become preoccupied by the relationship between the constantly transforming city and the traces and fragments of its former lives found on film; trespassing over the site of the former Gainsborough Studios as it is transformed, in a way that would surprise Googie Withers, into luxury apartments;[12]

scrutinising the film image for glimpses of long-demolished ABC Bakeries and Lyons Corner Houses. The transformation of the London East End, the devastation and redevelopment of the Docks and the penetration of this traditionally working-class area by finance capital in Spitalfields and Docklands is a constant provocation for anyone interested in London, but it has been King's Cross that has proved to me the power and poignancy of place on film. As Wim Wenders observes, the inadvertent archive quality of cinema insists, and I want to return, in this afterword, to where I started, King's Cross, and to bring some of these modes of melancholy together.

King's Cross features, with Soho, as the key low-life site of landmark London. As noted in the introductory chapter, the Copenhagen tunnel, the gas-holders, the Midland Hotel at St Pancras, Goods Way and Battlebridge Road feature in numerous films. It is to King's Cross that desperate provincial parents hasten in search of runaway children, and it is life in the infernal London on the streets around King's Cross that signifies the failure of the runaway's dream in films such as *Stella Does Tricks* (Coky Giedroyc, 1996), and which is explored in Sarah Miles's installation, *No Place*.[13] It is to King's Cross that middle-class social worker Ann (Barbara Murray) must be escorted by Bill (Max Bygraves) to find a missing mother in *A Cry from the Streets* (1958). It is King's Cross that is recreated for the 'meat-rack' scenes of *Mona Lisa* (1986), as discussed in Chapter 3, and it was in King's Cross, 'which has a reputation for sex and sleaze', that Isaac Julien staged the performance piece developed from his film *Looking for Langston* (1989).[14]

'The Triplets': three of the now dismantled gas holders in King's Cross photographed by Angela Inglis for her project on the area

I started this book with an old lady in King's Cross. Mrs Wilberforce, with her impossibly located, crooked house, walked confidently down the neighbouring streets to the police station to report what might have been a dream in a film that has been read as allegorical. Thirty years later, Mrs Bender (Edna Doré) visits her son in King's Cross at the end of Mike Leigh's 1988 film *High Hopes*. If Mrs Wilberforce was a relic of Victorian Britain, Mrs Bender remembers the Second World War and the post-war settlement. But she is marooned in a yuppiefying inner city. The working-class extended family has disappeared and her neighbours don't want to know her. The only help she can get in her neighbourhood is from a young shop assistant who doesn't really know how to help. *High Hopes* was made in 'deep Thatcherism', and, like *Wings of Desire*, before *Glaznost* and the fall of the Berlin Wall. One of the distinctive policies of this government was the selling of council (social) housing, and this film has a discernible concern with property owning. Leigh has subsequently observed,

> How the world has changed since we made this film only six short years ago … Cyril [the central male character] must be more deeply frustrated than ever by the gulf between how things are and how they ought to be, and how ever-increasingly hard it has become to do anything about it.[15]

The film opens with a very long, masked shot, of a man with a suitcase walking along a street – a strip of film in the middle of the screen which is then unmasked to reveal that he is in a very busy street, surrounded by pedestrians and traffic. This opening shot offers an arrival in the city in general. The subsequent shot, of the same man with the Gilbert Scott red-brick landmark of St Pancras on his right, signifies that this is a particular city, London, and it is clear that he does not know which way to turn. So these two establishing shots indicate that this film opens with a certain type of city story. The proximity of the station is maintained in the next sequence by the sound of whistles, as it is revealed that Wayne (Jason Watkins), clutching his suitcase and his carrier bag, is looking for his sister as he asks Cyril (Philip Davis), who is fiddling with his motorbike, if he knows where Ballswood House is. Wayne's arrival in London reworks a very familiar city story, the arrival of the ingénue from the countryside. Wayne doesn't understand the scale and anonymity of the city, 'My sister. Vivienne Bennett. Do you know her?' Nor does he understand what comprises an adequate address. Shirley (Ruth Sheen), Cyril's partner, can tell immediately that Vivienne lives in a block of council flats:

S: 'Well, Ballswood House is a block of flats.'
W: 'No, it's not. It's a house, see – 29, Ballswood House.'
S: 'Yeah, but … it's in a street … and you ain't got the street name.'

But Wayne doesn't come from the countryside, he comes from Byfleet in Surrey, and he doesn't fall among thieves, but among Cyril and Shirley, who recognise his vulnerability and naiveté and put him up for the night before firmly returning him to his mother the next day. So Wayne serves as a device to introduce the good-hearted city dwellers of this story who live in a squatted Victorian block of flats behind King's Cross. Wayne's unanticipated visit displays their small, dingy flat and their politics (a very spikey cactus is called Thatcher); under Cyril and Shirley's baggy, functional clothing beat hearts of gold.

Shirley and Cyril are the most rounded characters in the film, and their depth and interiority are developed through acting style and their lack of material goods. They are juxtaposed quite schematically with two other couples, the Booth-Braines and Cyril's sister and her husband, Valerie and Martin. The Booth-Braines are heartless, wealthy gentrifiers who live in an inner-city Victorian terraced house next door to Mrs Bender, Cyril and Valerie's mother, while Valerie and Martin live in the suburbs in semi-detached ostentatious vulgarity. Critical discussion of this film tends to circle around whether Leigh is 'fair' to the yuppie Booth-Braines and the more suburban Valerie and Martin.[16] I'm more interested, through the perverse gaze which Thom Andersen identifies as constituting attention to place in the cinema, in how Leigh uses the core characters to sketch out a map of London through the homes they inhabit. It is a London laid out with a diagrammatic simplicity, not of geographical location, but of types of housing and housing ownership. There is the social housing of Wayne's sister and Mrs Bender – a council block blossoming the new doors of privatisation and a poorly maintained Victorian terrace. Right next door to Mrs Bender there are the expensive curtains and modernised interior of the Booth-Braines, who drive a mud-spattered Saab, and who balance their intrepid foray into inner-city property owning with 'somewhere in the country'. In the suburbs, Valerie and Martin have less cultural capital and less money – and are arguably presented as slightly less loathsome – although Valerie's carefully chosen, ostentatiously fashionable 1980s interior is both ridiculed and used to reflect her shallow self-regard. With the privately rented flat of Martin's lover, and the squatted Victorian tenement of Cyril and Shirley, the film offers a mapping of London in terms of different possible relations between incomes and homes. This is London as it is lived through people of different circumstances in their different homes, necessarily thrown together. And it is a London that Leigh wishes to see possessed not by the Booth-Braines, who clearly have the most money, but by Shirley and Cyril and Mrs Bender. This is shown through the use of location shooting in the final scene of the film.

This concluding scene is set on the roof of Shirley and Cyril's flats and was filmed on one of the several Victorian blocks behind King's Cross which were preserved throughout the 1980s and 1990s as licensed squats.[17] Mrs Bender has stayed the night with Cyril and Shirley after an upsetting, climactic party at Valerie and Martin's. In the morning, Shirley and Cyril encourage her to climb up to the roof of the building where Shirley maintains a little container garden among the chimney stacks. The film uses the London landscape to provide an emotional resolution – literally, high hopes – for both greater family connection, and the possibility that there will be children for Cyril and Shirley. Mrs Bender seems confused at first, 'Where is this?', but begins to enjoy the vista as Cyril points out King's Cross, St Pancras, the gasworks and St Paul's 'like a big tit'. This is an unfamiliar view of these familiar landmarks – so close to the great arched glass and iron shed of St Pancras but still offering a panoramic London skyline – so it is not just Mrs Bender who has to get her bearings. The audience too, in a film that has been so very earthbound and interior, and in which family relations have been so resentful, must learn to adjust and to look at grimy London made new in the context of affection offered. We are with Mrs Bender when she exclaims with wonder that it is 'the top of the world'.

This is a dramatically satisfying resolution – holding in abeyance, as it does, what might happen, offering us only the vision of multitudinous, but located, possibility, presented as a 360-degree view of King's Cross. Within the terms of the fiction this panorama is an objective correlative for the tentative emotional rapprochement. It is, within its own terms, dramatically poignant, and the use of location is an integral part of this. It would not work with a studio panorama, and the fact that so much is given by a view which is regularly obscured by the chimney stacks offers a very fine rendition of the impoverished expectations of Mrs Bender and Cyril and Shirley. After they have reached the roof of the building, what they see is both a wonder to Mrs Bender, but also a moment in which, in Geoffrey Nowell-Smith's terms, the film 'yields up a sense of place that would have been impossible without the ontological link between nominal setting and actual location'.[18] This sense of place, its role as a spectacular gift for both Mrs Bender and the audience, is accentuated by its absence throughout most of the rest of the film.

However, the London in which Cyril encourages his mother to take hope is surely not the complex of luxury hotels and Eurostar freight depots currently being built on this site. Now Stanley Buildings stands alone in the indecipherable remains of Cheney Street and Battlebridge Road with the new, huge glass and steel roof of the new terminal almost brushing

Shirley (Ruth Sheen), Mrs Bender (Edna Doré) and Cyril (Philip Davis) on the roof of the flat in front of the arch of St Pancras station at the end of *High Hopes*: 'the top of the world'

against it. There is something very poignant in seeing a view from a now isolated building of an area that no longer exists, a poignancy not imagined when the film was made. As Laura Mulvey writes, 'The time of the film's original moment of registration can suddenly burst through its narrative time . . . the now-ness of story time gives way to the then-ness of the time when the movie was made.'[19]

Tony Reeves, author of *The Worldwide Guide to Movie Locations Presents London*, observes, in his walking guide to King's Cross,

> Return south on York Way and turn right into Goods Way. This small enclave of Victorian indus-
> trial buildings and cobbled streets, dominated by the unique group of linked gasometers, has
> been a favourite cinematic backdrop since the bullion robbery at the opening of *The Ladykillers*
> was filmed on Goods Way in 1955. However, the area was earmarked for the Channel Tunnel
> link, and disgracefully, a whole district of Grade II listed buildings has been demolished. As well
> as the buildings the splendid iron-frame Victorian gasometers have gone, and with them an irre-
> placeable part of Britain's film heritage.[20]

In 1990, Isaac Julien anticipated the redevelopment, observing, 'The whole space is going to be knocked down and renovated into a kind of Covent Garden yuppie village. It's barbaric.'[21]

It is in this redeveloping King's Cross that Anthony Minghella sets his 2006 film *Breaking and Entering*, making a narrative from the abrupt juxtaposition of, in the words of Ray Winstone's policeman, 'a fabulous building in a hostile community: crack village with a load of Somalis walking around with machetes'. This film brings together the London worlds of *Notting Hill* (1999) and *Dirty Pretty Things* (2002) discussed in Chapter 3 in a tale from the frontier gentrification of King's Cross. The liberal professional middle classes with the pale interiors of their remodelled nineteenth-century houses and refurbished former industrial buildings are juxtaposed with the street characters of King's Cross: prostitutes, illegal immigrants, asylum seekers, thieves and racketeers who live and work in holes and corners of a dirty, dis-integrating city. It is a London which is both Dickensian – boys used for audacious 'free-running' break-ins – and melodramatic in its shading of character and narrative develop-ment. And there is, at the centre of the film, an architectural model of the redevelopment of the area. Like the models in *Passport to Pimlico* (1949) and *The Long Good Friday* (1979) discussed in the last chapter, this model too bears symbolic weight within the film. Although regarded with enthusiasm within the fiction, 'this is brilliant, are you really going to do all this, put a canal through it', as the Winstone character asks, the model suggests another view of the area. For the simplicity of the yellow-bricked double arch of King's Cross Station and its sur-roundings is rendered in matt black, obliterating all the features and distinctions of the area. The new vision of the area is one in which everything that preceded it, including the untidy local businesses and the unruly poor – the mess of deprivation and exploitation – are oblit-erated.

Destruction and remaking is an essential part of the life of cities. However, there are cer-tainly arguments to be had about what should come down to put what in its place. For King's Cross, I'm with Tony Reeves, Isaac Julien, the King's Cross Railway Lands Groups, the pho-tographer Angela Inglis and the sculptor Richard Wentworth, who installed a periscope which offered similarly unfamiliar views of the same area in his exhibition, 'An Area of Out-standing Unnatural Beauty', held in the General Plumbing Supplies Building in York Way King's Cross.[22] The very preservation of St Pancras and the magnificent restoration of the railway hotel, in juxtaposition to the losses highlighted by Wentworth and Reeves, returns us to some of the arguments made by Katherine Shonfield. The redevelopment of King's Cross threatens to reconfigure the area, in Shonfield's terms, into a 'city of objects'. The rede-velopment has retained the 'tourist hardware' of the Midland Hotel, although the gas-hold-ers have gone (with a promise of partial return), but may eliminate the places in between, local London, where people actually live and work. The fact that this 'living and working' also involved, for some, drug-taking and prostitution as Simone (*Mona Lisa*) and Stella (*Stella Does Tricks*) testify, is not a problem that is solved by eliminating affordable residential housing and demolishing nineteenth-century buildings. Drug addiction, prostitution and the traf-ficking in both drugs and bodies are not spatial problems: they are social problems. 'Rubbish London' cannot just be crowded out of the city by luxury apartments, offices, hotel and 'live–work spaces'. I am not making an argument against change per se. Parts of the old King's Cross were pretty horrible to walk through, hard to live in, and, presumably, it was also pretty horrible to work the streets and score there.[23] Instead, I am making two different argu-ments, each of which involves a necessary attention to particularity. First, I am suggesting that there are historical reasons for the association of King's Cross with various types of pov-erty and street life. These are streets coloured mainly blue and grey (the poorest colours, with black poorest of all) on Booth's 1889 map of poverty in London, and the condition of the res-idents will not be improved by evicting them and removing the infrastructure of little local shops and suppliers that service them. Second, as so many argued with the redevelopment of the Docks, the social role and provision, nature and aesthetics of what is built is signifi-cant. The long-term social costs, which are visible all around in London, of development con-ducted for short-term financial gain, are easily apparent. The full consequences of the Spitalfields and Docklands redevelopment are yet to be felt although the aesthetic mess of much Docklands building is easily visible. The King's Cross development could easily exam-plify the city learning the wrong lessons from the cinema: the elimination of the local places in between the landmarks, which make up so much of everyday life, in favour of an archi-tecture of spectacle, a material montage of shiny surfaces and 'no-place' spaces like lobbies and atria.

So what is poignant about the final scene in *High Hopes* is not simply, in addition to its own planned dramatic poignancies, that the view Cyril shows his mother has disappeared, and that the beautiful proportions of the St Pancras arched glass roof have been spoilt by the alignment of the roof of the new terminal. It is not just that the area where both Mrs Wilber-force and Richard Wentworth lived out their days has been and is being redeveloped. It is the kind of redevelopment that is taking place, and that the possibility of ordinary improvement to particular places – a future for citizens – has been junked in favour of a much less specific 'international' vision. For while there is no consolation for many of the causes of melancholy, to have the particularity of place snatched away should give rise to protest. Raphael Samuel, writing of the paradoxical consequences of the partially successful conservationist battles in Spitalfields in an essay called 'The Pathos of Conservation', argues:

It should be evident that to plant an international banking centre in the midst of a district which for centuries has been devoted to industries and trades, to destroy its oldest occupation and in the process to flatten some 12 acres of buildings and appointments is not, as the developers claim, a 'regeneration' of Spitalfields but on the contrary, here as elsewhere, a recipe for office blight.[24]

Mike Leigh is horrible about the wealthy gentrifiers, the Booth-Braines, in *High Hopes*, but they are – he makes them – horrible, in a polemic against a hegemonic sensibility of the period. They have no sense of the local, no understanding of their neighbourhood and no interest in their neighbours. They do not participate in the civil society of the streets and their interest is in profit from property. If, on the one hand, 'regeneration' is too often conducted as the elimination of the local and indigenous, the dominance of the global financial industries, and the consequent (among many other consequences[25]) continual escalation of property prices in London, means that, increasingly, only the Booth-Braines can afford to live there.[26]

And a Chance Encounter

I want to finish by returning to *Wonderland* (1999), a film discussed in the 'Landmark London' chapter for its use of a London bus, and the way in which its narration moves in and out of particular characters' stories to a more abstract account of city life in general. *Wonderland* follows the lives of a south London family over the weekend of Bonfire Night (5 November), intercutting the stories of three sisters: Nadia (Gina McKee), who is searching for romance through the personal columns; Molly (Molly Parker), a married teacher who gives birth to her first child on the Sunday night; and Debbie (Shirley Henderson), a hairdresser who lives with her son Jack, with those of their parents, Debbie's ex-husband, their neighbours Donna (Ellen Thomas) and her son Franklyn (David Fahm), and their estranged brother, Darren, in London to celebrate his birthday with his girlfriend. The film is carefully scripted, providing all the information the attentive viewer needs to make sense of the interrelationships of the characters, but leaving it to the viewer to make the connections. Thus, on a first viewing, the connections between the characters seem to be created through montage – the juxtapositions of city life – rather than illustrative of family relations. For if this is the story of one family, and the boyfriends, girlfriends, husbands, ex-husbands, jobs, homes, accidents, neighbours and neighbours' dogs that make up the texture of their everyday life, these stories are constantly and firmly contextualised within the London that is the half-ironic wonderland of the title. This contextualisation is performed through a range of devices: exterior shots of the south London flats where most characters live; alternations between interiors and public spectacles such as football matches and firework displays; long shots of landmark London – St Paul's and the Post Office Tower – from the perspective or homes of individual characters; and the use of the Michael Nyman score to render almost abstract the spectacle of people in the streets; and sometimes, in conjunction with this use of music, the use of time lapse and slow motion for street sequences. Thus the strong, low-key, intimate performances of actors such as McKee, Jack Shepherd (Bill, the father), John Simm (Eddie, Molly's husband) and Ian Hart (Debbie's ex-husband) are repeatedly separated out so that we see each small drama as part of a much broader London pattern.

This film combines what Andrew Higson has seen as a characteristically British genre, the melodrama of everyday life[27], with elements of a form less commonly associated with British cinema, the city symphony. The intense familial relationships of melodrama – marriages endured, alienated children, sibling rivalries, the search for love – are repeatedly grounded in banal locations, while at moments, these intensely felt stories are swept up into the sense of a city 'full of folk', in which these intensities are multiplied many times over. The film presents London as a lived city in which the local and landmark London are integrated. This is achieved partly through location shooting and the film's attention to the unknown other people who surround the protagonists. The film was shot using a hand-held super 16mm camera, with minimal lighting, radio mikes and no extras, in locations that include a café, pubs, a bingo hall, a football match at Selhurst Park, Brixton police station, Lewisham Hospital and a firework display.[28] Both Nadia and Eddie at different points walk past the lighted windows of Soho bars where anonymous people are dancing and drinking. Dan's farcical failed date with the unknown who turns out to be Nadia finishes in a location-shot local pub where regulars are shown on an evening out much like any other. Eileen's (Kika Markham) brief respite is a bingo session in a large echoing hall with apparently hundreds of other poor middle-aged women. Nadia's mobility through the West End is marked by the camera's constant attention to the casualties of city life, such as the young homeless bedded down in the doorways of Shaftesbury Avenue and the coarser faces of the older alcoholics. In this film, there is another new trope for landmark London, one less likely than cultural diversity to find itself in promotional literature: the huddled homeless. The angry cinema of dispossession found in the 1980s break-up of the post-war settlement has huddled into the doorways and tourist thoroughfares of landmark London.

There is also a strong emphasis on the close proximity in which working-class people live. Eileen and Bill, Nadia and Debbie all live in south London estates, and the film chooses frequently to show these exteriors, the low- and high-rise buildings next to each, the banks of windows through which can occasionally be glimpsed St Paul's. Eileen is obsessed with the barking of the Portuguese neighbours' dog, finding herself unable to sleep or concentrate, and is also oppressed by their celebration of Bonfire Night. Returning home, or venturing out, exposes Eileen, Bill and their neighbour Donna to commentary and abuse from idling young people. But there is taken-for-granted-ness in some of the mixed cultures throughout the film, which suggests a pragmatic coming to terms with post-imperial Britain at a local everyday level. When Bill forgets his key, he goes round to Donna's and she makes them both cocktails and they dance. Similarly, it is the neighbourliness of Franklin's concern for Bill on the final Monday morning that permits the encounter on which the film ends. Franklin has been shown as solitary and unhappy throughout the film, working near Nadia in town, but apparently unacknowledged by her as a neighbour of her parents. On the Monday morning, he brings over an instruction book for the type of car with which Bill is perpetually fiddling, trying to fix this and that with the bonnet up. Nadia has dropped by to see her father, and as the two walk off, laughing, on their way to work together, the film clearly suggests that true love may be found closer to home than the personal column phone messages which have been Nadia's soundtrack from the beginning of the film.

Nadia (Gina McKee) and Franklyn (David Fahm) at the end of *Wonderland*

This is both a romantic ending, and an instance of a chance city encounter, bringing together the film's dual generic inheritance of melodrama and city symphony, as does the structure of the ending. For instead of ending on the Sunday night, as a family melodrama, with the birth of Molly's baby, the reconciliation of her parents and the decision to call her 'Alice', the film continues into the Monday morning and the encounter between Nadia, Bill and Franklin just described. It becomes clear that the film could go on endlessly: just like the city.

Notes

1. Ian Nairn, 'St Pancras Station', in his *Nairn's London* (Pleasantville, NY: The Akadine Press, 2002 [1966]), p. 106.
2. Paul Gilroy, *After Empire: Melancholia or Convivial Culture?* (London: Routledge, 2004).
3. Anthony Sutcliffe comments on Carl Mayer's failure to make a London equivalent to his *Berlin: die Symphonie einer Grossstadt*, 'Ironically, his last years saw the *Luftwaffe* exert a bigger influence on the cinematic portrayal of London than he had ever done.' 'The metropolis in the cinema', in A. Sutcliffe (ed.), *Metropolis: 1890–1940* (London: Mansell, 1984), p. 165.
4. Not just British films. See, for example, Ginette Vincendeau's discussion of the London interval, particularly the dancing-through-the Blitz scene in *Les Armée des ombres* in *Jean-Pierre Melville: An American in Paris* (London: BFI, 2003), pp. 83–5.
5. See, for example, Paul Willemen, 'Through a glass darkly: cinephilia reconsidered', *Looks and Frictions* (London: BFI, 1994); Kevin Robins, 'The city in the field of vision', *Into the Image* (London: Routledge, 1996); Susan Sontag, 'The decay of cinema', *New York Times Magazine*, 25 February 1996, pp. 60–1; Barbara Klinger, *Beyond the Multiplex* (Berkeley: University of California Press, 2006); Thomas Elsaesser, 'Cinephilia', plenary paper, SCMS Annual Conference, London, 2005.
6. Laura Mulvey, *Death at 24x a Second* (London: Reaktion, 2006), p. 8.
7. Ibid., p. 184
8. Phil Baker, 'Secret city: psychogeography and the East End of London', in Joe Kerr and Andrew Gibson (eds), *London from Punk to Blair* (London: Reaktion, 2003), p. 331.

9. Wim Wenders, from *The Act of Seeing* quoted in A. Graf, *The Cinema of Wim Wenders* (London: Wallflower Press, 2002), p. 118. Thanks to Alice Rothwell for bringing this to my attention.

10. The elderly Homer (Curt Bois) wanders the desolate wasteland close to the wall that was the Potsdamer Platz, remembering the coffee houses and the civilised debate of the public sphere of the Weimar Republic. See Andreas Huyssen (among many others) on the redevelopment of the Potsdamer Platz, *Present Pasts* (Stanford: Stanford University Press, 2003), pp. 72–84.

11. The opening of Kim Newman's review of Sorensen's *London on Film* serves as a warning, 'It would seem to have the musty smell of a garrulous old relative with a collection of century-old oddments …', *Empire* no. 84, June 1996, p. 129.

12. 'Gainsborough's Islington studios were abominable. To get there, you had to drive through slums. When you arrived, there was this awful old building and the dressing-rooms were dreadful. The make-up room was a box and the canteen food was uneatable.' Googie Withers, talking to Brian McFarlane in *Sixty Voices* (London: BFI, 1992), p. 234.

13. *No Place*, a two-site installation at King's Cross (17 July–13 August 2005) and King's Lynn (19–31 July 2005), which explored the country girl's journey to the city drawing on feature film imagery. Sarah Miles, *No Place* (Film and Video Umbrella in association with King's Lynn Arts Centre, 2005).

14. Isaac Julien in conversation with Paul Gilroy, 'Climbing the racial mountain', in Gilroy, *Small Acts* (London: Serpent's Tail, 1993), p. 167.

15. Mike Leigh, foreword to screenplay of *High Hopes*, in *Naked and Other Screenplays* (London: Faber and Faber, 1995), p. 188.

16. See John Hill, *British Cinema in the 1980s* (Oxford: Clarendon Press, 1999), pp. 192–8, for a discussion of debates.

17. This meant that their inhabitants could legally use and pay for gas, electricity and water and involved a negotiated agreement with the local council.

18. Geoffrey Nowell-Smith, 'Cities real and imagined', in Mark Shiel and Tony Fitzmaurice (eds), *Cinema and the City* (Oxford: Blackwell, 2001), p. 103.

19. Mulvey, *Death 24x a Second*, p. 31. I have omitted Mulvey's qualification 'Even in a Hollywood movie'.

20. Tony Reeves, *The Worldwide Guide to Movie Locations Presents London* (London: Titan, 2003), p. 65.

21. Julien in Gilroy, *Small Acts*, p. 167.

22. The King's Cross Railway Lands Group at <www.kxrlg.org.uk>; 'An Area of Outstanding Unnatural Beauty', 2002, see Introduction. This area was devastated in the nineteenth century by the building of the railways, a devastation of which there are many accounts. See *Victorian Babylon: people, streets and images in the nineteenth century* (London: New Haven and Yale University Press, 2000), pp. 34–46.

23. 'As the recession began to bite, so the entire area slid into decay, the darkening streets of King's Cross growing so crime-ridden that few people wanted to risk getting beaten up just to catch a creaky old horror movie in a venue [the Scala Cinema] that now counted rats and bad plumbing among its many attractions.' Richard Stanley, 'Dying light: an obituary for the great British horror movie' (writing of the early 1990s), in Steve Chibnall and Julian Petley (eds), *British Horror Cinema* (London: Routledge, 2002), p. 190.

24. Raphael Samuel, 'The pathos of conservation', in Mark Girouard, Dan Cruikshank, Raphael Samuel and others, *The Saving of Spitalfields*, (London: Spitalfields Historic Buildings Trust, 1989), p. 170.

25. See Doreen Massey, 'Throwntogetherness: the politics of the event of place', in her *For Space* (London: Sage, 2005), pp. 149–62.

26. The colonisation of previously gentrified areas by City money is meeting with more comment than the original gentrification of working-class areas partly because the early gentrifiers often have media-friendly networks. Thus, for example, Rachel Johnson's novel, about the Americanisation of Notting Hill, *Notting Hell* (London: Fig Tree/Penguin, 2006), and the journalist Michele Hanson's discussion of new London neighbours from hell, 'What is wrong with the newcomers? Are they insane? No. They're just a new breed: young, bossy and rich … like a new wave of land-owning gentry, surrounded by serfs', *The Guardian*, G2, 'The War of Mavis's wisteria', 9 October 2006, p. 19.

27. Andrew Higson, *Waving the Flag* (Oxford: The Clarendon Press, 1995), pp. 176–271.

28. Michael Winterbottom discussed his production procedures in several interviews on the film's release, emphasising the way in which some practices – such as not using clapperboards – just evolved. Interview with Michael Winterbottom, 'Through the looking-glass', *The Guardian*, 19 July 1999. The Director of Photography, Sean Bobbitt, came from a news/documentary background: 'What I liked when we did tests in Soho was he would just be right there and completely unfazed by it because that's what he does all the time … what Sean brought, because he's a documentary guy, is that when the actors were doing different things each time, he was used to the idea of trying to capture the moment, and trying to find the bit that's interesting. I felt that with the other people we talked to it would just become a stylistic thing; I didn't want it to be a stylistic thing. Sean was always trying to be at the right place and the right time, so that involves a camera movement. I think his hand-held is amazingly steady. Nothing is like wobbly-cam, that wasn't the point. We wanted to change the way we were working, rather than just do it as [a] device.' Andy Kaufman, 'Michael Winterbottom's *Wonderland*', *IndieWire.com*, 28 July 2000: <www.indiewire.com/people/int_Winter_Michael_00728.html>.

Selected Bibliography

Details of newspaper reviews and primary sources are given in notes and not repeated here.

Ackroyd, Peter, *London: The Biography* (London: Chatto and Windus, 2000).

Adams, Mark, *Location London* (London: New Holland, 2003).

Aldgate, Anthony, *Censorship and the Permissive Society* (Oxford: Clarendon Press, 1995).

Aldgate, Anthony and Richards, Jeffrey, *The Best of British: Cinema and Society from 1930 to the Present* (London: I. B. Tauris, 2002 [1999]).

Alexander, Karen, 'Black British cinema in the 90s: going going gone', in Robert Murphy (ed.), *British Cinema of the 90s* (London: BFI, 2000), pp. 109–14.

Alvarado, Manuel and Stewart, John (eds), *Made for Television: Euston Films Limited* (London: BFI, 1985).

Andrews, Julian, *London's War: The Shelter Drawings of Henry Moore* (Aldershot: Lund Humphries, 2002).

Ashby, Justine and Higson, Andrew (eds), *British Cinema: Past and Present* (London: Routledge, 2000).

Atkins, Marc and Sinclair, Iain, *Liquid City* (London: Reaktion, 1999).

Augé, Marc, *Non-Places: Introduction to an Anthropology of Super-modernity* (translated by John Howe) (London: Verso, 1995 [1992]).

Augé, Marc, *In The Metro* (translated by Tom Conley) (Minneapolis: University of Minnesota Press, 2002 [1986]).

Bakari, Imruh, 'A journey from the cold: rethinking Black film-making in Britain', in Kwesi Owusu (ed.), *Black British Culture and Society* (London: Routledge, 2000), pp.230–8.

Bakhtin, Mikhail, *The Dialogic Imagination* (edited by Michael Holquist, translated by Caryl Emerson and Michael Holquist) (Austin: University of Texas Press, 1981).

Balshaw, Maria and Kennedy, Liam, *Urban Space and Representation* (London: Pluto Press, 2000).

Barber, Stephen, *Projected Cities* (London: Reaktion, 2002).

Barefoot, Guy, *Gaslight Melodrama: From Victorian London to 1940s Hollywood* (London and New York: Continuum, 2001).

Barnwell, Jane, *Production Design: Architects of the Screen* (London: Wallflower, 2004).

Barr, Charles, *Ealing Studios* (Newton Abbot: Cameron and Tayleur in association with David and Charles, 1977).

Barr, Charles (ed.), *All Our Yesterdays* (London: BFI, 1986).

Barringer, Tim, '"Our English Thames" and "America's River": landscape painting and narratives of national identity', in Mark Dorrian and Gillian Rose (eds), *Landscapes and Politics* (London: Black Dog, 2003), pp. 24–39.

Barwell, Clare, 'Flâneur of London. Interview with Patrick Keiller', Pix 2, January 1997, pp. 158–65.

Baudelaire, Charles, 'The Painter of Modern Life' (translated by Jonathan Mayne), in Jonathan Mayne (ed.), *The Painter of Modern Life and Other Essays* (London: Phaidon, 1964 [1863]), pp. 1–41.

Benjamin, Walter, *Charles Baudelaire: A Lyric Poet in the Era of High Capitalism* (trans. Harry Zohn) (London: New Left Books, 1973).

Benjamin, Walter, *The Arcades Project* (translated by Howard Eiland and Kevin McLaughlin) (Cambridge, MA: Harvard University Press, 1999).

Berger, John and McBurney, Simon, *The Vertical Line* (London: Artangel and Theatre de Complicité, 1999).

Bergfelder, Tim, 'Extraterritorial fantasies: Edgar Wallace and the German crime film', in Tim Bergfelder, Erica Carter and Deniz Göktürk (eds), *The German Cinema Book* (London: BFI, 2002), pp. 39–47.

Bobrick, Benson, *Labyrinths of Iron: A History of the World's Subways* (New York: Newsweek Books, 1981).

Borden, Iain, Kerr, Joe, Pivaro, Alicia and Rendell, Jane, *Strangely Familiar* (London: Routledge, 1996).

Borden, Iain, Kerr, Joe, Pivaro, Alicia and Rendell, Jane, *The Unknown City* (Cambridge, MA: MIT Press, 2001).

Bourne, Stephen, *Brief Encounters: Lesbians and Gays in British Cinema 1930–1971* (London: Cassell, 1996).

Bourne, Stephen, *Black in the British Frame: Black People in British Film and Television 1896–1996* (London: Cassell, 1998).

Bradley, Lloyd, 'What's wrong with this picture?', *Empire*, June–July 1989, pp. 66–9.

Breward, Christopher, *Fashioning London: Clothing and the Modern Metropolis* (Oxford: Berg, 2004).

Breward, Christopher and Gilbert, David, *Fashion's World Cities* (Oxford: Berg, 2006).

Briggs, Asa, *Victorian Cities* (Harmondsworth: Penguin, 1990 [1963]).

Brooker, Peter, *Modernity and Metropolis: Writing, Film and Urban Formations* (Basingstoke: Palgrave, 2002).

Bruno, Giuliana, *Streetwalking on a Ruined Map* (Princeton, NJ: Princeton University Press, 1993).

Bruzzi, Stella, *New Documentary: A Critical Introduction* (London: Routledge, 2000).

Bullock, Nicholas, 'Imagining the post-war world: architecture, reconstruction and the British documentary film movement', in François Penz and Maureen Thomas (eds), *Cinema and Architecture* (London: BFI, 1997), pp. 52–61.

Burton, Alan, O'Sullivan, Tim and Wells, Paul (eds), *Liberal Directions: Basil Dearden and Postwar British Film Culture* (Trowbridge: Flicks Books, 1997).

Butler, Margaret, *Film and Community in Britain and France* (London: I. B. Tauris, 2004).

Calder, Angus, *The Myth of the Blitz* (London: Pimlico, 1992 [1991]).

Cameron, Ian (ed.), *The Movie Book of Film Noir* (London: Studio Vista, 1992).

Campbell, Russell, *Marked Women: Prostitutes and Prostitution in the Cinema* (Madison: University of Wisconsin Press, 2006).

Caughie, John, *The Companion to British and Irish Cinema* (London: Cassell and BFI, 1996).

Caughie, John, *Television Drama: Realism, Modernism and British Culture* (Oxford: Oxford University Press, 2000).

Chibnall, Steve, 'The teenage trilogy: *The Blue Lamp, I Believe in You* and *Violent Playground*' in Alan Burton, Tim O'Sullivan and Paul Wells (eds), *Liberal Directions* (Trowbridge: Flicks Books, 1997), pp. 37–153.

Chibnall, Steve, 'Travels in ladland: the British gangster film cycle 1998–2001', in Robert Murphy (ed.), *The British Cinema Book*, 2nd edn (London: BFI, 2001), pp. 281–91.

Chibnall, Steve and Murphy, Robert (eds), *British Crime Cinema* (London: Routledge, 1999).

Chibnall, Steve and Petley, Julian (eds), *British Horror Cinema* (London: Routledge, 2002).

Christie, Ian, 'Londres', in Thierry Jousse and Thierry Paquot (eds), *La Ville au cinéma* (Paris: Cahiers du cinéma, 2005), pp. 436–48.

Church Gibson, Pamela, 'Imaginary landscapes, jumbled topographies: cinematic London', in Joe Kerr and Andrew Gibson (eds), *London from Punk to Blair* (London: Reaktion, 2003), pp. 363–9.

Church Gibson, Pamela, 'New stars, new fashions and the female audience' in Christopher Brewer and David Gilbert (eds), *Fashion's World Cities* (Oxford: Berg, 2006), pp. 89–106.

Church Gibson, Pamela, 'From up north to up west? London on screen 1965–1967', *The London Journal* vol. 31 no. 1, 2006, pp. 85–108.

Clarke, David B. (ed.), *The Cinematic City* (London: Routledge, 1997).

Collier, John W., *A Film in the Making: It Always Rains on Sunday* (London: World Film, 1947).

Collins, Michael, *The Likes of Us: A Biography of the White Working Class* (London: Granta, 2004).

Conekin, Becky, Mort, Frank and Waters, Chris (eds), *Moments of Modernity* (London: Rivers Oram Press, 1999).

Conrich, Ian, 'Trashing London: the British colossal creature film and fantasies of mass destruction', in I. Q. Hunter (ed.), *British Science Fiction Cinema* (London: Routledge, 1999), pp. 88–98.

Cook, Pam, *Fashioning the Nation* (London: BFI, 1996).

Copjec, Joan (ed.), *Shades of Noir* (London: Verso, 1993).

Crawford, Alison, *Notting Hill: The History and Development of North Kensington* (London: Ealing College of Art, 1971).

Creeber, Glen, ' "Can't help lovin' dat man": Social Class and the Female Voice in *Nil By Mouth*', in Sally Munt (ed.), *Cultural Studies and the Working Class: Subject to Change* (London: Cassell, 2000), pp. 193–205.

Cresswell, Tim, *Place: A Short Introduction* (Oxford: Blackwell, 2004).

Daniels, Stephen, *Fields of Vision: Landscape Imagery and National Identity in England and the United States* (Cambridge: Polity Press, 1993).

Daniels, Stephen, 'Paris envy: Patrick Keiller's *London*', *History Workshop Journal* no. 40, Autumn 1995, pp. 220–2.

Dave, Paul, 'Representations of capitalism, history and nation in the work of Patrick Keiller', in Justine Ashby and Andrew Higson (eds), *British Cinema: Past and Present* (London: Routledge, 2000), pp. 339–51.

Dave, Paul, *Visions of England* (Oxford: Berg, 2006).

Davis, Mike, *City of Quartz* (London: Verso, 1990).

Dench, Geoff, Gavron, Kate and Young, Michael, *The New East End: Kinship, Race and Conflict* (London: Profile Books, 2006).

Desjardins, Mary, '"Free from the apron strings": representation of mothers in the maternal British state', in Lester Friedman (ed.), *British Cinema and Thatcherism* (London: UCL Press, 1993), pp. 130–44.

Dimendberg, Edward, *Film Noir and the Spaces of Modernity* (Cambridge, MA: Harvard University Press, 2004).

Dixon, Winston Wheeler (ed.), *Re-viewing British Cinema, 1900–1992* (Albany: State University of New York Press, 1994).

Doane, Mary Ann, *Femmes Fatales* (New York: Routledge, 1991).

Dodd, Kathryn and Dodd, Philip, 'From the East End to *EastEnders*: representations of the working class, 1890–1990', in D. Strinati and S. Wagg (eds), *Come on Down: Popular Media Culture* (London: Routledge, 1992), pp. 116–32.

Donald, James, *Imagining the Modern City* (London: Athlone Press, 1999).

Donald, James, 'Talking the talk, walking the walk', *Screen* vol. 40 no. 3, 1999, pp. 295–303.

Doré, Gustav and Jerrold, Blanchard, *London: A Pilgrimage* (New York: Dover, 1970 [1872]).

Dorrian, Mark and Rose, Gillian (eds), *Landscapes and Politics* (London: Black Dog, 2003).

Drazin, Charles, *The Finest Years: British Cinema of the 1940s* (London: André Deutsch, 1998).

Driver, Felix and Gilbert, David (eds), *Imperial Cities* (Manchester: Manchester University Press, 1999).

Drummond, Phillip, 'London, Fortress Europe and the cinema of migration', paper to Society for Cinema and Media Studies Conference, London, 2005.

Dupin, Christophe, *Free Cinema* booklet to accompany BFI 50th Anniversary DVD of *Free Cinema* (London: BFI, 2006).

Durgnat, Raymond, *A Mirror for England* (London: Faber and Faber, 1970).

Durgnat, Raymond, 'Two "social problem" films: *Sapphire* and *Victim*', in Alan Burton, Tim O'Sullivan and Paul Wells (eds), *Liberal Directions* (Trowbridge: Flicks Books, 1997), pp. 59–88.

Durgnat, Raymond, 'Some lines of enquiry into post-war British crimes', in Robert Murphy (ed.), *The British Cinema Book*, 2nd edn (London: BFI, 2001), pp. 135–45.

Dyer, Richard, '*Victim*: hegemonic project' [1977], in *The Matter of Images* (London: Routledge, 1993), pp. 93–110.

Dyer, Richard, *White* (London: Routledge, 1997).

Eade, John (ed.), *Living the Global City: Globalization as a Local Process* (London: Routledge, 1997), pp. 127–45.

Eade, John, *Placing London: From Imperial Capital to Global City* (Oxford and New York: Berghahn Books, 2000).

Elborough, Travis, *The Bus We Loved: London's Affair with the Routemaster* (London: Granta, 2005).

Eley, Geoff, '*Distant Voices, Still Lives*. The family is a dangerous place: memory, gender and the image of the working class', in Robert A. Rosenstone (ed.), *Film and the Construction of a New Past* (Princeton, NJ: Princeton University Press, 1995), pp. 17–43.

Ellis, John, 'Made in Ealing', *Screen* vol. 16 no. 1, Spring 1975, pp. 78–127.

Elms, Robert, *The Way We Wore: A Life in Threads* (London: Picador, 2006 [2005]).

Elsaesser, Thomas, 'Lulu and the meter man', *Screen* vol. 24 nos. 4–5, October 1983, pp. 4–36.

Emsley, Clive, 'The English bobby: an indulgent tradition', in Porter (ed.), *Myths of the English* (Cambridge: Polity Press, 1992), pp. 114–35.

English Heritage, *London Suburbs* (London: Merrell Holberton in Association with English Heritage, 1999).

Evans, Peter William, *Carol Reed* (Manchester: Manchester University Press, 2005).

Everett, Wendy and Goodbody, Axel (eds), *Revisiting Space: Space and Place in European Cinema* (Bern: Peter Lang, 2005).

Everson, William, 'British film noir', *Films in Review* vol. 38 no. 5, 1987, pp. 285–9 and vol. 38 no. 6, 1987, pp. 341–7.

Eyles, Allen, *Gaumont British Cinemas* (London: Cinema Theatre Association, 1996).

Eyles, Allen, *Odeon Cinemas 1* (London: Cinema Theatre Association, 2002).

Falcon, Richard, 'Last tango in Lewisham', *Sight and Sound* vol. 11 no. 7 (NS), July 2000, pp. 20–4.

Feldman, David and Stedman-Jones, Gareth (eds), *Metropolis – London: Histories and Representations since 1800* (London: Routledge, 1989).

Foster, Janet, *Docklands: Cultures in Conflict, Worlds in Collision* (London: Routledge, 2003 [1999]).

Freeman, Nick, 'London kills me: the English metropolis in British horror films of the 1970s', in Xavier Mendik (ed.), *Shocking Cinema of the Seventies* (Hereford: Noir, 2002), pp. 193–210.

Friedman, Lester (ed.), *British Cinema and Thatcherism* (London: UCL Press, 1993).

Friedman, Lester and Stewart, Scott, 'Keeping his own voice: an interview with Stephen Frears', in Wheeler Winston Dixon (ed.), *Re-viewing British Cinema* (Albany: State University of New York Press, 1994), pp. 221–40.

Fryer, Peter, *Staying Power* (London: Pluto Press, 1984).

Fyrth, Jim (ed.), *Labour's Promised Land* (London: Lawrence and Wishart, 1995).

Garland, Ken, *Mr Beck's Underground Map* (Harrow Weald: Capital Transport, 1994).

Geraghty, Christine, 'Women and sixties British cinema: the development of the *Darling* girl', in Robert Murphy (ed.), *The British Cinema Book* (London: BFI, 1997), pp. 154–63.

Geraghty, Christine, *British Cinema of the Fifties* (London: Routledge, 2000).

Geraghty, Christine, *My Beautiful Laundrette* (London: I. B. Tauris, 2005).

Geraghty, Christine, 'Paris, Hollywood and Kay Kendall', in Rachel Moseley (ed.), *Fashioning Film Stars* (London: BFI, 2005), pp. 121–32.

Gifford, Denis, *The British Film Catalogue, Volume 1: Fiction Film 1895–1994*, 3rd edn (London and Chicago: Fitzroy Dearborn, 2001).

Gifford, Denis, *The British Film Catalogue, Volume 2: Non-Fiction Film 1888–1994* (London and Chicago: Fitzroy Dearborn, 2001).

Gilbert, Pamela K. (ed.), *Imagined Londons* (Albany: State University of New York Press, 2002).

Gilbert, David and Henderson, Fiona, 'London and the tourist imagination', in Pamela K. Gilbert (ed.), *Imagined Londons* (Albany: State University of New York Press, 2002), pp. 121–36.

Gilbey, Ryan (ed.), *The Ultimate Film* (London: BFI, 2005).

Gillett, Philip, *The British Working Class in Postwar Film* (Manchester: Manchester University Press, 2003).

Gilroy, Paul, *Small Acts* (London: Serpent's Tail, 1993).

Gilroy, Paul, *After Empire: Melancholia or Convivial Culture?* (London: Routledge, 2004).

Girouard, Mark, Cruikshank, Dan, Samuel, Raphael and others (eds), *The Saving of Spitalfields* (London: Spitalfields Historic Buildings Trust, 1989).

Glancy, Mark, *When Hollywood Loved Britain* (Manchester: Manchester University Press, 1999).

Gledhill, Christine, *Reframing British Cinema 1918–28* (London: BFI, 2003).

Gledhill, Christine and Swanson, Gillian (eds), *Nationalising Femininity: Culture, Sexuality and British Cinema in the Second World War* (Manchester: Manchester University Press, 1996).

Glinert, Ed, *The London Compendium* (London: Penguin, 2004 [2003]).

Gough-Yates, Kevin, 'Jews and exiles in British cinema', *Leo Baeck Yearbook* no. xxxvii (1992), pp. 517–41.

Graf, Alexander, *The Cinema of Wim Wenders: the Celluloid Highway* (London: Wallflower Press, 2002).

Gregg, John, *The Shelter of the Tubes: Tube Sheltering in Wartime London* (Harrow Weald: Capital Transport, 2001).

Griffiths, Robin (ed.), *British Queer Cinema* (London: Routledge, 2006).

Grimble, Simon, 'Somewhere to stand: descriptive writing and cultural criticism in Iain Sinclair's *Lights Out for the Territory*', in Mark Dorrian and Gillian Rose (eds), *Landscapes and Politics* (London: Black Dog, 2003), pp. 175–81.

Gross, John, *Double Thread: a Childhood in Mile End and Beyond* (London: Vintage, 2002 [2001]).

Guy, Stephen, ' "Someone presses a button and it's goodbye Sally": *Seven Days to Noon* and the threat of the atomic bomb', in Alan Burton, Tim O'Sullivan and Paul Wells (eds), *The Family Way: The Boulting Brothers and British Film Culture* (Trowbridge: Flicks Books, 2000), pp. 143–54.

Halliday, Stephen, *Underground to Everywhere: London's Underground Railway in the Life of the Capital* (Stroud: Sutton, 2001).

Hamnett, Chris, *Unequal City: London in the Global Arena* (London: Routledge, 2003).

Hardy, Phil (ed.), *The BFI Companion to Crime* (London: BFI, 1997).

Harper, Sue, *Picturing the Past* (London: BFI, 1994).

Harper, Sue, *Women in British Cinema: Mad, Bad and Dangerous to Know* (London: Continuum, 2000).

Harper, Sue and Porter, Vincent, *British Cinema of the 1950s* (Oxford: Oxford University Press, 2003).

Hebdige, Dick, *Hiding in the Light* (London: Comedia, 1988).

Highmore, Ben, *Cityscapes* (Basingstoke: Palgrave Macmillan, 2005).

Higson, Andrew, 'Space, place, spectacle', *Screen* vol. 25 nos. 4–5, July–October 1985, pp. 2–21.

Higson, Andrew, *Waving the Flag* (Oxford: Clarendon Press, 1995).

Higson, Andrew (ed.), *Dissolving Views* (London: Cassell, 1996).

Higson, Andrew, 'Pool of London', in Alan Burton, Tim O'Sullivan and Paul Wells (eds), *Liberal Direction* (Trowbridge: Flicks Books, 1997), pp. 162–71.

Higson, Andrew, *English Heritage, English Cinema* (Oxford: Oxford University Press, 2003).

Hill, John, *Sex, Class and Realism: British Cinema 1956–63* (London: BFI, 1986).

Hill, John, 'Allegorising the nation: British gangster films of the 1980s', in Steve Chibnall and Robert Murphy (eds), *British Crime Cinema* (London: BFI, 1999), pp. 160–71.

Hill, John, *British Cinema in the 1980s* (Oxford: Clarendon Press, 1999).

Hill, John, 'Failure and utopianism: representations of the working class in British cinema of the 1990s', in Robert Murphy (ed.), *British Cinema of the 90s* (London: BFI, 2000), pp. 178–87.

Hjort, Mette, 'Themes of nation', in M. Hjort and S. Mackenzie (eds), *Cinema and Nation* (London: Routledge, 2000), pp 103–17.

Hobbs, Dick, *Doing the Business: Entrepreneurship, Detectives and the Working Class in the East End of London* (Oxford: Oxford University Press, 1992 [1988]).

Hodgson, Clive, 'Interview with Horace Ové', *Film (BFFS)* no. 64, August 1978.

Hoggart, Richard, *The Uses of Literacy* (Harmondsworth: Penguin, 1958 [1957]).

hooks, bell, *Black Looks: Race and Representation* (Boston: South End Press, 1992).

Hopkins, Harry, *The New Look: A Social History of the Forties and Fifties* (London: Secker and Warburg, 1964).

Houlbrook, Matt, *Queer London: Perils and Pleasures in the Sexual Metropolis, 1918–1957* (Chicago and London: University of Chicago Press, 2005).

Hughes, David, 'The Spivs', in Michael Sissons and Philip French (eds), *Age of Austerity, 1945–51* (Oxford: Oxford University Press, 1986), pp. 69–88.

Hunt, Leon, *British Low Culture: from Safari Suits to Sexploitation* (London: Routledge, 1998).

Hunter, I. Q., *British Science Fiction Cinema* (London: Routledge, 1999).

Hutchings, Peter, '*Frenzy*: return to Britain', in Charles Barr (ed.), *All Our Yesterdays* (London: BFI, 1986), pp. 368–74.

Hutchings, Peter, *Hammer and Beyond: the British Horror Film* (Manchester: Manchester University Press, 1993).

Hutchings, Peter, '"We're the Martians now"', in I. Q. Hunter (ed.), *British Science Fiction Cinema* (London: Routledge, 1999), pp. 33–47.

Hutchings, Peter, *Dracula* (London: I. B. Tauris, 2003).

Hutchings, Peter, 'Uncanny landscapes in British film and television', *Visual Culture in Britain* vol. 5 no. 2, 2004, pp. 27–40.

Huyssen, Andreas, *Present Pasts* (Stanford: Stanford University Press, 2003).

Inwood, Stephen, *A History of London* (London: Macmillan, 1988).

Iris, 'European Precursors of Film Noir', no. 21, Spring 1996.

Jacobs, Jane M., *The Edge of Empire: Postcolonialism and the City* (London: Routledge, 1996).

James, Joy, 'Black femmes fatales and sexual abuse in progressive "white" cinema: Neil Jordan's *Mona Lisa* and *The Crying Game*', *Camera Obscura* no. 36, September 1995, pp. 33–47.

James, Nick, 'Being there: interview with Hugo Luczyc-Wyhowski', *Sight and Sound* vol. 7 no. 10 (NS), October 1997, pp. 6–9.

James, Nick, 'Farewell to Napoli', *Sight and Sound* vol. 9 no. 5 (NS), May 1999, pp. 20–2.

Jancovich, Mark and Lucy Faire, with Sarah Stubbings, *The Place of the Audience: Cultural Geographies of Film Consumption* (London: BFI, 2003).

Jephcott, Pearl, *A Troubled Area: Notes on Notting Hill* (London: Faber and Faber, 1964).

Jordan, Neil and Leland, David, *Mona Lisa* (London: Faber and Faber, 1986).

Jousse, Thierry and Paquot, Thierry (eds), *La Ville au cinéma* (Paris: Cahiers du cinéma, 2005).

Kaplan, E. Ann, *Women and Film Noir* (London: BFI, 1998 [1978]).

Keefe, Barry, 'Haunting Friday', *Sight and Sound* vol. 6 no. 8, August 1996, pp. 20–1.

Kemp, Philip, *Lethal Innocence: The Cinema of Alexander Mackendrick* (London: Methuen, 1991).

Kemp, Philip, 'The long shadow: Robert Hamer after Ealing', *Film Comment* vol. 31 no. 3 (May–June 1995), pp. 71–8.

Kerr, Joe and Gibson, Andrew (eds), *London from Punk to Blair* (London: Reaktion, 2003), pp. 257–71, 371–6.

King, Anthony D., *Global Cities* (London: Routledge, 1990).

Kirby, Lynne, *Parallel Tracks: The Railroad and Silent Cinema* (Durham: Duke University Press, 1997).

Kirkham, Pat, 'Dress, dance, dreams and desire: fashion and fantasy in *Dance Hall*', *Journal of Design History* vol. 8 no. 3, 1995, pp. 195–214.

Klinger, Barbara, *Beyond the Multiplex: Cinema, New Technologies and the Home* (Berkeley: University of California Press, 2006).

Konstantarakos, Myrto (ed.), *Spaces in European Cinema* (Exeter: Intellect, 2000).

Kracauer, Siegfried, *Theory of Film: The Redemption of Physical Reality* (Oxford: Oxford University Press, 1960).

Krause, Linda and Petro, Patrice (eds), *Global Cities: Cinema, Architecture and Urbanism in a Digital Age* (New Brunswick: Rutgers University Press, 2003).

Krutnik, Frank, *In a Lonely Street* (London: Routledge, 1991).

Kuhn, Annette, *Family Secrets: Acts of Memory and Imagination* (London: Verso, 1995).

Kuhn, Annette, *An Everyday Magic: Cinema and Cultural Memory* (London: I. B. Tauris, 2002).

Kureishi, Hanif, *London Kills Me: Three Screenplays and Four Essays* (London: Penguin, 1992).

Landy, Marcia, *British Genres: Cinema and Society, 1930–1960* (Princeton, NJ: Princeton University Press, 1991).

Landy, Marcia, *The Cinematic Uses of the Past* (Minneapolis: University of Minnesota Press, 1996).

Lant, Antonia, *Blackout: Reinventing Women for Wartime British Cinema* (Princeton, NJ: Princeton University Press, 1991).

Leach, Neil (ed.), *The Hieroglyphics of Space* (London: Routledge, 2002).

Leigh, Jacob, *The Cinema of Ken Loach: Art in the Service of the People* (London: Wallflower Press, 2002).

Leigh, Mike, *Naked and Other Screenplays* (London: Faber and Faber, 1995).

Lejeune, Anthony (ed.), *The C. A. Lejeune Film Reader* (Manchester: Carcanet, 1991).

Luckett, Moya, 'Image and nation in 90s British cinema', in Robert Murphy (ed.), *British Cinema of the 90s* (London: BFI, 2000), pp. 88–99.

Luckett, Moya, 'Travel and mobility: femininity and national identity in Swinging London Films', in Justine Ashby and Andrew Higson (eds), *British Cinema: Past and Present* (London: Routledge, 2000), pp. 223–46.

Luckhurst, Roger, 'Occult London', in Joe Kerr and Andrew Gibson (eds), *London from Punk to Blair* (London: Reaktion, 2003), pp. 335–40.

Lynch, Kevin, *The Image of the City* (Cambridge, MA: MIT Press, 1960).

MacCabe, Colin, *Performance* (London: BFI, 1998).

MacCabe, Colin, 'Interview: Hanif Kureishi on London', *Critical Quarterly* vol. 41 no. 3, Autumn 1999, pp. 37–56.

MacNab, Geoffrey, *Searching for Stars: Stardom and Screen Acting in British Cinema* (London: Cassell, 2000).

Malik, Sarita, *Representing Black Britain: Black and Asian Images on Television* (London: Sage, 2002).

Marriott, Oliver, *The Property Boom* (London: Pan Books, 1969 [1967]).

Marris, Paul, 'Northern realism: an exhausted tradition?', *Cinéaste* XXVI no. 4, 2001, pp. 47–50.

Martin-Jones, David, 'Two Stories, One Right, One Wrong: Narrative, National Identity and Globalization in *Sliding Doors*', *CinéAction* no. 24, 2004, pp. 18–27.

Martin-Jones, David, *Deleuze, Cinema and National Identity* (Edinburgh: Edinburgh University Press, 2006).

Mash, Melinda, 'Stepping out or out of step? Austerity, affluence and femininity in two post-war films', in Christine Gledhill and Gillian Swanson (eds), *Nationalising Femininity: Culture, Sexuality and British Cinema in the Second World War* (Manchester: Manchester University Press, 1996), pp. 257–63.

Massey, Doreen, *Space, Place and Gender* (Cambridge: Polity, 1994).

Massey, Doreen, *For Space* (London: Sage, 2005).

Massood, Paula J., 'City Spaces and City Times: Bakhtin's Chronotope and Recent African-American Film', in Mark Shiel and Tony Fitzmaurice (eds), *Screening the City* (London: Verso, 2003), pp. 200–15.

Mather, Nigel, *Tears of Laughter: Comedy-drama in 1990s British Cinema* (Manchester: Manchester University Press, 2006).

Matless, David, *Landscape and Englishness* (London: Reaktion, 1998).

Mazierska, Ewa and Rascaroli, Laura, *From Moscow to Madrid: Postmodern Cities, European Cinema* (London: I. B. Tauris, 2003).

McArthur, Colin, *Underworld USA* (London: Secker and Warburg, 1972).

McArthur, Colin, 'Chinese boxes and russian dolls: tracking the elusive cinematic city', in David B. Clarke (ed.), *The Cinematic City* (London: Routledge, 1997), pp. 19–45.

McFarlane, Brian (ed.), *Sixty Voices* (London: BFI, 1992).

McFarlane, Brian (ed.), *The Encyclopaedia of British Film* (London: Methuen and BFI, 2003).

McFarlane, Brian (ed.), *The Cinema of Britain and Ireland* (London: Wallflower Press, 2005).

McKernan, Luke, 'London on film', in Brian McFarlane (ed.), *The Encyclopaedia of British Film* (London: Methuen and BFI, 2003), pp. 403–4.

McLeod, John, *Postcolonial London: Rewriting the Metropolis* (London: Routledge, 2004).

Medhurst, Andy, 'Victim: text as context', *Screen* vol 25 nos. 4–5, July–October 1984, pp. 222–35.

Medhurst, Andy, 'Dirk Bogarde', in Charles Barr (ed.), *All Our Yesterdays* (London: BFI, 1986), pp. 335–64.

Medhurst, Andy, 'Myths of consensus and fables of escape', in Jim Fyrth (ed.), *Labour's Promised Land* (London: Lawrence and Wishart, 1995).

Meikle, Denis, *Jack the Ripper: the Murders and the Movies* (London: Reynolds and Hearn, 2002).

Mercer, Kobena (ed.), *Black Film/British Cinema* (London: Institute of Contemporary Arts, 1988).

Mercer, Kobena, *Welcome to the Jungle* (London: Routledge, 1994).

Mighall, Robert, *A Geography of Victorian Gothic Fiction* (Oxford: Oxford University Press, 1999).

Mighall, Robert, 'Crime and memory in the capital', in Joe Kerr and Andrew Gibson (eds), *London from Punk to Blair* (London: Reaktion, 2003), pp. 371–6.

Miller, Laurence, 'Evidence for a British film noir cycle', in Wheeler Winston Dixon (ed.), *Reviewing British Cinema 1990–1992* (Albany: State University of New York Press, 1994).

Minden, Michael, 'The city in early cinema: *Metropolis*, *Berlin* and *October*', in Edward Timms (ed.), *Unreal City: Urban Experience in Modern European Literature and Art* (Manchester: Manchester University Press, 1984), pp. 193–213.

Monk, Claire, 'From underworld to underclass: crime and British cinema in the 1990s', in Steve Chibnall and Robert Murphy (eds), *British Crime Cinema* (London: Routledge, 1999), pp. 172–88.

Monk, Claire, 'Men in the 90s', in Robert Murphy (ed.), *British Cinema of the 90s* (London: BFI, 2000), pp. 156–66.

Monk, Claire, 'Underbelly UK: the 1990s Underclass film, masculinity and ideologies of "New" Britain', in Justine Ashby and Andrew Higson (eds), *British Cinema: Past and Present* (London: Routledge, 2000), pp. 274–87.

Monk, Claire, 'Projecting a new Britain', *Cinéaste* XXVI Contemporary British Cinema Supplement, Autumn 2001, pp. 34–7.

Monk, Claire and Sargeant, Amy (eds), *British Historical Cinema* (London: Routledge, 2002).

Monks, Sarah, 'The visual economies of the downriver Thames in eighteenth-century British art', *Visual Culture in Britain* vol. 7 no. 1, 2006, pp. 1–20.

Moretti, Franco, *Atlas of the European Novel 1800–1900* (London: Verso, 1998).

Morley, David and Robins, Kevin, *Spaces of Identity* (London: Routledge, 1995).

Mort, Frank, 'Mapping sexual London: the Wolfenden Committee on Homosexual Offences and Prostitution 1954–57', *New Formations* no. 37, Spring 1999, pp. 92–113.

Mort, Frank, 'Fantasies of metropolitan life: planning London in the 1940s', *Journal of British Studies* 43, January 2004, pp. 120–51.

Mort, Frank, 'Scandalous events: metropolitan culture and moral change in post-second World War London', *Representations* 93, 2006, pp. 106–37.

Mort, Frank, and Nead, Lynda, 'Introduction', *New Formations* no. 39, 'Sexual Geographies', Spring 1999, pp. 5–10.

Mort, Frank and Ogborn, Miles, 'Transforming Metropolitan London 1750-1960', *Journal of British Studies* vol. 43 no. 1, 2005, pp. 1–14.

Moseley, Rachel, *Growing Up with Audrey Hepburn* (Manchester: Manchester University Press, 2002).

Moseley-Wood, Rachel, '"Colonizin Englan in reverse"', *Visual Culture in Britain* vol. 5 no. 1, 2004, pp. 91–104.

Mulvey, Laura, *Death at 24x a Second: Stillness and the Moving Image* (London: Reaktion, 2006).

Murphy, Robert, 'Riff-raff: British cinema and the underworld', in Charles Barr (ed.), *All Our Yesterdays* (London: BFI, 1986), pp. 286–305.

Murphy, Robert, *Realism and Tinsel: Cinema and Society in Britain, 1939–48* (London: Routledge, 1989).

Murphy, Robert, *Sixties British Cinema* (London: BFI, 1992).

Murphy, Robert, *Smash and Grab: Gangsters in the London Underworld* (London: Faber and Faber, 1993).

Murphy, Robert (ed.), *The British Cinema Book* (London: BFI, 1997 [2nd edn 2001]).

Murphy, Robert (ed.), *British Cinema of the 90s* (London: BFI, 2000).

Murphy, Robert, 'City life: urban fairytales in late 90s British cinema', in Robert Murphy (ed.), *The British Cinema Book*, 2nd edn (London: BFI, 2001), pp. 292–300.

Murphy, Robert, 'Dark shadows around Pinewood and Ealing', *Film International* vol. 2 no. 7, January 2004, pp. 29–35.

Murphy, Robert, '*The Long Memory*', in Brian McFarlane (ed.), *The Cinema of Britain and Ireland* (London: Wallflower Press, 2005), pp. 85–93.

Naficy, Hamid, *An Accented Cinema: Exilic and Diasporic Filmmaking* (Princeton, NJ: Princeton University Press, 2001).

Nairn, Ian, *Nairn's London* (Pleasantville, NY: The Akadine Press, 2002 [1966]).

Naremore, James, *More Than Night: Film Noir in its Contexts* (Berkeley and Los Angeles: University of California Press, 1998).

Nead, Lynda, *Victorian Babylon: People, Streets and Images in Nineteenth-Century London* (New Haven and London: Yale University Press, 2000).

Neumann, Dietrich (ed.), *Film Architecture: Set Designs from Metropolis to Blade Runner* (Munich: Prestel Verlag, 1999).

Newman, Kim, '*The Krays*', *Monthly Film Bulletin* vol. 57 no. 675, April 1990, pp. 110–11.

Newman, Kim, 'Jack the Ripper', in Phil Hardy (ed.), *The BFI Companion to Crime* (London: BFI, 1997), pp. 183–5.

Nowell-Smith, Geoffrey, 'Cities real and imagined', in Mark Shiel and Tony Fitzmaurice (eds), *Cinema and the City* (Oxford: Blackwell, 2001), pp. 99–108.

Ogborn, Miles, 'Mapping words', *New Formations* no. 57, 2005, pp. 145–9.

Oldman, Gary, '*Nil by Mouth*' *Script* (Suffolk: ScreenPress, 1997).

Orr, John, *The Art and Politics of Film* (Edinburgh: Edinburgh University Press, 2000).

Orr, John, 'Traducing Realisms: *Naked* and *Nil By Mouth*', *Journal of Popular British Cinema* no. 5, 2002, pp. 104–13.

Ovenden, Mark, *Metro Maps of the World* (Harrow Weald: Capital Transport, 2003).

Owusu, Kwesi (ed.), *Black British Culture and Society: A Text Reader* (London: Routledge, 2000).

Pascoe, David, *Airspaces* (London: Reaktion, 2001).

Patterson, Sheila, *Dark Strangers* (London: Tavistock, 1963).

Pearson, John, *The Profession of Violence: The Rise and Fall of the Kray Twins* (London: HarperCollins, 1995 [1972]).

Pendreigh, Brian, *On Location: The Film Fan's Guide to Britain and Ireland* (Edinburgh: Mainstream, 1995).

Penz, François and Thomas, Maureen (eds), *Cinema and Architecture* (London: BFI, 1997).

Perks, Marcelle, 'A descent into the underworld: *Deathline*', in Steve Chibnall and Julian Petley (eds), *British Horror Cinema* (London: Routledge, 2002), pp. 145–55.

Pettit, Lance, 'Philip Donnellan, Ireland and dissident documentary', *Historical Journal of Film, Radio and Television* vol. 20 no. 3, 2000, pp. 352–65.

Pettit, Lance, *Screening Ireland: Film and Television Representation* (Manchester: Manchester University Press, 2000).

Phillips, Caryl, *Playing Away* (London: Faber and Faber, 1987).

Phillips, Charlie and Phillips, Mike, *Notting Hill in the Sixties* (London: Lawrence and Wishart, 1991).

Pike, David, 'Modernist space and the transformation of Underground London', in Pamela K. Gilbert (ed.), *Imagined Londons* (Albany: State University of New York Press, 2002), pp. 101–19.

Pile, Steve, '"The problem of London", or, how to explore the moods of the city', in Neil Leach (ed.), *The Hieroglyphics of Space* (London: Routledge, 2002), pp. 139–51.

Pines, Jim, 'Black Independent Film in Britain: an historical overview', in John Twitchin (ed.), *The Black and White Media Book* (Stoke-on-Trent: Trentham, 1988), pp. 103–10.

Pines, Jim, *Black and White in Colour: Black People in British Television since 1936* (London: BFI, 1992).

Pirie, David, *A Heritage of Horror: The English Gothic Cinema 1946–1972* (London: Gordon Fraser, 1973).

Pollock, Griselda, *Vision and Difference* (London: Routledge, 1988).

Porter, Roy (ed.), *Myths of the English* (Cambridge: Polity Press, 1992).

Porter, Roy, *London: A Social History* (London: Penguin, 1996 [1994]).

Pulleine, Tim, 'A song and dance at the local: thoughts on Ealing', in Robert Murphy (ed.), *The British Cinema Book* (London: BFI, 1997), pp. 114–21.

Rabinowitz, Paula, *Black and White Noir: America's Pulp Modernism* (New York: Columbia University Press, 2002).

Rappaport, Erika, *Shopping for Pleasure: Women in the Making of London's West End* (Princeton, NJ: Princeton University Press, 2000).

Reeves, Tony, *The Worldwide Guide to Movie Locations Presents London* (London: Titan, 2003).

Rich, Nathaniel, *San Francisco Noir* (New York: The Little Bookroom, 2005).

Richards, Jeffrey, *The Age of the Dream Palace* (London: Routledge, 1984).

Richards, Jeffrey, *Films and British National Identity* (Manchester: Manchester University Press, 1997).

Richards, Jeffrey, 'Cul-de-sac England: *The Ladykillers*', in Anthony Aldgate and Jeffrey Richards (eds), *The Best of British: Cinema and Society from 1930 to the Present* (London: I. B. Tauris, 2002 [1999]), pp. 148–65.

Richards, Jeffrey and Sheridan, Dorothy (eds), *Mass Observation at the Movies* (London: Routledge and Kegan Paul, 1987).

Robbins, David (ed.), *The Independent Group: Postwar Britain and the Aesthetics of Plenty* (Cambridge, MA, and London: MIT Press, 1990).

Robertson, James C., *The Hidden Cinema* (London: Routledge, 1989).

Robertson, James, 'The censors and British gangland', in Steve Chibnall and Robert Murphy (eds), *British Crime Cinema* (London: Routledge, 1999), pp. 16–26.

Robins, Kevin, 'The city in the field of vision', *Into the Image* (London: Routledge, 1996), pp. 127–46.

Rose, Jonathan, *The Intellectual Life of the British Working Classes* (New Haven and London: Yale University Press, 2001).

Rowbotham, Sheila and Beynon, Huw, *Looking at Class: Film, Television and the Working Class in Britain* (London: Rivers Oram, 2001).

Rumbelow, Donald, *The Complete Jack the Ripper* (London: Penguin, 2005 [1992]).

Russell, Dave, *Looking North: Northern England and the National Imagination* (Manchester: Manchester University Press, 2004).

Ryall, Tom, 'England's dreaming/Urban legends: London', *Sight and Sound* vol. 11 no. 8 (NS), August 2001, pp. 30–3.

Samuel, Raphael, 'The pathos of conservation', in Mark Girouard, Dan Cruikshank, Raphael Samuel and others, *The Saving of Spitalfields* (London: Spitalfields Historic Buildings Trust, 1989), pp. 135–71.

Samuel, Raphael, *Theatres of Memory* (London: Verso, 1994).

Sandhu, Sukhev, *London Calling* (London: HarperCollins, 2003).

Sargeant, Amy, 'The content and the form: invoking past-ness in three contemporary films', in Claire Monk and Amy Sargeant (eds), *British Historical Cinema* (London: Routledge, 2002), pp. 199–215.

Sargeant, Amy, *British Cinema* (London: BFI, 2005).

Sassen, Saskia, *The Global City: New York, London, Tokyo* (London: Routledge, 1990).

Saunders, James, *Celluloid Skyline: New York and the Movies* (London: Bloomsbury, 2002 [2001]).

Scalway, Helen, *Travelling Blind* (Artist's Book, 1999). Copy held at Chelsea School of Art and Design Library, The London Institute.

Scalway, Helen, 'Travelling Blind', in Steve Pile and Nigel Thrift (eds), *City A–Z* (London: Routledge, 2000).

Schivelbusch, Wolfgang, *The Railway Journey: The Industrialization and Perception of Time and Space* (Berkeley: University of California Press, 1986).

Schivelbusch, Wolfgang, *Disenchanted Night: The Industrialization of Light in the Nineteenth Century* (translated by Angela Davies) (Berkeley: University of California Press, 1995 [1983]).

Schlör, Joachim, *Nights in the Big City: Paris, Berlin, London 1840–1930* (translated by Pierre Gottfried Imhof and Dafydd Rees Roberts) (London: Reaktion, 1998 [1991]).

Schwarz, Bill, '"The only white man in there": The re-racialization of England, 1956–68', *Race and Class* vol. 38 no. 1, 1996, pp. 65–78.

Schwarz, Bill, 'Postcolonial times: the visible and the invisible', in F. Driver and D. Gilbert (eds), *Imperial Cities* (Manchester: Manchester University Press, 1999), pp. 268–72.

Schwarz, Bill, 'Reveries of race: the closing of the imperial moment', in Becky Conekin, Frank Mort and Chris Waters (eds), *Moments of Modernity* (London: Rivers Oram, 1999), pp. 189–207.

Selvon, Samuel, *The Lonely Londoners* (Harlow: Pearson Educational, 2004 [1956]).

Shiel, Mark and Fitzmaurice, Tony (eds), *Cinema and the City* (Oxford: Blackwell, 2001).

Shiel, Mark and Fitzmaurice, Tony (eds), *Screening the City* (London: Verso, 2003).

Shields, Rob, *Places on the Margin: Alternative Geographies of Modernity* (London and New York: Routledge, 1991).

Shonfield, Katherine, *Walls Have Feelings: Architecture, Film and the City* (London: Routledge, 2000).

Silver, Alain and Ursini, James (eds), *Film Noir Reader* (New York: Limelight, 1996 [1970]).

Simmel, Georg, 'The metropolis and mental life', in David Frisby and Mike Featherstone (eds), *Simmel on Culture* (London: Sage, 1997), pp. 174–85.

Sinclair, Iain, 'Necropolis of fretful ghosts', *Sight and Sound* vol. 4 no. 6, June 1994, pp. 12–15.

Sinclair, Iain, 'Smart guys', *Sight and Sound* vol. 6 no. 8 (NS), August 1996, pp. 22–4.

Sinclair, Iain, *Lights Out for the Territory* (London: Granta, 1997).

Sinclair, Iain, 'Heartsnatch Hotel', *Sight & Sound* vol. 12 no. 12 (NS), December 2002, pp. 32–4.

Sinclair, Iain, 'Paint me a river', *The Guardian Review* 5, February 2005, pp. 16–17.

Sinclair, Iain, *London: City of Disappearances* (London: Hamish Hamilton, 2006).

Sissons, Michael and French, Philip (eds), *Age of Austerity 1945–51* (Oxford: Oxford University Press, 1986).

Smith, Murray, *Trainspotting* (London: BFI, 2002).

Smith, Stephen, *Underground London* (London: Little, Brown, 2004).

Sorensen, Colin, *London on Film: 100 Years of Film-making in London* (London: Museum of London, 1996).

Sorlin, Pierre, *European Cinemas, European Societies 1939–90* (London: Routledge, 1991).

Spicer, Andrew, *Film Noir* (Harlow: Longman, 2002).

Spicer, Andrew, *Typical Men: the Representation of Masculinity in Popular British Cinema* (London: I. B. Tauris, 2003 [2001]).

Stedman-Jones, Gareth, 'The "cockney" and the nation, 1780–1988', in David Feldman and Gareth Stedman-Jones (eds), *Metropolis – London: Histories and Representations since 1800* (London: Routledge, 1989), pp. 272–324.

Street, Sarah, *British National Cinema* (London: Routledge, 1997).

Street, Sarah, *Costume and Cinema* (London: Wallflower Press, 2001).

Sutcliffe, A. (ed.), *Metropolis: 1890–1940* (London: Mansell, 1984).

Sutcliffe, Anthony, 'The metropolis in the cinema', in A. Sutcliffe (ed.), *Metropolis: 1890–1940* (London: Mansell, 1984), pp. 147–71.

Sydney Smith, Susan, *Beyond Dixon of Dock Green* (London: I. B. Tauris, 2002).

Tallack, Douglas, ' "Waiting, waiting": the hotel lobby in the modern city', in Neil Leach (ed.), *The Hieroglyphics of Space* (London: Routledge, 2002), pp. 139–51.

Tashiro, C. S., *Pretty Pictures: Production Design and the History Film* (Austin: University of Texas Press, 1998).

Taylor, John, *A Dream of England* (Manchester: Manchester University Press, 1994).

Thomson, David, *A Biographical Dictionary of Cinema* (London: Secker and Warburg, 1980 [1975]).

Timms, Edward (ed.), *Unreal City: Urban Experience in Modern European Literature and Art* (Manchester: Manchester University Press, 1984).

Trench, Richard and Hillman, Ellis, *London Under London: A Subterranean Guide* (London: Murray, 1993 [1984]).

Turvey, Gerry, 'The moment of *It Always Rains on Sunday*', *Framework* 9, 1978/9, pp. 13–26.

Twitchin, John (ed.), *The Black and White Media Book: Handbook for the Study of Racism and Television* (Stoke-on-Trent: Trentham, 1988).

Urry, John, *The Tourist Gaze: Leisure and Travel in Contemporary Societies* (London: Sage, 1990).

Vidler, Anthony, *The Architectural Uncanny* (Cambridge, MA: MIT Press, 1992).

Walker, Alexander, *Hollywood UK* (London: Harrap, 1986 [1974]).

Walker, Alexander, *National Heroes: British Cinema in the Seventies and Eighties* (London: Orion, 2005 [1985]).

Walkowitz, Judith R., *City of Dreadful Night: Narratives of Sexual Danger in Victorian London* (London: Virago, 1992).

Warshow, Robert, 'The gangster as tragic hero', in Robert Warshow (ed.), *The Immediate Experience* (Cambridge: Harvard University Press, 2001 [1948]), pp. 97–103.

Webster, Wendy, *Imagining Home: Gender, 'Race' and National Identity, 1945–64* (London: UCL Press, 1998).

Weinreb, Ben and Hibbert, Christopher, *The London Encyclopaedia* (London: Macmillan, 1993[1983]).

Wentworth, Richard, '"The accident of where I live" – journeys on the Caledonian Road', in Iain Borden, Joe Kerr, Jane Rendell with Alice Pivaro (eds), *Unknown City* (Cambridge, MA: MIT Press, 2001), pp. 386–404.

Whitaker, Sheila, '*It Always Rains on Sunday* part ii', *Framework* 9, 1978/9, pp. 13–26.

White, Jerry, *London in the Twentieth Century: a City and its People* (London: Penguin, 2002).

Williams, Raymond, *The Country and the City* (London: Chatto and Windus, 1973).

Williams, Rosalind, *Notes on the Underground: An Essay on Technology, Society and the Imagination* (Cambridge, MA: MIT Press, 1990).

Williams, Tony, *Structures of Desire: British Cinema 1939–55* (Albany: State University of New York Press, 2000).

Wilson, Elizabeth, *The Sphinx in the City* (London: Virago Press, 1991).

Wilson, Elizabeth, 'The invisible flâneur', *New Left Review* no. 191, 1992, pp. 90–110.

Wolff, Janet, 'The invisible flâneuse: women and the literature of modernity', *Theory, Culture and Society* vol. 2 no. 3, 1985, pp. 37–46.

Wolfreys, Julian, *Writing London volume 2: Materiality, Memory, Spectrality* (Basingstoke: Palgrave, 2004).

Wollen, Peter, 'Ontology and materialism in film', *Screen* vol. 17 no. 1, 1976, pp. 7–25.

Wollen, Peter, *Paris Hollywood: Writings on Film* (London: Verso, 2002).

Wolmar, Christian, *The Subterranean Railway* (London: Atlantic, 2005 [2004]).

Wright, Patrick, *On Living in an Old Country: the National Past in Contemporary Britain* (London: Verso, 1985).

Wright, Patrick, *A Journey through the Ruins: The Last Days of London* (London: Radius, 1991).

Wright, Patrick, *The River* (London: BBC, 1999).

Young, Lola, *Fear of the Dark: 'Race', Gender and Sexuality in the Cinema* (London: Routledge, 1996).

Young, Michael and Willmott, Peter, *Family and Kinship in East London* (London: Harmondsworth, 1962 [1957]).

Zukin, Sharon, *Loft Living* (London: Radius, 1988 [1982]).

Zukin, Sharon, *Landscapes of Power: from Detroit to Disneyworld* (Berkeley and Los Angeles: University of California Press, 1991).

Zukin, Sharon, *The Cultures of Cities* (Oxford: Blackwell, 1995).

Unpublished Material Consulted

British Film Institute Special Collections (with the assistance of Janet Moat): Michael Balcon Collection;
    Carol Reed Collection; Material on Robert Hamer and *The Long Memory*; Papers of the British Film
    Institute Production Board (with advice from Christophe Dupin).
London's Transport Museum (with the assistance of Simon Murphy and Helen Kennedy): Miscellaneous
    files on fluffers, filming underground and the Underground on film. Details of cited material given
    in Chapter 4.
Transport for London Archives and Records Management (with the assistance of Francis Maunze).
    Files on dust exposure of fluffers.
Donnellan, Philip, 'We were the BBC: An alternative view of a producer's responsibility 1948–1984',
    unpublished manuscript, courtesy of the Donnellan family and Paul Long.
Haggith, Toby, '"Castles in the Air": British Film and the Reconstruction of the Built Environment
    1939–51', PhD thesis, University of Warwick, 1998.
Newland, Paul, 'A Howling Sea of Human Wreckage: the Discursive Construction of the East End of
    London', PhD thesis, University of Exeter, 2005.

Exhibitions Cited

Peter Ackroyd, 'Thames', Millennium Bridge, London SEI, 16–25 June 2006.
Wentworth, Richard, Exhibition: 'An Area of Outstanding Unnatural Beauty' (Artangel),
    General Plumbing Supplies Building, York Way, 4 September–17 November 2002.
Museum of the River Thames, The Bargehouse, Oxo Tower Wharf, 24 March–1 July 2001.

Film and Television Dates

Films are dated on first appearance in the text, and occasionally this date is repeated at the beginning
of a longer discussion of the film. For films made before 1994, dates are taken from Denis Gifford, *The
British Film Catalogue*. Following 1994, dates are taken from *Sight and Sound*. Full details of most films
discussed can be found either in Gifford, in *Sight and Sound*, or on the BFI's website, BFI Screenonline:
<www.screenonline.org.uk> or <www.imdb.com>. Television programmes are given a transmission date
and minimum credits in footnotes.

Index

Page numbers in *italic* denote illustrations; those in **bold** indicate detailed analysis.
n = endnote.

List of Illustrations

While considerable effort has been made to correctly identify the copyright holders, this has not been possible in all cases. We apologise for any apparent negligence and any omissions or corrections brought to our attention will be remedied in future editions.